SAGE was founded in 1965 by Sara Miller McCune to support the dissemination of usable knowledge by publishing innovative and high-quality research and teaching content. Today, we publish over 900 journals, including those of more than 400 learned societies, more than 800 new books per year, and a growing range of library products including archives, data, case studies, reports, and video. SAGE remains majority-owned by our founder, and after Sara's lifetime will become owned by a charitable trust that secures our continued independence.

Los Angeles | London | New Delhi | Singapore | Washington DC | Melbourne

THE ROHINGYA CRISIS

THE ROHINGYA CRISIS

Human Rights Issues, Policy Concerns and Burden Sharing

Edited by
NASIR UDDIN

Los Angeles | London | New Delhi
Singapore | Washington DC | Melbourne

First published in 2022 by

SAGE Publications India Pvt Ltd
B1/I-1 Mohan Cooperative Industrial Area
Mathura Road, New Delhi 110 044, India
www.sagepub.in

SAGE Publications Inc
2455 Teller Road
Thousand Oaks, California 91320, USA

SAGE Publications Ltd
1 Oliver's Yard, 55 City Road
London EC1Y 1SP, United Kingdom

SAGE Publications Asia-Pacific Pte Ltd
18 Cross Street #10-10/11/12
China Square Central
Singapore 048423

Published by Vivek Mehra for SAGE Publications India Pvt Ltd and typeset in 10.5/13 pt Adobe Caslon Pro by AG Infographics, Delhi.

Library of Congress Control Number: 2021917424

ISBN: 978-93-5479-130-7 (HB)

SAGE Team: Amrita Dutta, Ankit Verma, and Rajinder Kaur

To
Bangabandhu Sheikh Mujibur Rahman,
the Father of the Nation, on his birth centenary
and
the people of Bangladesh
on the golden jubilee of Independence

Thank you for choosing a SAGE product!
If you have any comment, observation or feedback,
I would like to personally hear from you.

Please write to me at **contactceo@sagepub.in**

Vivek Mehra, Managing Director and CEO, SAGE India.

Contents

Part V: New Developments

List of Figures

List of Tables

List of Abbreviations

AAP	Accountability to Affected Population
ACF	Action Contre La Faim
ADAB	Association of Development Agencies Bangladesh
AFD	Armed Forces Division
AJS	Acute jaundice syndrome
ARSA	Arakan Rohingya Salvation Army
ASEAN	Association for Southeast Asian Nations
AWD	Acute watery diarrhoea
BBC	British Broadcasting Corporation
BDR	Bangladesh Border Patrol
BJP	Bharatiya Janata Party
BRI	Belt and Road Initiative
BSFP	Blanket Supplementary Feeding Programmes
BRAC	Bangladesh Rural Advancement Committee
CA	Citizenship Act
CAA	Citizenship Amendment Act
CERD	Convention on the Elimination of Racial Discrimination
CEDAW	Convention on the Elimination of Discrimination against Women
CFS	Child Friendly Spaces
CHT	Chittagong Hill Tracts
CIC	Camp-in-Charge
CRC	Convention on the Rights of the Child
CSO	Civil Society Organization
CMR	Clinical management of rape
COVA	Confederation of Voluntary Associations
CP	Child protection
CPIMS	Child Protection Information Management System
CPP	Cyclone Preparedness Programme

CSS	Critical social science
CwC	Communicating with communities
DC	Deputy commissioner
DG	Director general
DOS	Dark object subtraction
DPHE	Department of Public Health Engineering
DSS	Department of Social Services
DTF	District Task Force
ETS	Emergency Telecommunications Sector
EU	European Union
FCN	Family Counting Number
FCC	False colour composite
FDMN	Forcibly Displaced Myanmar Nationals
FGD	Focus group discussion
FNB	Federation of NGOs in Bangladesh
FTS	Financial Tracking Service
GBV	Gender-based violence
GDP	Growth domestic product
GFD	General food distribution
GIS	Geographical information system
GoB	Government of Bangladesh
GoM	Government of Myanmar
GT	Grounded theory
HRW	Human Rights Watch
ICC	International Criminal Court
ICCPR	International Convention on Civil and Political Rights
ICDDR,B	International Centre for Diarrheal Disease Research, Bangladesh
ICESCR	International Covenant on Economic, Social and Cultural Rights
ICJ	International Court of Justice
ICU	Intensive care unit
IDPs	Internally displaced persons
IFI	International financial institutions
IHP	International Humanitarian Partnership
IM	Information management
INGO	International non-governmental organization

IOM	International Organization for Migration
IMDT	Immigration determination by Tribunal Act
IPC	Infection prevention and control
IPD	Immigration and Population Department
IRC	International Rescue Committee
ISS	Interpretive social science
IUU	Illegal, unreported and unregulated
JeM	Jaish-e-Mohammed
JICA	Japan International Cooperation Agency
J-MSNA	Joint Multi-Sector Needs Assessment
ISCG	Inter-Sector Coordination Group
IYCF	Infant and young child feeding
JMB	Jamaat-ul-Mujahideen Bangladesh
JRP	Joint Response Plan
LeT	Lashkar-e-Taiba
LPG	Liquid petroleum gas
LSE	Land surface emissivity
LST	Land surface temperature
LTV	Long-term visas
MAM	Moderate acute malnutrition
MHPSS	Mental health and psychosocial support
MoDMR	Ministry of Disaster Management and Relief
MoFA	Ministry of Foreign Affairs
MoHA	Ministry of Home Affairs
MoHFW	Ministry of Health and Family Welfare
MoPME	Ministry of Primary and Mass Education
MSF	Medecins Sans Frontiers
MSNA	Multi-Sector Needs Assessment
NAHAB	National Alliance of Humanitarian Actors Bangladesh
NCD	Non-communicable diseases
NDPHR	National Democratic Party for Human Rights
NFI	Non-food items
NGO	Non-governmental organization
NGOAB	Non-Governmental Organization Affairs Bureau
NIA	National Investigating Agency
NIRAPA	Network for Information, Response and Preparedness Activities on Disaster

NLD	National League for Democracy
NPM	Needs and Population Monitoring
NPP	National Panthers Party
NRC	National Register of Citizens
NTF	National Task Force
ODA	Overseas development assistance
OTP	Outpatient Therapeutic Programme
PERU	Protection Emergency Response Unit
PFA	Psychological first aid
PHE	Public health engineer
PLW	Pregnant and lactating women
PSEA	Protection against sexual exploitation and abuse
PSS	Psychosocial support
PSS	Positivist social science
PTSD	Post-traumatic stress disorder
PWG	Protection Working Group/Sector
REVA	Refugee Influx Emergency Vulnerability Assessment
RF	Random forest
RRRC	Refugee Relief and Repatriation Commissioner
RSD	Refugee Status Determination
RTI	Reproductive tract infections
SAARC	South Asian Association for Regional Cooperation
SAM	Severe acute malnutrition
SARI	Severe acute respiratory infection
SARI ITCs	Severe Acute Respiratory Infection Isolation and Treatment Centres
SEG	Strategic Executive Group
SIMEX	Simulation Exercise
SLORC	State Law and Order Restoration Council
SMEP	Site Management and Engineering Project
SMS	Site Management Support
SMSD	Site Management and Site Development
SO	Strategic objective
SOP	Standard operating procedures
SPARRSO	Space Research and Remote Sensing Organization
SPDC	State Peace and Development Council
SPSS	Statistical Package for the Social Sciences

SSC	Secondary School Certificate
SSWG	Safe spaces for women and girls
STI	Sexually transmitted infections
TDK	Tie-down kits
TOA	Top of atmosphere
TRC	Temporary registration card
TSFP	Targeted Supplementary Feeding Programme
UASC	Unaccompanied and separated children
UCL	University College London
UDHR	Universal Declaration of Human Rights
UNDP	United Nations Development Programme
UNFPA	United Nations Population Fund
UNHCR	United Nations High Commissioner for Refugees
UNHRC	United Nations Human Rights Council
UNICEF	United Nations International Children's Emergency Fund
UNSC	United Nations Security Council
UNO	Upazila Nirbahi Officer
UPR	Universal Periodic Review
USCR	US Committee for Refugees
WASH	Water, sanitation and hygiene
WB	World Bank
WFP	World Food Programme
WG	Working group
WHO	World Health Organization
WSJ	Wall Street Journal

Preface

This book is a collection of some recent, authentic and very good quality research on the Rohingya crisis written by some established scholars, mid-career researchers and studious dissertation researchers. This book covers the Rohingya crisis from a comprehensive perspective both regionally and thematically since it showcases the plight of the Rohingya in Bangladesh, India, Myanmar, Southeast Asia and the West, particularly in Canada. It does so by covering their struggles for survival, health issues, environmental impacts in Bangladesh, citizenship issues in the framework of legality and illegality in India, critical conditions in Myanmar and their diasporic situation in the Western countries. This book also concerns the policy issues including the dynamics of repatriation, the roles of the international community and the global civil society under the framework of 'responsibilities sharing' and 'global justice'. All the relevant chapters have touched upon the recent military coup in Myanmar which has changed many future predictions of the resolution to the Rohingya crisis and many policy issues dealt with by the international community. This book is comprehensive in its nature, diversity and articulation. During the last couple of years, many edited volumes and single-authored books came out on the Rohingya crisis, but this book due to its comprehensive contents will provide different perspectives and frameworks to address and redress the Rohingya crisis. The rest depends on readers who are the judges to assess the quality of research, the validity of the analysis and the claims of originality.

Acknowledgements

Any book in its making is always a journey of relations, emotions, cooperation and serious academic engagement, which finally shape the book contextually, intellectually and physically. This book has received endless support, cordial cooperation, loving care and spontaneous inspiration from different individuals associated with me and beyond including colleagues, friends, fellows, associates, critics, students, relatives, reviewers, cover designer, typesetters, editorial team and production team. First and foremost, I express my heartfelt gratitude to all contributors of this volume for their valuable contributions with quality research and incredible patience to respond to my repeated and numerous editorial queries. At every stage of editorial process, all contributors have very cordially responded to my tireless knocks without which this book would have not seen the light of the day and taken the shape of this sort.

I would like to acknowledge my colleagues at the University of Chittagong Professor S. M. Monriul Hassan, Professor Dr Abdullah Al Faruk, Professor Dr Shyamol Ranjan Chakrabarty, Professor Dr Alak Paul, Professor Dr Khairul Islam, Professor Dr Ala Uddin and Professor Dr Nazmul Islam Khan for their support and constant encouragement.

I am also indebted to my research assistants, Nusrat Kabir Preom, Aisha Yeasmin, Tonmoy Chowdhury, Tuni Chakma, Md. Mohin Uddin, Rezaul Karim and Ranel Chakma, who were my thesis students working under my supervision to complete their graduation in the Department of Anthropology at the University of Chittagong. They were always a wonderful source of inspiration and fresh minds and I always try to find myself in the renewed thinking of my thesis students what they often uphold with high esteem.

I acknowledge my deep gratitude to the wonderful editorial team, particularly Ms Amrita Dutta and the brilliant production team for their tremendous efforts and high level of professional outputs which have made this book an aesthetically bright one.

Finally, I owe my indefinite debt to my partner, Mrs Farzana Ahmed, who always takes care of all non-academic issues of my life to allow me full time to engage in my academic and professional activities. I must say sorry to my two daughters, Mrittika Rahman and Neelima Rahman, because I have deprived them of their required time and due attention which I have invested in this book.

Introduction

The Rohingya Crisis—Unfolding Some Issues and Concerns

Nasir Uddin

I.1. Beginning

The Rohingya people, declared by the United Nations (UN) as 'the world's most persecuted minority' (UNHRC 2017), have been facing various forms of discrimination, exploitation, oppression and deprivation of basic human rights for decades in Burma/Myanmar. However, the deadly campaign named *clearance operation* carried out by Tatmadaw, Myanmar military forces, in August 2017 superseded all precedents of atrocity and the degree of brutality (Uddin 2020a) which drew deep attention of the international community. Much has been written about what happened to the Rohingya people in Rakhine state on and after 25 August 2017, perpetrated by Myanmar military forces and vigilantes. A few impressively edited volumes meanwhile came out covering the numerous issues of the Rohingya crisis during the pre- and post-2017 mass exodus. Among these, *The Plight of the Stateless Rohingyas: Responses of the State, Society & the International Community Migration and Citizenship Legal Practice* (2010), edited by Ahmed; *To Host or To Hurt: Counter-Native on the Rohingya Refugee Issues in Bangladesh* (2012), edited by Uddin; *The Rohingya in South*

Asia (2018), edited by Chowdhury and Sammadar and *Citizenship, Nationalism and Refugeehood of Rohingyas in Southern Asia* (2020); edited by Chowdhory and Mohanty have substantially contributed to the scholarship on the Rohingya. However, both Chowdhury and Sammadar's and Chowdhory and Mohanty's volumes covered the Rohingya crisis within the South Asia countries on the one hand. And Ahmed's and Uddin's volumes covered various aspects of the Rohingya crises within Bangladesh only. But this book covers the Rohingya crisis, apart from its thematic diversities, across the globe including Bangladesh, Myanmar, India, Southeast Asian countries, the Rohingya diaspora social movement particularly in the West, the duties of global civil society and the roles of the international community in the context of global justice and burden-sharing. Upon arrival in Bangladesh, traumatized Rohingya shared their horrible experiences of killing, rape, torture and burning which unfolded the intensity of brutality of what happened to the civilian Rohingya in the Rakhine state (Lee 2021). However, following the deadly *operation* which triggered about 750,000 Rohingya to leave their homeland, how they have been surviving in 34 temporary refugee camps in Bangladesh under what conditions and with what sort of necessity and scarcity have largely been left out in the academic literature that mushroomed during the post-influx period. Therefore, it requires addressing some unreported aspects of Rohingya's lives in the camps amid their everyday need for food, sanitation, healthcare, housing, education, water supply, cooking materials, childcare, maternity support, networking and daily essentials. Some other issues ranging from the dynamics of camp management, growing concerns of supposed ecological decline, the current state of state policy in dealing with the Rohingya crisis, the extent of the repatriation process to the future of the Rohingya crisis, etc., demand critical discussion with empirical evidence. Besides, there is a transforming public discourse about Rohingya presence in Bangladesh (Yasmin and Akhter 2020) changing the relationship between the host community and the refugees, escalating tension in connection with inter-group and intra-group conflicts among the Rohingya (Uddin 2018), declining law and order situations in and around the camp, growing cases of sexual abuse and child–women trafficking (Tayeb 2019), mounting aid-crises due to decreasing international support

(Uddin 2020b) and the critical roles of non-governmental organizations (NGOs) in relation to repatriations. Moreover the increasing mistrust between the Rohingya and the state of Bangladesh deserves special attention to understand the Rohingya crisis from the perspective of migration. Apart from Bangladesh, there is a growing curiosity to know the state of Rohingya in India, Myanmar and other parts of the world to record their post-2017 conditions and global activism. This book is about the current state of Rohingya in the places of migration (Bangladesh, India, Southeast Asia and other parts of the world), but the place of origin (Myanmar) is not apart from it since the place of origin is intimately linked with the place of migration. The Rohingya thus are locked in different countries with a critical present and an uncertain future that should be discussed with detailed empirical data to understand the broader continuum of the Rohingya crisis. This book accordingly takes on their critical past in Rakhine, the struggling present in their places of migration and an uncertain future in nowhere as nobody knows yet, but it concerns with priority the dynamics of lives and living of Rohingya refugees in Bangladesh, India and Myanmar. This book also touches upon the state of Rohingya in Southeast Asian countries and other parts of the world to unfold the Rohingya in crisis. Having briefly stated the aforementioned issues, the chapter as an introduction aims to present the summary of some very recent, fresh and good quality research on the Rohingya living in Bangladesh, Myanmar, India and other countries conducted by acclaimed academics, professional researchers and committed activists from across the world. The central attention of the chapter is to provide the readers with a comprehensive overview of the contents of this book. However, the chapter briefly sets out the history of the Rohingya in the larger canvas of Burma's/Myanmar political history as well as in the realm of statelessness, refugee-hood, political asylums and diaspora activism concerning the Rohingya crisis.

Following a brief introduction, the chapter is structurally organized into five sections: (a) the Rohingya refugees in Bangladesh, (b) the Rohingya refugees in India and South Asia, (c) the Rohingya in other parts of the world, (d) the Rohingya crisis: policy issue, global justice and responsibilities sharing and (e) new developments.

I.2. Political History of Rohingya Displacement

Available historical records (see for details, Buchanan 1799; Hamilton 1820; Harvey 2000 [1925]; Phayre 1883) confirm that the Rohingya have been living in Arakan, now called Rakhine after 1989, for centuries with different ethnic identities like Arakanese Muslims, Rooinga, Ruinga and Rohingya. Following the decolonization, the Rohingya had an honourable space in the state formation and nation-building in the Union of Burma since a few Rohingya politicians, such as Abdul Gaffar and Sultan Ahmed were representing the Rohingya people in the Constituent Assembly as an elected member of the Parliament (Uddin 2020a). Burma's first elected president Sao Shwe Thaike, who himself was a member of Shan ethnic group, in a public speech in 1954 said, 'Muslims of the Arakan certainly belong to one of the indigenous races of Burma. If they do not belong to the indigenous races, we [Shan] also cannot be taken as indigenous races' (Rogers 2016, 158). And in another public speech on 25 September 1954, the first Prime Minister of Burma U Nu said, 'The Rohingya has the equal status of nationality with Kachin, Kayah, Karen, Mon, Rakhine and Shan' (Ibrahim 2018, 48). But soon after General Ne Win took over the state power amid a military coup in 1962, the Rohingya people started experiencing various forms of discrimination, exploitations, oppression and state violence (Uddin 2015). The military continued in office until 2011 and so did the discrimination of the Rohingya in various social, cultural, economic and political contexts. During this long period, the history of Rohingya turned into the history of physical torture, killing, frequent rape of the Rohingya girls and women, burning of houses and properties (see for details, Green, Thomas and Alicia 2015; Zarni and Cowley 2014). The military junta launched *operation nagamin* (called *dragon king*) in 1978 to drive about 200,000 Rohingya out of the country who then took shelter in south-eastern Bangladesh (Ahmed, ed. 2010). The fundamental attack came to Rohingya life, living and existence in 1983 when the Burmese government enacted a *Citizenship Law* conferring citizenship to 135 nationals excluding the Rohingya. This *Law* formally made the Rohingya non-citizens and rendered them stateless (Uddin 2015). Following such a constitutional and legal exclusion in the state structure, junta government launched a second massive campaign called *Operation Clean and Beautiful Nation* in 1991–1992 which forced 250,000 Rohingya to flee Myanmar to Bangladesh (Ahmed 2010). Under a tripartite agreement with the involvement of the United Nations Human Rights Office of the High Commissioner (UNHCR 2017), 236,000 Rohingya were repatriated to Myanmar during 1992–1996, but most of them came back later on through illegal ways since the Rakhine state remained unsafe for them (Uddin 2019). The next massive influx took place in 2012, when around 120,000 Rohingya crossed the border and sheltered in Bangladesh, which was followed by about 87,000 in 2016 (Uddin 2021). Finally, about 750,000 Rohingya fled Rakhine state in 2017 when brutal genocidal attacks, called *clearance operation*, on the civilian Rohingya were executed by the Myanmar military in the name of counter-insurgency. According to an independent facts finding commission formed by the UN, about 10,000 Rohingya were killed in two months since 25 August 2017, 1,900 girls and women were raped and about 400 villages were completely destroyed in the campaign (Uddin 2020c). The Rohingya people were dealt with by the Myanmar military along with some Buddhist fundamentalists and some Bamar ethnic extremists as if they were lesser than human beings, what Uddin theorizes as 'subhuman' life (Uddin 2020a). Now, Bangladesh hosts more than one million Rohingya, but Myanmar has about 500,000 and 130,000 of them as Internally Displaced Persons confined in camps in Rakhine state (Wade 2017). Rohingya people do not enjoy even refugee status in Bangladesh as an ultimate and immediate place of migration since Bangladesh recognizes them as Forcibly Displaced Myanmar Nationals (Uddin 2020a). Around 40,000 Rohingya live in India, 300,000 in Southeast Asian countries including 150,000 in Malaysia, 50,000 in Pakistan, 250,000 in the Middle East including 190,000 in Saudi Arabia and around 20,000 in Western countries including 12,000 in the United States (USA) (Uddin 2017). Rohingya people have a strong diaspora activist network across the world that is working for their citizenship rights, justice for genocidal survivors and mobilizing the international community to make Myanmar accountable for the life and safety of the Rohingya remaining in Rakhine state (Yuriko 2019). Bangladesh is trying its level best to execute repatriation agreements so that the Rohingya could be sent back to Rakhine (Siddiqi 2021). The International Court of Justice (ICJ) is trialling Myanmar for a genocidal accusation in a case lodged by Gambia. International Criminal Court also gave an order to investigate the accusation against Myanmar for committing crimes against humanity in the form of deportation (Uddin 2020b). But nothing promising has happened till to give a ray of hope anywhere, particularly in Myanmar, Bangladesh and India, which could reduce the sufferings of the Rohingya in their places of migration and the place of origin. This book will provide readers with a vivid portrait of the Rohingya crisis and what the Rohingya people have experienced across the world.

I.3. The Rohingya Refugees in Bangladesh

As a place of migration, Bangladesh is the ultimate destination for the Rohingya as it is the nearest neighbouring country. The Government of Bangladesh (GoB) set up 34 temporary refugee camps to accommodate the refugees. Combined with the previous ones—around 400,000–450,000[1] who came in 1978, 1991–1992, 2012, and 2016—more than one million Rohingya now live in Bangladesh, which has made it the largest Rohingya hosting country. Though meeting the increasing needs is always challenging, the GoB in collaboration with national and international NGOs is trying its best to support Rohingya refugees. However, there are still various forms of deficiencies and critical conditionality which are making the life of Rohingya challenging in the world's largest refugee camp.[2] Particularly, frequent monsoon rains seriously hamper their normal course of life. On top of that, the appearance of the COVID-19 pandemic has made their life

---

[1] There was no concrete numerical figure before 2017 about how many Rohingya refugee used to live in Bangladesh. There were two official camps—Kutupalong in Ukhia and Nayapara in Teknaf—and two makeshift camps—*Taal* in Ukhia and *Leda* in Teknaf—but many Rohingya who were living there were not recorded. Besides, many Rohingya were living in Ukhia, Teknaf, Cox's Bazar and other parts of Bangladesh who were remained undocumented. But my research findings confirm that about 400,000–450,000 Rohingya were living in Bangladesh before the massive influx of 2017.

[2] The United Nations Office for the Coordination of Human Affairs. 2018.

more difficult in the camps. This section covers various issues which unfold the current state of Rohingya in Bangladesh.

Chapter 1 deals with the health status of the Rohingya women and girls amidst the coping experiences from refugee camps in Bangladesh. Alak Paul, Shaila Sharmin, Bebek Kanti Das and Morsheduzzaman discuss that refugees across the globe are at risk of deteriorating physical and mental health. Though health is a universal human right, refugee women and adolescent girls are the most vulnerable and neglected groups in many places. In Bangladesh, Rohingya refugee females (women and girls) are found to be the worst sufferers and vulnerable due to unhygienic environment, poor access to healthcare and health education. The chapter discusses how the Rohingya refugee females living in the camps are at health risk due to their health status and adopted coping strategies. The chapter explores two central questions: what are the major diseases and depression faced by refugee females and why? Which contexts put them into these vulnerabilities? The study based on which the chapter is prepared found that most of the refugee females have physical health problems and different forms of mental disorders. The authors recommend that an integrated development programme be formulated for the female refugees to reduce prevalence of health risks and mental depression among them.

Chapter 2, by Jenny Lamb, with an understanding of the Rohingya particularities and nuances, presents the interactions within the water, sanitation and hygiene staff and between the Rohingya when implementing sanitation activities in Cox's Bazar camp. The metaphor 'floating' is often used by the Rohingya to describe their predicament, that they belong neither to Myanmar nor to Bangladesh. The scale, speed and competencies of the water, sanitation and hygiene staff in some instances, as Lamp argues, stripped them of their social values, humanity and dignity. Yet, the Rohingya demonstrated their agency, tenacity and resourcefulness by substituting and developing their sanitation infrastructure in the camp. So, if the water, sanitation and hygiene staff are serious about providing humanitarian assistance, then it needs to embrace the social, cultural and emotional components rather than a techno-centric one. The chapter illustrates the Rohingya have been stripped of their civil, political, economic, social and human rights for a lifetime which has aided ongoing suffering to a great extent. It suggests that the Rohingya apartheid system needs to be dismantled once and for all.

In Chapter 3, Meherun Ahmed and Syeda Kaosar Jahan Barkha argue that the potential threat of an uncontrollable spread of diseases remains a serious concern as most of the camps are densely populated. In the face of this humanitarian crisis, NGOs are playing a vital role. The authors focus mostly on the intervention areas of health as the pandemic poses the greatest health risk for the refugees. They critically review the existing reports of international humanitarian agencies, NGOs operating on the ground and media reports providing a summary of available services. They discuss the efficiency and efficacy of service delivery by identifying the gaps between demand and supply. They claim that they observe from the existing body of literature that several of the public health preventive measures that were strictly enforced throughout the pandemic—including limitations on access to humanitarian aid and services, internet barring and the restriction on mobility—further marginalizes and puts the Rohingya community at risk of exclusion. They also find that strict COVID-19 containment measures may have curbed the spread of the virus but hindered and threatened the Rohingya's physical and mental health and human rights. Finally, they conclude by offering some policy directions imperative to improve the well-being of the Rohingya refugees in the camps.

In Chapter 4, Md. Atiqur Rahman and Alak Paul discuss that new makeshift camps were built to host the new arrivals of more than 750,000 Rohingya refugees by clearing forested lands and vegetation in large numbers near the existing refugee settlements of Kutupalong and Nayapara. The protected forests and wildlife habitats have been marked endangered considering the extreme pace and scale of refugee inflow in that particular area. The high density of the population living in such proximity has a huge toll on the environment and biodiversity of the surrounding regions as well. They argue that geographical changes in physical and human environments have occurred in the area due to this massive influx. Most of the existing studies on Rohingya influx cover the humanitarian and relevant socio-economic issues, but environmental perspectives have received less academic attention until today. Considering the issues, this chapter investigates the level of physical changes in comparison to the same of the past; the future trends of physical changes in refugee camps and their surrounding areas; and, how these physical changes increase environmental concerns for the region. The authors expect that the outcomes could contribute to a better understanding of the environmental impacts of Rohingya refugee camps in addition to the existing socio-economic stresses.

I.4. The Rohingya in India

Officially, India hosts 40,000 Rohingya refugees though unofficially the figure should be higher. During the Modi-regime, a serious anti-Rohingya sentiment in India has emerged among the general public; particularly among the BJP leaders and activists. This chapter of the book entirely covers the state of Rohingya living in India. This chapter discusses the complex situation of the Rohingya in the interface of the new citizenship law, religious identity in a more complicated political turmoil and geopolitical dynamics of hosting/hurting Rohingya in Indian land. Though the discussion of Chapter 5 is not limited to only India, but it is included in this part as it thematically goes with the other two chapters in Part II of this book. The other two chapters present a lucid picture of Rohingya refugees living in India.

Sagarika Naik in Chapter 5 explains how the Rohingya people have faced organized discrimination, statelessness and targeted violence in Rakhine state, Myanmar. The severity of ruthlessness was so intense in 2017 that the UN called it a 'textbook example of ethnic cleansing'. In the contemporary scenario, they are the world's most numerous 'stateless' people, who have left wondering whether they will ever receive the legitimate claim on their inhabited land. When the question comes to refugee protection and livelihood there is abundant research that has been concentrated on the common obligation of refugee accessibility or distribution of basic necessity, public healthcare and living condition. At the same time, the refugee-hosting nations themselves experience some vulnerable conditions like forced and bonded labour, arbitrary arrest, sexual exploitation; domestic abuse and human trafficking are highly prevalent. In addition to that, the creation of exploitive conditions, which deny the Rohingya equal opportunity to establish secure livelihoods, illustrated that the journey, initiated in search of safety has terminated with despair, destitution and abuse. Besides, she has explored and examined that the current situation is an outcome of the failure of the nation state, absence of effective governance, transnational governance and the legal infrastructure in the hosting nations of South Asia.

In Chapter 6, Manas Dutta argues that at the onset of the colonially inherited violence of postcolonial Myanmar and the waves of inhuman persecutions towards the Rohingya Muslims in the form of a state-sponsored campaign of massacre and atrocity by the security forces and vigilantes in recent times have forced them to flee to India especially for shelter and a better livelihood. While Bangladesh proved to be vulnerable for the Rohingya, Indian states, particularly Hyderabad and Jammu and Kashmir proved to be a deliberate and natural choice for them merely on account of the substantial Muslim population in those regions. The situation has started deteriorating while the anti-Rohingya eviction campaigns have gained momentum in these regions by local-based political parties, right-wing groups and other intolerant stakeholders. The so-called Muslim identity of the Rohingya makes them an easy target in the highly polarized society of Hyderabad and Jammu. Later, labelling the Rohingya as a 'ticking time bomb' and a 'threat to communal harmony' has helped mobilize public opinion against them and play into the hands of communally driven groups. Even, the politics of hate against the Rohingya further intensified as 'catch and kill every Rohingya' campaign in Jammu and Hyderabad. This chapter provides a theoretically grounded and discursive explanation as well as examines different steps taken by the Government of India to project the Rohingya as a threat to India's national security and looks at the response, by explaining the underlying paradigm of politics of such anti-Rohingya campaign and the question of infiltration associated with them.

Parvin Sultana in Chapter 7 discusses that in the post-2000 period, violence and expulsion began which triggered the Rohingya to flee Myanmar and enter neighbouring countries like Bangladesh and India. In India, while they are only 40,000 in number, they have faced terrible vilification. Most Rohingya entered India before 2012 and a smaller number entered at different points of time. But it was only post-2014 that they came to be portrayed as a 'national security threat'. With the Narendra Modi-led government coming to power in 2014, a new narrative was put in place which portrayed Muslims as the 'other', a perennial outsider as opposed to Hindus whose 'natural home' is India. Interestingly, India has a substantial number of refugees from Tibet, Afghanistan and even Chin Burmese from Myanmar. But the Rohingya came to be vilified when the ruling BJP party decided to amend India's Citizenship Act to provide easier access to citizenship to non-Muslim immigrants from Bangladesh, Pakistan, and Afghanistan. In this new binary—Rohingya Muslims were seen as perennial outsiders for their religious affiliation. This chapter locates the Rohingya living in India in this larger context of the changing narrative of India's citizenship by bringing the element of religion in India's Citizenship Act, which has rendered a communal tone to a human rights issue. This chapter points out the inherent contradiction in the situation—on the one hand, India's Citizenship Act is amended to accommodate persecuted minorities of the neighbouring countries and on the other hand, a minority in a similar situation is being forced to face further persecution.

I.5. The Rohingya in Other Parts of the World

Apart from Bangladesh and India, Rohingya live in Myanmar, Southeast Asian countries and Western countries. Though Myanmar is their place of origin, other countries are their places of migration which are the centre of attention of this book for a better understanding of the Rohingya crisis. This part covers the state of Rohingya in Myanmar and Southeast Asian countries as well as the Rohingya diaspora in Canada.

In Chapter 8, Yuriko Cowper-Smith explains that as one of the main mechanisms of Rohingya's social movement in Canada, highlighting the importance of knowledge-practices around the collective-self that the movement generated since 2017. Knowledge-practices of collective-self refer to the ethos and political visions of a movement. She argues that knowledge-practices around the collective-self are crucial mechanisms that support the work of Rohingya's social movement in Canada. To make this case, this chapter analyses a data set of interviews (n = 70) and participant observation of meetings, conferences and various other advocacy events to understand the development of the ethos and visions of the movement. First, the movement has developed an ethos around the collective feelings of responsibility, awareness and resolution. Second, the movement has shaped its political visions around the geopolitical realities of Myanmar, the international community's desire for intervention, Islamophobia in Canada, issues with resettlement and difficulty with community-building in the diaspora. She concludes that in recognition of these structural obstacles, the movement's political vision is to bring recognition of the crisis to the Canadian public, and in doing so, reinstate the human rights and citizenship of Rohingya people in Myanmar by holding the government accountable and responsible.

Syeda Naushin Parnini in Chapter 9 argues that the politics of ethnicity can have serious repercussions if the balance of interests is not maintained, and this can lead to internal destabilization of states. This is the case in Myanmar, a situation that has brought suffering and deaths of thousands, effectively raising concerns and opprobrium against the government of Myanmar. Minority groups like Rohingya in Myanmar are greatly oppressed, though recent proceedings have seen the democratically elected government trying to avert the situation while facing great restraints from the military, which has been in control of the government for decades. The transformation process to uphold minority rights is marred by controversy as systematic alienation of the Rohingya has persisted even in the new political dispensation. Discriminatory, cumbrous bureaucratic tendencies are constantly used to control and manipulate the Rohingya to force them out of the country, a system which is ultimately backed by state-sponsored violence. This chapter, therefore, seeks to critically examine how the bureaucratic systems in Myanmar have been weaponized to systematically suppress the rights of the Rohingya. She argues that the doctrine of sovereignty has largely remained the salvation harbouring and facilitating the continuity of repressive regimes despite the existence of the doctrine of limited sovereignty. The chapter concludes that there is a need to create a global authority with executive-legislative, judiciary, military and constitutional authority to exert authority over governments.

Matteo Fumagalli in Chapter 10 critiques and unpacks the notion of groupness, which has traditionally framed how ethnic groups are studied in a variety of fields, from political science to sociology and nationalism studies. This is especially true as regards the Rohingya in Myanmar. The study of ethnicity and religion in Myanmar has collapsed all diversities, contradictions and complexities—of which there are many—into one meta-group, in fact, a 'meta-other' Muslims. This of course ignores both the diversity within Myanmar's Rohingya communities and the considerable differences across the country's Muslim groups and the religious variations within different ethnic groups. The chapter aims to shed some light on this diversity by complicating how Rohingya and Islam should be approached and researched in Myanmar. Drawing on fieldwork carried out during 2013–2019, the chapter unpacks the alleged groupness of Myanmar's Rohingya and, more generally, Muslim communities. What emerges is a picture of 'plural others' and multilevel minority complexes. This is especially evident in Rakhine state, on the Bangladesh border, but it is also apparent across the whole country, in ethnic states and the regions.

I.6. The Rohingya Crisis: Policy Issue, Global Justice and Responsibility Sharing

This part discusses the issues of refugee policy, global justice and burden-sharing since the Rohingya people find no light of hope about how to resolve their crisis and they live in acute uncertainty and obscurity. Though burden-sharing is a global principle to host refugees on earth, the international community is gradually unloading the burden from their shoulders leaving the Rohingya alone on Bangladesh and Myanmar. Then the question comes up about global justice and the roles of the international communities to uphold it. This part comprehensively covers human rights issues, various policy concerns, the question of global justice and the roles of the international community under the principles of 'burden sharing'.

Azeem Ibrahim in Chapter 11 explains that insofar as the persecution of the Rohingya was noted, it was part and parcel of the wider
human rights abuses by the regime. After 2011, world simply wanted
to believe that the National League for Democracy (NLD) and Aung
San Suu Kyi were a democratic movement that wanted the best for
all citizens including the Rohingya living in the Rakhine state. This
myopia led to a muted response to the violence aimed at the Rohingya
in 2012–2013, their exclusion from the 2015 elections and the clear
evidence that the NLD's leadership fully embraced the anti-Rohingya
prejudices of the military regime. This started to slowly change as
persecution carried on after 2015, but it took the 2017–2018 mass
exoduses to provoke a response both by external states and international bodies. Even so, this remains muted as Myanmar has become
yet another region contested between the Chinese and the West.
Nonetheless, the expulsion of more than one million people has been
impossible to ignore, and this has led to formal proceedings against
Myanmar at the ICJ. Ibrahim argues that unfortunately, the wider
response by the international community remains muted. China (and
Russia) will back their client regime at the UN, the USA is afraid that
China will extend its domination in Myanmar if they challenge the
regime and the European Union (EU) remains, predictably, irrelevant.
This chapter explores the role of the international community, especially since 2011, to redress the Rohingya crisis and what needs to be
done to ensure the Rohingya can safely and with dignity return to the
country of their birth.

Paul Chaney in Chapter 12 explores the crisis facing an estimated
more than one million Rohingya people, a Muslim minority group
that has fled persecution in the Rakhine state. They are now stateless
people regarded as 'non-citizens' by both Myanmar and Bangladesh.
This chapter makes a timely and original contribution by exploring the
'situated knowledge' set out in civil society accounts of the emergency.
It presents the findings of longitudinal data analysis spanning over a
decade. Specifically, it uses discourse analysis to examine hundreds of
submissions by civil society organizations (CSOs) working with the
Rohingya refugees in Bangladesh and covering three cycles of UN's
Universal Periodic Review; the monitoring mechanism associated
with the UN human rights treaties. This rich data set shows how

Rohingya refugees are subject to inhuman treatment, oppression and rights denial. Thus, the chapter provides new insights into a range of issues associated with the crisis including gender-based oppression and discrimination; legal and international treaty failings; suppression of civil society and intimidation of human rights defenders; the negative impact on local, indigenous people and a growing environmental disaster. From an epistemological perspective, this new account shows how the 'situated knowledge' of CSOs' discourse has much to offer in understanding current challenges and finding paths to resolution.

Bayes Ahmed and others in Chapter 13 explain that the Rohingya fled the northern Rakhine state to escape serious human rights violations, genocide and war crimes perpetrated by the Myanmar army. Now they live in camps but are not allowed to work. They are being subject to human trafficking, exploitation, domestic violence and uncertainties. To redress such crisis, it is essential to repatriate them with safety and dignity to their ancestral land in Myanmar. Against this background, the authors aim to understand the barriers and challenges for voluntary and sustainable repatriation in Myanmar. The chapter shows that the Rohingya are keen to repatriate to Myanmar, subject to assurance of their free movement, religious freedom and protection against sexual violence against women. They also demand land and property ownership, healthcare facilities and recognizing their Rohingya identity. Lastly, they require access to employment, education, marriage and citizenship rights, no military attacks in their villages and justice for them (low priority). No influence of demography and socio-economic conditions were found in their decision making. The chapter presents Rohingya voices which are necessary for voluntary and sustainable repatriation in Myanmar with safety and dignity.

Bulbul Siddiqi in Chapter 14 discusses that the constant delay of repatriation has already made the crisis uncertain, complex and multifaceted. The current progress with the repatriation shows no greater hope for these displaced Rohingya in Bangladesh. Thus, the current Rohingya crisis may follow the same path if there is no strong initiative taken to facilitate their repatriation by Bangladesh with the active help of various international communities. The chapter aims at exploring the nature of vulnerabilities as the repatriation has remained as a 'myth' so far. The trust and sympathized relationship between the host and the Rohingya refugees may decrease significantly in Ukhia and Tekhnaf, and it may also create anxiety and tension between the two coexisting parties. The increasing nature of frustration in camps without a long-term vision has already pressurized many Rohingya to adopt various means of unsafe migration. Thus, human trafficking has become a harsh reality for many. Finally, there has been a growing concern for the decreasing pattern of donor support among the international community that may complicate the crisis further. Considering all this, the chapter presents a wide spectrum of sufferings the Rohingya refugees might go through especially due to the delay of repatriation.

Nasir Uddin in Chapter 15 examines the various forms of myths and realities regarding Bhasan Char and Rohingya relocation process. There is a serious dearth of knowledge about Bhasan Char among the international partners, general public of Bangladesh and the Rohingya refugees. Besides, why human rights organizations are opposing this Rohingya relocation to Bhasan Char is also quite ambiguous. The chapter critically analyses the GoB's initiatives to relocate Rohingya to Bhasan Char while the UN, EU and the human rights organizations raised questions about the move. It also discusses the settings, preparation and management of Bhasan Char against the misunderstanding and rumours about cyclones, floods, tidal surges and monsoon rains. It also covers the perspectives of the Rohingya, the international community and the people in Bangladesh about the Rohingya relocation to Bhasan Char. The chapter based on ethnographic evidence and netnography (Kozinets 2010) examines the claims and blames between the voluntary relocations and coerced migrations beneath the discourse of myths and realities regarding Bhasan Char.

I.7. Conclusion

The introductory chapter has presented the summary of different chapters in an attempt to provide readers with a preliminary feeling of what this book is about. We know that the present is the product of the past but reproduces the future. The Rohingya across the globe are in transition because Myanmar as their place of birth is certainly uncertain about what to do with the Rohingya crisis and how to redress it. Bangladesh, an immediate destination of Rohingya migration, seems increasingly reluctant in hosting massive Rohingya refugees in its land. The Rohingya in other parts, particularly in India, Malaysia, Pakistan, Thailand, some middle eastern countries including Saudi Arabia, are dealt with as unwelcome guests and hence living in inhuman conditions in most cases. Therefore, with the increasing pressure from the international community, hearable sought of the international rights bodies, constant media portrayal of Rohingya vulnerability and continued knocks from Bangladesh might force Myanmar to re-initiate the Rohingya repatriation process, but it would fail again for sure because there is no lasting trust, reliable promise and tangible preparation from Myanmar's part for the Rohingya people to return to their 'homeland' voluntarily. Bangladesh will not host more than one million Rohingya willingly forever, gives no space for social integration and takes no attempts for third country resettlement on the one hand. Myanmar, on the other hand, will not willingly bring them back. Considering the bilateral and multilateral dilemmas, the Rohingya people lead their lives with extreme uncertainty as they are in a trap of a critical present with no future. The chapters of this book show no strong light of hope except their struggling present and an uncertain future. The question now is: what needs to be done for the Rohingya for their future? We strongly expect, with a renewed appeal, the international community to uphold the idea of 'burden-sharing' to help Bangladesh as well as to form a 'collective & global force' to compel Myanmar to comply with the UN Human Rights resolutions to bring the Rohingya back to Myanmar with safety, dignity and legal recognition by conferring citizenship to them.

References

Ahmed, Imtiaz, ed. 2010. *The Plight of the Stateless Rohingyas: Responses of the State, Society & the International Community Migration and Citizenship Legal Practice*. Dhaka: The University Press Limited.

Buchanan, Francis. 1799. 'A Comparative Vocabulary of Some of the Languages Spoken in the Burma Empire'. *Asiatic Researches* 5: 219–240.

Chaudhury, S. B. R., and R. Samaddar, eds. 2018. *The Rohingya in South Asia*. London: Routledge.

Chowdhory, Nasreen and Biswajit Mohanty, eds. 2020. *Citizenship, Nationalism and Refugeehood of Rohingyas in Southern Asia.* Singapore: Springer.

Cowper-Smith, Yuriko. 2019. 'The Global Rohingya Diaspora Throws Lifelines to Bangladesh and Myanmar.' *The Conversation* July 05. Available at: https://theconversation.com/the-global-rohingya-diaspora-throws-lifelines-to-bangladesh-and-myanmar-117881 (accessed on April 20, 2021).

Farzana, K. Fahmida. 2017. *Memories of Burmese Rohingya Refugees: Contested Identities and Belonging.* London: Palgrave MacMillan.

Green, Penny, Thomas MacManus, and Alicia de la Cour Venning. 2015. *Countdown Annihilation: Genocide in Myanmar.* London: International State Crime Initiative.

Hamilton, W. 1820. *Geographical, Statistical, and Historical Description of Hindostan and its Adjacent Countries.* London, Albemarle Street: John Murray.

Harvey, G. E. *History of Burma: From the Earliest Time to the 10 March, the Beginning of the English Conquest.* (New Delhi and Madras: Asian Education Services, 2000 [1925]).

Ibrahim, Azeem. 2018. *The Rohingya: Inside Myanmar's Hidden Genocide.* London: Hurts Publication.

Kozinets, Robert. 2010. *Netnography: Doing Ethnographic Research Online.* London: SAGE Publications.

Lee, Ronan. 2021. *Myanmar's Rohingya Genocide: Identity, History and Hate Speech.* London: Bloomsbury.

Phayre, A. P. 1883. *History of Burma Including Burma People, Pegu, Taungu, Tenasserim, and Arakan.* London: Trubner & Co.

Rogers, Benedict. 2016. *Burma: A Nation at Crossroad* [Revised Edition]. London: Rider Books.

Siddiqi, Bulbul. 2021. 'The "Myth" of Repatriation: The Prolonged Sufferings of the Rohingya'. In *The Rohingya Crisis: Human Rights, Policy Concerns and Burden Sharing*, edited by Nasir Uddin [this volume]. New Delhi: SAGE Publications.

Tayeb, Tasneem. 2019. 'Trafficking in Rohingya: Exploiting the Desperate'. *The Daily Star*, Dhaka, 7 December. Available at: https://www.thedailystar.net/opinion/closer-look/news/trafficking-rohingya-exploiting-the-desperate-1836772 (accessed on 15 January 2021).

The United Nations Human Rights Office of the High Commissioner (UNHCR). 2017. '*Human Rights Council Opens Special Session on the Situation of Human Rights of the Rohingya and Other Minorities in Rakhine State in Myanmar*'. UNHCR, 5 December 2017. Available at: https://www.ohchr.org/EN/NewsEvents/Pages/DisplayNews.aspx?NewsID=22491&LangID=E (accessed on 5 March 2021).

The United Nations Office for the Coordination of Human Affairs. 2018. 'The Rohingya Crisis'. 29 August 2018. Available at: https://www.unocha.org/rohingya-refugee-crisis (accessed on January 5, 2021).

Uddin, Nasir. 2020. *The Rohingya: An Ethnography of 'Subhuman' Life*. Delhi: Oxford University Press.

Uddin, Nasir, ed. 2012. *To Host or to Hurt: Counter Narratives on Rohingya Refugee Issue in Bangladesh*. Dhaka: Institute for Culture and Development Research.

Uddin, R. Nasir. 2017. *Not Rohingya, But Royanga: Stateless People in the Struggle for Existence* (in Bengali). Dhaka: Murdhonno.

Uddin, Nasir, 'Rohingya Refugees in Bangladesh: Five Challenges for the Future', *South Asia (blog)*, SE, London School of Economics, University of London, November 21, 2018, https://blogs.lse.ac.uk/southasia/2018/11/21/rohingya-refugees-in-bangladesh-five-challenges-for-the-future/ (accessed on 2 July 2020.)

Uddin, Nasir, 2020. 'Three Years On: What's Next for Rohingya Refugees in Bangladesh?'. *The Daily Star*, Dhaka, 25 August. Available at: https://www.thedailystar.net/opinion/news/three-years-whats-next-rohingya-refugees-bangladesh-1950253 (accessed on 3 March 2021).

Uddin, Nasir. 2015. 'State of Stateless People: The Plight of Rohingya Refugees in Bangladesh'. In *Human Rights to Citizens: A Slippery Concept*, edited by Rhoda Howard-Hassmann and Margaret Walton-Roberts, 62–77. Philadelphia, PA: University of Pennsylvania Press.

Uddin, Nasir. 2019. 'The State, Vulnerability, and Transborder Movement: The Rohingyas in Myanmar and Bangladesh'. In *Deterritorialised Identity and Transborder Movements in South Asia*, edited by Nasir Uddin and Nasreen Chowdhory, 73–90. Singapore: Springer.

Uddin, Nasir. 2020. 'Pressuring Bangladesh to Do More will not Help the Rohingya', *Al-Jazeera*, 25 August. Available at: https://www.aljazeera.com/opinions/2020/8/25/pressuring-bangladesh-to-do-more-will-not-help-the-rohingya (accessed on 5 January 2021).

Uddin, Nasir. 2021. 'The Rohingya Relocation to Bhasan Char: Myths and Realities', this volume. Delhi: SAGE Publications.

Wade, Francis. 2017. *Myanmar's Enemy Within: Buddhist Violence and the Making of a Muslim 'Other'*. London: ZED Books.

Yasmin, Lailufar and Sayeda Akhter. 2020. 'The Locals and the Rohingyas: Trapped with an Uncertain Future'. *Asian Journal of Comparative Politics* 5 (2): 104–120.

Zarni, Maung and Alice Cowley. 2014. 'Slow-Burning Genocide of Myanmar's Rohingyas'. *Pacific Rim Law & Policy Journal* 23 (3): 683–754.

Part I

The Rohingya Refugees in Bangladesh

CHAPTER 1

Disease and Depression among Female Rohingya Refugees in Bangladesh

Alak Paul, Shaila Sharmin, Bebek Kanti Das and Mursheduzzaman

1.1. Introduction

Globally, there are an estimated 68.5 million people forcibly displaced, with 25.4 million of these crossing international borders for protection (WHO 2020a). Displaced people's health is mainly affected by infectious diseases, mental health problems and chronic diseases, and the health status of this displaced population depends on their geographic origin, refugee camp conditions and their personal, physical and psychological conditions (Palinkas et al. 2003). The Rohingya are a stateless Muslim minority in Myanmar (Uddin 2019), who have been surviving a 'subhuman' life (Uddin 2020). Since 25 August 2017, more than 750,000 Rohingya refugees from Myanmar fled to Bangladesh following a deadly violence in the Rakhine state (UNHCR 2020) perpetrated by the Myanmar security forces. Rohingya refugees have received tremendous support from the people of Bangladesh as well as Bangladesh government (Alam 2017). According to Amnesty International, the Rohingya have suffered human rights violations under past military dictatorships in Myanmar (previous Burma) since 1962 (Imran and Mian 2014). Stateless Rohingya refugees, especially women and children are vulnerable to various types of risks, particularly communicable disease outbreaks, malnutrition and mental health problems due to different contexts.

The complexity of refugees' socio-economic condition and psychological behaviour makes the health situation more vulnerable, especially of the women and girls in the camp setting (Sultana 2011). Akhter and Kusakabe (2014) studied the gender-based violence among the documented Rohingya refugees in Bangladesh. Mahmood et al. (2017) described the status of health, human rights and identity crisis of Rohingya people. Riley et al. (2017) found that daily stressors, trauma exposure and mental health distress among the stateless Rohingya refugees in Bangladesh are very high. Pocock (2017) assessed the condition inside the camps in terms of living conditions and health of the refugees. White (2017) portrayed the sufferings of the refugees right after the influx in terms of health emergencies, lack of drinkable water, adequate shelters, etc. Milton et al. (2017) determined the water, sanitation and hygiene (WASH) condition in the camps before the recent influx and found that potable water per person is scarce in quantity, number of refugees per latrine is high and percentage of defecation into a toilet is really high. Summers et al. (2018) tried to define the diarrhoea and acute respiratory infection among the refugees as well as the vaccination coverage in the camps. Islam and Nuzhath (2018) tried to describe the unplanned nature of the camp, WASH services which may worsen health crisis of the refugees after the influx. Chan et al. (2018) tried to determine the health risks of the refugees with respect to water, sanitation, food, nutrition, shelter and non-food items.

Although there is no dearth of studies on refugees in the academia, health issues related to women have so far received little research attention. The Rohingya women, who take shelter in those refugee camps, face various types of health vulnerabilities especially physical, mental, social vulnerabilities which should be addressed by the researcher using both quantitative and qualitative methods. This chapter is actually inspired by this fact and intends to find out the issues related with health vulnerabilities of the Rohingya refugees (women and girls) in Bangladesh. The current chapter will explore the health vulnerabilities of the Rohingya women in the refugee camps situated in the south-eastern part of Bangladesh. The objective is to find out answers to some basic questions including: what type of major diseases mostly affects the physical and mental health of refugee women? What are the causes of health vulnerabilities, especially depression, and how do they cope with these vulnerabilities?

1.2. Methods

1.2.1. Site Selection

In this study, researchers visited five refugee camps of Kutupalong, Balukhali, Unchiprang, Shamlapur and Leda (all situated in Ukhia and Teknaf *upazila* of Cox's Bazar district) to explore the facts about how Rohingya refugee women have been confronting the health sufferings and prejudice. All the study sites (Table 1.1) were chosen based on the number of Rohingya refugee women and girls who were the subject of this study.

1.2.2. Ethical Approach of the Research

Ethical consideration should be given the prime importance while designing a research (Green and Thorogood 2004; Paul 2020). As the study has a profound focus on the health vulnerabilities of the

Table 1.1 *Study Area*

Upazila	Camp Location	Camp Number
Ukhia	Kutupalong Mega Camp	2W
Ukhia	Balukhali Mega Camp	18
Teknaf	Unchiprang (Makeshift Camp)	22
Teknaf	Shamlapur (Baharchara)	23
Teknaf	Leda	24

Rohingya women, it mandates some ethical issues to be taken in consideration. Therefore, to ensure the appropriate application of the ethical approach, before starting the survey the researcher took permission from them. As the Rohingya women and girls are conservative, researchers didn't insist them to speak up on sensitive health topics, rather they used a friendly approach with them. Researchers offered light food like chocolates and biscuits. As part of the study, the researchers interviewed some NGO and government officials and assured about not using their name and identity to any kind of publications. In this chapter, all names of respondents have been changed to keep the anonymity.

1.2.3. Limitations of the Study

Refugee camps are generally very crowded areas. Researchers faced many problems during the research period. It was quite difficult to collect appropriate data from many respondents as most of the respondents were illiterate. Sometimes, respondents gave misleading information about their health problems, though it was cross-checked by the NGO workers. Many of the respondents were not aware about their diseases. They didn't know the name of diseases they suffered from and the researcher couldn't identify some of the diseases they were told about. Moreover, there were some questions on RTI, STI and family planning issues, etc. As these were of a sensitive nature, some respondents felt shy and didn't give answers properly, while some of them tried to escape those types of questions. However, many refugee females were in a hurry to collect relief which hampered the interview sessions.

1.2.4. Data Collection

Primary data collection through questionnaire was originally started in March 2018 in Kutupalong and Leda camps and all qualitative forms of data were gathered between June and October, 2020 in all camps. Participant observation method was used throughout the study. For example, researchers spent almost the whole day with the refugees in their poorly structured houses by gossiping. Sometimes, the team offered food to the kids of refugee families. In addition, some refugee women were observed for few hours at the NGO health centres or service points. A total of 20 in-depth interviews were conducted to know the major health risks and their causes, available healthcare facilities for the vulnerable females in the refugee camps, etc. To gather an in-depth knowledge about the women's sufferings, limited numbers of case studies (10) were conducted on the worst sufferers. A significant number of focus group discussions (FGDs) (10) were conducted in five camps based on a predefined theme to understand the overall health status of adult refugee women. FGDs help to ascertain the major health problems and their causes, sanitation system, lifestyle, or basic needs of the Rohingya females. A semi-structured questionnaire was prepared on the basis of the objectives of the study to conduct personal interview following random sampling technique. A total of 200 questionnaires were used to conduct the study on women aged 13–50 years in the household level. Opinions of some health workers who work in NGOs have been considered for some policy recommendations. Digital voice recorder was used during the entire data collection time. Some photographs were also taken to show the actual condition of refugee camps and the sufferers. Some secondary data were gathered from different books, journals, newspaper, different NGOs, upazila office, dissertations and online documents.

1.2.5. Data Analysis

The qualitative data collected by in-depth interviews, FGDs, participant observations, case studies and opinion surveys during the study were analysed following Grounded Theory (GT) method. Kitchin and Tate (2001) emphasized different strategies of coding and analysing qualitative data by GT method which consists of description, classification and making connections between data. On the other hand, questionnaire data were processed and analysed in a sequential manner after collecting the data. Data were processed and analysed by descriptive statistics using MS Excel 2007.

1.3. Nature of Women Refugees' Health Challenges

The refugees are at the great risk of health vulnerabilities due to the limited healthcare services and lack of healthy environment in the refugee camps. According to Palinkas et al. (2003), refugees face a threefold challenge to their health and well-being and those are: (a) psychiatric disorders precipitated by the refugee experience, (b) infectious and parasitic diseases endemic to countries of origin and (c) chronic diseases endemic to host countries. Swanson et al. (2012) mentioned that high rates of mental health problems like post-traumatic stress disorder, depression, anxiety and somatization are common among different refugee populations. Cross-border movements increase the vulnerability of migrants to communicable and non-communicable diseases (WHO 2017). According to World Health Organization (WHO 2018), migrant populations have heightened risks of malnutrition, substance abuse and maternal and neonatal mortality. The tendency of spreading of communicable diseases such as measles, diphtheria and acute jaundice syndrome is high among the Rohingya community which is denoted as public health emergency (Ahmed et al. 2018; WHO 2018). There are also respiratory diseases and increasing health problems due to domestic violence (Arie 2019). Moreover, the incidence of waterborne diseases usually rises during the monsoon season (Hossain et al. 2019). However, having seen the atrocities of the genocide refugees are reported to suffer from frequent nightmares, sleeplessness, anxiety, severe stress, eating disorder and even speaking disorder. Human Rights Watch found that during the genocide on villages, Burmese security forces raped and sexually assaulted both women and adolescent girls (HRW 2017). The following section describes the Rohingya women's physical and mental health challenges.

1.3.1. Physical Health Problems

The overall health and hygienic situation in the Rohingya camps are poor. The refugee's symptomatic perception and health workers opinion reveals that most of the women refugees (about 85%) have physical health problems. Among them, communicable diseases found to be the most prevalent. The most common communicable disease is skin diseases (35%). Various skin diseases like ring worm, abscess, eczema, itching, scabies, heat rash, pox, infection, etc., are common among Rohingya refugee women and girls (Table 1.2). In group discussions, the participants insisted that these diseases have been caused

Table 1.2 Prevalence of CDs, NCDs and STI–RTIs among the Rohingya Women

CDs	%	NCDs	%	STIs and RTIs	%
Skin diseases	35.1	High fever	16.4	Vaginal discharge	32.8
Tuberculosis	6.8	Gastric/Heartburn	26.2	Fungal infection	6.3
Hepatitis	5.8	Eye/Dental illness	8.2	Uterine prolapse	1.6
Chickenpox	2.4	Blood pressure	10.7	Urine infection	14.1
Cholera	2.7	Anaemia	2.5	Fistula	6.3
Diarrhoea	10.8	Joint pain	12.3	Gonorrhoea	1.6
Dysentery	7.9	Diabetes	5.7	Syphilis	6.3
Typhoid	8.5	Severe headache	7.4	Painful periods	20.3
Seasonal flu	14.9	Heart pain	2.5	Abnormal menstrual	4.7
Others	5.1	Others	5.7	Others	6.0
Total	100	Total	100	Total	100

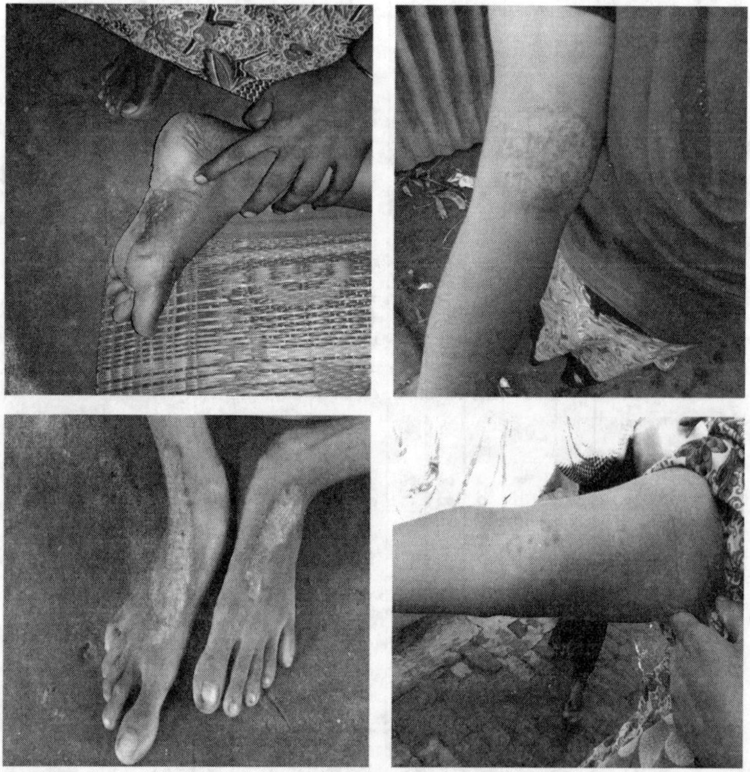

Figure 1.1 *Prevalence of Skin Diseases among Female Refugees*

by the excess heat that they are facing (see Figure 1.1). They commented that due to heavy deforestation in the whole region after the influx period, heat increased substantially which may increase diseases among the refugees as well. According to the interviewed physicians unhygienic conditions and increasing heat are the major causes of these skin diseases. Many of those health practitioners believed that several communicable diseases have already been experienced by the refugee families due to lack of space in the confined shelter environment. A refugee woman of Shamlapur camp, Sabera (33) told:

> I have been suffering from skin problems for the last two years;
> I think I got this disease from my next-door neighbour; when the

temperature rises, it results terrible itching; at first, it started in between my hand fingers then slowly it spread on my whole body.

About 30 per cent refugee women suffer from waterborne diseases of which, diarrhoea, typhoid, dysentery, cholera are very common in the refugee camps. Participants in group discussions agreed that poor water quality is the prime cause of waterborne diseases. They mentioned that in summer months due to increased heat, the waterborne diseases increase. A girl of Leda camp, Sabina (14) mentioned that:

> You can consider our refugee camps as a breeding ground for so many diseases like skin disease, diarrhoea, malaria, typhoid, dysentery, diphtheria, measles etc.; I think, most of our diseases come from dirty water and latrine.

The interviewed doctors suggested that these diseases exacerbate in the monsoon months.

About 15 per cent women experience seasonal flu. Some health workers mentioned that several women are suffering from respiratory diseases. Respiratory problems, cough, pneumonia, asthma and bronchitis are common among the refugees. In group discussions, the participants implied that dust pollution is responsible for their respiratory problems. The interviewed doctors also suggested that seasonal variations might have a link with this type of diseases. About 7 per cent women think that they have the symptoms of tuberculosis (TB), and many of them are getting treatment from the health centres. In FGDs, many women mentioned that bad cough with blood, chest pain, weight loss and weakness are the common symptoms for TB. Some women refugees hinted that they have the signs of jaundice (about 6%). In group discussions, many women described the jaundice as 'yellow disease'. Their skin, eyes and urine become yellowish while they have this disease. Healthcare workers think that water and food contamination is responsible for jaundice. Moreover, some women are suffering from other diseases such as small pox, chicken pox, dengue, and so on.

On the other hand, according to health workers, gastric, heart diseases, blood pressure-related problems, diabetes, dental problems, chronic kidney diseases are also prevalent among the Rohingya refugees. Cold and cough is the most happened non-communicable diseases among the refugee women due to unhealthy conditions of their houses and seasonal change (Table 1.2). About 16 per cent females suffer from high fever around the year. Heartburn is a common problem among the refugee women. More than one woman out of four experiences the gastric problem in the recent history. In FGDs, most females told that they have burning sensation in the chest, stomach pain, vomiting tendency, indigestion problem, appetite loss, etc. Health workers mentioned that a good number of their patients have been suffering from gastric problems. They think that Rohingya's food habit, especially spicy food intake may be the main reason of having gastric. Symptoms of arthritis or joint pain are almost common among the elderly refugee females. About 12 per cent respondents replied that they have family members who experience this problem. The Rohingya females have blood pressure problems. In group discussions, they mentioned that they like to take more raw salt in their foods that may contribute high blood pressure problem. At the same time, malnutrition may cause the low blood pressure symptoms among them. A good number of Rohingya females suffer from eye and dental illnesses. Many elderly women complain that they have no remedies for low vision. On the contrary, a good number of young girls have tooth pain and decay problems. According to respondents, bad headaches, diabetes, anaemia and heart pain are new phenomena as disease to the refugee females. Some respondents are affected by other diseases which are unknown to them. Moreover, many Rohingya female refugees are affected by various sexually transmitted infections (STI) and reproductive tract infections (RTI). According to health workers, leucorrhoea, menstrual period-related problems, urine infection, etc., are the most common diseases among the refugee females. About 33 per cent refugee women experience Leucorrhoea which may be a sign of vaginal infection. Painful period (20%) is also common among them, especially girls. About 14 per cent Rohingya women are suffering from urinary infection. Fungal infection of the genital area is also seen among 6 per cent of the women. Syphilis, late period and fistula are experienced by 6.3 per cent, 5 per cent and 6.3 per cent women respectively. However, respondents reported that during seasonal changes they (mostly adolescents and old people) suffer from RTI. A female doctor in the refugee health unit, Kutupalong stated,

> We receive more RTI cases in the camp when the season changes specially beginning of summer or winter; itching and various infections in the girl's genital area prevail throughout the year among the adolescents because of unhealthy lifestyle.

1.3.2. Mental Depression

The effect of displacement on the mental health of the forcefully displaced refugees is noteworthy. From the survey, it is found that fear is the highest mental effect among the Rohingya females. About 40 per cent respondents told about the frightening situation in the camp. In the group discussions, many of them mentioned that their previous worst memories and present situation have increased their vulnerability. A refugee woman of Unchiprang camp, Shahana (28) told with tears:

> We don't have any future; don't know whether it would be possible to go back to motherland; sometimes we feel very unfortunate as we are stateless people in the world; though receiving many reliefs or helps from many countries, there is always a feeling of frustration and anxiety for our future.

It is clear that most of the refugees are mentally stressed. Depression and anxiety are the common mental effects of the refugee women for various factors. About 38 per cent refugees think that they have to live with depression and anxiety in the camps (Table 1.3). Especially, a number of emotional problems can arise when someone is pregnant or have had a baby. A lot of effects can add to feelings of stress, anxiety, depression during pregnancy or after the baby arrives. When it is asked how the adolescent girls pass their everyday life in Rohingya camp, many adolescent girls expressed their pessimism about life. A number of them mentioned that they have lack of interest in daily activities due to isolation in the family and increased stress and anxiety in the camps. Many of them told us that they don't see a positive future and no destiny as well. As consequences, they suffer from various mental

Table 1.3 *Factors and Effects of Increasing Mental Problems among the Refugee Females*

Factors	%	Effects	%
Migration history	23.2	Sleeping disorder	5.8
Loss of family members	9.7	Fear	39.6
Physical problems	33.1	Depression	24.9
Money and family crisis	20.8	Anxiety	13.2
Neighbours	5.9	Abnormal behaviour	5.4
Don't know	7.3	Don't know	11.1
Total	100	Total	100

disorders like anger, sleeping disturbance, appetite loss, etc. Similarly, many refugee women replied when it is asked what the status of their mental health. Many women complained that they have a poor relation with their husbands in the family which made them always angry and stressful. Feeling of hopelessness is very common among refugee women due to their previous physical and mental tortures upon them in Myanmar before influx that provoke them for lacking interest in life. Hafiza (28) is a refugee living in the Leda camp with symptoms of depression and anxiety. She told:

> Few days ago, my husband assaulted me and at one point I got injured in the head; every night he forces me for sex which makes me very sick; for many days, I have been suffering from fistula; sometimes, I find blood in my genital organ; recently he got married again with a teenage girl and shifted to his new wife; therefore, now I am living a helpless life with my two children, having constant financial crisis.

1.4. Conditions of Refugee Camps and Context of Health Challenges

The refugees live in emergency-like situation which is low quality and unhealthy. The majority of the refugees are undernourished which hampers their physical and mental development (MSF 2002). They need food, clean water and shelter to survive, but above all they need to feel safe. Globally, refugee women and children reported facing gender-based violence including gang rapes resulting in infections, vaginal tears and posttraumatic disorders (Swanson et al. 2012). However, people are living in makeshift tents in hugely overcrowded settlements. Conditions in the camps are woefully inadequate and unhealthy, with overflowing latrines and contaminated water. The living conditions in the Rohingya refugee camps are very congested and poor in terms of access to WASH particularly to women and children (Banerjee 2019). Some studies (Chan et al. 2018; Hossain et al. 2019; Islam and Nuzhath 2018; Summers et al. 2018) found that poor hygiene and nutritional status, lack of access to safe water, food and sanitation, overcrowding, inadequate access to vaccination and health needs are fuelling various diseases among the refugees. However, decreasing groundwater level, increase of land surface temperature (LST), massive vegetation and other resources loss due to camp expansion, etc., can be considered as other environmental threats in the Rohingya refugee camps which are linked with health risks (Rahman and Paul 2021). Moreover, Rohingya females are particularly vulnerable to abuse, exploitation and trafficking (Oxfam 2017). Tay et al. (2018) noted that many refugees became quite emotional regarding their vulnerable situation and lack of hope. Conditions of the refugee camps and context of health challenges faced by Rohingya refugee women are discussed in the following.

1.4.1. Context of Physical Health Concerns

More than 75 per cent refugee females are concerned about their health risk. Table 1.4 shows that about six women in the refugee camps out of 10 consider their health risk from various diseases as high and very high. About 18 per cent Rohingya women think the matter as moderate. About 20 per cent females almost ignore their physical problems and consider the health risk as low and very low. A refugee woman named Moslema (42) of Leda camp who considered herself as an NGO volunteer mentioned that:

> We are always at health risk since we came here in the camp; among the women, adolescents face many health risk because they cannot seek help when they face physical problems because of sensitivity;

on the other hand, aged women suffer much as they become the family 'liability'.

Rohingya women living in the refugee camps illustrated many contexts for causing of physical diseases in both settings of FGD and questionnaire survey. Surrounding unhygienic environment and living condition are playing a key role for causing various types of diseases in the refugee camps (Table 1.4). About 29.6 per cent females think that the causes of diseases are mostly unhygienic environment. These camps become the 'breeding ground' for many diseases, especially infectious because of unhygienic condition in the camps. As the refugee camps are situated in the hilly area, there is abundance of mosquitoes which are the main reason of parasitic diseases. Cold and cough and high fever are mostly caused by unhygienic environment. A good number of female refugees (23.3%) think

Table 1.4 *Perception of Risk, Causes of Disease and Cleanliness in the Refugee Camps*

Risk	%	Causes of Disease	%	Camp Points	Observation Findings
Very high	27.4	Poor quality of water and dirty latrine	23.3	Surrounding area	Mostly dirty and unhygienic
High	31.1	Unhygienic environment	29.6	Latrine	Mostly dirty and unhygienic
Moderate	17.9	Lack of quality food and proper nutrition	23.8	Inside the house	Mostly clean
Low	10.3	Increasing pollution in and around camps	13.5	Kitchen	Mostly dirty
Very low	9.7	Lifestyle and food habit	8.1	Courtyard	Mostly clean
No idea	3.6	No idea	1.7	Children playground	Mostly dirty and unhygienic
Total	100	Total	100		

that contaminated water and dirty latrine causes waterborne diseases like bloody/haemorrhagic diarrhoea, cholera, typhoid, etc. In rainy season, these types of diseases spread quickly. Poor bathing conditions have also been marked by women as another threat for their health. In an FGD with aged women, most of them said that water source scarcity, poor drainage and lack of effective sanitation facilities, especially insufficient latrines are the main factors responsible for waterborne and infectious diseases among the refugee women. Sabera (33) of Unchiprang camp told:

> Some latrines are very close to water collection points in the camp, so water can be contaminated by human waste or the water in the latrine or its (latrine) smell; disease can come to us very easily.

Some respondents (23.8%) said that lack of quality food and nutrition is the cause of many non-communicable diseases (NCD). In FGDs, good numbers of women think that malnutrition is the sole factor for catching diseases by the refugee women. Insufficient and unhygienic food may push them into health risk. Beside these, pollution in and around the camps may be considered as the important cause for many diseases by many refugee females (13.5%). It is mentionable that deforestation and hill cutting cause many diseases due to air pollution. In group discussion, almost all respondents mentioned about the excessive heat/hot temperature in the camp area which may be considered as a common factor for disease occurrence among the refugees, especially in the girls. Few recent studies (Hassan et al. 2018; Rashid et al. 2020) show that massive deforestation set into motion by huge Rohingya influx since the end of 2017 has been causing the increase of LST in the refugee camps and its neighbourhoods. About 8.1 per cent females think that Rohingya's food habits and their 'uncontrolled' lifestyle may be the cause of many diseases. A mid-aged woman (41) named Shufia of Kutupalong camp stated:

> I have been suffering from gastric from long time; (I) always feel vomiting tendency and chest burning after taking meals; actually, we prefer spicy dishes and like to take green chilies with rice; red chili mash with dry fish is very popular among us; maybe these are the reasons for catching such stomach diseases.

In FGDs, refugee females mentioned that tiny dwelling space of the refugees and camp structure has been blamed as important risk factors for disease occurrence among many refugee women. Due to high conservative nature among the Rohingya, most of the refugee women are compelled to stay at home during the daytime also, which ultimately reduces their social networking and health support from neighbours. Polygamy is very common among the Rohingya. It is common that many of the Rohingya males have illegal sexual relations which may be one of the major reasons of STI among the women respondents. In addition, it is mentionable that most of the Rohingya girls get married in their early age, especially in their adolescence. Lack of hygiene products and their uses have been considered as health threat for the adolescent girls. Many respondents commented that after the influx of refugees, the number of RTI patients has increased due to environmental pollution. Poor light and ventilation facilities inside the camp houses have also been considered as a major threat for the adolescents. Few girls (1.7%) have no idea about the causes of diseases they face in the refugee camps. Through observation, cleanliness in the refugee camps has been illustrated. Surrounding area, latrine, kitchen and children's playground in the camps appear dirty and unhygienic (Table 1.4).

1.4.2. Background of Mental Fear

The Rohingya refugees live in emergency-like conditions that are substandard and unhealthy. Mental problems of the Rohingya women in the camp have been increasing day by day and they are expected to grow. It is commonly observed that many women, girls and children have different forms of mental disorders. The brutality they faced caused different forms of mental problems. Apart from previous traumatic experiences, various sufferings in the camp are also increasing their mental problems. Gender-based violence, neighbourhood, forced migration, loss of family members, physical health risks, etc., act as factors. Many women and girls are not comfortable in the refugee camps. They are having a number of mental disorders. Among these, insomnia, depression, anxiety, fear, abnormal behaviour are severe.

When they were asked about the factors for their increasing mental problems, one third of the respondents replied that various physical diseases make them upset. In the group discussions, a significant number of females mentioned that many women don't get proper treatment in the NGO health centres. Some NGO healthcare providers told that despite of insufficient number of doctor's chambers compared to huge number of refugees, sensitivity is the main culprit where women don't want to share their confidential physical matters to the doctors or healthcare providers. Women may think that they would be stigmatized due to their health problems which might increase their mental sufferings further. A 15-year-old girl of Balukhali camp, Sabina told:

> Sometime I feel very helpless when I face some physical problems, especially urinal infections; when I seek attention of my mother for its remedy, she just asks me to drink water; one day, I shared the matter with a female NGO worker for some medicine, but within few days I come to know that people somehow knew the matter and they blamed me; many of them consider the problem as a bad disease which ultimately made me upset.

Rohingya females have seen violence, murder, rape. Many of them directly faced the torture in Myanmar. All of these have made them mentally vulnerable. About 33 per cent women told that their previous migration histories from Myanmar to Bangladesh and loss of family members by Burmese soldiers before the refugee influx make them mentally very disturbed (Table 1.3). Regarding the different types of mental problems, Parveen Akter (20), a refugee of Kutupalong New Extension camp said:

> I came to the refugee camp in Bangladesh with my son Ali being a single mother when he was only 8 months old; Burmese soldiers abducted my husband in 2017 when I was pregnant and, since then I don't know my husband's fate, although I presume that he is dead; it is very devastating for me; when the sadness and frustration become overwhelming, I become abnormal and often harm Ali; these abnormalities are increasing day by day; sometimes, I feel worried about my Ali's future.

In this study, we found many girls and women who carry many terrible memories with them. In Kutupalong new extension camp, a refugee girl named Sofura (17) shared her story about what she faced at the age of 14.

> Before coming here (in Bangladesh) I was kidnapped by Burmese soldiers for 2 months; it was a terrible history of being tortured and sexually assaulted by them; what a time I passed over there! Meanwhile, I lost my father and other relatives; still I feel pain in my whole body.

Apart from the previous history and family member loss by the conflict, refugee women feel that recent financial and family crisis is one of the responsible factors for increasing their mental problems in the camps. About one woman out of five feels stressed for money shortage and bad relation in the family. Daily stressors associated with the life in the camps including food problem and money crises are also increasing the mental dissatisfaction. In the group discussions, many female refugees mentioned that they become hopeless due to their insolvent status in the family which ultimately leads to many family crises. Bad relations with neighbours are another factor for refugee women's mental stress. Quarrel is very common in the refugee camps with abusive and vulgar words. Many women recollected the quarrels with the next-door neighbour and bad relations in the group discussion setting. However, few refugee women in the surveyed camps cannot recognize their causes of mental unhappiness.

1.5. Healthcare Facility for Rohingya Refugees

Local, national and international NGOs raised concerns because of the future generations and current humanitarian crisis of the Rohingya refugees (Tylor and Garmirian 2019). To improve the quality of life of the refugees, NGOs are assisting the government of Bangladesh (GoB) and UN agencies effectively. The humanitarian condition of the camp is seemingly stable due to the effective role of NGOs (Ahmed and Ahmad 2020). More than 100 national, international NGOs and UN agencies are playing big role for ensuring refugees essential health services along with other programmes like nutrition, WASH, site management services, etc., in the camp setting in Ukhia and Teknaf in association with the GoB (WHO 2020b). Working national, international NGOs and UN agencies give special focus on sexual, reproductive, maternal, neonatal, child and adolescent health; mental health and psychosocial support and non-communicable diseases (ISCG 2020). The partners in the health sector include 62 international partners, 59 national NGOs and eight UN agencies which adopted a three-tiered coordination structure. At the top level, a strategic advisory group, with representatives from Ministry of Health, Director General of Health Services, RRRC Health unit, Health sector working group coordinators, INGO and NGO health agencies serves as an advisory to the health sector (WHO 2020b). They manage all types of disease outbreaks in the refugee camps (ISCG 2020). The perception of female refugees regarding healthcare facility provided by development partners is discussed in the following.

1.5.1. Healthcare Support Types and Sources

Refugee women's problems may take place from biological, emotional or social perspectives. Regarding the source of healthcare, refugee women visit some places where they can receive their healthcare services. Some popular healthcare points in refugee camps are Medecins Sans Frontieres (MSF), International Organization for Migration (IOM), United Nations High Commissioner for Refugees (UNHCR), etc. MSF provides quality healthcare like outpatient consultations and inpatient admissions along with emergency service and medicine access. They also have door-to-door visiting programme in the camp. For women, they give maternal healthcare services with delivery and sexual and reproductive health services. Study shows that (Table 1.5) about 50 per cent refugee women visited their health centres once in their camp life. In terms of healthcare service, IOM also ensures door-to-door primary healthcare services along with referral services. One out of four refugee females used to go their health centres. UNHCR works on community health with the service of referral system. About 10 per cent of women like their services. Gonosatho Kendro provides sexual and reproductive awareness among the adolescents. International Centre for Diarrheal Disease Research, Bangladesh (ICDDR'B) helps to prevent the disease spreading, especially diarrhoea. Bangladesh Red Crescent Society (BDRCS) works on child protection with vaccination and case management along with first-aid support. Moreover, many

Table 1.5 *Sources of Healthcare for Increasing Physical and Mental Problems among Refugees*

Sources of Physical Healthcare	%	Sources of Mental Healthcare	%
MSF	49.6	UNHCR	25.1
IOM	23.9	ACF	19.7
ICDDR'B/BDRCS	3.2	MSF	19.3
UNHCR	9.7	BRAC	14.7
Gonoshasto Kendro	3.5	IOM	11.8
Others	10.1	Others	9.4
Total	100	Total	100

local and international agencies (UNFPA, WHO, UNICEF, HOPE, BRAC, RTMI, CARE, Action Contre La Faim [ACF]) give their services for managing gender-based violence, adolescent health, community health awareness, nutrition, etc., in the refugee camps.

Though violence and oppression are very common in the life of a refugee, women suffer more often both inside and outside the home. The changing mobility profile and the increasing economic role of the women lead to more violence against women. This study finds that refugee women have a high level of psychological distress, especially poor sleep and unexplored mental abnormality. Many elderly women described that sleeplessness is very common and they have to even use some herbal medicines for remedies about insomnia. In addition, some young married women mentioned that they can recognize and understand their anger, laziness, absent-mindedness, appetite loss, etc., as abnormal behaviour. One Rohingya woman of Balukhali camp, Rabeya (29) said:

> Although we had many resources in Myanmar, (but) there was no peace or satisfaction; on the contrary, in Bangladesh, we live here with mental peace but without resources.

For many of them, depression come from the sense of mental peace they have. Most of the girls and women think that they owned many belongings without mental peace while they were in Myanmar. Although they are penniless now, they have mental tranquillity. However, about 11 per cent women do not understand why they are mentally dissatisfied. Regarding the mental healthcare support, some international agencies and local NGOs have been providing psychosocial support in various camps to the Rohingya refugees. Among the service providers (Table 1.5), UNHCR is in the top for their quality services. They usually provide mental health and psychosocial support to their respondents. About 25 per cent female refugees have taken their services. ACF gives mental health and psychosocial support through counselling, community consultation and awareness making. They have the clinical support as well where one female out of five take their support. MSF provides individual psychosocial and mental health consultation for all refugees through counselling. About 20 per cent females take their mental support. BRAC, one of the leading NGOs of Bangladesh, provides mental health and clinical support to the victims and potential vulnerable females. Moreover, IOM, Handicap International, BDRCS, RTMI, CARE, etc., support the mental health victims. Here, it is mentionable that most of the agencies and NGOs provide meditation and breathing exercise (Yoga), physical exercise, life-skill training, coping techniques for survival, etc., and many of them involve clinical psychologists in their programmes.

1.6. Conclusion and Recommendations

Although our knowledge about the relationship between migration and women's health is increasing, we still have a limited knowledge of the health vulnerabilities of refugee females. Rohingya refugee women and girls' health status and related problems have been prioritized in this chapter. The chapter aimed to assess major health vulnerabilities focusing on the physical and mental health of Rohingya refugee females and exploring their causes. Unhygienic and over-crowded refugee camps have been affecting the physical and mental well-being of these female refugees. Many infectious or contagious diseases and waterborne diseases may spread both in the camps and its neighbouring localities due to lack of clean water and sanitary facilities and unhygienic condition. Recently, a good number of HIV/AIDS and COVID-19 cases have been identified among the Rohingya refugees which can be considered as a serious health threat for both the local men and women due to social and cultural practices, beliefs and attitude and inadequate healthcare facilities. In addition, many health vulnerabilities have been gradually increasing among the female refugees in many camps. Many female Rohingya refugees need emergency health services, including care for different types of communicable and non-communicable diseases. They also need more access to pure drinking water, clean latrines, hygiene practices and vaccination coverage. Apart from physical health service, different healthcare providers need to increase availability and access to specialized mental health services for the refugees, especially females. However, reforestation programme should be introduced immediately in this area to reduce the LST and heat-induced health concerns. Thus, both behavioural and structural changes can reduce many communicable diseases, NCDs and psychiatric disorders of the female Rohingya refugees. Camp authorities need coordination among the health service providers and quality of healthcare services. Coordination is also needed between the international funding agencies and local implementing organizations. Finally, it is a matter of hope that many UN agencies, international charity organizations, Bangladeshi NGOs, along with different wings of Bangladesh government will ensure healthcare services for the Rohingya refugees, especially women and children.

Acknowledgement

The authors are thankful to the Research and Publication cell, Chittagong University, Bangladesh for funding the project and Department of Geography and Environmental Studies, CU for different forms of support during the study. We are thankful to the NGO officials for assistance and grateful to the respondents who participated in the survey in various refugee camps.

References

Ahmed, M. Z., and A. Ahmad. 2020. 'Reclaiming Fate of Rohingya Refugees: Role of Local and International NGO's'. *International Non-Governmental Organizations Congress - NGO'19*, November: 1–3. Available at https://www. researchgate.net/publication/339106476 (accessed on 18 April 2021).

Ahmed, B., M. Orcutt, P. Sammonds, R. Burns, R. Issa, I. Abubakar, and D. Devakumar. 2018. 'Humanitarian Disaster for Rohingya Refugees: Impending Natural Hazards and Worsening Public Health Crises', *The Lancet Global Health* 6 (5): 487–488.

Akhter, S., and K. Kusakabe. 2014. 'Gender-based Violence among Documented Rohingya Refugees in Bangladesh', *Indian Journal of Gender Studies* 21 (2): 225–246.

Alam, M. 2017. 'Women and Girls at Risk in the Rohingya Refugee Crisis', *Council on Foreign Relations*. Available at https://www.cfr.org/blog/women-and-girls-risk-rohingya-refugee-crisis (accessed on 30 November 2020).

Arie, S. 2019. 'Healthcare for the Rohingya People: Traumatized by Violence Trapped in Squalor'. *British Medical Journal* (Online) 364–366.

Banerjee, S. 2019. *The Rohingya Crisis: A Health Situation Analysis of Refugee Camps in Bangladesh.* ORF Special Report No. 91. Kolkata: Observer Research Foundation.

Chan, E. Y., C. P. Chiu, and G. K. Chan. 2018. 'Medical and Health Risks Associated with Communicable Diseases of Rohingya Refugees in Bangladesh 2017'. *International Journal of Infectious Diseases* 68: 39–43.

Green, J., and N. Thorogood. 2004. *Qualitative Methods for Health Research.* London: SAGE Publications.

Hassan, M., A. Smith, K. Walker, M. Rahman, and J. Southworth. 2018. 'Rohingya Refugee Crisis and Forest Cover Change in Teknaf, Bangladesh'. *Remote Sensing* 10(5): 689.

Hossain, A., S. Ahmed, M. Shahjalal, and G. U. Ahsan. 2019. 'Health Risks of Rohingya Children in Bangladesh: 2 Years On'. Available at https://www.rohingyapost.com/health-risks-of-rohingya-children-in-bangladesh-2-years-on/ (accessed on 21 December 2020).

HRW, 2017. 'All of my Body was Pain—Sexual Violence against Rohingya Women and Girls in Burma, Human Rights Watch'. Available at https://www.hrw.org/sites/default/files/report_pdf/burma1117_web_1.pdf (accessed on 2 November 2020).

Imran, H. F., and N. Mian. 2014. 'The Rohingya Refugees in Bangladesh: A Vulnerable Group in Law and Policy'. *Journal of Studies in Social Sciences* 8 (2). Available at https://infinitypress.info/index.php/jsss/article/view/776 (accessed on 2 December 2020).

ISCG. 2020. '2020 Mid-Term Review: Rohingya Humanitarian Crisis January–July 2020'. *The Strategic Executive Group and Partners*. Available at www.humanitarianresponse.info/en/operations/bangladesh (accessed on 5 January 2021).

Islam, M. M., and T. Nuzhath. 2018. 'Health Risks of Rohingya Refugee Population in Bangladesh: A Call for Global Attention'. *Journal of Global Health* 8 (2): 020309.

Kitchin, R., and N. J. Tate. 2001. *Conducting Research into Human Geography: Theory, Methodology and Practice.* London: Prentice Hall.

Mahmood, S. S., E. Wroe, A. Fuller and J. Leaning. 2017. 'The Rohingya People of Myanmar: Health, Human Rights, and Identity', *The Lancet* 389 (10081):1841–1850.

Milton, A. H., M. Rahman, S. Hussain, C. Jindal, S. Choudhury, S. Akter and J. T. Efird. 2017. 'Trapped in Statelessness: Rohingya Refugees in Bangladesh'. *International Journal of Environmental Research and Public Health* 14 (8): 942–949.

MSF 2002. '10 years for the Rohingya Refugees in Bangladesh: Past, Present and Future'. *Médecins Sans Frontières-Holland.* Available at https://www.msf.org/ten-years-rohingya-refugeespast-present-and-future-report-summary. (accessed on 23 December 2020).

OXFAM. 2017. 'Bangladesh Rohingya Refugee Crisis, Oxfam International'. Available at https://www.oxfam.org/en/what-we-do/emergencies/bangladesh-rohingya-refugee-crisis (accessed on 7 January 2021).

Palinkas, L. A., S. M. Pickwell, K. Brandstein, T. J. Clark, L. L. Hill, R. J. Moser and A. Osman. 2003. 'The Journey to Wellness: Stages of Refugee Health Promotion and Disease Prevention'. *Journal of Immigrant Health* 5 (1): 19–28.

Paul, A. 2020. *HIV/AIDS in Bangladesh: Stigmatized People, Policy and Place.* London: Springer. Available at https://www.springer.com/gp/book/9783030576493 (accessed on 13 December 2020).

Pocock, N. S. 2017. *Occupational Risks, Health Needs and Victim Identification of Trafficked Fishermen in the Greater Mekong Sub region (GMS).* Doctoral Dissertation, London School of Hygiene & Tropical Medicine, University of London, UK.

Rahman, M. A., and A. Paul. 2021. Geo-environmental Changes in Rohingya Refugee Neighbourhoods: Spatio-temporal Evidences. In *Living with Uncertainties: The Rohingya in Bangladesh, India and at the Global Scale*, edited by N. Uddin. New Delhi: SAGE Publications.

Rashid, K. J., M. A. Hoque, T. A. Esha, M. A. Rahman and A. Paul. 2020. 'Spatiotemporal Changes of Vegetation and Land Surface Temperature in the Refugee Camps and its Surrounding Areas of Bangladesh after the Rohingya Infux from Myanmar'. *Environment, Development and Sustainability.* Available at https://link.springer.com/article/10.1007/s10668-020-00733-x (accessed on 18 December 2020).

Riley, A., A. Varner, P. Ventevogel, H. M. M. Taimur and C. Welton-Mitchell. 2017. 'Daily Stressors, Trauma Exposure, and Mental Health among Stateless Rohingya Refugees in Bangladesh'. *Transcultural Psychiatry* 54 (3): 304–331.

Sultana, N. 2011. 'Healthcare at Rohingya Refugee Camp: A Case Study on RTM Initiative'. *RTM International.* Available at https://healthmarketin-novations.org/sites/default/files/Healthcare_Refugee_Camp.pdf (accessed on 11 January 2021).

Summers, A., A. Humphreys, E. Leidman, L. T. V. Mil, C. Wilkinson, A. Narayan, M. L. Miah, B. G. Cramer and O. Bilukha. 2018. 'Notes from the Field: Diarrhea and Acute Respiratory Infection, Oral Cholera Vaccination Coverage, and Care-Seeking Behaviors of Rohingya Refugees-Cox's Bazar, Bangladesh, October–November 2017'. *Morbidity and Mortality Weekly Report* 67 (18): 533–535.

Swanson, S. J., C. R. Phares, B. Mamo, K. E. Smith, M. S. Cetron and W. M. Stauffer. 2012. 'Albendazole Therapy and Enteric Parasites in United States-bound Refugees'. *The New England Journal of Medicine* 366 (16): 1498–1507.

Tay, A. K., R. Islam, A. Riley, C. Welton-Mitchell, B. Duchesne, V. Waters, A. Varner, D. Silove and P. Ventevogel. 2018. 'Culture, Context and Mental Health of Rohingya Refugees: A Review for Staff in Mental Health and Psychosocial Support Programmes for Rohingya Refugees'. Geneva: United Nations High Commissioner for Refugees (UNHCR).

Tylor, E., and C. Garmirian. 2019. 'Sixty-one NGOs Warn of Worsening Crisis in Myanmar, Call for Refugees' Engagement on Safe, Voluntary'. Available at https://www.savethechildren.org/us/about-us/media-and-news/2019-press-releases/ngos-warn-of-worsening-crisis-in-myanmar (accessed on 5 February 2021).

Uddin, N. 2019. 'The State, Vulnerability, and Transborder Movements: The Rohingya People in Myanmar and Bangladesh'. In *Deterritorialised Identity and Transborder Movement in South Asia*, edited by N. Uddin and N. Chowdhory, 73–90. Singapore: Springer.

Uddin, N. 2020. *The Rohingya: An Ethnography of 'Subhuman' Life.* New Delhi: Oxford University Press.

UNHCR. 2020. 'Rohingya Emergency'. Available at https://www.unhcr.org/rohingya-emergency.html (accessed on 3 January 2021).

White, K. 2017. 'Rohingya in Bangladesh: An Unfolding Public Health Emergency'. *The Lancet* 390 (10106): 1947.

WHO. 2017. 'Health Emergency and Disaster Risk Management Communicable Diseases, Health Emergency and Disaster Risk Management Fact Sheets, December 2017'. Available at https://www.who.int/hac/techguidance/preparedness/risk-management-communicable-diseases-december2017.pdf (accessed on 9 January 2021).

WHO. 2018. 'EWARS Epidemiological Bulletin—Cox's Bazar, W21'. Available at https://www.who.int/docs/default-source/searo/bangladesh/bangladesh---rohingya-crisis---pdf-reports/ewars/ewars---2018/ewars-w21-2018.pdf?sfvrsn=127c77bf_2 (accessed on 21 December 2020).

WHO. 2020a. 'Refugee and Migrant Health'. World Health Organization. Available at https://www.who.int/migrants/en/ (accessed on 4 March 2021)

WHO. 2020b. *Bangladesh Emergency: Rohingya Refugee Crisis in Cox's Bazar District Reporting Period: January–June 2020.* Geneva: WHO.

CHAPTER 2

Floating Voices from Within

Listening to the Rohingya Victims in Bangladesh

Jenny Lamb

2.1. Introduction

The plight of the Rohingya in Myanmar is grave and one which has gone on for decades with little respite, justice and future. They have been stripped of their civil, political, economic, social and human rights. The United Nations (UN) identified them as one of the most persecuted minority groups in the world. Yet, the Rohingya do not wish to be seen and viewed as stateless but rather as one of the 135 nationals of Myanmar—something they have fought for a lifetime. The metaphor—floating—is often used by the Rohingya to describe their predicament that they belong to neither Myanmar nor Bangladesh. The Rohingya apartheid system needs to be dismantled once and for all.

The Rohingya cite their presence in 1826 as natives of Arakan (Rakhine State) where they called themselves 'Rooinga' or 'Rohang' (Mahmood et al. 2017, 463). There was a time when both Rakhine

(Buddhists) and Rohingya (Muslims) shared a compatible life sharing resources, trading and working together. But this has been suppressed by various powerholders, such as the Tatmadaw (military), the Government of Myanmar (GoM) and the MaBaTha[1] given their joint sentiments of 'the Muslims of Myanmar had become to be seen as the outsiders bent on bringing the nation, and its majority Buddhist belief system, to ruin' (Wade 2017, 16).

More recently, in August 2017, clashes in Rakhine State broke out after a militant group known as the Arakan Rohingya Salvation Army (ARSA) claimed responsibility for attacks on police and army posts. Declaring them a terrorist group, Tatmadaw launched a brutal campaign that destroyed hundreds of Rohingya villages and displaced a large majority of them to Bangladesh. This brutal campaign included rape, torture, murder, arson and many more atrocities which forced more than 750,000 Rohingya to flee to Bangladesh. The UN Myanmar Fact-Finding Mission found that these brutal attacks were done with 'genocidal intent' (Human Rights Council 2018) and that their perpetrators must be investigated and prosecuted for genocide. The UN Secretary-General acknowledged this as 'the world's worst largest humanitarian and human rights crisis' (Guterres 2018) with more than one million Rohingya living in Bangladesh (Inter Section Coordination Group 2019). Throughout all of this, Aung San Suu Kyi (the former first State Counsellor of Myanmar and leader of the National League for Democracy), who had been known for her struggle for democracy and human rights, had not responded to the persecution in the fashion she had been known for, but had rather withdrawn from human rights, and tragically so, given the deep-rooted persecution and marginalization of the Rohingya.

The provision of water, sanitation and hygiene (WASH) is essential in displacement contexts to reduce public health risks through the access to and use of appropriate, safe and dignified WASH infrastructure. Typically, the WASH team comprises a public

---

[1] Group of high-profile monks who openly promote anti-Muslim narratives targeting the Rohingya.

health engineer (PHE) and a public health promoter (PHP) who are responsible for community engagement, design, implementation and monitoring of WASH-related activities and infrastructure. But the failure of WASH staff to produce solutions for refugees, like the Rohingya, is attributed to several reasons, which is the subject of this chapter.

The chapter aims to communicate the different characteristics of life for the Rohingya in Myanmar and Bangladesh, with an understanding of the different agencies[2] between the Rohingya and WASH staff when implementing sanitation activities in Cox's Bazar camps in Bangladesh.

First, the chapter will present the different life characteristics for the Rohingya living in either Bangladesh or Myanmar and how they cope with encampment and liminality. Second, looking through an anthropological lens, one will examine what agencies the Rohingya have in resisting, substituting and inventing sanitation infrastructure in the camps in Cox's Bazar; plus what interaction and relations exist among the WASH staff which translates to action when responding to the sanitation needs of the Rohingya.

2.2. Conceptual Framework and Methodology

2.2.1. Definitions

Van Gennep described liminality as the *rites of passage* with three stages: 'separation, liminal period, and assimilation' (Gennep 1960), while Turner defined the concept of liminality as 'neither here nor there; they are betwixt and between' (Turner 1969). Scholars have communicated a shift of emphasis from displacement to emplacement and life in camps as characterized by a state of both liminal and permanent precariousness (Agier 2011; Malkki 1995a). These definitions resonate how the Rohingya felt, as many echoed their sentiments of neither belonging in Bangladesh (*neither here*) nor in Myanmar (*nor there*) despite their longing for assimilation, recognition and justice—'it

---

[2] One's agency is the capacity of individuals to act independently.

is like we are floating, we have fear in our heart'—Rohima, adult female.

Regrettably, there are countless terms used to categorize the Rohingya from Myanmar and Bangladesh. These terms are politically loaded, which have grave consequences on their human rights or rather lack of. Some of these terms include 'Bengali immigrants', 'illegal Burmese migrants', 'Muslim terrorists', 'Burmaya' and 'forcibly displaced Myanmar nationals'. The latter term, ascribed by the Government of Bangladesh (GoB) in their biometric database is the current one—which is like a glass half full, with extreme notions of 'biopower, and biopolitics of otherness' (Fassin 2011, 214)—they recognize them as Myanmar nationals, yet they do not mention their refugee status, nor as Rohingya. I have a moral dilemma here, should I acknowledge this term 'forcibly displaced Myanmar nationals'—no, is an answer to this—given it is politically loaded—it is incorrect to not recognize them as refugees but also not to recognize them as Rohingya. Rights to being human and humanity are complex (i.e., their universality, upholding them in a meaningful way). I will concur and refer to them as Rohingya as I have done during my fieldwork and based on their self-identification as 'we are Rohingya'.

2.2.2. Ethnographic Fieldwork

Ethnographic fieldwork carried out in June 2019, targeted the camps and host areas in Nayapara and Unchiprang of Teknaf and Kutupalong and Balukhali of Ukhia. These locations provided an opportunity to consult with Rohingya who had been displaced in 1991, 2017 (different waves of displacement). Moreover, these areas have varying levels of population density between Kutupalong and Balukhali.

The justification for ethnographic fieldwork provided an opportunity to immerse oneself in as many aspects of the Rohingya's daily life (as appropriate) to understand their social and cultural norms, behaviours and interactions, and thereafter support them with anthropological interpretations. The detailed understanding and description of a particular time and location is known as a 'thick description' (Geertz 1972) which explores their behaviours, perspectives and the protracted context, with anthropological interpretations (i.e., encampment and liminality). Given their plight, I wished to tell their story with respect and humanity. The focus was listening and observing, with the goal of producing a snapshot of the Rohingya life, by allowing them to be open and steer the conversation.

A local translator supported the conversations with the Rohingya and thereafter transcribed the recordings. We were unable to stay overnight in the camps and were limited to a daily travel restriction from Cox's Bazar town to the camps. Given this limitation, we concentrated our efforts on building rapport with a small number of Rohingya to build depth and rigour, rather than a vast and shallow set of perspectives. Discussions ranged in length from 120 minutes to 240 minutes, with the latter atypical given the willingness of the Rohingya to engage, trust and talk with me.

Humanitarian informants included a range of WASH staff, journalists, the UN, the GoB and communications specialists at the aforementioned locations. Compliance with research ethics is key to any research and more so in the participant-sensitive context of the Rohingya crisis. I have consulted with only research participants who were willing to communicate voluntarily, and in no uncertain terms have they been persuaded to do so. Verbal consent from informants was obtained from the outset, all research data have been anonymized, and I have used pseudonyms for the Rohingya and WASH staff voices.

In summary, transect walks, participant observation (where I documented my observations, what I heard, and thereafter my reflections), unstructured and semi-structured discussions were carried out, which all played a pivotal role in the ethnographic fieldwork carried out in the Rohingya camps in Bangladesh.

2.3. Encampment and Liminality

Figures 2.1 and 2.2 provide a perspective of the resourcefulness and terrain where the Rohingya live but also a stark reminder of their congested and precarious life.

Figure 2.1 *Multicoloured Materials Characteristic of the Camp*
Source: Fieldwork in Cox Bazar, June 2019.

2.4. Belonging and Identity

2.4.1. 'We Are Rohingya'

Arakan State, now known as Rakhine State, is home to two major ethnic groups—Rakhine Buddhists and Rohingya Muslims. The Rakhine are followers of Theravada Buddhism and ethnically close to Burman. The Rohingya Muslims trace their ancestry to ancient Indian people of the Chandra dynasty of Arakan, plus Arabs, Turks, Persians, Bengalis. Evidence communicates that the Rohingya have been settled in present-day Arakan state for many centuries. The Arakanese had their first contact with Muslims in the 9th century when Arab merchants docked at an Arakan port and thereafter this seeded their descendance to Arakan between the 9th and 15th centuries (Uddin 2015, 66). In 1872, a British colonial census report identified an indigenous race living in Arakan and referred to them as 'Arakanese

Figure 2.2 *Drainage Art Forms*

Source: Fieldwork in Cox Bazar, June 2019.

Mussulman' (Haque 2017, 464), and the last colonial census in 1931, recognized them as Rohingya, and one of Burma's affirmed ethnic groups. Burma achieved independence from Britain in 1948. U Nu between 1948 and 1962 also officially declared Rohingya as one of the indigenous ethnic groups of Burma, but this was crushed by the military coup of General Ne Win in 1962, which stripped them of their civil, political, economic, social and human rights. In 1978, the Tatmadaw implemented a nationwide project called *Operation Dragon King* to register all citizens and aliens ahead of the national population census. This led to 200,000 Rohingya fleeing to Bangladesh, amid allegation of human rights violations. By 1982, it was set at 135 ethnic groups when the Rohingya were denied citizenship under the *Citizenship Law*, rendering them stateless. Burma was renamed Myanmar by the military junta in 1989. In 2014, Myanmar's first census in 30 years initially permitted to include Rohingya, but the Buddhist nationalists threatened to boycott the census, and the GoM had to revoke this and only register them as Bengali.

Literature and accounts from the research participants highlight there was a time when both the Rakhine and Rohingya shared a compatible life. They worked together on farms, in rice mills and brick kilns and they traded with one another. But this was put to a complete stop (by Tatmadaw, GoM and MaBaTha), and there were repercussions if one did not comply with these restrictions. This echoes the Rwanda crisis during which the Hutus were targeted if they had aided the Tutsis (Wade 2017).

The Rohingya also suffer from a lack of legal frameworks to protect them. Bangladesh is not a signatory to the UN 1951 Convention Relating to the Status of Refugees (UNHCR 1951). But there exist constitutional provisions and laws which, in principle, do cover the basic rights of the Rohingya in Bangladesh. Too often, the Rohingya displacement is treated arbitrarily as a bilateral issue between Myanmar and Bangladesh, rather than a matter requiring international accountability. Plus, the GoB has stated that rather than granting refugee status, it wishes to focus towards 'a safe, dignified, voluntary return to Myanmar' (UK House of Commons International Development Committee 2018). An NGO research informant echoed their frustration and dilemma, 'our hands are tied, we fear to have a voice - how do we deal with a rights-based response when we are perpetuating it by responding to the camps both in Myanmar and Bangladesh'.

Within the ethnographic findings, the Rohingya research participants acknowledged the following ethnic groups where they originated: Sheing, Kesheng, Murong, Burma, Chakma, Magh, Borowa,

Hindu, and Dara Foir—this most certainly echoes multiculturalism in one state, and that it is not simply Rohingya versus Rakhine (Gupta and Ferguson 1992, 7).

2.4.2. A Refugee? Stateless? Or the Rohingya from Myanmar?

A 'slippery citizenship' (Uddin 2015) is echoed by Rohima and Usman:

> 'It is like we are floating. The card is given to us so we can stay here. We think we have been registered here in Bangladesh, but they might not keep us here and might send us back. We have that fear in our heart.
>
> Rohima, an adult female

> It's like a punishment here. Our number one request is the GoM provides us with an ID card, our land, our houses and let us practice our religion. We want nothing more.'
>
> Usman, an adult male

Local integration is defined by *de facto* and *de jure* (Hovil 2014). *De facto* integration is an informal process where the stateless Rohingya negotiate their belonging in a locality through economic, social, cultural means—this I would argue is characteristic of the self-settled Rohingya who I spoke to in the host areas of Cox's Bazar. Whereas, *de jure* integration is a formal process, where one obtains new citizenship, which is evidently a political process and dependant on acceptance in a particular society—this I would argue is characteristic of the Rohingya who said they dreamt of being repatriated overseas or provided with a 'new code of citizenship' in Myanmar (Hammond 2004).

2.5. Social and Cultural Norms

2.5.1. Purdah

Purdah is an Urdu word meaning 'curtain' and is common among Muslims and some Hindu communities across South Asia. For the Rohingya women, its use is twofold: covering one's body from the gaze of men who are not part of the immediate family and gender segregation, which is achieved by remaining inside their homes. Female informants described purdah as their dignity. Men too believed that the purdah preserved their dignity given it linked to their economic ability. Some women prioritized their self-reliance and broke purdah to work outside the home (e.g., a Community Health Volunteers (CHVs) or in the rice fields) to support their families given the liminal predicament faced both in Cox's Bazar and Rakhine State.

2.5.2. Gender Roles and Relations

As mentioned earlier, Rohingya is a patriarchal conservative society. A guiding principle of NGOs is gender justice and empowerment, which calls for equal participation of both men and women in programme activities. With all good intentions and principles—the employment of an equal ratio of male and female CHVs in WASH led to the Rohingya women being threatened by certain powerholders in the camp and religious leaders for working for NGOs, as their employment disrespected Rohingya values (purdah). During this time, NGOs suspended activities and later resumed with no pressure or expectations made of female volunteers to return. Hasina, a CHV confided in an emotive way, whilst she stroked my headscarf that I had taken off whilst we sat outside the NGO office—it was almost her comfort blanket as she recounted her life and predicament.

> My eldest son was beaten because I worked for an NGO. They asked him, why I had been allowed to work.... I had to work, as my husband is sick, and I needed to provide for my family. I asked for help from the Majhi. I did not wear my NGO t-shirt, nor carry my volunteer bag so people did not suspect that I was going to work, but rather to visit the market. Back in Myanmar, I worked too—in the paddy fields and grew vegetables.

These changes, justified by NGOs, undoubtedly have changed the Rohingya society, providing women freedom of movement and opportunities to voice their ideas during decision making. But one must be cognizant that such changes can lead to social tension, especially when men who used to be the main powerholder find their wives and daughters provided with opportunities. This shared phenomenon of earning an income could facilitate a change in the patriarchal society—but one should be conscious of how this evolves, in the short and long term, and any repercussions.

2.6. Encampment

2.6.1. Encampment in Myanmar

Anthropology has presented the forced migration studies with a range of binaries, such as 'belonging and identity; displacement and emplacement; territoriality and liminality; camp-based and self-settled' (Chatty 2014). These binaries are critically relevant to understand the life that prevails for the Rohingya.

The Human Rights Council report on the findings of the Independent International Fact-Finding Mission on Myanmar (Human Rights Council 2018) together with my ethnographic field-work and my past humanitarian experience in Myanmar inform that the Rohingya, before the August 2017 unrest, often had their land, food and livestock confiscated, were denied freedom of movement and access to healthcare or curfews imposed upon them. Whilst the aforementioned do not explicitly mean that the Rohingya were living in a restricted camp per se—in reality, their family life had a refugee camp-like environment restricted upon them. The Rohingya did find measures to overcome these restrictions. They examined competencies in their community and designated teachers, traditional birth attendants, traditional healers and Imans to provide the essential structures and basic services for their community, which the Rakhine State was not willing to provide.

Overall, this crisis has persisted from the long and ongoing silence of humanitarian actors inside Myanmar who have frustratingly watched this crisis develop over time—their hands have been tied with unacceptable compromises due to intimidation by the state, resulting in negative repercussions for the Rohingya. Mahony powerfully alluded this to 'subsidising apartheid and paying for illegal prisons' (Mahony 2018, 9). Adding insult to injury, Myanmar demand that the NGO staff working in Rakhine refrain from using the word 'Rohingya' at all and most complied, thus assisting the state in erasing their identity. This is something I can relate to and grappled with personally. Whilst working in Rakhine, I referred to them as Rohingya and had several reprimands from management and technical Rakhine staff. I too had to compromise, given this intimidation and the lack of cooperation from the Rakhine staff I was working with at the time. This is unacceptable despite our efforts to institutionalize the humanitarian ethos and human rights principles within our teams. We 'need better defensive strategies for confronting state pressures and intimidation to sustain the humanitarian and human rights principles we stand for' (Mahony 2018, 4).

2.6.2. Encampment in Bangladesh

Scholars (Agier 2011; Horst 2006; Malkki 1995b) showed how displaced populations shape the social order of a camp and manage to transform from displacement into emplacement (placemaking). Dadaab of Kenya, Mishamo in Tanzania, and Cox's Bazar in Bangladesh all illustrate displaced populations emplace themselves in a camp space, where with time social networks provide a robust support mechanism.

Malkki's ethnography on the Hutu refugees living in the Mishamo camp is similar in fashion to the Rohingya who wished to hold on to their identity as the displaced Rohingya in Cox's Bazar. Whilst in contrast, Malkki found that the urban refugees in Tanzania wished to lose one's identity and the Rohingya families also wished to assimilate alongside the Bangladeshi community. She related her findings to a mythico-history narrative (true members of Burundi) where 'Hutu/Tutsi relations in Burundi were structurally reproduced in the refugee/Tanzanian relations within the camp' (Malkki 1995a, 121). The Hutu refugees in Mishamo did not wish to relinquish their 'up rootedness' and 'remain in a categorical state of displacement, both legally and socially' (Malkki 1995a, 209)—this could be said the same scenario for the Rohingya in the Cox's Bazar camps.

Feldman said that the life of refugees is shaped by a 'camp as a humanitarian space, as a political space, and an emotional space', and camp life 'is a nexus of constraint and possibility' (Feldman 2015, 245). This is echoed during an informative discussion I had with a group of adolescent boys, aged 13–18 years. Their 'humanitarian and emotional space' pleaded for access to education and a shaded area where they could meet with their friends. All anxiously mentioned how important their education was to them—'our studies have stopped—we are growing younger now', said Mohammod. They said they were not able to access a consistent education, nor pitched at the right level—as most NGOs offered activities for younger children, and an Iman at a madrasa communicated 'we were instructed by GoB to not permit non-Bengalis to attend here'. Despite this gap, their tenacity and resourcefulness were evident—as they had found Rohingya teachers who organized private lessons and others reaped the benefits of their diasporic connections and social media by connecting on WhatsApp to teachings by the Rohingya living in Malaysia.

The Rohingya have self-settled in villages along with Bangladeshi communities, but competition for employment and resources is an issue. Daily labour, fishing, boat making, working in brickfields, agriculture and carpentry are all sources of employment. Given the precarious life of the Rohingya, they sell their labour at a cheaper rate than the locals do, which strips the Bangladeshis of employment. NGO staff recruits the Rohingya as paid volunteers, whilst others engage in clandestine activities, working illegally and for low wages. This further supports the predicament with 'Article 17—right to engage in wage-earning employment' of the Convention Relating to the Status of Refugees (1951), as too often humanitarian organizations have their hands tied when the GoB and/or donors do not permit displaced people to work. This puts into question the universality of such a Convention and moreover the lacklustre of the accountability in upholding these rights in the first place.

2.7. Liminality

Liminality as highlighted previously is when people feel 'neither here or there; they are betwixt and between' (Turner 1969). Ali in Nayapara acknowledged this liminal flux of not knowing where home might be 'the thought of Myanmar gives me goosebumps—I fear to hear the name. Without justice, our rights, access to our home and land—how can one go home?'—adult male.

Rohingya research informants, Perez Murcia (2016) and Malkki (1995a, 518) refer to refugeeness with the metaphor 'floating', 'a floating world either beyond or above politics and beyond or above history—a world in which they are simply "victims" ... and become a deeply dehumanizing environment for refugees'. Floating a common metaphor for the Rohingya, as they found themselves accepted *neither here* in Bangladesh *nor there* in Myanmar (Turner 1969). Rohima said, 'it is like we are floating, we have fear in our heart'—adult female.

In Nayapara registered camp, Fatema and Alauddin (an elderly couple) recounted their precarious situation, as they have been living in the camp since the 1990s. Their son, Tarek had taken his future into his own hands by becoming a teacher in Malaysia. However, news about Tarek's journey—that he was fit and well—took four years to reach his parents. Fatema said, 'when we heard from him after four years I felt at ease—but I had lost my eyes crying for him'. In other words, Fatema's eyesight had deteriorated given the volume of tears shed for her son, who she thought had died. Whilst her husband Alauddin said,

> 'We wish for our citizenship in Burma, we wish for our land under our feet, we wish to have jobs and when we die, we wish to be buried in our country. We wish for a future for our children. Allah is the one to provide us peace.'

Their resilience and emotion are illustrative of the sheer frustration of not knowing their future, and the unbeknown territory of when children like Tarek take their liminal life into their own hands. Here, the camp has become part of their identities and bodies, providing a notion of 'historical embodiment' where the body is the site of incorporated history (Bourdieu 1991, cited in Sigona 2015, 9).

Malkki (1995a, 509) raises a thought-provoking point, which I too asked myself: 'To go home is where one belongs. But is it?' Some feel their rooted homeland to be Rakhine, despite the precarious life there. Whereas some no longer wish to consider it as 'home' given the atrocities they faced there. Repatriation to Myanmar for all is perhaps too much an assumed ideology—as one's actual homeland is heterogenous for the Rohingya.

2.8. Anthropology of WASH Infrastructure

Toyoba said 'the latrines are not separate – so we don't know if it is a man or a woman. That's a problem.'

'We did not have time—from the beginning, it was all about numbers, and coverage of latrines' (National WASH—Male).

'We only had time to ask people where to locate the latrines, not the details and the actual design' (National WASH—Male).

'We implement too much with a technical lens, and we have lost our emotional sense' (National WASH—Female).

WASH is essential in displacement contexts to reduce public health risks through the provision of safe and dignified access and use of facilities, which are appropriate for all cultures, gender and age. The WASH team includes PHE and PHP staff who are responsible for engaging and consulting communities on design, implementation and management of WASH-related activities.

The following sections will present an understanding of the interactions and relations, which exist between WASH staff, and how this translates in their agency when responding to the sanitation needs of the Rohingya. Moreover, it will provide an overview of the levels of agency, which the Rohingya have in resisting, substituting and inventing WASH infrastructure upon their liminal life in Cox's Bazar.

2.9. Brokers, Translators and Aid

Anthropologists are critical of development and aid. Too often, it is full of buzz words, where NGOs dive in headfirst without understanding the complexities and subsequently oversimplify their failures and successes. Emma Crewe wrote that 'our aim is not to arbitrate between these groups and decide upon either success or failure, but to comment

Figure 2.3 *Emergency Latrines*

Source: Fieldwork in Cox's Bazar, June 2019.

on the perceptions about good or bad programmes reveal about the workings of development' (Crewe 1998). I can relate to this, and I endeavour to 'reveal humanitarian workings' between the Rohingya and the WASH team.

Within the humanitarian discourse, there is the issue and question of 'who defines what is technical?' (Crewe 1998, 107). This question, raised commonly among the PHP and PHEs, is personality dependent, competency-based and depends on how one can translate theory into practice.

Brokers represent local populations and work as mediators. Community-based ethnographies like this one can inform structural, policy-level and technical transformations at the local, national and international levels. Brokers in this context include Rohingya themselves, PHPs, PHEs and I—whereby the Rohingya heterogenous life is deconstructed and translated into a material and conceptual order of a successful project (Lewis and Mosse 2006, 12, 14).

2.10. Engagement and Participation

Community engagement and participation in humanitarianism suffer from 'a cosmetic label'—where it is included in programme strategies and donor contracts, is rather tokenistic, and the notions of participation are 'our' project and not 'their' project. Chambers calls for a 'paradigm shift from things to people', to ask ourselves 'whose reality counts?' and 'rather we (NGOs) participate in their project and empower them to take control of their analysis and decisions' (Chambers 1995, 30). Their reality, gender, social and cultural norms and the notion of their project are asserted through self-built latrines in their homes for use by women, girls and the elderly.

Referring to Figure 2.4, I would like to draw readers to the ladder concept for citizen participation by Arnstein, which communicates the extent of citizen participation and how much power people hold to determine their processes and outcomes—'citizen participation is citizen power' (Arnstein 1969, 216). In non-participation, powerholders 'cure or educate participants', for tokenism; 'participants views are heard but not headed', and then for citizen control participants 'negotiate and engage powerholders over decision making'.

For the last few years, a concerted effort and attention have been paid by the WASH sector to community engagement and

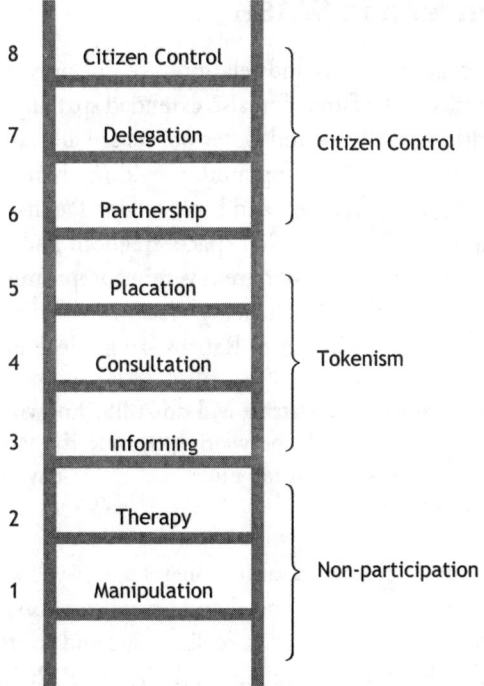

Degrees of Citizen Participation

Figure 2.4 *Arnstein's Ladder of Citizen Participation*
Source: Arnstein (1969).

participation. This seed is founded by learnings from the Ebola response in West Africa, and also the need for PHP to move away from a top-down approach; with too much focus on providing hygiene kits and hygiene messages in a. didactic fashion—which have mixed levels of success and impact (Oxfam 2016). This community engagement renaissance is long-awaited—that is, to sit down, listen, learn, empower and pass the responsibility to communities to take ownership in decision making and action (Niederberger, Knight, and O'reilly 2018). Not forgetting, this requires substance, capacity with both emotional and technical intelligence and changes in behaviour in WASH teams and other humanitarian professionals—'otherwise it will not be more than partial' (Chambers 1995, 41).

2.11. Gender and WASH

In Myanmar, gender roles and relations are not only defined for the division of tasks in the family but also extended spatially in their home. Latrines, bathing facilities and water points are allocated for women and girls at the rear of the compound, providing them with necessary privacy and dignity. The men and boys' latrine facility is at the front of the compound. This dignified space, freedom and clear-cut division of basic services by gender are severely compromised since their arrival at Cox's Bazar—which many research participants raised as being problematic. According to Rabeya, an adult female,

> 'I don't like going to the latrine as I don't like knowing that men are watching me or could be waiting outside the latrine after I finish. I don't drink nor eat too much during the day, or I go with someone else.'

A study in India highlighted sanitation-related psychosocial stressors attributed to environmental, social and sexual stressors, which can be attributed to access to infrastructure, life stage and contextual factors, thus leading to behavioural regulation (Sahoo et al. 2015). This argument is applicable here for Rohingya—as with the women's and girls' social and cultural norms (purdah), their limited access to latrines has led them to carry out regulatory behaviours, such as withholding food and drink, travelling in groups, going during dusk and dawn or defecating within their home (in a bucket or makeshift latrine). Behaviour is influenced by a person's environment—and the NGO community have been absent in listening and observing the Rohingya of their social and cultural norms, which has acerbated their liminal and encampment life, leaving them little or no option but to assimilate their own makeshift latrines.

2.12. Lettin or Latrine

2.12.1. Rohingya and Their Agency

'We were not consulted about the design of *lettins*—we were just asked where it could be built'—Khaleda, adult female. This correlates with the non-participation in Arnstein's ladder (1969) in

Figure 2.4, where Rohingya accepted the transaction of a latrine being built for them.

'We don't feel comfortable using *lettins* here, so we either go at night, go in a group, or make a hole in the shelter or use children's potties'—Nuru, adult female.

Nuru and Khaleda highlight the endemic issue of sanitation responses in the humanitarian WASH sector. Sanitation psychosocial stressors and latrines not being fit for purpose are a common issue. The field reality is WASH staff build communal latrines in the first phase (which should be segregated by gender), which progressively adapt to family shared (3–5 families per latrine) or individual household latrines (1 per household) as the context evolves. The report 'We're Listening' communicated that 'strong consultation and strong follow-through to implementation of community solutions appeared to lead to more appropriate latrines' and that 'first-phase latrines could act as rapid prototypes, which communities could co-create and provide feedback, promoting iterations' (Sandison 2019, 6, 7).

The separation of social spaces in respect to gender roles and relations is critically important for the Rohingya. The camp environment and WASH response have quashed this, resulting in them taking it into their own hands by resisting, substituting and inventing their own *lettin* inside their shelters. They had to exercise their agency (initiative) as a coping mechanism to deal with sanitation psychosocial stressors' characteristic of the camp.

The environmental stressors expressed by the Rohingya included: latrines are built too far from their shelter, on steep hillsides, with no privacy screens, locks or lighting, or were shared with many other people both male and female. Since their social stressors ranged from lack of privacy, dignity and social restrictions for women and girls, it intensified sexual stressors, with fear of gender-based violence, compromised privacy and dignity and meeting men whilst at the latrine.

Figure 2.5 illustrates the assumed comprehension of Western gender signs, plus the proximity of the latrines side by side (signs in English where most of the Rohingya are illiterate). Figure 2.6 illustrates a rather

Figure 2.5 *Male and Female Latrine Side (L)*
Source: Fieldwork in Cox's Bazar, June 2019.

tokenism attempt in erecting a screen between the two—at least an NGO tried, but one does wonder if this is sufficiently better to enlist both men and women to use the latrines or rather for them to continue through their own means.

Figure 2.6 A Tokenistic Effort of a Privacy Screen (R)
Source: Fieldwork in Cox's Bazar, June 2019.

These predicaments should never be something that women, girls and their families should need to do and rather more be avoided by meaningful consultation, empathy, compassion and putting oneself into their shoes—that is, ask ourselves how we would like to be consulted, what social values are part of family life, how is our home laid out, what WASH infrastructure do we have, what would we like a latrine to look like?

In summary, sanitation for the Rohingya suffers from 'social nakedness' (Shacknove 1985). Why this happens in the first place is a critical question. There are reams of guidance, best practice and policies which inform the absolute minimum that should be considered and included in latrine infrastructure. WASH research informants acknowledged this sheer negligence due to several reasons, which will be explained in the next section.

2.12.2. WASH Staff and Their Agency

The WASH sector objectives within the JRP for Rohingya Humanitarian Crisis are populated with equitable and effective WASH services that the Rohingya are encouraged to adopt individual and collective measures to mitigate public health risks, and that WASH promotes protection, safety and dignity (Inter Section Coordination Group 2019, 43).

The geographical landscape in Cox's Bazar—which the Rohingya and WASH staff had to contend with—is hilly terrain, prone to landslides, which suffered from a lack of space and time for planning. Nevertheless, I conducted fieldwork in June 2019 and the major displacement took place between August and December 2017. This time frame echoes surely a sufficient time to solve this endemic sanitation issue—should it not?

The Sphere Humanitarian Handbook (Sphere 2018) is the 'go to' guidelines for humanitarian workers and states that 'defaecation with dignity is a highly personal matter, plus appropriateness is determined by cultural practices, people's daily customs and habits, preferences.' The Pakistan earthquake response provided a stark example of a can-do attitude and awareness of social-culture norms. Latrine, bathing and menstruation hygiene management units were designed in response to the conservative and religious society of Pakistan. The fundamental question is—we have a wealth of experience, best practices and guidance, yet, we still have many latrines not fit for purpose and Rohingya adopting their own strategies. WHY? This question informed discussions with national and international PHE and PHP staff.

In short, the WASH response suffered from a cultural hierarchy—which is perhaps a stereotype atypical of Asia. National PHE staff acknowledged that they 'followed the standard designs' given by their senior PHE and got on with the job in hand with little scope for 'neither thinking out of the box, nor ask questions or to scope out reiterations with the Rohingya'.

A body metaphor again—but this time is 'blind', not naked. A PHE (Nat M) said, 'we engineers are blind. PHPs do the consultation and provide us with a weekly report that we follow up on'. Whilst a

PHP (Nat F) said, 'time is the essence for PHEs, and they believe in action, whereas we PHPs believe in community engagement and then action—this is the problem we have!'

During the first phase of the response, two senior WASH staff acknowledged that the sanitation response did not match the standards and expectations of the Rohingya and the WASH sector.

'Space and access were a grave issue, but is this is a genuine excuse to forget the absolute minimums? Locks are simple (small even!); I have no idea why they are always an afterthought and missed out. We need to translate this to our local teams—that's our failure' (International WASH—Lorna, female).

'Too many engineers are male, we need more female engineers', said Barsha, Nat. F.

Sally said, 'the first situation report is not valid if you have not respected the minimum standards, that is, does the community use the facilities and would you? It needs to be more than a number.'

One engineer said, 'We lack people who understand the social construct in WASH. Empathy and technical competence: how many of us have both of these competencies? The emotional burden is a massive component in WASH; how can we reduce this? It is not just only about building toilets' (International WASH—Male).

All of the aforementioned research participant comments provide a glaring nudge to seek help—and one NGO initiated latrine user groups, water user groups and listening groups and a *Women's Social Architecture Project* (WSAP; Oxfam 2018). The latter project enlisted architects (two local and two international, all female) as brokers and translators to bring a fresh pair of eyes to engage Rohingya women and girls and WASH staff to co-create, design and construct WASH facilities. The broker skill set of the architects 'engaged in blending, translating and reworking' diverging interests and perspectives (Koster and Leynseele 2018, 803).

WSAP led to a good level of interest from the WASH sector and Oxfam had requests to share their designs with other WASH NGOs. Credit to Oxfam—they said no, as they did not wish for designs to be equivalent to 'cookie cutters' and be replicated everywhere. Every camp is different, and families living within each block are different ('some wished to have the latrines segregated, and some were willing to share with other families', said Sarah, National WASH—Female). The WASH staff wished to educate and advocate that WSAP was a 'process' and not another cogwheel of standard designs being churned out and used by the masses. The unfortunate thing about WSAP, it occurred rather late in the response, small in output and lacked ownership at the field level, and that community engagement needs to be embraced by the PHEs and not just left to the PHPs.

Ruby said 'I liked the WSAP—it did not create anything new, but it rather repackaged better. It simply illustrated that you don't need 15-years of technical experience—but simply listening skills, putting yourself in their shoes, with appropriate action'—International WASH—Female.

This discussion calls for emotional intelligence, which relies on being self-aware, empathy, relationship management and effective communication. Emotions—inside and out—are at a height in humanitarian crises for the displaced community. The Rohingya in Cox's Bazar felt that their supposed safe, private and dignified needs of latrines and bathing areas were simply transactional for WASH staff. Jamila stated that 'they simply asked us where we could put it, and we were not asked about we liked, and needed', whilst Hassem acknowledged that 'later after a while, we were asked but by that time it was too late'. The WASH staff have suggested that they suffer 'too much from a technical lens' and that 'an emotional sense' is lacking.

I wonder if a WASH NGO would be willing to 'undertake a study aiming to learn about their staff's everyday practices – what they are doing, as distinct from what they are reporting – and their effects' (Eyben 2010, 384) what I endorse. This together with asking how people would like to be consulted, how can local and international staff be influenced for the better—is it an emotional trigger that is necessary? This would certainly open up a Pandora's Box, which is hugely necessary for the step change required to eradicate the allusions that the PHE and PHPs have built the perfect toilet. The Rohingya would welcome this, and anthropologists as 'brokers, and translators' could help this endeavour.

2.13 Conclusion

This chapter has described how the Rohingya cope with encampment and liminality and also examined the development and impact of sanitation infrastructure, through discussions with WASH staff in both Myanmar and Bangladesh.

The term 'floating' is symbolic of their precarious liminal life as their self-identification; 'we are Rohingya' has never been endorsed and accepted 'neither here' in Bangladesh 'nor there' in Myanmar (Turner 1969). The Rohingya have had to embrace an 'ethno-religious uniformity' (Wade 2017, 18), which has stripped them of their civil, political, economic, social and human rights. Despite this, their tenacity and resourcefulness are demonstrated by their proactiveness in seeking work, connecting on WhatsApp to teachings by the Rohingya living in Malaysia through their diasporic connections, and moreover alleviation of their sanitation psychosocial stressors through building their own latrines.

Sanitation errors have stripped them of their social values, their humanity and dignity. Informants attributed this due to the fact— there are not enough female engineers, there is too much a reliance on standardized designs, there was not sufficient time to consult users— PHEs plough on and PHPs catch up, that it was a numbers game to build as many latrines but moreover simply a lack of compassion and emotional responsiveness.

Overall, I still feel there are unresolved questions. This is about PHE and PHP staff being better equipped to understand the humanitarian context they are responding to—by putting aside their 'technical lens' and rather opening their eyes and ears to enable a benevolent understanding of the communities they are supporting from the outset. WASH staff in all seriousness have no excuse but to consider at least the 'quick wins' of including locks, privacy screens, lighting and gender segregation. This is a call for action, and I invite the first NGO who will undertake the study suggested by Eyben 'to examine staff's everyday practices – what they are doing, as distinct from what they are reporting – and their effects'. Maybe this emotional trigger is what we need, along with the regularity of suggesting WASH staff to put themselves in the shoes of the Rohingya and ask them what their minimum attributes of a latrine would be?

I will now conclude with this powerful quote, which highlights that different cultures and belief systems are a worthwhile diversity to fight for.

'Myanmar is a rainbow nation, and its vast array of different cultures and belief systems could all make a unique and important contribution to its future if they were allowed.' (Wade 2017, 132)

References

Agier, M. 2011. *Managing the Undesirables: Refugee Camps and Humanitarian Government*. Cambridge: Polity.

Arnstein, S. R. 1969. 'A Ladder of Citizen Participation.' *Journal of the American Institute of Planners* 35: 216–224.

Chambers, R. 1995. 'Paradigm Shifts and the Practice of Participatory Research and Development.' In *Power and Participatory Development: Theory and Practice*, 30–42. London: Intermediate Technology Publications. Available at https://opendocs.ids.ac.uk/opendocs/handle/123456789/690 (accessed on 10 September 2019).

Chatty, D. 2014. 'Part I Approaches: Old and New, Chapter 6: Anthropology and forced migration.' In *The Oxford Handbook of Refugee and Forced Migration Studies*, edited by E. Fiddian-Qasmiyeh, G. Loescher, K. Long, and N. Sigona, 74–85. 1st ed. Oxford: Oxford University Press.

Crewe, E. 1998. *Whose Development?: An Ethnography of Aid*. London: ZED Books.

Eyben, R. 2010. 'Hiding Relations: The Irony of "Effective Aid."' *European Journal of Development Research* 22: 382–397.

Fassin, D. 2011. 'Policing Borders, Producing Boundaries. The Governmentality of Immigration in Dark Times.' *Annual Review of Anthropology* 40: 213–226.

Feldman, I. K. 2015. 'What Is a Camp? Legitimate Refugee Lives in Spaces of Long-term Displacement.' *Geoforum* 66: 244–252.

Geertz, C. 1972. 'Deep Play: Notes on the Balinese Cockfight.' *Daedalus* 101: 1–37.

Gennep, A. V. 1960. *The Rites of Passage*. East Sussex: Psychology Press.

Gupta, A., and J. Ferguson. 1992. 'Beyond "Culture": Space, Identity, and the Politics of Difference.' *Cultural Anthropology* 7: 6–23.

Guterres, A. 2018. 'Myanmar's Refugee Problem among World's Worst Humanitarian, Human Rights Crises.' UN Secretary General. Available at https://www.un.org/press/en/2018/sc13469.doc.htm (accessed on 18 August 2019).

Hammond, L. 2004. 'Chapter 10: The Making of a Good Citizen in an Ethiopian Returnee Settlement.' In *Coming Home? Refugees, Migrants, and Those Who Stayed Behind*, edited by L. Long and E. Oxfeld, 187–205. Philadelphia, PA: University of Pennsylvania Press.

Haque, M. M. 2017. 'Rohingya Ethnic Muslim Minority and the 1982 Citizenship Law in Burma.' *Journal of Muslim Minority Affairs* 37: 454–469.

Horst, C. 2006. *Transnational Nomads: How Somalis Cope with Refugee Life in the Dadaab Camps of Kenya*. New York, NY: Berghahn.

Hovil, L. 2014. 'Local Integration.' In *The Oxford Handbook of Refugee and Forced Migration Studies*, edited by E. Fiddian-Qasmiyeh, G. Loescher, K. Long, and N. Sigona, 488–499, 1st ed. Oxford: Oxford University Press.

Human Rights Council. 2018. 'Report of the Independent International Fact-finding Mission on Myanmar—A/HRC/39/64.' Available at https://www.ohchr.org/EN/HRBodies/HRC/MyanmarFFM/Pages/ReportoftheMyanmarFFM.aspx (accessed on 18 August 2019).

Inter Section Coordination Group. 2019. 'Joint Response Plan (2019) for Rohingya Humanitarian Crisis—Snapshot.' Available at https://www.humanitarianresponse.info/en/operations/bangladesh/infographic/2019-joint-response-plan-rohingya-humanitarian-crisis-snapshot (accessed on 31 August 2019).

Koster, M., and Y. Van Leynseele. 2018. 'Brokers as Assemblers: Studying Development through the Lens of Brokerage.' *Ethnos* 83: 803–813.

Kundnani, A. 2014. *The Muslims Are Coming!: Islamophobia, Extremism, and the Domestic War on Terror*. London: Verso.

Lewis, D., and D. Mosse, eds. 2006. *Development Brokers and Translators: The Ethnography of Aid and Agencies*. Bloomfield, CT: Kumarian Press.

Mahmood, S. S., E. Wroe, A. Fuller, and J. Leaning. 2017. 'The Rohingya People of Myanmar: Health, Human Rights, and Identity.' *The Lancet* 389: 1841–1850.

Mahony, L. 2018. *Time to Break Old Habits—Shifting from Complicity to Protection of the Rohingya in Myanmar (Advancing Field Protection and Human Rights)*. Edison, NJ: Fieldview Solutions.

Malkki, L. H. 1995a. Refugees and Exile: From 'Refugee Studies' to the National Order of Things. *Annual Review of Anthropology* 24: 495–523.

———. 1995b. *Purity and Exile: Violence, Memory and National Cosmology among Hutu Refugees in Tanzania*. Chicago, IL: University of Chicago Press. Available at https://library.soas.ac.uk/Record/107487 (accessed on 2 June 2019).

Niederberger, E., L. Knight, and M. O'Reilly. 2018. *An Introduction to Community Engagement in WASH*. Oxford: Oxfam.

Oxfam. 2016. 'Guide to Community Engagement in WASH—a Practitioners' Guide, Based on Lessons from Ebola.' Available at https://www.oxfam.org/en/research/guide-community-engagement-wash (accessed on 14 September 2019).

———. 2018. 'Oxfam Rohingya Response: Women's Social Architecture Project, Phase 1 Final Report—Bangladesh.' Available at https://reliefweb.int/report/

bangladesh/oxfam-rohingya-response-womens-social-architecture-project-phase-1-final-report (accessed on 15 September 2019).

Perez Murcia, L. E. 2016. 'Losing and Remaking Home—Conflict and Displacement in Columbia.' Global Development Institute. Available at https://social.shorthand.com/GlobalDevInst/jgks7bGvMf/losing-and-remaking-home (accessed on 23 August 2019).

Sahoo, K. C., K. R. S. Hulland, B. A. Caruso, R. Swain, M. C. Freeman, P. Panigrahi, and R. Dreibelbis. 2015. Sanitation-related Psychosocial Stress: A Grounded Theory Study of Women across the Life-Course in Odisha, India. *Social Science & Medicine* 139: 80–89.

Sandison, P. 2019. 'We're Listening: An Evaluation of User-Centred Community Engagement in Emergency Sanitation. Bangladesh, Iraq, Lebanon and Uganda.' Available at https://reliefweb.int/sites/reliefweb.int/files/resources/gd-listening-community-engagement-emergency-sanitation-050219-en.pdf (accessed on).

Shacknove, A. E. 1985. Who Is a Refugee? *Ethics* 95: 274–284.

Sigona, N. 2015. 'Campzenship: Reimagining the Camp as a Social and Political Space.' *Citizenship Studies* 19: 1–15.

Sphere. 2018. *The Sphere Handbook—Humanitarian Charter and Minimum Standards in Humanitarian Response.* Available at https://handbook.spher-estandards.org/en/sphere/#ch001 (accessed on 14 September 2019).

Turner, V. 1969. *The Ritual Process: Structure and Anti-structure.* The Lewis Henry Morgan lectures. London: Routledge and K. Paul.

Uddin, N. 2015. 'State of Stateless People: The Plight of Rohingya Refugees in Bangladesh.' In *The Human Right to Citizenship—a Slippery Concept,* edited by R. E. Howard-Hassmann and M. Walton-Roberts, 62–78. University of Pennsylvania Press. Available at https://www.researchgate.net/publication/324442978_State_of_stateless_people_The_plight_of_rohingya_refugees_in_Bangladesh (accessed on 1 September 2019).

UK House of Commons International Development Committee. 2018. 'Bangladesh and Burma: the Rohingya Crisis.' Available at https://publications.parliament.uk/pa/cm201719/cmselect/cmintdev/504/50409.htm#footnote-118 (accessed on 31 August 2019).

UNHCR. 1951. 'Convention and Protocol Relating to the Status of Refugees.' Available at: https://www.unhcr.org/protection/basic/3b66c2aa10/convention-protocol-relating-status-refugees.html (accessed on 6 September 2019).

Wade, F. 2017. *Myanmar's Enemy Within.* London: ZED Books. Available at https://www.dawsonera.com/readonline/9781783605309 (accessed on 6 August 2019).

CHAPTER 3

Health Consequences of COVID-19 in Rohingya Camps

Roles Played by NGOs

**Meherun Ahmed and
Syeda Kaosar Jahan Barkha**

3.1. Introduction

The World Health Organization (WHO) on 11 March 2020, declared the COVID-19 outbreak to be a global pandemic, setting off a wave of nationwide lockdowns and declarations of national emergency. The Government of Bangladesh (GoB) immediately instituted measures to contain the spread of COVID-19—establishing quarantines and social distancing norms. The United Nations High Commissioner for Refugees (UNHCR) reports that globally 21,000 refugees across 97 countries tested positive for the novel coronavirus till September 2020 (Godin 2020). On 14 May 2020, the GoB confirmed the first cases of COVID-19 in the Rohingya camps of Cox's Bazar (Assessment Capacities Project 2020). At the end of September, 32 new cases were reported leading the tally close to 90 (WHO 2020b). Initially, it appeared that the world's largest refugee camp has been spared the predicted devastation of the coronavirus pandemic, but many human rights groups recently reported that COVID-19 infection rates are on the rise hinting at alarming consequences for this vulnerable group who fled the Rakhine State to secure refuge in a foreign land (Amnesty International 2020b) particularly in the desolated and crowded camps of Cox's Bazar.

Most high-income donor countries are facing deteriorating macroeconomic conditions due to COVID-19 situation with a decline in GDP growth, rising unemployment and debts. Prior studies have shown that, in times of recession, the donor countries reduce their foreign development assistance and redirect resources for resolution of domestic crises (Worley 2020). Despite commitments of the donor countries, the first five months of 2020 saw a 30 per cent decline in the Official Development Assistance as compared to 2019 (Morozkina 2020). Humanitarian assistance provided by donor countries constitutes an important source of financing for the refugee relief initiatives. Only 29 per cent of the United Nations' (UN) appeal for humanitarian assistance for 2020 was funded which will have serious negative consequences for the refugee response plans (Homaira, Islam, and Haider 2020).

The reduction in humanitarian funding will lead to food shortages and inadequate supply of essential services, for example, education, health, water, sanitation, nutrition, shelter and protection, etc. Even though we focus on the COVID-19 crisis affecting the health of the Rohingya in the camps, we acknowledge that service delivery of all basic human needs is intrinsically tied and exacerbates the negative long-run consequences of the COVID-19 pandemic on their lives. The critical services such as health, food security, nutrition, clean water, gas, hygiene, sanitation, waste management, etc. are highly correlated influencing each other. Inadequate short-term supplies in service delivery impede the short-run health response to coronavirus and have long-term negative health consequences (Human Rights Watch 2020).

António Guterres, the Secretary-General of the UN warned that diverting resources from humanitarian needs during this pandemic time would generate an environment in which multi-morbidity would flourish, for the elderly, women and children and other high-risk vulnerable groups. Cholera, measles and meningitis and other communicable diseases would thrive, even more children would become stunted and malnourished, maternal and neonatal mortality rates would spike, overall hospitalization and death rates would rise. It would also propagate the coronavirus disease itself which would simultaneously accelerate the likelihood of multi-morbidity, creating a vicious cycle. The long-run compounded consequences of all of these could be dire for the entire world, not just the refugees (UNOCHA 2020).

The camps in Ukhiya and Teknaf are among the most densely populated places on earth where social distancing is extremely challenging. In some of these camps, approximately 65,787 people live per square kilometre. While it was quite difficult to provide basic sanitation due to the high population density in the camps, it is next to impossible to maintain proper hand hygiene, social distancing, which are the minimum requirements to prevent the spread of coronavirus. The existing healthcare system in the camps was already under severe strain before the COVID-19 pandemic (JRP 2020b). The overcrowding and unhygienic conditions in the camps exacerbate the likelihood of a rapid spread of communicable diseases like COVID-19 which is alarming. Alemi et al. (2020) warned that the COVID-19 outbreak might 'exhaust medical resources and overwhelm camp hospitals within 58 days, which would lead to a rise in deaths from other infectious diseases, such as malaria'. The refugees' concern of getting deported or being isolated from their families in quarantines might also result in minimal voluntary testing. As a result, the true number of infected may be much higher. Without adequate precautions, they could grow significantly in the months and years to come (McPherson and Paul 2020). The economic impact of COVID-19 could also be dire. Reports suggest that the livelihoods of the majority residing in the camps have been adversely affected, which has compounded concerns in many social, economic and health sectors (Sutton 2020). The hardships confronting the refugees in recent months have made life inside the camps in Cox's Bazar immensely and increasingly difficult. The stark reality is that COVID-19 prevention will require not merely short-term preventative measures but also a long-term transformational response that would both be inclusive and sustainable. Without it, the fallout from a lack of preparation and disease control in camps will not only lead to the further spread of COVID-19 but also heighten the long-standing crises confronting the Rohingya refugee community.

The chapter is based on secondary sources as we critically review the existing reports of international humanitarian agencies, NGOs operating on the ground and media reports providing a summary of available services discuss the efficiency and efficacy of service delivery. It aims to analyse the roles that government and non-government organizations played during this pandemic in the Rohingya refugee camps. We focus mostly on the intervention areas of health as the pandemic poses the greatest health risk for the refugees to assess the current steps taken by the humanitarian initiatives in securing the camps from the spread of COVID-19 and improve service delivery in health, prevention and awareness. We also analyse the difficulties faced by the NGOs. Finally, we conclude by offering a set of policy guidelines designed to improve the well-being of the Rohingya refugees in the camps.

3.2. Extent of Spread of COVID-19 in the Camps

It is observed that in the first six months of the pandemic, starting from March 2020, case rates remained far lower than anticipated. The imposition of strict lockdown measures to curb the spread by the GoB, almost complete isolation from the neighbouring host communities, inadequate testing, low levels of voluntary testing due to stigma and fear of being isolated from families or deportation could explain why such a low number of cases have been reported.

Government authorities have enforced stricter restrictions on mobility in and out of the camps allowing only 20 per cent of the usual number of humanitarian workers access to the camps during the first few months of lockdown. Infrequent deliveries were made to reduce the risks of potential transmission of the virus. According to the UNHCR majority of the refugees are very young, close to the age of 18 or below, making them relatively less susceptible. A shortage of testing supplies and trained medical personnel to carry out the tests make screening difficult. Amnesty International (2020b) reported that in Cox's Bazar less than 1 per cent of the Rohingya population has been tested. It is thus possible that, with some cases of COVID-19 being undetected in camps, the officially reported infection rate is underestimated. The actual number of infected could be much higher (Monir 2020). On 14 May 2020, two Rohingya tested positive as the first cases of COVID-19 in the refugee camps of Cox's Bazar. Within a month, the WHO reported that the number of infected refugees rose to 38 by 17 June 2020. Till May 2021, the total positive cases of affected Rohingya refugees reached 996 cases with 13 confirmed deaths.

From the beginning of the pandemic, several studies predicted that the outbreak in the camps would be alarming if not timely controlled. Kamal et al. (2020) in their study of 23 camps with 600,000 residents projected that the hospitalization rate of COVID-19 positive patients will range from 2,391 to 6,143 in a slow transmission process which has the potential to rise to 8,228–15,865 in a high transmission process. In another study, Truelove et al. (2020) mentioned that they predict (with 95% Prediction Interval) 18 (in low transmission scenario), 54 (in moderate transmission) and 370 (in high transmission scenario) people among the total Rohingya population will be infected respectively within the first 30 days of the outburst (Truelove et al. 2020). Modelling data from the Johns Hopkins University projections, extrapolated to include all 34 camps, indicate that in a high transmission scenario approximately 16,000 refugees could require hospitalization in a single day during the peak (Truelove et al., 'COVID-19', 2020).

In the face of this humanitarian crisis, as per the JRP 2020a, the NGOs, in coordination and collaboration with the government, funding bodies and international humanitarian agencies are providing sustenance for the refugees who are almost solely reliant on this aid for their survival. It is thus of great importance to examine the supply-side initiatives taken by the civil society organizations not only to review the gaps but also to investigate the scope of improvement in terms of identification of priority areas, efficient management of the aid disbursement, etc.

3.3. COVID-19-related Assistance in the Camps

3.3.1. Essential Service Delivery: The Joint Response Plan 2020

At the onset of the COVID-19 crisis, the humanitarian community, led by the Inter-Sector Coordination Group (ISCG) and Strategic Executive Group (SEG), in close collaboration with the GoB provided a road map to prevent the negative consequences of the pandemic. They strategized the pathways to address the needs of the Rohingya refugees and provide life-saving assistance. Their plans also included mitigation of the crisis faced by the host communities. The JRP 2020b is a complete base for the Rohingya refugees in Bangladesh as a response to their necessity and requisites. The JRP is renewed every year since its inception in 2018 after taking stock of the conditions and needs of the Rohingya refugees and neighbouring host communities.

The JRP 2020 acknowledges that the main response strategy for the health sector is to decrease mortality and morbidity due to COVID-19 by taking measures collaborating with the government and non-government actors. The focus for establishing the response strategy is to build the following nine pillars: (a) coordination, planning and monitoring, (b) risk communication and community engagement, (c) surveillance, (d) camp points of entry, (e) field laboratory for Cox's Bazar district, (f) infection prevention and control (IPC), (g) case management, (h) minimum essential health service and (i) operational support and logistics (JRP 2020).

The first pillar will be particularly guided, coordinated and supervised by the WHO along with collaboration with other organizations to connect other stakeholders and publicize technical guidelines to all the partners. The second pillar will supervise and communicate the health risk factors and conduct 'community health engagement activities' (JRP 2020). For the third pillar surveillance-trained investigation team was appointed in each camp who will conduct contact tracing of COVID-19 within a day for any kind of outbreak. For the fourth pillar government authorities in collaboration with partners will ensure the activities of hand-washing stations and screening of temperatures. The capacity of Cox's Bazar field laboratory will be increased for conducting tests within time and labs will be facilitated with new diagnostic methods, which is the fifth pillar. The sixth pillar is infection prevention and control (IPC) department which will assure their quality for perfect assessment of medical and non-medical capabilities. The seventh pillar of case management will have facilities with screening areas and separate management for identified suspects of COVID-19 patients keeping the gender-based protection concept in mind. JRP 2020 reports that this sector 'aims to establish approximately 1,600 beds in isolation and treatment facilities in and around the camps including twelve new SARI (Severe Acute Respiratory Infection), ITCs (Isolation and Treatment Centre)'. The eighth and ninth pillars will secure minimal health service when needed and will cooperate to ensure the accessibility of logistics like oxygen cylinders, PPE, medical equipment and supplies. According to JRP 2020 analysis, the health sector requires US$160 million, of which US$86.5 million is allocated for COVID-19 requirements and the remaining US$73.5 million is for JRP priority requirements. JRP (2020) will execute its strategic planning in mitigating this humanitarian crisis with the help of 117 NGO partners (local, 61; international, 48; and UN agencies, 8). JRP has 20 sector projects for the health sector; 10 of which are focused on COVID-19. For the health sector, there are 20 appealing partners and 35 are implementing partners.

3.3.2. Joint Multi-Sector Needs Assessment, 2020

To gauge the current humanitarian needs of the Rohingya refugees, their living conditions and potential gaps in the coverage of humanitarian responses, ISCG in collaboration with other organizations, implemented a survey-based assessment in 34 camps in Cox's Bazar, called 'The Joint Multi-Sector Needs Assessment (J-MSNA)'. Several MSNAs have been implemented so far. The J-MSNA (2020) surveyed a total of 836 households consisting of 4,293 refugees to provide a precise and detailed snapshot of the situation in the camps for providing data-driven needs assessment to inform the 2021 Joint Response Plan and analyse the changes in the sectoral needs that arose due to COVID-19 pandemic. J-MSNA (2020) finds that only 3 per cent of the sample households reported COVID-19-related sickness. An overwhelming majority, more than 90 per cent of the Rohingya were well informed through the awareness programmes about the precautionary measures, symptoms of the disease and the contact points in case of sickness. But they reported that they were reluctant to receive treatment for other illnesses from the health centres in fear of contracting the disease. Lack of skilled medical personnel, inferior treatment options and misbehaviour by the staff, closing of health centres, mobility restrictions and travel expenses were cited as major reasons for not availing health services within the camps.

Table 3.1 reports the overall healthcare initiatives taken from June 2020 to October 2020 by the government and non-government organizations and the inadequate provision of hospital beds, ICUs,

Table 3.1 *Healthcare Initiatives for Preventing COVID-19 and Gaps in Meeting the Requirements in Rohingya Camps*

Healthcare Initiatives Taken by June 2020	Healthcare Initiatives Taken by October 2020	Gaps in Requirements
409 isolation and treatment beds were ready with a target to prepare 1,900 beds.	1,106 isolation and treatment beds were ready with a target to prepare 1,900 beds.	Fear among the refugees for getting tested and sending for isolation, lack of transport for patients, permission to move out of the camps.
6 new Severe Acute Respiratory Infection Isolation and Treatment Centres (SARI ITCs) were opened with a target to open 12.	14 new Severe Acute Respiratory Infection Isolation and Treatment Centres (SARI ITCs) were opened with a target to open 14 more.	Though the organizations are successful in reaching their target, these are still inadequate for fighting any high outbreak.
257,400 cloth masks were distributed with a target to distribute 1.5 million.	1,429,138 cloth masks were distributed with a target to distribute 1.5 million.	Despite proper distribution, the authorities are facing difficulties in ensuring wearing masks among the refugees.
10 ICU beds with 8 HDI beds (high dependency) were provided.	38 ICU beds with few ventilator facilities.	This is the only ICU facility for both the locals and the refugees, which is inadequate for all.

Source: Authors' compilation from ISCG (2020a); WHO (2020b).

ventilators, testing centres. In line with JRP (2020) and MNSA (2020), they highlight the intervention areas which require the immediate attention of the NGOs, which would be more effective in preventing the transmission of COVID-19.

Even though efforts are underway to prevent the pandemic outbreak, the literature indicates that much needs to be done. The consequences could be dire, otherwise, not only for the refugees but also for the host communities.

3.3.3. Support for Mental Health

Mental health has turned to be an alarming issue worldwide due to the COVID-19 pandemic. Various studies show that people are facing mental health issues that cause lack of sleep, infuriating temper, suicidal tendency, lack of appetite as an effect of the deadly coronavirus. A study shows that economic hardship, lack of jobs, interruption in formal education, lack of socializing are the main causes for people to suffer through deteriorating mental health conditions (Didar-Ul et al. 2020). When the general citizens of the country are facing mental health issues, then it is almost terrifying to think about the mental health condition in the Rohingya refugee camps. At present, the lockdown condition due to the pandemic imposed on the camp areas worsened the mental health condition of the Rohingya refugees. Haider (2020) mentioned that most of the refugees are comfortable seeking support from religious leaders (Imam) and some of them seek help from NGO workers for counselling. This has been badly hampered due to the current COVID-19 situation, as the NGO workers or the religious leaders are not able to reach out to them due to the pandemic (Haider 2020).

Organizations like UNHCR, WHO, IASC and many other government organizations and NGOs took the mental health issues of the Rohingya refugees very seriously. The UNHCR mental health and psychosocial support (MHPSS) team supported the other partners to continue service for improving the mental health conditions in the refugee camps. According to a UNHCR report, 43 national psychologists from the partner organizations were trained for giving consultation. Also, an additional 500 people were trained as community psychosocial volunteers, health workers and counsellors to promote psychological well-being (UNHCR 2020). The WHO at the beginning of the pandemic trained 200 health workers with Mental Health Gap Action Programme (mhGAP). This training plays a vital role for the healthcare workers to realize the mental health needs during the crisis and provide psychosocial support confidentially to patients in the midst of inadequate medical care facilities. The UNHCR decided to provide psychological first aid (PFA) to adapt the notions of the PFA keeping COVID-19 in mind so that mental health support can be given remotely too.

The J-MSNA mentioned that among the Rohingya refugees, mostly the women and children are facing increased mental health issues. They targeted mostly the adolescent and the youth for providing mental health support, as they are the most affected among the vulnerable refugees. The children are mostly afraid and uncomfortable to share their feelings after the trauma they went through. The lockdown, lack of socialization and isolation in a limited space are affecting their mental health condition and making it worse over time. J-MSNA mentioned that their child protection training for the health and social workers should collaborate with mental health and MHPSS care teams to ensure safety and develop some child-friendly promotion and development activities. Also, the JRP (2020) provides mental health and psychosocial support to their targeted Rohingya and host communities. JRP (2020) reported that per year a total of 1,224,000 Rohingya refugees and host communities need mental health consultations. JRP targeted to provide 25 per cent more consultancy in 2020 compared to 2019, accounting for about 24,000 more people. They also mentioned that about 294,516 girls and boys of Rohingya refugees and 33,913 of the host communities require mental health and psychosocial support services, where the target of JRP (2020) is to provide mental health support to at least 117,627 of the refugees and 11,375 from the host communities (JRP 2020).

All these numbers and facts related to the mental health condition of the Rohingya refugees indicate immediate attention with utmost importance should be given to this problem by all the working organizations and GoB to handle any long-term consequences.

The mental health condition of the refugees should be given equal priority as all other basic needs, as this directly deteriorates the health conditions.

3.3.4. Distribution of Protective Gears, Hygiene Kits

Partners of JRP implemented coronavirus emergency response and distributed hygiene kits, including masks, sanitizers, soaps, detergents and provided testing kits, skilled health personnel and an isolation centre as soon as the first COVID-19 positive case was identified back in May 2020. Other organizations like Helvetas, through Rohingya volunteers, distributed vouchers for hygiene kits containing a 20-litre bucket, a 1.5-litre container for water, soap with a soap dish, disinfectant and powder for making a disinfectant solution (Hafner 2020).

In the overall scenario, there is a scarcity of gears and trained health personnel in the Rohingya camps. The authorities are trying to expand medical facilities inside the camp with the help of aid organizations. According to Mohammad and Yeasir (2020), community engagement under the JRP team created 13,500 handwashing booths in the camp area, which are still inadequate for the overall Rohingya population. They also created four quarantine centres and four severe acute respiratory infection isolation and treatment centres, which provide 1,900 beds for patients. Till October 2020, the only intensive care unit with 10 beds, 11 ventilators and two portable ventilators along eight HDU beds is in Cox's Bazar District Hospital according to a UNHCR report (UNHCR 2020). By increasing, primary healthcare and contributing basic medicines, the UN agencies and other care organizations are helping the government to increase the response capacity in the Rohingya camps (Islam and Yunus 2020). The on-duty health workers need to protect themselves from COVID-19 to keep the refugees free from danger, which is a huge challenge with the limited supply of masks, PPE and other medical equipment. We can safely predict that if these personal protective gears are not in sufficient supply for the health personnel, the prevention efforts and early detection and prompt response will be hindered, and the outbreak cannot be controlled when the refugees start getting infected at higher rates.

3.3.5. Healthcare Awareness for COVID-19

Since the start of the pandemic in March 2020, government organizations and NGOs have conducted camp-wide public awareness campaigns on physical distancing, hand washing, mask-wearing and other health measures. Health workers went door to door to alert and inform people about the signs and symptoms of the disease, early prevention response and treatment measures. About 600 Rohingya faith leaders, Muslim and Hindus, were engaged to get coronavirus prevention messages out quickly (World Vision Bangladesh 2020). Action Aid also provided mask-making training in the camps. Rohingya health volunteers were trained who distributed health vouchers and leaflets in their language for easy understanding. The leaflets were about the disease, its causes, symptoms, transmission routes and prevention measures. The awareness programme also informed about available hospital beds, test centres, healthcare facilities, hygiene kits and basic medicine, etc. But, outside of the refugee camps there were no obvious instructions for the Rohingya refugees to get treatment from the government hospitals (Kamal et al. 2020).

The focus of the Communication with Community (CwC) strategic partners is to implement proper community engagement approaches for raising awareness, integrating gender and their protection, engaging the community to participate in applying public health measures and designing ideas to prevent COVID-19. JRP 2020a reported that along with civil surgeon, other sectors of the CwC group will 'promote Risk Communication and Community Engagement (RCCE) for COVID-19'. The design of this RCCE strategy is developed with the opinions, insights and advice of the partners, keeping audio and visual approaches in mind with proper languages. For example, posters, placards, murals, paintings, advertisements, videos and other promotional media that will be used have been structured according to the community's responsive view. People working for this sector will keep updating strategies by collecting the recent community perceptions and their thoughts to make proper decisions about the facilities.

Arranging awareness spreading by the volunteers and workers through radio stations, religious leaders in mosques and temples with loudspeakers, using hand microphones and speakers while riding in vehicles like rickshaw, tom-tom, etc. has been planned to inform the refugees residing deep inside their community far from the town. Other strategic activities of this CwC sector include replying to queries and concerns regarding COVID-19 through Hotlines, WhatsApp, Social Media pages and Interactive Voice Response (IVR) to spread verified information and make people aware of the rumours that they might encounter. This overall plan requires a budget of US$12.8 million (JRP 2020b).

3.3.6. Other Media Advocacy Work

The DW report (2019) mentioned that a local radio station is working hard to spread awareness in the Rohingya refugee camp through their broadcasts. They are informing people by playing traditional songs with awareness-raising lyrics about the coronavirus, which is an easier way to reach the Rohingya people rather than loudspeaker broadcasting or distributing placards. According to them, it is a short and easy way to inform through entertainment regarding hygiene, instructions about washing hands and sharing proper information about COVID-19. The DW added that around 70 per cent of the refugees in Cox's Bazar are illiterate, so reaching out through radio is the most effective way to convey the message (Rietdorf and Marshall 2020). As access to other media or technologies like smartphones, Facebook, external radio station is difficult for the refugees, Radio Naf (local radio) is the only community radio station working inside the camps. Volunteers receive training from the weekly show of this radio station named 'Palonger Hota' (Voice of Palong). According to DW Akademie, 'Palonger Hota (Voice of Palong) is a radio magazine program that runs for 30 minutes on everyday matters in the Rohingya refugee settlements as well as the surrounding Palong host community villages in Bangladesh' (DW Akademie 2019). The top priority of this show is to inform people of coughing manners, maintaining social distancing, addressing mental health issues due to the pandemic, dealing with the dead due to the COVID-19 and their burial procedure (Rietdorf and Marshall 2020).

The aforementioned programmes and initiatives by the NGOs have proven effective to a large extent in securing the refugees from the COVID-19 pandemic. We now delineate the difficulties experienced by these humanitarian organizations.

3.4. Challenges Encountered by Humanitarian Organizations

Since 2017, the sudden and massive influx of Rohingya refugees has made life in the 34 camps in Cox's Bazar significantly challenging due to the existing overcrowded and dilapidated living arrangements. In the past three years, the UN agencies along with the local and international NGOs in collaboration with the GoB and funding bodies have been working relentlessly to effectively address the demand–supply gaps in providing life-sustaining support for the Rohingya in the camps.

But this worldwide outbreak of COVID-19 has made it difficult for many of these organizations to work efficiently in the camps. The major difficulties encountered by humanitarian agencies are fund shortage, lack of mobility due to enforcement of lockdown by the government, inadequate availability of testing kits, lack of treatment facilities and skilled personnel, inappropriate distribution of the relief materials and many other types of mismanagement in the system, host community resistance, government red tape and bureaucratic hassles, government barring of internet in the camps, etc.

The worldwide economic recession following the onset of the pandemic has created financial constraints in every sector and hence developed countries are cutting off foreign humanitarian assistance (BBC 2020). As a result, the resource and the supply capacity of many NGOs have dramatically decreased. Many of them had to shut down their operations from Rohingya camps. Many staff became sick adding layers of difficulties in terms of smooth operations. It is noteworthy that at the very beginning of April 2020, the GoB took initiative to seal the refugee camps in Cox's Bazar as the international aid organizations warned of a catastrophic result in the refugee camps due to COVID-19. Public movement was restricted by the law enforcement group by putting roadblocks and constant police patrols. NGOs were given only

20 per cent access compared to the pre-COVID situation. This created a hurdle in terms of essential services delivery. The NGOs had to also ensure protection for their staff who were allowed to enter the camps.

Many NGOs approached the GoB offering help in distributing relief materials or medical supplies but faced bureaucratic complexity and other bottlenecks in the file process. Though many non-government agencies like 'National Alliance of Humanitarian Actors, Bangladesh (NAHAB), Bangladesh CSO-NGO Coordination Process, Network for Information, Response and Preparedness Activities on Disaster (NIRAPA), Disaster Forum, Association of Development Agencies Bangladesh (ADAB) and Federation of NGOs Bangladesh (FNB)' are working in emergency COVID management in the camps, many other small- or medium-scale NGOs were turned down by the government and they had to stop working (Ahmad 2020).

The GoB blocked internet access in the Rohingya camps since September 2019 to stop any kind of violence that was anticipated for the second anniversary of the forced migration of the Rohingya refugees (*The Guardian* 2019). Information about the threat of COVID-19 could not be widely circulated via the internet. According to a news report, refugees still got connections to unstable internet facilities even after the internet blackout. But the humanitarian organizations are negatively affected as they cannot reap the full potential of internet-based awareness campaigns fighting the pandemic (Ebbighausen 2020b). The International Rescue Committee (IRC) mentioned that restrictions on cell phones and the internet have restricted the agencies from taking action rapidly right after they find any reported case of COVID-19 (Ebbighausen 2020a). This significantly hindered the online awareness campaigns during the pandemic until the GoB restored the internet and mobile access in August 2020.

An impressive well-coordinated aid operation has stabilized the humanitarian crisis to a large extent and managed the COVID-19 pandemic keeping the infection rate under control despite many constraints faced by the humanitarian agencies. Under the multifaceted collaborative response from over 100 NGOs, the situation has gradually begun to stabilize even though it is nowhere near optimal. COVID-19 mitigation efforts were reasonable with the provision of basic assistance in health, food, nutrition and sanitation. However, despite the efforts of these organizations in achieving some progress, the fate of the Rohingya remains extremely perilous and uncertain. With no sustainable solution for the refugees in sight, attention must now be given to short- and medium-run goals of improving their lives and livelihoods in Bangladesh.

3.5. Future Directions for Effectively Managing the COVID-19 Pandemic

The COVID-19 pandemic poses a serious risk for the Rohingya community because of their congested living conditions. Most of the refugees are denied or have limited access to mobile phones, the internet, sanitary conditions and cleaning products which increases the likelihood of transmission of the virus. Since the declaration of the pandemic, under domestic and international pressure, the GoB has enacted strict preventive measures to protect the Rohingya from widespread infection. A widespread COVID-19 outbreak has been thwarted so far, but several of the measures enforced by the GoB, including limitations on humanitarian access, internet ban and the restriction on mobility, have led to further exclusion of the Rohingya community.

In accordance with the guidelines of the policy reports 'COVID-19: Bangladesh Multi-Sectoral Anticipatory Impact and Needs Analysis' (2020) and 'The Joint Response Plan' (2020), the following suggestions address the immediate, medium- and long-term goals for the Rohingya and the relevant players such as NGOs, government institutions, donor states, members of the UN Security Council, the European Union and the Association of Southeast Asian Nations (ASEAN) need to work on.

3.5.1. Immediate Needs and Priorities

- Capacity building: Training needed on evidence-based surveillance; biosafety, biosecurity and laboratory biosafety protocols; specimen collection and transport; RTPCR; case management; IPC, including on donning and doffing of PPE for relevant health and lab professionals.

- Equipment and reagent: Stocking up and ensure a steady supply of ventilators; pulse oximeter with cardiac monitoring; N95 masks; closed coloured bins; PPE; biohazard bags; autoclaves; Viral transport media with swabs; large medical oxygen cylinders; RNA extractor; reagents and laboratory consumables.
- Human resource: National consultants for contact tracing and surveillance; national consultants for monitoring quality of in vitro diagnostics and other devices with a focus on isolated camp areas.
- Others: Provision of ambulance service in the camps for transporting COVID-19 patients.

3.5.2. Anticipated Medium-term Needs and Priorities

- Prevent contagion and transmission including reducing secondary infections among close contacts and healthcare workers;
- Prevent transmission and amplification events and enhance infection prevention and control in community and healthcare settings;
- Identify, isolate and care for patients at an early stage;
- Communicate critical risk and event information to the communities and counter misinformation and
- Minimize social and economic impact through multi-sectoral partnerships.

3.5.3. Launch Long-term Transformational Aid Response

The unprecedented challenges posed by COVID-19 call for an unprecedented global response that moves beyond the standard operations of Overseas Development Assistance (ODA). It is imperative that states move rapidly and boldly to ensure that the Rohingya receive the required support.

- A vital role for the international financial institutions (IFI): Shareholders of IFI need to commit to increasing support for the at-risk communities, particularly in Bangladesh. Any aid to Myanmar must include a strong accountability clause to ensure proper and targeted utilization of funding for the Rohingya and prevent misallocation and diversion.

- Scale-up sanitation assistance: Particularly in Cox's Bazar, it is imperative that assistance support the weak and overburdened sanitation systems.
- Public information campaigns: Information must reach those who require it. Public information campaigns must be designed to reflect the realities of IDP and refugee camps.
- Cash injections to the refugees: It is important that assistance be provided to get money directly into the hands of households, to stimulate buying power and to maintain economic solvency.
- Immunizations. There is a major risk that cholera, measles and malaria will be compounded as a consequence of pauses to routine vaccinations. Immunizations should be scaled up to account for the growing need.

It is imperative to take steps as soon as possible to protect both the Rohingya and the host communities from widespread infection. They should create conditions whereby future devastation can be prevented. This can only be achieved through an integrated, inclusive and international response that places both the short- and long-term concerns of the Rohingya community at its core.

3.6. Concluding Remarks

This chapter is premised on the assumption that a genuinely effective response to the COVID-19 pandemic in the refugee camps of Cox's Bazar can be forged only when conceived with and by those most vulnerable to it: the Rohingya refugees themselves. Ultimately, a sustainable response for the situation of COVID-19 calls for both short-term and long-term policies, which must recognize and address the root drivers of the hardships and vulnerability faced by the Rohingya refugees—their systematic marginalization and persecution inside their homeland of Myanmar.

On the other hand, the government organizations and NGOs that provide funds to these refugees along with the humanitarian agencies have been devastated financially due to the raging pandemic. With limited resources, these agencies and the supporting organizations should prioritize supporting and educating the refugees who are susceptible to other health diseases and more likely to get affected by this deadly virus. These measures will help the vulnerable refugees to control multi-morbidity, avoid high health risks and reduce the spread of COVID-19.

The elderly and other vulnerable people with pre-existing/underlying health conditions are at higher risk of death from COVID-19. High-risk co-morbidities of these vulnerable groups include hypertension, cardiovascular disease, diabetes mellitus, liver disease, tuberculosis, chronic lung disease, renal failure, immunosuppressive disorders, severe acute malnutrition (SAM) and severe anaemia. The prevalence of high levels of malnutrition, stunting and other negative health conditions make the Rohingya susceptible to multiple chronic diseases or multi-morbidity. Multi-morbidity patients have complex and costly care needs and puts considerable strain on the already overburdened and inadequate health systems in the camps. Thus, systematic public health preventive measures, integrated food security, nutrition, sanitation and awareness building that will go a long way to protect the Rohingya facing the double burden of infectious and chronic diseases should be on the agenda of the non-government agencies.

Alemi et al. (2020) further state that social stigma might influence preventive measures and reduce the urgency of taking treatment among the refugees. It is vital for the care providers to prevent this fear, stigma and fallacies linked to COVID-19 to reduce the spread. The government, non-government and other public health organizations working in these camps should focus also on the mental health conditions of the refugees, as the pandemic has negatively changed their socio-economic status and increased the uncertainty that they faced after migrating (Alemi et al. 2020).

There is hopeful news from the GoB about including the Rohingya community in the vaccination plan. The WHO along with the support of the GoB and other humanitarian organizations is working closely for the allocation of AstraZeneca or Oxford vaccine from the COVAX facility of Bangladesh (UNHCR 2021). The effectiveness of the designed COVID-19 vaccine campaign by WHO (2021) is still a concern as plans are yet to be finalized by the first quarter of 2021. A large-scale vaccination drive covering all 34 camps is a massive logistical challenge even if the vaccine is made available for the Rohingya.

The concerned authorities and stakeholders need to plan strategically and prioritize the elderly and high-risk vulnerable groups, especially with chronic illness and disabilities, to receive the vaccine and prevent any mismanagement regarding the distribution.

The Rohingya people have suffered decades of systematic discrimination, statelessness, persecution and targeted violence leading to 'ethnic cleansing' in Rakhine State, Myanmar and fled to Bangladesh to secure refuge. The unfortunate reality for the refugees is that there is no near-term prospect of returning to their home country as the root causes of their plight in Myanmar have not been resolved by the Myanmar government. The recent military coup in Myanmar makes the repatriation efforts next to impossible for the Rohingya. With the uncertain future, they continue to remain vulnerable, utterly dependent on aid provided by NGOs and live in extremely difficult and hazardous environments exposed to the vagaries of weather and infectious diseases.

References

Ahmad, M. 2020, 6 May. 'The COVID-19 Outbreak: A Testing Time for NGOs in Bangladesh.' E-International Relations. Available at https://www.e-ir.info/2020/05/06/the-covid-19-outbreak-a-testing-time-for-ngos-in-bangladesh/ (accessed on 6 August 2021).

Alemi, Q., C. Stempel, H. Siddiq, and E. Kim. 2020. 'Refugees and COVID-19: Achieving a Comprehensive Public Health Response.' *Bulletin of the World Health Organization* 98, no. 8: 510. Available at https://www.ncbi.nlm.nih.gov/pmc/articles/PMC7411314/ (accessed on 6 August 2021).

Amnesty International. 2020a, 28 January. 'Bangladesh: Rohingya Children Get Access to Education.' Available at https://www.amnesty.org/en/latest/news/2020/01/bangladesh-rohingya-children-get-access-to-education/ (accessed on 6 August 2021).

———. 2020b, April 6. 'Bangladesh: COVID-19 Response Flaws Put Older Rohingya Refugees in Imminent Danger.' Available at https://www.amnesty.org/en/latest/news/2020/04/bangladesh-covid-19-response-flaws-put-older-rohingya-refugees-in-imminent-danger/ (accessed on 6 August 2021).

Assessment Capacities Project. 2020. 'Bangladesh.' Available at https://www.acaps.org/sites/acaps/files/products/files/20200608_acaps_coxs_bazar_analysis_hub_rohingya_response_covid19_and_gender_0.pdf

BBC. 2020, 23 July. 'Coronavirus: UK Foreign Aid Spending Cut by £2.9bn amid Economic Downturn.' BBC News. Available at https://www.bbc.com/news/uk-politics-53508933 (accessed on 6 August 2021).

Didar-Ul, S. M., Mariam Binte Safiq, Md. Bodrud-Doza, and Mohammed A. Mamun. 2020, November 13. 'Perception and Attitudes toward PPE-related Waste Disposal amid COVID-19 in Bangladesh: An Exploratory Study.' Frontiers in Public Health. Available at https://www.frontiersin.org/articles/10.3389/fpubh.2020.592345/full (accessed on 6 August 2021).

DW Akademie. 2019, 20 July 20. 'Palonger Hota/Voice of Palong a Weekly Radio Show by and for Rohingya and Bangladesh Local Communities.' Available at http://www.thisisplace.org/i/?id=82a61859-c840-436a-ac64-828c20b549b9

Ebbighausen, R. 2020a, 15 May. 'Bangladesh: Coronavirus Reaches Largest Refugee Camp in the World.' Deutsche Welle. Available at https://www.dw.com/en/bangladesh-coronavirus-reaches-largest-refugee-camp-in-the-world/a-53456506 (accessed on 6 August 2021).

———. 2020b, June 19. 'In Rohingya Refugee Camps, Coronavirus is under Control—for Now.' Deutsche Welle. Available at https://www.dw.com/en/in-rohingya-refugee-camps-coronavirus-is-under-control-for-now/a-53873931 (accessed on 6 August 2021).

Godin, M. 2020, 9 October.' COVID-19 Outbreaks Are Now Emerging in Refugee Camps. Why Did It Take so Long for the Virus to Reach Them.' Time. Available at https://time.com/5893135/covid-19-refugee-camps/ (accessed on 6 August 2021).

Hafner, Katrin. 2020, 24 August. 'Helvetas Supports the Rohingya in the World's Largest Refugee Camp in the Fight against COVID-19—Three Years after the Exodus.' HELVETAS Swiss Intercooperation. Available at www.helvetas.org/Helvetas-Supports-the-Rohingya-in-the-World-s-Largest-Refugee-Camp-in-the-Fight-Against-COVID-19-Three-Years-After-the-Exodus_pressrelease_7060 (accessed on 6 August 2021).

Haider, Sharif. 2020, 17 June. 'The Mental Health and Well-Being of the Rohingya in Bangladesh beyond COVID-19.' Refugee Research Online. Available at https://refugeeresearchonline.org/the-mental-health-and-well-being-of-the-rohingya-in-bangladesh-beyond-covid-19/ (accessed on 6 August 2021).

Homaira, N., M. S. Islam, and N. Haider. 2020. 'COVID-19 in the Rohingya Refugee Camps of Bangladesh: Challenges and Mitigation Strategies.' *Global Biosecurity* 1, no. 4. Available at https://jglobalbiosecurity.com/articles/10.31646/gbio.84/ (accessed on 6 August 2021).

Human Rights Watch. 2020, 28 April. 'Bangladesh: Covid-19 Aid Limits Imperil Rohingya.' Human Rights Watch. Available at https://www.hrw.org/news/2020/04/28/bangladesh-covid-19-aid-limits-imperil-rohingya (accessed on 6 August 2021).

ISCG. 2020a, June. 'Situation Report Rohingya Refugee Crisis.' ReliefWeb. Available at https://reliefweb.int/sites/reliefweb.int/files/resources/ISCG%20Situation%20Report%20-%20Rohingya%20Refugee%20Crisis%2C%20Cox%E2%80%99s%20Bazar%2C%20June%202020.pdf (accessed on 6 August 2021).

ISCG. 2020b, October. 'Situation Report Rohingya Refugee Crisis.' ReliefWeb. Available at https://reliefweb.int/sites/reliefweb.int/files/resources/final_october_sitrep_en.pdf (accessed on 6 August 2021).

J-MSNA. 2020, 12 November. 'Joint Multi-Sector Needs Assessment (J-MSNA): Bangladesh Host Communities | July–August 2020.' Reliefweb. Available at https://reliefweb.int/report/bangladesh/joint-multi-sector-needs-assessment-j-msna-bangladesh-host-communities-july-august (accessed on 6 August 2021).

JRP. 2020a, 3 March. 'Joint Response Plan: Rohingya Humanitarian Crisis (January–December 2020)—Bangladesh.' Reliefweb. Available at https://reliefweb.int/report/bangladesh/2020-joint-response-plan-rohingya-humanitarian-crisis-january-december-2020 (accessed on 6 August 2021).

———. 2020b. '2020 COVID-19 Response Plan Addendum to the Joint Response Plan 2020 Rohingya Humanitarian Crisis.' Humanitarian Response. Available at https://www.humanitarianresponse.info/sites/www.humanitarianresponse.info/files/documents/files/covid-19_addendum_rohingya_refugee_response_020720.pdf (accessed on 6 August 2021).

Kamal, A., M. Huda, C. Dell, S. Hossain, and S. Ahmed. 2020. 'Translational Strategies to Control and Prevent Spread of COVID-19 in the Rohingya Refugee Camps in Bangladesh.' *Global Biosecurity*. Available at https://jglobalbiosecurity.com/articles/10.31646/gbio.77/ (accessed on 6 August 2021).

McPherson, P., and R. Paul. 2020, 5 June. 'Fear Stops Rohingya Getting Tested as Virus Hits Refugee Camps.' Available at https://www.reuters.com/article/us-health-coronavirus-rohingya-refugees/fear-stops-rohingya-getting-tested-as-virus-hits-refugee-campsidUSKBN23C1GV (accessed on 6 August 2021).

MNSA. 2020, April. 'COVID-19: Bangladesh Multi-Sectoral Anticipatory Impact and Needs Analysis by Needs Assessment Working Group Bangladesh.' ResearchGate. Available at https://www.researchgate.net/publication/340778069_COVID-19_Bangladesh_Multi-Sectoral_Anticipatory_Impact_and_Needs_Analysis_by_Needs_Assessment_Working_Group_Bangladesh (accessed on 6 August 2021).

Mohammad, and M. D. Yeasir. 2020, 25 June. 'Rohingya Refugees at High Risk of COVID-19 in Bangladesh.' Available at https://www.ncbi.nlm.nih.gov/pmc/articles/PMC7316456/ (accessed on 6 August 2021).

Monir, F. 2020, 15 September. 'Bangladesh: Rohingya Refugees Must Participate in Decisions Affecting Their Lives.' Amnesty International. Available at https://www.amnesty.org/en/latest/news/2020/09/bangladesh-rohingya-refugees-must-participate-in-decisions-affecting-their-lives/ (accessed on 6 August 2021).

Morozkina, Aleksandra. 2020, 21 September. 'Impact of COVID19 on International Development Assistance System.' Observation Research Foundation. Available at https://www.orfonline.org/expert-speak/impact-of-covid19-on-international-development-assistance-system/ (accessed on 6 August 2021).

Rietdorf, J., and A. Marshall. 2020, 8 April. 'Bangladesh: Reporting the Coronavirus at a Rohingya Camp.' Deutsche Welle. Available at https://www. dw.com/en/reporting-the-coronavirus-at-a-rohingya-camp-saving-lives-is-now-the-most-important-task/a-53061759 (accessed on 6 August 2021).

Sutton, R., ed. 2020. *Rohingya Experiences of Covid-19 in Cox's Bazar Camps (PSRP Research Report: Covid-19 Series)*. Edinburgh: Global Justice Academy, University of Edinburgh.

The Guardian. 2020, 5 September. 'Bangladesh Imposes Mobile Phone Blackout in Rohingya Refugee Camps.' Guardian News and Media. Available at www. theguardian.com/global-development/2019/sep/05/bangladesh-imposes-mobile-phone-blackout-in-rohingya-refugee-camps (accessed on 6 August 2021).

Truelove, Shaun, O. Abrahim, C. Altare, A. S. Azman, and P. B. Spiegel. 2020, 25 March. 'COVID-19: Projecting the Impact in Rohingya Refugee Camps and Beyond.' Available at http://hopkinshumanitarianhealth.org/assets/documents/COVID-19__Rohinya_Refugees__Beyond_-_Summary_FINAL_March_25_2020.pdf (accessed on 6 August 2021).

Truelove, S., O. Abrahim, C. Altare, S. A. Lauer, K. H. Grantz, A. S. Azman, and P. Spiegel. 2020. 'The Potential Impact of COVID-19 in Refugee Camps in Bangladesh and Beyond: A Modeling Study.' *PLoS Medicine* 17, no. 6: e1003144. Available at https://journals.plos.org/plosmedicine/article/file?id=10.1371/journal.pmed.1003144&type=printable (accessed on 6 August 2021).

UNHCR. 2020, 11 June. 'Emerging Practices: Mental Health and Psychosocial Support in Refugee Operations during the COVID-19 Pandemic—World.' ReliefWeb. Available at https://reliefweb.int/report/world/emerging-practices-mental-health-and-psychosocial-support-refugee-operations-during (accessed on 6 August 2021).

UNOCHA. 2020. 'Global Humanitarian Response Plan COVID-19.' Available at https://www.unocha.org/sites/unocha/files/Global-Humanitarian-Response-Plan-COVID-19.pdf (accessed on 6 August 2021).

WHO. 2020a, 17 September. 'Emergency: Rohingya Crisis—WHO Bangladesh Situation Report #23, 17 September 2020 (Period Covered: Week 37: 7 September–13 September 2020) – Bangladesh.' ReliefWeb. Available at https://www.who.int/docs/default-source/searo/bangladesh/bangladesh--rohingya-crisis---pdf-reports/sitreps/sitreps-2020/who-cxb-situation-report-23.pdf?sfvrsn=f82e45a3_2 (accessed on 6 August 2021).

———. 2020b, 24 September. 'Emergency: Rohingya Crisis—WHO Bangladesh Situation Report #24, 24 September 2020 (Period Covered: Week 38: 14 September–20 September 2020)—Bangladesh.' ReliefWeb. Available at https://reliefweb.int/report/bangladesh/emergency-rohingya-crisis-who-bangladesh-situation-report-24-24-september-2020 (accessed on 6 August 2021).

———. 2020c, 3 November. 'Emergency: Rohingya Crisis—WHO Bangladesh Situation Report #30, 3 November 2020 (Period Covered: Week 44: 26

October–1 November 2020)—Bangladesh.' ReliefWeb. Available at https://reliefweb.int/sites/reliefweb.int/files/resources/who-cxb-situation-report-30.pdf (accessed on 6 August 2021).

WHO. 2020d. 'Rohingya Crisis (Period Covered: February–April 2020)—Bangladesh.' ReliefWeb. Available at https://www.who.int/docs/default-source/searo/bangladesh/bangladesh---rohingya-crisis---pdf-reports/donor-alerts/donor-update-feb-apr-2020.pdf?sfvrsn=27eb6fee_10 (accessed on 6 August 2021).

———. 2021, 16 April. 'Rohingya Crisis—WHO Bangladesh Situation Report #7, 16 April 2021 (Period Covered: Week 13–14: 01–14 April 2021)—Bangladesh.' ReliefWeb. Available at https://cdn.who.int/media/docs/default-source/searo/bangladesh/bangladesh---rohingya-crisis---pdf-reports/sitreps/2021/who-cox-s-bazar-situation-report-7.pdf?sfvrsn=a53fffc2_11 (accessed on 6 August 2021).

World Vision Bangladesh. 2020. 'Three Years On: Rohingya Refugee Response Report 2020.' Available at https://reliefweb.int/sites/reliefweb.int/files/resources/RRR_Annual%2BReport%2B2020.pdf (accessed on 6 August 2021).

Worley, W. 2020, 3 December 3. 'UK Aid Cuts Will Deny Millions of Water and Vaccines, NGOs Say.' Available at https://www.devex.com/news/uk-aid-cuts-will-deny-millions-of-water-and-vaccines-ngos-say-98703 (accessed on 6 August 2021).

CHAPTER 4

Geo-environmental Changes in Rohingya Refugee Neighbourhoods
Spatiotemporal Evidences
Md. Atiqur Rahman and Alak Paul

4.1. Introduction

Since the early 1990s, the Rohingya people have continued to flee in huge numbers from the Rakhine State and enter Cox's Bazar district of Bangladesh (Hassan et al. 2018). On 25 August 2017, a massive influx occurred and about 750,000 people fled Myanmar to Bangladesh within two months due to genocidal attacks by the military. The United Nations High Commissioner for Refugees (UNHCR 2019) reported that besides the existing refugee settlements in Ukhia and Teknaf of Cox's Bazar, 34 makeshift camps were constructed clearing forested lands and vegetation to accommodate the new arrivals. The spontaneous settlement process has caused great environmental damage in the regions (Imtiaz 2018). It was estimated by Abrar (2018) that the initial loss of forest area is 3,500 acres due to Rohingya incursion in Cox's Bazar, while the total forest area is around 2,092,016 acres. It means a loss of 0.167 per cent of the forest area of Cox's Bazar and a loss of 0.05 per cent of the total national forest area of Bangladesh (Abrar 2001; Sobrino et al. 2004; Sultana 2013). Thus, the available forest resources at Ukhia range of Cox's Bazar are facing significant direct impacts. Since the majority of the Rohingya live in this area, it has become the most adversely affected area due to the crisis.

Moreover, out of the total 1,485 hectares of encroached forest land of Ukhia, about 700 hectares were planted area. Huge, forested areas of the region have been cleared up to inhabit the Rohingya (Khatun 2017). Refugees have settled in unstructured sites in more out-of-the-way and remote hilly areas in addition to settling in congested existing camps (IOM 2017). A significant number of researchers (Ahmed et al. 2019; Hassan et al. 2018; Imtiaz 2018; Rashid et al. 2020) have observed that the widespread ecological and environmental damages due to such unprecedented speed and scale of the refugee incursion have resulted in the degradation of reserved forest lands and the destruction of critical flora and fauna habitat. It is estimated that nearly 4,000 acres of forested hills have been cleared since August 2017 in order to build the makeshift camps (Hassan et al. 2018; Rashid et al. 2020). Also, the Rohingya people have encroached the nearby forests for collecting fuelwood and for other necessities. Moreover, this part of the country is well known for several natural disasters such as tropical cyclones, storm surges and floods (30% of the Kutupalong–Balukhali) which would throw the region to greater risks of environmental threats.

The vanishing of the natural forests and naked interference of the people on other natural resources will lead to social clashes between the Bangladeshi nationals and the Rohingya people (Kudrat-E-Khuda 2020). The Energy & Environment Technical Working Group (2018) mentioned that the daily requirement of fuelwood for the refugees is approximately 700 tonnes—equivalent to more than four football fields of forest. Such rampant use of woods in the area is alarming for the existing forests. The physical settings of the terrain of the slopes have been disoriented due to random cutting of hills to put up shelters for the refugees. According to a report of the United

Nations Development Programme (UNDP), a major portion of the hilly areas already shows large-scale degradation due to vegetation loss. Due to frequent camp activities, the fertile topsoil and other loose soils have lost their hydrological settings and become vulnerable. It is predicted that this vulnerability can result in frequent landslides in these hilly regions in the near future. It is estimated that about 50 per cent of the hills have been entirely uncovered in the incursion area (Khatun 2017). If the unrestricted growth of spontaneous refugee camps continues, it may cause brisk biomass reduction, the disappearance of species and wildlife habitat, dissipation of wildlife corridor and extinction of wildlife (UNDP and UN Women 2018). Earlier, the number and density of human population in the area were not as high as they are today. Thus, the pressure of the increased population has many other types of impacts on the physical settings of the natural environment of the area. For instance, Rashid et al. (2020) investigated the impacts of the Rohingya influx on the land surface temperature (LST) of the area and found significant changes in it. However, the overall changes and impacts due to the massive influx of the Rohingya are yet to be known. The chapter examines the possible changes in the physical environment of the area based on available data from different sources. It presents a better understanding of the environmental impacts of Rohingya refugee camps in addition to the existing socio-economic stresses.

4.2. Methodology

4.2.1. Study Area

The chapter is based on a study which has divided the total area into four major clusters of refugee camps within Ukhia, Teknaf and Cox's Bazar Sadar administrative units. The largest cluster (C1) is located at Ukhia upazila and comprises Kutupalong, Balukhali, Burma para, Hakim para, Thangkhali, Baggoha and Choukali camps. Around 717,000 refugees live in this cluster. The camp numbers included in C1 are Kutupalong RC, Camps 1E, 1W, 2E, 2W, 3, 4, 4Ext, 5-7, 8E, 8W, 9-20, 20Ext. The second cluster (C2) is at Baharchara area, which has 10,494 refugees in Camp 23. The third cluster (C3) is close to Noapara, the camp number of which is 22, and it has about 21,206

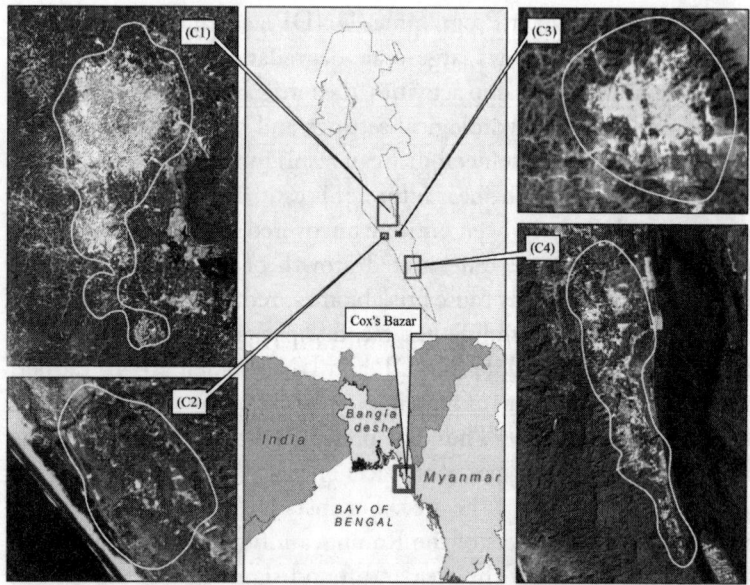

Figure 4.1 *Map of the Study Area in Makeshift Camps of the Rohingya*

Disclaimer: This figure has been redrawn and is not to scale. It does not represent any authentic national or international boundaries and is used for illustrative purposes only.

Source: Maps shown are prepared by the authors and the google images are redrawn by the authors.

refugees. The fourth cluster (C4) of this study consists of Nayapara RC, with camps numbered 24–27 and has around 111,230 refugees. The clusters used in this study have included the camp area and their surrounding areas considering an estimated buffer zone around the camps. This is because the environmental impacts are not always limited within the camp areas demarcated by humans. The whole study area is shown in Figure 4.1 with necessary maps and illustrations.

4.2.2. Data Sources

The main data source is satellite imageries collected from the USGS website (freely available). Two types of images are used in the study—sentinel-2 and Landsat. Sentinel-2 images were used to examine

Table 4.1 Sentinel-2 Image Information Used in the Study to Determine LULC and Vegetation Loss

Sensor	Source	Dates	Bands/Scale
Sentinel-2	US Geological Survey	4 Feb 2016, 18 Feb 2017, 23 Feb 2018, 23 Feb 2019, 28 Feb 2020	Band (2, 3, 4, 8)/10 m

Source: Compiled by the authors.

Table 4.2 Landsat Image Information Used in the Study to Know the NDVI and LST

Sensors	Image IDs (Path: 136, Row: 45, clouds = 0%-30%)	Resolution (m)	Date
Landsat 8 OLI/ TIRS C1 Level 1	LC08_L1TP_136045_2020 0510_20200526_01_T1	30	10 May 2020
Landsat 8 OLI/ TIRS C1 Level 1	LC08_L1TP_136045_2015 0513_20170409_01_T1	30	13 May 2015
Landsat 7 ETM + C1 Level 1	LE07_L1TP_136045_2010 0507_20161215_01_T1	30	7 May 2010
Landsat 4-5, TM C1 Level 1	LT05_L1TP_136045_2005 0501_20161126_01_T1	30	1 May 2005
Landsat 4-5, TM C1 Level 1	LT05_L1TP_136045_2000 0503_20161214_01_T1	30	3 May 2000

Source: Compiled by the authors.

the land use land cover (LULC) change in the study area. Landsat images were applied to check the *normalized difference vegetation index* (NDVI) and LST. The advantage of using the sentinel image is that it provides much better resolution (10 m) than Landsat images (30 m). However, sentinel data is not available for a longer period to see chronological changes. Table 4.1 presents sentinel-2 image information and Table 4.2 portrays the image information of Landsat satellite. Fieldworks were part of the study to examine the changes in the physical environment of the area.

In addition to the satellite images, the study has used LST data of NASA LP DAAC at the USGS EROS Center collected from

MOD11A1.006 Terra Land Surface Temperature and Emissivity Daily Global 1 km source. All these data sources were checked through the necessary processes to ensure their quality and usability for achieving the objectives of the study. Image processing and map preparation were done using both QGIS 3.4 and ArcGIS10.5. Other types of data processing and plotting were done using R programming.

4.2.3. Image Pre-processing

Pixel-based change detection is done by using Landsat L1TP and it is geometrically corrected with the help of ground control points. Semi-automatic Classification Plugin in QGIS 3.4 is used for radiometric calibrations and atmospheric corrections. Yankovich, Yankovich, and Baranovskiy (2019) argued that Landsat images are accessible as DN (digital numbers) values that have no substantial implication. For digital processing, it is mandatory to convert bands into reflectance or radiance. Top of atmosphere (TOA) reflectance and radiance were obtained by transforming the OLI and TIRS bands in this study. For further analysis, Dark Object Subtraction (DOS) method was applied for atmospheric correction in order to process the images. For sentinel images, only four bands (red, green, blue, near infrared) of the 10-metre resolution were converted into surface reflectance for further analysis. The DOS1 method in QGIS was applied for atmospheric corrections. A composite of corrected four bands and an NDVI layer were prepared for each year. Samples were collected applying false-colour composite (FCC) on the images for LULC classifications. After that, a random forest (RF) algorithm was applied to classify images. RF algorithm uses two-thirds of the samples as training data and the other one-third is used for validation. Figure 4.2 represents the schematic diagram of LULC change detection method using satellite images. Table 4.3 illustrates the classification schemes of sentinel images used in the study.

4.2.4. Calculation of Vegetation Change

Random forest (RF) method was adopted to calculate the vegetation change in the camp area. It is a nonparametric machine learning algorithm which is widely used in modelling high-degree non-linear relationship between the targeted and forecasted variables (Breiman

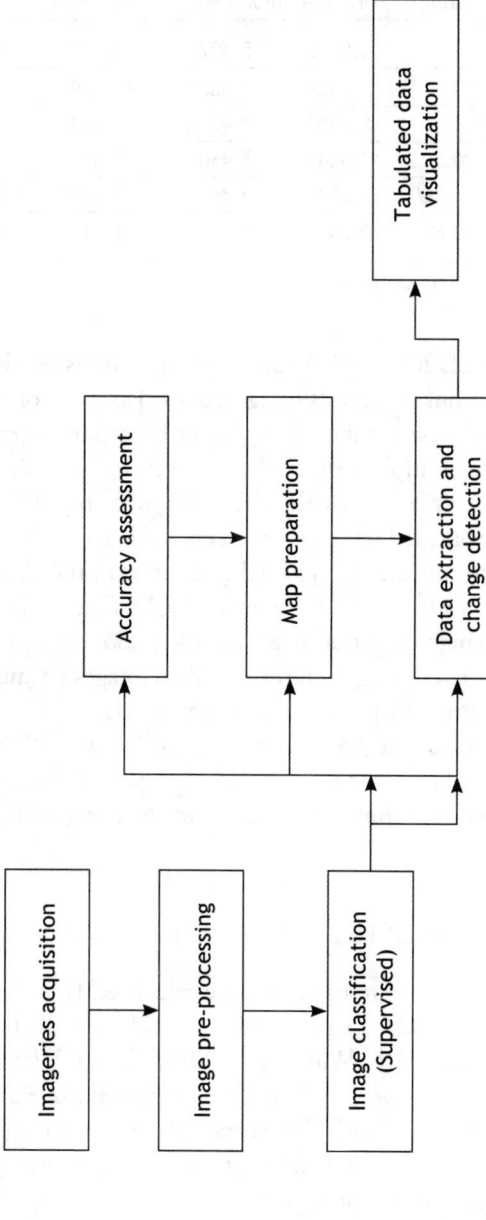

Figure 4.2 *Typical LULC Detection Method Followed in the Study*

Source: Compiled by the authors.

Table 4.3 *Classification Scheme of Sentinel Images*

Date	Forest	Camp	Bare Soil	Inland Water	Non-forest	Coastal_Naf
2000	27.4878	0	1.0413	5.4927	9.1404	0.8685
2005	25.1424	0	1.1934	6.8661	10.8198	-
2010	13.1265	0	8.1909	10.4292	12.2841	-
2015	14.6115	0	13.5846	5.4306	10.404	-
2018	11.2239	5.7807	17.0946	5.841	3.6711	0.4194
2020	9.28	10.89	10.25	6.56	6.41	0.64

Source: Compiled by the authors.

2001; Ghosh et al. 2014). RF creates a group of decision classes and each of the decisions provides a categorization label, out of which the most nominated class is taken. Bagging or bootstrap aggregation is used to generate multiple formations of subsets for achieving a range of classes (Breiman 2001). In RF algorithm, one-third of the training samples are omitted which is called out-of-bag (OOB) data, and these are used to run an unprejudiced estimation of the classification error (Belgiu and Drăguţ 2016; Breiman 2001). One of the simplest methods for change detection is post-classification comparison and it is achieved by overlaying both the classified images (Almutairi and Warner 2010). Pixel-to-pixel changes between classes of two images are calculated in this method (Almutairi and Warner 2010; Raja et al. 2013). To produce a change detection image, both independently classified images were compared in the study by using SCP plugin in QGIS 3.4.

4.2.5. Calculation of LST

A significant number of researchers have calculated LST in different ways (Amiri et al. 2009; Li et al. 2013; Rashid et al. 2020; Sahana, Ahmed, and Sajjad 2016; Wang et al. 2019; Zhang, Wang, and Li 2006), and different algorithms have been developed to estimate LST. For LST computation of both TIRS bands, Planck equation (Equation 4.1) is used in this study. Change detection images were produced from the averages for final mapping.

$$T_s = \frac{BT}{\left\{1 + \left[\dfrac{\lambda BT}{\rho}\right].\ln\varepsilon\right\}} - 273.15 \qquad (4.1)$$

Here, T_s is the LST (°C); BT is the at-sensor brightness temperature (K); λ is the wavelength of the emitted radiance; ρ is the ($h \times c/\sigma$) = 1.438×10^{-2} mK and ε is the land surface emissivity (LSE). A significant number of researchers (Avdan and Jovanovska 2016; Bharath, Rajan, and Ramachandra 2013; Liu and Zhang 2011; Qin et al. 2001) have claimed that they have applied Planck equation for the derivation of LST from different thermal sensors. This method is simple to use and does not necessitate atmospheric parameters (Avdan and Jovanovska 2016; Ndossi and Avdan 2016b) unlike other algorithms (e.g., SCA and SWA). LST for different Landsat sensors were calculated by Ndossi and Avdan (2016a), and they observed that Planck function produces best results from Landsat 8 TIRS. It is imperative to correct the brightness temperature against LSE to obtain the LST. The capacity of radiation of any surface with reference to an ideal blackbody is known as emissivity of that surface. It is usually determined by calculating the terrestrial composition (Gondwe, Muchena, and Boys 2018; Ndossi and Avdan 2016a). In this regard, NDVI is highly promising for the calculation of LSE. NDVI is calculated from the difference between NIR and red bands divided by their sum. It is used to find the vegetation proportion (Pv) from Equation (4.2) (Carlson and Ripley 1997).

$$Pv = \left[\frac{(NDVI - NDVImin)}{(NDVImax - NDVImin)}\right]^2 \qquad (4.2)$$

Pv is then applied in Equation (4.3) by Sobrino et al. (2004) for LSE.

$$\varepsilon = 0.004\ Pv + 0.986 \qquad (4.3)$$

4.3. Findings and Discussions

Multidimensional environmental changes and impacts are observed in the study region due to the excessive use of natural resources by the refugees along with the local people. Though the refugees are not solely responsible for environmental degradation of the area, the huge influx of Rohingya people have contributed in a significant way. The reason behind this is that the increased number of people have created pressure on the carrying capacity of the natural environment of the area. The significant visible changes include land use and land cover changes, vegetation loss, geomorphologic changes due to hill cutting, settlement growth in unplanned ways. Some of the invisible and intangible changes in the environment include groundwater level depletion, air and sound pollution, changes in soil fertility and moisture and loss of natural settings. At the same time, both these sorts of tangible and intangible changes in the physical environment destroy the natural balance, which enhances the risk of occurrence of different geo-environmental hazards. However, this chapter will focus on the most significant and visible changes in the physical environment and the associated impacts.

4.3.1. Land Use and Land Cover Changes

Land use and land cover changes in the study area were examined by splitting the Rohingya occupied areas into four major clusters as mentioned earlier in the description of the study area. The changes were investigated from 2016 to 2020 to provide a reliable picture. From Figure 4.3, we can see significant changes in the LULC in all four clusters during the period. As we know, the massive refugee influx occurred in 2017, and pre influx and post influx differences exhibit the changes. For cluster 1, no significant change is observed between 2016 and 2017 images, but a drastic change occurred after 2017, that is, after the influx. A vast vegetated/forested area is replaced by built-up areas because of the newly built makeshifts to inhabit the refugees. This cluster is located at Ukhia upazila and comprises Kutupalong, Balukhali, Burma para, Hakim para, Thangkhali, Baggoha, Choukali camps. There are 26 identified camps in this largest cluster, and about 717,000 refugees live there. The study area is classified into five classes to investigate the LULC. So, it was not possible to take into account the small land use classes in the study other than these five classes. In 2018, a significant part of the cluster was open soil (not barren soil) as the outcome of cutting trees and hills by the refugees. However, in the next year, in 2019, those open soil were also occupied by makeshift camps to accommodate the increased number of refugees. It means

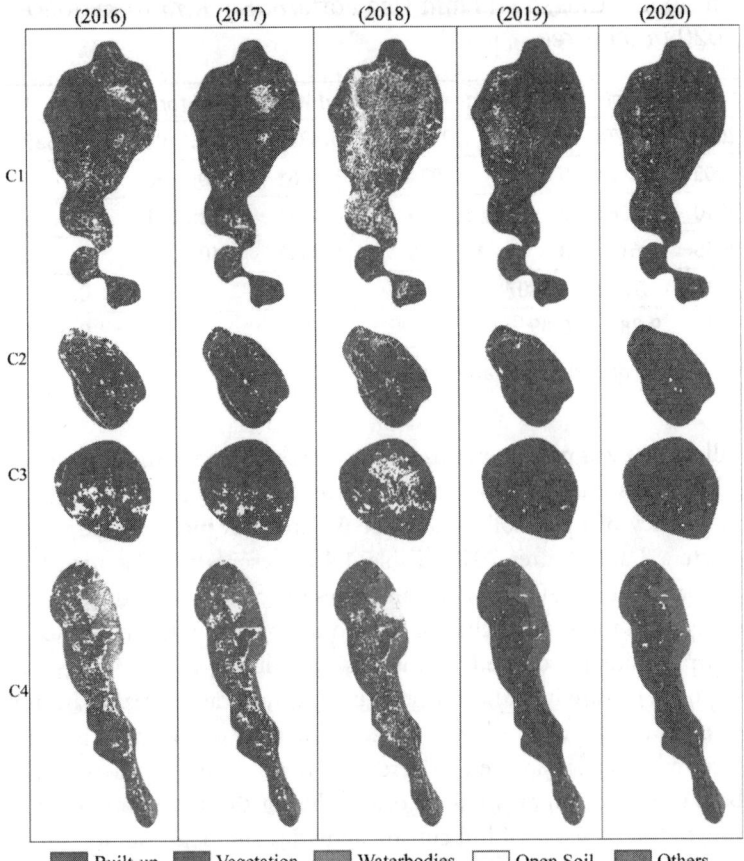

Figure 4.3 *Land Use Pattern in the Study Area during Pre- and Post-influx Periods*

Source: Processed and prepared by the authors.

the number of refugees and makeshift camps have increased between 2019 and 2020. The findings of the current study conform to the observations of the fieldwork team.

In the case of the second cluster, the changes in LULC are not remarkable, but some scattered built-up area is visible in the eastern part. However, a substantial increase in the built-up area in this cluster is observed after 2017 and it increased up to the year 2020. Notably,

Table 4.4 Classified Land Use Pattern (Sq. Km) from 2000 to 2020 in the Area

Date	Forest	Camp	Bare Soil	Inland Water	Non-forest	Coastal_Naf
2000	27.4878	0	1.0413	5.4927	9.1404	0.8685
2005	25.1424	0	1.1934	6.8661	10.8198	-
2010	13.1265	0	8.1909	10.4292	12.2841	-
2015	14.6115	0	13.5846	5.4306	10.404	-
2018	11.2239	5.7807	17.0946	5.841	3.6711	0.4194
2020	9.28	10.89	10.25	6.56	6.41	0.64

Source: Compiled by the authors.

hill cutting was present in this cluster even before the influx incidence. The same scenario is observed in cluster 3 regarding hill cutting and occupancy of open soil. The built-up area has increased largely in clusters 3 and 4 after 2017. Table 4.4 represents the classified land use pattern from 2000 to 2020 and gives the picture of gradual change along with the sudden change in land use pattern after the influx. A sharp decline of forested area is observed during the period and an opposite picture is found for built-up area and camp areas. The area of inland water bodies has also decreased after the influx. The non-forested area also showed a decreasing trend during the period. But bare soil occupied area has increased during the same period which proves the presence of hill cutting activities and deforestation in the area. Other types of land use which includes river side land and salt fields are found mostly in clusters 2 and 4. A common characteristic of all four clusters is that deforestation and hill cutting were an ongoing activity that was prior to building makeshift camps.

4.3.2. Vegetation Loss

Vegetation loss was the first visible environmental impact of Rohingya influx in the study area. A huge area of forestland was deforested by cutting trees to build makeshift settlements for the refugees. Fuel-wood, fruits and vegetables, house building materials including bamboo and cane, medicinal plants, cattle fodder are collected by the refugees from the nearby forests. Such extensive collection and use of natural resources may create ecological imbalance. The Rohingya who arrived between 1960 and 1970 on an average own about 0.09 hectares of encroached-upon land and around 92.5 per cent of the refugees were solely dependent on forest products for their daily household needs (Khan, Uddin, and Haque 2012). They also leased land from the local people for different purposes. By analysing the satellite images of the clusters from 2017 to 2020, it was observed that major vegetation loss occurred in cluster 1 and about 75 per cent area of the cluster has experienced vegetation loss. The remaining vegetated area of the cluster is also under threat because of the extreme pressure of the refugees on the existing resources. The carrying capacity of the area is already much lower than that required for the population living in the area. Thus, resource scarcity (land, water, forest) in the area is very severe and it has created unbearable stress on the physical environment and degrading the natural environment. Hassan et al. (2018) noticed that between 2016 and 2017, a significant growth in the number of refugee settlements occurred in nearby refugee camp sites, with an increase of land occupancy from 175 to 1,530 hectares. Hassan et al. (2018) observed the highest growth in the Kutupalong–Balukhali site also with a net increase of 1,219 hectares in the same period of time. However, Braun, Fakhri, and Hochschild (2019) observed the highest increase between July 2017 and February 2018. The camp area amplified tenfold at that time within only a few months. Ecological imbalance and disturbed wildlife habitats were the immediate outcome of such hasty dilapidation of forest land in the area (Imtiaz 2018). Islam and Weil (2000) observed various harmful impacts on the environment due to anthropogenic reasons of deforestation. Such environmental degradation driven by deforestation includes soil erosion, wildlife habitat loss and imbalance in hydrological cycle and other sorts of ecological risks. Newell and Stavins (2000) noticed that changes of forest cover also influence the ability of forest biomass to store carbon, bring changes in the diurnal temperature variation which has an impact on local climate, thereby leaving a footprint on global climate change also. The risk of occurrence of geo-environmental hazards is also accelerated by reckless deforestation. Risk of landslides is reduced by vegetation by protecting the soil and making the slope stable (Sarker and Rashid 2013). A pivotal role is also played by big trees which ensure strong root formation in the earth which fasten the soil and protect it from erosion (Sultana 2013).

Land cover change is an important issue in soil failure. But, for the relocation of refugees, huge vegetation cover is destroyed (Choudury 2019; Rahman et al. 2018; Rashid et al. 2020), which enhances the risk of different hazardous events. Similar findings were observed in the case of the current study. In addition, there are many (82 plant species) medicinal plants in the area (Uddin, Ratna, and Faruque 2013) which are being destroyed because of uncontrolled vegetation loss in the area. The makeshift camps are destroying not only the trees and medicinal plants but also other types of shrubs and herbs which provide shelter and foods for insects, birds and microorganisms. Thus, the vegetation loss occurring in the area is causing a great loss to the biodiversity. As we can see from Figure 4.4, a huge area of C1 experienced vegetation loss after the refugee influx which continued up to the year 2020. For C2, a moderate level of vegetation loss was noticed and the trend was almost similar for the years under consideration. However, both the vegetation loss and gain were sensible for C3 and C4 for the period from 2016 to 2020. Overall, the area experienced a huge loss of vegetation after the influx, but it was not homogeneous in all the clusters. Vegetation gain which was observed in some parts was due to the concerted efforts of managing and proper use of the land by the local people and NGOs to keep the impacts of vegetation loss at minimum level.

During the NDVI analysis (Figure 4.5), which is a simple graphical indicator of assessing whether or not the target land mass contains live green vegetation, it was noticed that C1 is experiencing a sharp decreasing trend of NDVI. However, the scenario was different for three other clusters which do not represent any significant loss of vegetation coverage in the area. C2 depicts a stable trend, while C3 and C4 showed a slight increasing trend of NDVI. This could be due to very limited number of plantation activities occurring in these areas. However, further studies are required to know the exact reason of such findings in the case of clusters 3 and 4.

4.3.3. Hill Cutting and Land Degradation

Hill cutting and land degradation are observed in the study area; this is a consequence of building makeshift camps for the refugees. Beginning of hill cutting is usually initiated by cutting trees and shrubs of the hills and then the shape of hills is changed to make them suitable for

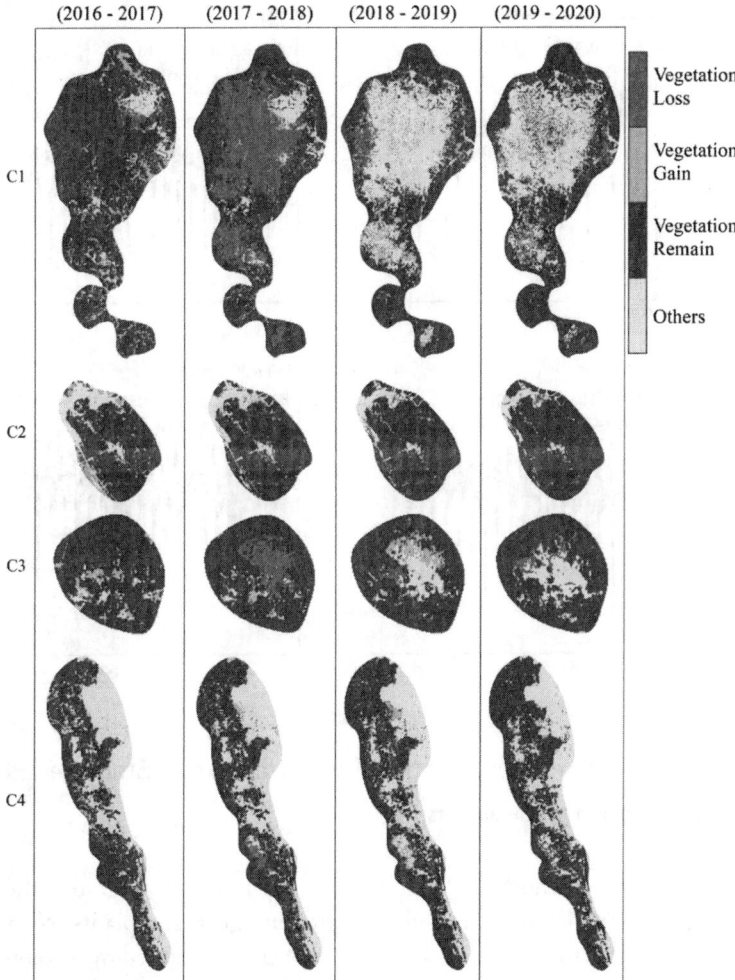

Figure 4.4 *Changes in Vegetation Cover of the Clusters during Pre- and Post-influx Periods*

Source: Processed and prepared by the authors.

erecting the shelters. Sometimes, they make steps on the hill slopes using spades to go up the hills to make more structures to accommodate more people. This makes the sandy hilly soil particles to loosen and erosion occurs there during both the rainy and the dry season.

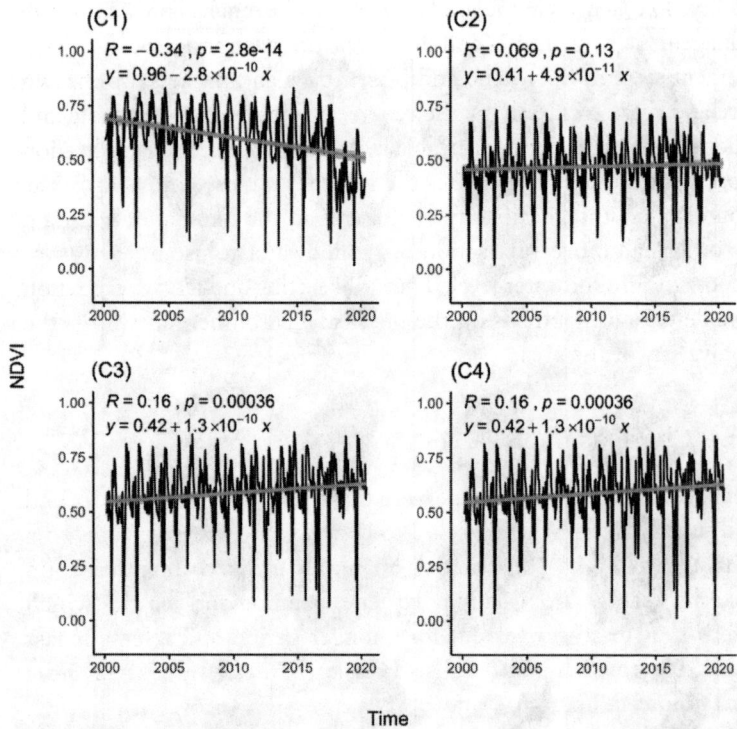

Figure 4.5 *NDVI Trends of the Clusters during the Study Period*
Source: Prepared by the authors.

The loss of soil moisture because of topsoil erosion degrades the soil quality and destroys its ability of growing grass and plants. Next time, plants cannot grow easily on the infertile soil caused by erosion and topsoil loss. Moreover, the eroded soil particles are carried away by rainwater to the nearby water bodies, the water quality of which is degraded due to the increased turbidity of water. In addition, the eroded soil particles deposited in the river bed/water bodies reduce the depth of water and the aquatic lives of those water bodies face challenges to survive. It is noticeable from Figure 4.3 that huge areas of clusters 1, 3 and 4 are bare lands which indicate the presence of eroded hills without trees or plants and also the existence of deposited sandy soils. During the dry season, the soil particles are carried by wind resulting in increased dust particles in air thereby worsening the air quality. The densely populated area of the clusters has no solid waste management programmes and there is no drainage and sewerage management system. Polythene and plastic bags and packets are thrown here and there recklessly by the refugees. These non-degradable and solid wastes create an impermeable layer which reduces the infiltration capacity of the soil. It increases the run-off and leave impacts on the groundwater storage capacity of the area in the one hand; while on the other hand, over-extraction of groundwater to use in the camps reduces the groundwater level. Thus, hill cutting and land degradation have deteriorating effects on the physical environment as well as the biodiversity of the area.

4.3.4. Changes in LST

Changes in LST, as assumed, were the result of vegetation loss and land use change in the area due to converting natural settings to a built-up area. The construction materials utilized for putting up makeshift camps are usually polythene, bamboo and plastics which absorb heat to a great extent for a longer period and release it fast comparing to plants and soils. This leads to significant increase in day-time temperature and decrease in night-time temperature. Deforestation also brings about changes in the microclimate of the area by changing the heat-absorbing and heat-releasing capacity of the surface. A change in microclimate is associated with local changes in different climatic parameters including temperature, precipitation, relative humidity, etc. For instance, converting to a built-up area will increase the temperature difference between day and night because of faster heat absorbing and releasing capacity of the construction materials. Thus, day-time temperature of the clusters area will be much higher than that of the surroundings. The living organisms, both flora and fauna, of the area will experience a different thermal environment which may affect their life cycle. The increased temperature will evaporate more water from soil and water bodies which may alter the soil quality negatively and may hamper the growth of plants. Changes in LST are also associated with moisture-holding capacity of air, and it influences the precipitation formation and quantity. If the rising LST continues to increase, the area may experience less rainfall than it usually receives. Figure 4.6 depicts the changes in LST

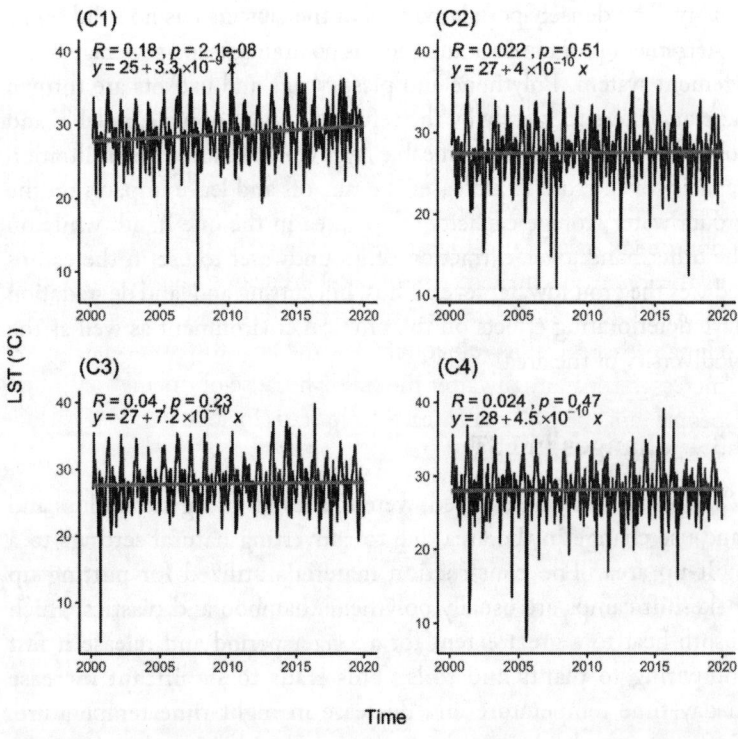

Figure 4.6 *Changes in LST in the Clusters during the Study Periods*

Source: Prepared by the authors.

between pre- and post-influx period in the four clusters. Cluster-1 which has experienced the highest amount of vegetation losses along with the changes in LULC shows the clear trend of rising LST, which indicates a temperature rise of 3–4 °C during the study period. Clusters 2, 3 and 4 also reveal a rising trend of LST, shown using linear regression lines in Figure 4.6. It means LST has increased in all clusters because of deforestation, putting up camp shelters and other sorts of LULC. The rising LST of the area is a matter of concern considering the climate change impacts in Bangladesh, especially for its geographical location and the increasing vulnerability for the huge population.

4.3.5. Changes in Physical Environment and Factors Affecting Hazard Occurrence

An unprecedented influx of the Rohingya refugees into Cox's Bazar district of Bangladesh has put the ecologically fragile region on the brink of an environmental disaster. The Rohingya refugee camps are located in the south-eastern coastal areas of Bangladesh. The elevation of the area is also high and considered as hilly areas. This part of the country is at high risk of several hazards due to geographical location, geological features, rainfall pattern and in the context of climate change. The vulnerability of the area to natural hazards has increased substantially after the influx because of the high number of people inhabiting a small area. The hazards include frequent cyclones, storm surges and floods.

Moreover, the formation of informal settlements on hill slopes with unplanned hill cutting increases the risk of hazardous events occurrence such as landslides. According to the geological time scale, the hilly areas of Bangladesh were developed in the tertiary age and composed of mainly unconsolidated sedimentary rocks such as sandstone, siltstone, shale and conglomerate. The composition of the soil of the hilly regions is complex, and the young rocks have higher content of easily weatherable feldspars (Khan and Hoque 2002). Due to the acid properties, hilly soil is easily saturated with water, and the bedrock and soil structure of the hills of the south-eastern region are not stable (Patwary 2013). Therefore, the soil of this hilly region is very much susceptible to landslide risks during heavy rains carried by the monsoon wind system (Ahmed et al. 2020; Sarker and Rashid 2013). Heavy rainfall and hill cutting cause massive soil erosion also. Similar observations were found from the fieldworks conducted by the investigators of this study.

It is known that the south-eastern coastal area including Cox's Bazar district is in a high-risk zone for high tidal surges. Besides, storm surges are a very frequent phenomenon in this region, which result in coastal flooding, erosion and salinity problem due to global climate change (Wahl 2017) and sea-level rise; the situation may aggravate in the future and may enhance the frequent cyclone and surge effect. Hill cutting and soil erosion will accelerate the damage of cyclone and storm surge. Groundwater level declining may speed up the salinity intrusion to groundwater as well as to the freshwater reservoirs since the area is close to the sea. This may create a drinking water crisis in the area in near future. Moreover, the eastern part of the country including the refugee settlement area lies along a highly oblique convergent boundary fault, which puts the area at high risk of earthquake occurrence. A former study showed that, on an average 6.3–7.5 magnitude earthquakes occurred once in 30–50 years in the secondary active structure in Chittagong–Tripura Fold Belt (Bilham and Hough 2006). Thus, the area is at risk of earthquake occurrence and the vulnerability of earthquake has further increased due to hill cutting, deforestation and massive LULC.

4.4. Conclusion

This chapter discussed the major types and reasons of physical changes in the area associated with the influx of the Rohingya. Land use and land cover changes, loss of vegetation, changes in LST were directly assessed in the study using satellite imagery analysis techniques. The result showed that the LULC has changed significantly in the area, massive deforestation has occurred and the LST has increased considerably. Hazard occurrence possibilities based on the physical environment change were also discussed. However, some types of changes like environmental hygiene, sound, air and light pollution were not assessable using the method adopted for the study. Further studies are recommended to know the impacts of the highlighted problems. It is imperative to note that the methods used in the study have a number of limitations, but still those are considered as the best option to investigate LULC change, vegetation loss and NDVI and LST of vast area where plot-to-plot survey is quite difficult and requires huge time and money investment. The Government of Bangladesh has been trying since the beginning of the problem to send back the Rohingya people to their birthplace through diplomatic initiatives, which is the ultimate solution of the problem. However, some steps have been taken by the government with the help of international agencies and NGOs as the immediate measures to reduce the sufferings of the refugees, minimize the conflict with the local people and to control the environmental loss. These steps include keeping the Rohingya people within the camp area, supporting them with everyday necessities including food and to relocate the refugees to Bhasan Char, an island in the Bay of Bengal. Obviously, the humanitarian issues were the prime concern of the government and international agencies to reduce the sufferings of the refugees and local people. Thus, the environmental aspect did not get much attention. However, it is expected that the outcomes of the current study will contribute to a better understanding of the environmental problems in the areas in the refugee camps and their neighbourhoods.

Acknowledgement

This research work was funded by Research and Publication Cell, University of Chittagong, Bangladesh.

References

Abrar, C. R. 2001. 'On the Margin: Refugees, Migrants and Minorities.' *Refugee Survey Quarterly* 20, no. 1: 235–240.

Ahmed B., M. S. Rahman, P. Sammonds, R. Islam, and K. Uddin. 2020. 'Application of Geospatial Technologies in Developing a Dynamic Landslide Early Warning System in a Humanitarian Context: The Rohingya Refugee Crisis in Cox's Bazar, Bangladesh.' *Geomatics, Natural Hazards Risk* 11, no. 1: 446–468.

Ahmed N., M. N. Islam, M. F. Hasan, T. Motahar, and M. Sujauddin. 2019. 'Understanding the Political Ecology of Forced Migration and Deforestation through a Multi-algorithm Classification Approach: The Case of Rohingya Displacement in the Southeastern Border Region of Bangladesh.' *Geology, Ecology, Landscapes* 3, no. 4: 282–294.

Almutairi, A., and T. A. Warner. 2010. 'Change Detection Accuracy and Image Properties: A Study Using Simulated Data.' *Remote Sensing* 2, no. 6: 1508–1529.

Amiri, R., Q. Weng, A. Alimohammadi, and S. K. Alavipanah. 2009. 'Spatial–Temporal Dynamics of Land Surface Temperature in Relation to Fractional Vegetation Cover and Land Use/Cover in the Tabriz Urban Area, Iran.' *Remote Sensing of Environment* 113, no. 12: 2606–2617.

Avdan, U., and G. Jovanovska. 2016. 'Algorithm for Automated Mapping of Land Surface Temperature Using LANDSAT 8 Satellite Data.' *Journal of Sensors*, no. 2: 1–8.

Belgiu, M., and L. Drăguţ. 2016. 'Random Forest in Remote Sensing: A Review of Applications and Future Directions.' *ISPRS Journal of Photogrammetry and Remote Sensing* 114: 24–31.

Bharath, S., K. Rajan, and T. Ramachandra. 2013. 'Land Surface Temperature Responses to Land Use Land Cover Dynamics.' *Geoinfor Geostat: An Overview* 1, no. 4: 1–10.

Bilham, R., and S. Hough. 2006. 'Future Earthquakes on the Indian Subcontinent: Inevitable Hazard, Preventable Risk.' *South Asian Journal* 12, no. 5: 1–9.

Braun, A., F. Fakhri, and V. Hochschild. 2019. 'Refugee Camp Monitoring and Environmental Change Assessment of Kutupalong, Bangladesh, Based on Radar Imagery of Sentinel-1 and ALOS-2.' *Remote Sensing* 11: 2047.

Breiman, L. 2001. 'Random Forests.' *Machine Learning* 45, no. 1: 5–32.

Carlson, T. N., and D. A. Ripley. 1997. 'On the Relation between NDVI, Fractional Vegetation Cover, and Leaf Area Index.' *Remote Sensing of Environment* 62, no. 3: 241–252.

Choudury, A. H., and M. Fazlulkader. 2019. 'Rohingya Refugee Crisis in Bangladesh: An Analysis of the Socio-economic and Environmental Problems in Bangladesh Myanmar Border Area.' *European Journal of Research* 87: 106.

Energy & Environment Technical Working Group. 2018. 'Support to Bangladesh Host Communities and Institutions in the Rohingya Refugee Response: Environmental Activities Overview.' Available at https://www.humanitarian-response.info/sites/www.humanitarianresponse.info/files/documents/files/environment-2018-5-9_twopage_eetwg_summary9.pdf (accessed on 31 July 2020).

Ghosh, A., R. Sharma, and P. K. Joshi. 2014. 'Random Forest Classification of Urban Landscape Using Landsat Archive and Ancillary Data: Combining Seasonal Maps with Decision Level Fusion.' *Applied Geography* 48: 31–41.

Gondwe, S. V., R. Muchena, and J. Boys. 2018. 'Detecting Land Use and Land Cover and Land Surface Temperature Change in Lilongwe City, Malawi.' *Journal of Remote Sensing & GIS* 9, no. 2: 17–26.

Hassan, M. M., A. C. Smith, K. Walker, M. K. Rahman, and J. Southworth. 2018. 'Rohingya Refugee Crisis and Forest Cover Change in Teknaf, Bangladesh.' *Remote Sensing* 10: 689.

Imtiaz, S. 2018. 'Ecological Impact of Rohingya Refugees on Forest Resources: Remote Sensing Analysis of Vegetation Cover Change in Teknaf Peninsula in Bangladesh.' *Ecocycles* 4: 16–19.

IOM. 2017. 'Needs and Population Monitoring Cox's Bazar, Bangladesh.' Available at http://www.globaldtm.info/bangladesh (accessed on 23 October 2020).

Islam, K. R., and R. R. Weil. 2000. 'Land Use Effects on Soil Quality in a Tropical Forest Ecosystem of Bangladesh.' *Agriculture, Ecosystems & Environment* 79: 9–16.

Khan, A. A., and M. A. Hoque. 2002. 'Quaternary Paleo-geography and Geohazard Scenario of the Bengal Delta of Bangladesh.' *Oriental Geographer* 46, no. 2: 1–16.

Khan, M., M. Uddin, and C. E. Haque. 2012. 'Rural Livelihoods of Rohingya Refugees in Bangladesh and Their Impacts on Forests: The Case of Teknaf Wildlife Sanctuary.' In *Counter-Narratives on Rohingya Refugees Issue: Re-look at Migration, Security and Integration*, edited by N. Uddin. Chittagong: SSRI, Chittagong University.

Khatun, F. 2017. 'Implications of the Rohingya Crisis for Bangladesh.' Dhaka: Centre for Policy Dialogue.

Kudrat-E-Khuda. 2020. 'The Impacts and Challenges to Host Country Bangladesh due to Sheltering the Rohingya Refugees.' *Cogent Social Sciences* 6, no. 1: 1770943.

Li, Z. L., B. H. Tang, H. Wu, H. Ren, G. Yan, and Z. Wan. 2013. 'Satellite-derived Land Surface Temperature: Current Status and Perspectives.' *Remote Sensing of Environment* 131: 14–37.

Liu, L., and Y. Zhang. 2011. 'Urban Heat Island Analysis Using the Landsat TM Data and ASTER Data: A Case Study in Hong Kong.' *Remote Sensing* 3, no. 7: 1535–1552.

Ndossi, M. I., and U. Avdan. 2016a. 'Application of Open Source Coding Technologies in the Production of Land Surface Temperature (LST) Maps from Landsat: A Pyqgis Plugin.' *Remote Sensing* 8, no. 5: 413.

———. 2016b. 'Inversion of Land Surface Temperature (LST) Using Terra Aster Data: A Comparison of Three Algorithms.' *Remote Sensing* 8, no. 12: 1–19.

Newell, R. G., and R. N. Stavins. 2000. 'Climate Change and Forest Sinks: Factors Affecting the Costs of Carbon Sequestration.' *Journal of Environmental Economics Management* 40: 211–235.

Patwary, M. A. A. 2013. 'Hazard Assessment Using Open Source Data: A Case Study for Chittagong, Bangladesh.' Master's thesis, Geo-Information Science (MGI), Wageningen University, Wageningen.

Qin, Z., G. Dall'Olmo, A. Karnieli, and P. Berliner. 2001. 'Derivation of Split Window Algorithm and Its Sensitivity Analysis for Retrieving Land Surface Temperature from NOAA-Advanced Very High Resolution Radiometer Data.' *Journal of Geophysical Research Atmospheres* 106, no. D19: 22655–22670.

Rahman, M., M. Islam, and T. Chowdhury. 2018. 'Change of Vegetation Cover at Rohingya Refugee Occupied Areas in Cox's Bazar District of Bangladesh: Evidence from Remotely Sensed Data.' *Journal of Environmental Science and Natural Resources* 11, no. 1–2: 9–16.

Raja, R. A., V. Anand, A. S. Kumar, S. Maithani, and V. A. Kumar. 2013. 'Wavelet Based Post Classification Change Detection Technique for Urban Growth Monitoring.' *Journal of the Indian Society of Remote Sensing* 41, no. 1: 35–43.

Rashid, K. J., M. A. Hoque, T. A. Esha, M. A. Rahman, and A. Paul. 2020. 'Spatiotemporal Changes of Vegetation and Land Surface Temperature in the Refugee Camps and Its Surrounding Areas of Bangladesh after the Rohingya Influx from Myanmar.' *Environment Development and Sustainability* 23, no. 3: 1–16.

Sahana, M., R. Ahmed, and H. Sajjad. 2016. 'Analyzing Land Surface Temperature Distribution in Response to Land Use/Land Cover Change Using Split Window Algorithm and Spectral Radiance Model in Sundarban Biosphere Reserve, India.' *Modeling Earth Systems and Environment* 2, no. 2: 81.

Sarker, A. A., and A. M. Rashid. 2013. 'Landslide and Flashflood in Bangladesh.' In *Disaster Risk Reduction Approaches in Bangladesh*, edited by Rajib Shaw, Fuad Mallick, and Aminul Islam, 165–189. Tokyo: Springer.

Sobrino, J. A., J. C. Jimenez-Munoz, and L. Paolini. (2004). 'Land Surface Temperature Retrieval from LANDSAT TM 5. *Remote Sensing of Environment* 90, no. 4: 434–440.

Sultana, N. (2011). 'Health Care at Rohingya Refugee Camp A Case Study on RTM Initiative. ACCESS Health International, RTM International, 6.

Uddin, S. B., R. S. Ratna, and M. O. Faruque. 2013. 'Ethnobotanical Study on Medicinal Plants of Rakhaing Indigenous Community of Cox's Bazar District of Bangladesh.' *Journal of Pharmacognosy and Phytochemistry* 2, no. 4: 164–174.

UNDP and UN Women. 2018. 'Environmental Impact of Rohingya Influx.' Available at https://reliefweb.int/report/bangladesh/report-environmental-impact-rohingya-influx-executive-summary (accessed on 29 October 2020).

UNHCR. 2019. 'Rohingya Emergency.' Available at https://www.unhcr.org/en-us/rohingya-emergency.html?query=rohingya%20crisis (accessed on 19 October 2020).

Wahl, T. 2017. 'Sea-level Rise and Storm Surges, Relationship Status: Complicated.' *Environmental Research Letters* 12, no. 11: 111001.

Wang, M., G. He, Z. Zhang, G., Wang, Z. Wang, and R. Yin. 2019. 'A Radiance-based Split-window Algorithm for Land Surface Temperature Retrieval: Theory and Application to MODIS Data.' *International Journal of Applied Earth Observation and Geoinformation* 76: 204–217.

Yankovich, K. S., E. P. Yankovich, and N. V. Baranovskiy. 2019. 'Classification of Vegetation to Estimate Forest Fire Danger Using Landsat 8 Images: Case Study.' *Mathematical Problems in Engineering* 2019: 1–14.

Zhang, J., Y. Wang, and Y. Li. 2006. 'A C++ Program for Retrieving Land Surface Temperature from the Data of Landsat TM/ETM+ band6.' *Computers & Geosciences* 32, no. 10: 1796–1805.

Part II

The Rohingya Refugees in India and South Asia

CHAPTER 5

Representation of Refugee, Migration and Displacement

Sagarika Naik

5.1. Introduction

Though Hannah Arendt (1973, 267–302) advocated for the rights of stateless people in the form of having citizenship, which is also related to the entitlements of human rights, (Bernstein 2005, 46–60) the UN 1945 definition confirms statelessness as a person without protection under any state's protections act (UNHCR 1945). Therefore, there were approximately 12 million stateless people, as per the United Nations Human Rights Office of the High Commissioner (UNHCR) estimation, in the world living with a vulnerable condition, lacking basic services such as education, employment, or healthcare, discrimination and exploitations. Given these circumstances, the massive existence of statelessness imposes a challenge to the fundamentals of international law and human rights discourses (Blitz 2009). To justify this assessment, there are approximately 10 million people who reside in South Asia, and South East Asia, among them the Rohingya of Myanmar are considered as the single largest stateless group in the world, where they consist of more than a million people according to the UNHCR's stateless mandate (European Parliament 2017). In addition to that, the 'Global Trend Report' also exposed the brutal ethnic cleansing campaign of 2017 led by the military junta that has created a massive displacement, forced migration situation in Rakhine State (Institute on Statelessness and Inclusion Analysis 2018). In particular, the 2017 massive destruction has forced the Rohingya to different parts of South Asia or Southeast Asia, making them vulnerable, the statelessness status becoming a key challenge for their security. Or we can say the forcibly migrated Rohingya are one such group, who constantly claimed their belongingness to their inherited land of Myanmar/Burma by historic evidence, which has continuously been repudiated by the Burmese government (Farzana 2017).

The Rohingya considered the world's most persecuted minority constitute the largest groups of stateless persons since the 1982 Citizenship Law in Burma was enacted. The undemocratic, authoritarian Citizenship Law has violated the most fundamental motto/principle of the Universal Declaration of Human Rights (1948) which broadly confirms, 'everyone has the right to a nationality'. In these worst scenarios, the plight of stateless Rohingya further deteriorated due to the dominant presence of the state in their everyday life (Uddin 2019).

In the context of the so-called enactment of the Citizenship Law, Brad Blitz (2009) has clearly stated,

[T]he Rohingya of Myanmar who had perpetually lost their citizenship/nationality right, further, where their rights were rescinded by the 'law in the 1980s' are permanently excluded from the national homogenization ethnic membership which often connected with the loyalty and this has been a major factor for denial and granting of citizenship.

This ethnic cleansing campaign also revealed that there is a severe crack and weakness in the political system and governance, and that the state administrative mechanism failed to act as a primary guarantor of human rights. Therefore, the contemporary crisis or the brutal and authoritarian action which was led by the military junta exposed the danger towards the democracy of Myanmar. As historian Thant Myint-U (2021) said,

> [T]he doors just opened to a very different future. I have a plummeting feeling that no one will able to control what will comes next. And remember Myanmar as a country currently awash in weapons with deep divisions across ethnic & religious lines, where millions can barely feed themselves.

As the magnitude of this, the Rohingya are treated as the stateless victim, and left outside the national boundary and hence become the major victim to abuses, poverty, and marginalization in all its forms (Banerjee Paula, et al. 2015). Nevertheless, in Myanmar, the Rohingya have always been treated as *de facto* stateless people who are even incompetent to generate proof of their nationality, residency, or other means of qualifying needs for citizenship, as the government denied their historical claim over the Arakan land. As Jeff Kingston (2019) has argued in the *Politics of Religion*,

> Rohingya are always treated as the gypsies and unwanted people according to a local ethnic Rakhine Buddhist monk.... they were only temporary migrants, named as Kalar, a vulgar slur for South Asians that is widely used to refer to the swarthy Rohingya.

One of the central focuses of this chapter is to address the plight of the Rohingya which has created a new chapter in the contemporary history of statelessness. Through exploring or contextualizing statelessness through legal, theoretical, and practical lenses, the chapter presents a broader analysis of the Rohingya refugee crisis. The chapter also outlines the difficulties of the Rohingya stateless population and trace the relationship between statelessness and human trafficking, as recently the Global Slavery Index and the US State Department highlighted that the Rohingya refugee is vulnerable to modern-day slavery-like trafficking, forced labour and debt bondage in Southeast Asia (Weiner 1993). Furthermore, the chapter also investigates the gendered dimension of contemporary servitude focusing on the fastest-growing trafficking network where the Rohingya women and children have become the major victims of abuses and domination, also used as an object for commercial sex purpose across the state boundaries. In addition to that, I am trying to analyse why the state has failed to provide a transparent government to its own citizens. The chapter follows a diverse approach to give a clear idea to its reader regarding the question on the why Myanmar has failed to take necessary measures to resolve the Rohingya crisis as it also questions the silence of its *de facto* leader, the Nobel laureate and the democratic icon Aung San Suu Kyi who has ignored the genocide done by the military junta and testified that, 'while it is possible war crimes that have been committed against the Rohingya, however, those crimes did not constitute genocide.' The chapter concludes with recommendations and solutions, what needs to be done, as the ASEAN state failed to recognize Rohingya as one of the world's persecuted minority and seeking immediate help from them. Also it shows, how the member of the ASEAN countries has completely reluctant to adopt a holistic strategy to resolve this Rakhine issue (*The Washington Post*).

5.2. Statelessness, Citizenship Crisis in South Asia: Contextualizing the Beginning

As Justice Earl Warren has correctly remarked, 'citizenship has considered as human fundamental right…, the deprivation of [citizenship right] … it, deprives of the right to assert any right.'[1] In particular, the concept of 'the right to have rights' has signified or advocated the state and its responsibilities to defend or naturalized its citizenship rights against all the efforts which have to denaturalize them. Indeed, by all means, state responsibility is to play a key role or prime custodial role to protect its citizenship rights and protect its liberty, freedom and fraternity (Benhabib 2004). In the current era, the global society is radically out of balance as the nation states are more concerned towards the creation of homogenous identity; as a repercussion of that, the interest of the minority has always been neglected and underestimated. The initial question can be raised here, that what is the nature of the state

---

[1] Among the other Asian states, the Rohingya is one example of a stateless and persecuted group being displaced and forced to seek refuge in multiple countries. See Maizura (2018).

of Myanmar? And how this question on citizenship and statelessness can fit into the contexts?

As we can see from the military-led genocide where the minority rights, their claims on the citizenship right 'become much more imperiled' and which has created an alarming condition for the global governance to take instantaneous steps to protect these fundamental rights of the stateless victims in South Asia. In the contemporary scenario, statelessness is considered as more ... *a set of circumstances that has limited the rights of citizens* ... (Frelick and Lynch 2015). Bill and Lynch have argued that citizenship rights or nationality is the connection between an individual and the state. Also, the denial of identity, status and rights generates uncertainty, fear amongst people and individuals/groups who are excluded and inhabit a liminal 'in-between position' (Chowdhory 2018). As noted earlier, the Rohingya in Myanmar are often confronted with the constant denial of citizenship rights, denial of freedom of movement, eviction campaigns, forced labour, expulsion from their lands and property, sometimes violence and physical torture (Ahmed 2010).

Even this constant denial of citizenship has made the Rohingya especially vulnerable to different types of exploitation, forced labour, and abuses done by the state, given the xenophobic attitude of the current regime in Myanmar. However, their problems associated with citizenship status or nationality had not started until 1983. As Brad Blitz has argued, in 1983, the Burmese government completed a nationwide census where the Rohingya were intentionally excluded or were not accounted for in the survey, rendering them stateless through exclusion (Blitz 2011). According to Berlie Jean it is the 1982 Citizenship Act that permanently legalized this exclusion and created two separate categories for the citizens: 'full citizens' and 'subordinate citizens'. Also, their status as stateless was officially declared after the enforcement of 1982 Burmese Citizenship Law, which distinguished three categories of citizenship and particularly excluding the Rohingya from each (Razzaq and Haque 1995).

Nevertheless, the Rohingya are excluded from both groups as they failed to substantiate their lineage as 'associated with Burma' before 1948 (Berlie 2008). Amnesty International underlined that the 1982

Law has introduced a form of government-controlled 'Central Body' or 'Central Administration' that controlled a wide range of powers which has regulated the specific citizenship-related issues. The 1982 *Citizenship Act* is not only an unpretentious legal mechanism through which the Rohingya experience systematic and legalized discrimination, but it also acts as the 'anchor' that holds the discriminatory legal framework that designed to severely cripple the Rohingya as a group of falsely damned illegals and non-citizens. As Maung Zarni (2014) has argued, apart from the citizenship entitlement, the Rohingya have been going through a process of slow-burning genocide over years. The government has frequently denied the Rohingya claim over citizenship rights, as the 1982 Citizenship Act legalized its provision. Consequently, the members of the Rohingya community are therefore treated as illegitimate or classified as ineligible for getting the citizenship status in Myanmar.[2] In this given context, we can say that the constant denial of their lawful citizenship right by the Myanmar government is a major factor for their suffering. In addition to that, the government-sponsored inclusion completely visible in 1989, not only it reinforced different citizenship categories, but also it announces the so called color coded identity cards including pink cards for full citizens, blue cards for the associated citizens and the green cards for naturalized citizenship (Andersen 1997). The most important factor behind the entire statelessness claim, and the citizenship crisis is, they are never treated as the natives of this land, sometimes they are categorized as the 'people who came from the border region', particularly, the Rohingya are labelled as the *'people from the west'*, that they do not belong to Myanmar. In *Memories of Burmese Rohingya Refugees: Contested Identity and Belonging*, Farzana argued that this is indicative of the weak political nature of the legal system, and for that, the Rohingya in Myanmar cannot withstand the state.

Later, we can see the colour-specific identity cards temporarily given by the State Peace and Development Council (SPDC) has also

---

[2] According to Article 3, Chapter II, nationals such as the Kachin, Kayah, Karen, Chin, Burman, Mon, Rakhine or Shan and ethnic groups as have settled in any of the territories included within the state as their permanent home from a period anterior to 1185 BC, 1823 AD are Burma citizens. This specifies that the Rohingya are excluded from the Burma Citizenship Law.

failed to guarantee them citizenship right, instead, it provided citizenship right to those Rohingya who were repatriated from Bangladesh. In July 1995, the Myanmar Immigration and Population Department (IPD) had given the Rohingya Temporary Registration Card (TRC) or the white card. However, due to the lack of transparency or its limited circulation in rural areas, all the Rohingya have not received this card, even though later it denied its legitimate claim as evidence of citizenship (Andersen 1997). I have argued how the Burmese government has violated the fundamental constitutional principle ... it supposed to protect its citizen's rights, under the section of Right of Equality Article 13, as its clearly stated that 'all citizens irrespective of their birth, religion, sex or race are equal before law; that is to say, there shall not any arbitrary discrimination between one citizen or class of citizens and another' (Constituent Assembly 1947).

However, the research vividly shows how the Burmese societies have been considered as one of the most ethnically diverse society in the world. Within this '135 distinctive classification', the state was slow to formulate a common national identity for its citizens. This also reflects the exclusion of Rohingya who were considered as alien and illegal community not even listed on the government-created 135 recognized distinctive 'ethnic nationalities' as per the International Federation of Humanities Rights League (2000). Most importantly, in 1997, on the basis of national categorization the SPDC, which was interchanged with the Burma Socialist Party Programme, has rejected their existence in Myanmar; however, it has also denied 'the presence of a separate ethnic group called Rohingya'. Despite the presence of international organizations such as the UNHCR, the Rohingya continue to suffer by the state (military)-controlled violence amounting to sometimes extreme discrimination, forced migration, forced labour based on their ethnicity, and various restrictions and abuses at the hands of local Myanmar administrative bodies. Afterwards, those who flee are deported back to Burma and are often imprisoned for leaving the country illegitimately. With their absence, their names are gradually removed from the Myanmar draconian household registration system that keeps track of people's movements, and they are often handed rigid fines and sometimes imprisoned (Amnesty International 1997).

5.3. Violence, Restriction and Struggle for Everyday Life in Rakhine

Lack of citizenship rights has created a bigger problem for the Rohingya. As they are not given the right to citizenship, they eventually are subjected to heavy restriction on their movement within the Rakhine, and to other parts of the country (Lynch 2005). The freedom of movement is a fundamental right upon which other human rights are truly dependent, inappropriately that has been repudiated or restricted for the Rohingya. As I am trying to bring the reader's attention here that, this wide range of restrictions on the free movement on Rohingya is completely illegal or unethical. Chris Lewa argued that without the appropriate documentation the Rohingya constantly face exploitation by the corrupt administrators, as they must pay bribes to them to obtain a travel document (Lewa 2003). Or can this explanation be justified that all the restrictions were imposed on them just because they are Rohingya and are not any other community?[3]

Another abuse told by the refugees also related to the denial of citizenship right is the violation of the fundamental right which includes forced unpaid labour and the restriction upon getting an adequate standard of living. As a refugee shared his experience that, 'the Burmese government does not even allow us to work as their laborer. We work as their Kuli, and they do not even pay for or service.'[4] The austere brutality can be also observed from the experience of a 40-year-old Rohingya man from northern Maungdaw, who opined his inability to earn a living due to the travel restrictions.

[S]ince our movements are restricted, I cannot even go to another village to find a job. I am a carpenter and the daily wage of a carpenter is 2,500 kyat, but in my village, I can hardly find work

---

[3] See Articles 23 and 25 of UDHR which have clearly stated that 'everyone has right to work, to free of choice of employment to just and favorable conditions work and to protection against unemployment'. Available at https://www.un.org/en/universal-declaration-human-rights/ (accessed on 9 August 2021).

[4] Kulis/Coolies are people who carry weight for others.

foresight or 10 days a month. (Amnesty International 2004; Arakan Project 2016)

Historical narrative has always expressed the Rohingya identity and their relationship to Burma which can be traced back to centuries. However, it is the politics behind globalization and the land grabbing competition in South Asia that have forcefully created a xenophobic atmosphere or have created a rigorous competition between minority versus majority which has resulted in the exclusion of the Rohingya from the citizenship right and given them a statelessness status (Chatterjee 2012). During the colonial expansion and the consolidation process, the South Asians are derogatorily referred to as kala (foreigner/ emigrants) in Burma, but often, the Rohingya are viewed as beneath even this level of disdain. This was starkly in evidence in February 2009, wherein a letter from the Burmese Consul-General in Hong Kong, Ye Myint Aung, to his fellow heads of mission mentioned:

> In reality, Rohingya are neither 'Myanmar People' nor Myanmar's ethnic group. You will see in the photos that their complexion is 'dark brown'. The complexion of Myanmar people is fair and soft, good looking as well. It is quite different from what you have seen and read in the papers. (They are as ugly as ogres.)[5]

There were many instances when the Rohingya were not allowed to use their own property. As the confiscation of land resulted in displace-ment, which legitimizes the government claim on the Rohingya native land. Their everyday life becomes quashed due to restriction, violence, fear and anxiety. Moreover, there are cases that show the destruction of religious shrines, madrasa and cemeteries and pagodas established in their place. These instances are indicative of massive human rights violation in South Asia against a particular community that has been forcefully assigned a stateless indemnity, as the consequence of it, they have become the victim of trafficking, forced labour and exploitations.

[5] Letter from Ye Myint Aung, Consul General of Myanmar in Hong Kong, to heads of Mission, Consul Corps, Hong Kong and Macau SAR (2009); Human Rights Watch (2009).

5.4. Stateless Rohingya: Displaced and Uprooted in South Asia and Southeast Asia

As the earlier discussion suggests, the Rohingya Refugee crisis is an outcome of the state-sponsored camping, decade-long persecution and violation of their fundamental rights. The Rohingya non-recognition of citizenship status which was created institutionally by the state has led to inequalities between citizens and non-citizens. Yet, it was in August 2017 that triggered by far the largest and fastest Rohingya refugee influx into South Asian countries including Bangladesh, India, Sri Lanka, and Pakistan. Since then, an estimated 7,50,000 Rohingya including more than 400,000 children have fled into Cox's Bazar and other parts of South Asia and Southeast Asia. Recent documents show till March 2019, approximately one million stateless Rohingya refugees reside in Ukhiya and Tenknaf upazilas of Bangladesh. However, it has been frequently reported that the Bangladeshi government's frequent raids on the illegal drug trade, which includes severe allegations of terrorizing the Rohingya. In addition to that, the intensifying clashes are also putting everyone in the camps at even greater risk.

Hopelessly, many Rohingya refugees are fleeing to Sri Lanka, India, Pakistan and Bangladesh, which has created an increased anti-Muslim and anti-refugee sentiments in these regions. The anti-Muslim sentiments encouraged by India's Hindutva-aligned ruling government's Citizenship Amendment Act 2019 (CAA), National Register of Citizens 2013 (NRC) have not only excluded the minority interest but also is the biggest threat to the country's democracy. Similarly, Pakistan experiences sectarian violence, surprisingly, despite being a country for all Muslims it is pushing back the integration of the Rohingya refugees. Even Sri Lanka, a country that was recently impacted by a bloody civil war based on ethnic divisions, has seen an emerging rise of communal violence or a threat due to the Rohingya migrants (Sharma 2017).

The 2017 Rohingya human rights violation, which was state-sponsored destruction, has not only affected Bangladesh and its periphery but also caused strife in other parts of Southeast Asian countries including Malaysia, Indonesia, and Thailand. Thailand and

Indonesia have become a wayward station for Rohingya who are seeking refuge in Malaysia. Likewise, the Rohingya refugee community in Thailand have lived in a fearful situation, anxious and terrorized with the fear of sudden arrest and deportation by Thai authorities. As frequently as, *The diplomat* has reported, in Thailand, the 'Rohingya are considered the biggest threat to the security system' (Beech 2020). If 'the authorities do not take the necessary action to repress the violence and protect refugees, there's a serious risk of further bloodshed' (Hammadi 2020).

In 2016, during the adaptation of the New York Declaration, the UN Secretary-General and seven member states had emphasized global responsibility-sharing for refugees. At that summit, 47 states committed to a legal policy to change the basic amenities for the refugees including access to education, lawful employment and social services, substantially increase humanitarian aid and expanded access to the third country solutions (UNHCR 2020). Therefore, it can be argued that the countries in Southeast Asia, including Thailand, Malaysia and Indonesia, have never ratified the International Refugee Convention as well as New York Declaration and failed to take any kind of drastic steps in order to protect the asylum seekers and refugees. However, as per the records, all three have signed regional frameworks to halt the flow of migrants due to the violence and prosecution in Myanmar; unfortunately, they failed to keep their promises.

In this chapter, I am trying to question that, how statelessness is a contributing factor in the continual failure of the repatriation process in South Asia or in Southeast Asia. According to the UNHCR (2014), there are millions of people who still suffer the lifelong denial of their human rights because they are stateless. Moreover, statelessness can lead to a devastating cycle of deprivation and vulnerability. The notion of being stateless is underlined by various forms of deprivation and subjugation. This also reminds us to return to the idea of why the denial of citizenship right is so important in shaping people's identity. Because a lot of these abuses and exploitation are based on their access to, or denial of, citizenship, which in turn is interrelated with rights and entitlements.

5.5. The Rohingya at Risk: Trafficking, Forced Labour and Debt Bondage

Statelessness and human trafficking are grave and widespread human rights challenges for the international community in this 21st century (Lori 2017). Reportedly the US State Department has warned the statelessness of Rohingya increases their vulnerability towards human trafficking and debt bondage. Therefore, statelessness can be both a cause and a consequence of human trafficking. Inter-connectedly, these two issues have a similar linkage as statelessness puts a person at a greater risk of trafficking (US State Department 2018). However, the fundamental link between statelessness and trafficking has never been decisively demonstrated. Particularly in this chapter, I am trying to analyse the vulnerable condition of the Rohingya refugees and how their statelessness status is putting them at an everyday risk towards human trafficking, forced labour, sexual exploitation and debt bondage. Without any legal identity, stateless Rohingya were more exposed to trafficking, as certain rackets are actively working in the camps. Some studies also have shown that there are numerous allegations that the Rohingya camps at Cox's Bazar are frequently being used in drug and human trafficking and other forms of illegal activities (*The Daily Star* 2004; The Irrawaddy 2009).

Recently, the global estimate has shown that human trafficking is a US$30–US$45 billion industry. Human trafficking is not only the most profitable business in the world but also emerging as the fastest growing underground industry (Walk Free Foundation 2018). Furthermore, globalization has created a worldwide platform where the present-day slaves are easy to procure, easy to transport and easy to exploit and easy to transit through trafficking (Kara 2010).

Consistently, the world's economies grow faster and highly interdependent, because of which the opportunity gap between people grows wider and wider (Appadurai 1991). Also, the Third World countries are prone to ethnic conflicts, subjugation and genocide, which create a favourable space for trafficking and exploitation. As a result, the statelessness status has pushed them towards the greater risk of exploitation; thus, the journey initiated in the search of safety and employment has turned in to risk, forced labour, destitution and abuses (Naik 2021a). Recently, the International Organization on Migration (IOM) has reported there are thousands of Rohingya refugees in Bangladesh who are at a greater risk of falling prey to human traffickers who exploit them sexually and for forced labour. The US State Department has already warned the risk on Rohingya women who are recruited from the refugee camps for various domestic works and being transferred to Saudi Arabia for sex work.

Simultaneously, the Rohingya women became the major victim of both national and transnational sex trafficking. Neither the hosting nation Bangladesh nor the neighbouring states Kathmandu and Kolkata has failed to provide the adequate security, even due to the high demand some of these girls are 'traded' between traffickers over the internet. To contextualize the forced migration and trafficking, Naik argued, to maintain the basic amenities and livelihood that were neither provided by the homeland nor in the hoisting countries, the Rohingya women have been forced to serve as sex workers in the expensive industries in Thailand, brothels market in Malaysia and bars in Indonesia (Naik 2021b).

Another dimension of this study shows, men also experience exploitation and abuses, debt bondage in the refugee camps (US State Department 2020). Therefore, the situation of the Rohingya men is worse than that of any other. There are even instances like Rohingya men who fled to Bangladesh from Burma decades ago have been trapped in debt bondage to Bangladeshi fishermen for 20 years. In the recent past, some Rohingya and Bangladeshi migrants who travelled by boat to Southeast Asian regions were subjected to exploitation when they were unable to pay ransoms and were instead sold into forced labour. According to the statement of a victim, 'I was held captive by the smugglers for one and a half months until my family paid the debt' (Rohingya refugee, 44 years old, male; UNHCR 2019). Transnationally, the Rohingya are very vulnerable to the Thai fishing industry where human trafficking as well as forced, bonded and slave labour are highly prevalent (Goldberg 2015).

The 21st-century statelessness status has a significant human rights repercussions for children in today's world, jeopardizing their access to fundamental social protections and entitlements that many take for granted. The dramatic abuses were started in Myanmar, as the Rohingya children are not allowed to go to state-run schools beyond the primary education level, as secondary education was preserved for only citizens (Bhabha 2010). Although, the situation became worst in camps, recently it has been reported that, there are more than one million victims who are sexually exploited, among them 21 per cent are children under the age of 18 years. Indeed, these numbers are creating an alarming situation for the international community, which has urged immediate action. As the ILO's Worst Forms of Child Labour Convention, 1999 (No. 182), shows that in the South Asian regions maximum of children are being forced to do sex works, domestic services and involved in different criminal activities.

What is perhaps the most disturbing for the Rohingya is the insecure future of their children in the host nation. Among the many communities in Malaysia, the Rohingya children are more exposed to danger and exploitation. As Aegile Fernandez, from the anti-trafficking organization, *Tenganita* said 'there is a demand now for more and more children, it is very clear; the market is there for these kids to be used and violated' (Allchin 2009). 'The biggest group we deal with are the Rohingya ... they are the most vulnerable,' said Dr Ziauddin, of the Nur-a-Salam organization for street children (Human Rights Watch 2019).

This study shows that the denial of the citizenship rights and the stateless status make the Rohingyas even more vulnerable to trafficking. Most of the South Asian states have the legal provisions for condemning trafficking, yet their implementation is often unsatisfactory.

5.6. Statelessness and Protection: Weak Intervention of Regional and International Actors

Indeed, both the regional and international actors are slow to recognize or slow to register these human rights violations. For instance, there are repetitive reports about the Bangladesh camp officials involved in a wide range of illegal activities every day, including domestic, sexual and gender-based violence and trafficking, but in practice, no such implication has been registered or documented yet. As Bangladesh has come under the tier 2 watch list of US state department's 2019 Trafficking in Persons Report, following which the government maintains minimal anti-trafficking law enforcement efforts and took some minimal steps for its preventions. Therefore, to take advantage of this, the law enforcement officials have decreased the investigations and continued to reject such allegations which have been registered by the Rohingya. Despite the hundreds of credible reports on forced labour and sex trafficking, the officials did not even open any investigations to verify these reports. Even it has also been reported that the Bangladesh High Court did not entertain any anti-trafficking cases filed by the Rohingya, despite the law allowing them to file trafficking cases in Bangladesh courts. The international organizations also alleged some Bangladesh officials' role in facilitating the Rohingya trafficking that includes accepting bribes from the human trafficking racket, which was actively working in the camps. A few cases have drawn wider attention from the media. For instance, in 2018, there were at least 100 credible reports on forced labour and sex trafficking of Rohingya within Bangladesh; unfortunately, the Bangladesh High Court did not entertain any trafficking case that was filed by the Rohingya refugees. It clearly shows the government of Bangladesh does not take even the minimum action for the elimination of trafficking (US State Department 2019).

Likewise, *The Guardian* reported how Thailand's export-oriented seafood business has become the major centre of the vast trafficking network, where thousands of the Rohingya who were held captive in jungle camps are now highly vulnerable to this (Equal Right Trust and Institute of Human Rights and Peace Studies 2014). Over the last five years, both the US State Department and European Commission have issued a formal warning to Thailand about its illegal fishing industry. Recently, the US State Department downgraded Thailand to the most horrible possible rating to tier 3 on its Trafficking in Persons Report, for failing to combat human trafficking, while the European Commission issued an 'yellow card' warning to Thailand for failing to combat IUU (Illegal, Unreported and Unregulated) fishing that could lead to a ban on importing Thai seafood products into the European Union. Sometimes, the government-amended policies such as sending back the Rohingya asylum seekers to their native lands also violate the international principle. It is highly recommended that the countries like Malaysia, Thailand, and Indonesia should end their policies of maritime pushbacks and instead undertake coordinated efforts to respond to boats in distress, enact search-and-rescue operations, bring boats ashore to the nearest safe port and provide humanitarian aid. It can also be suggested that it is a crucial time for the UN Refugee Agency, UNHCR, to be granted immediate access to any Rohingya asylum seekers who arrive by boat or overland to assess their claims for protection following international standards.

The Association of Southeast Asian Nations (ASEAN) has also failed to respond effectively to the Rohingya refugee crisis in Myanmar as it shows lack of leadership and the 10-member organization's inability to grasp the scale of human rights crisis. Until ASEAN and many other global actors acknowledge the conditions in Myanmar that forced the Rohingya out of the Rakhine state, there is little hope for peace in Rakhine state (Lego 2017). Now, South Asia or Southeast Asian leaders should have urgently adopted a concrete plan to solve this humanitarian emergency. Since 'ASEAN leaders, having done almost nothing for years,' said Brad Adams, Asia director, 'a coordinated regional response is desperately needed to protect Rohingya in Myanmar' (Human Rights Watch 2020).

5.7. Conclusion

This chapter discussed the way in which the Rohingya identity and their stateless status have been formulated and politicized and its repercussion on the community. The chapter explained how the Rohingya are largely treated in Myanmar and beyond. After the constant denial of citizenship rights, denial of freedom of movement, eviction campaigns, forced labour, expulsion from their lands and property, violence and physical torture have created a severe human rights challenge in South Asia and Southeast Asia (Ahmed 2020). The exiled live in camps and their restricted life is an outcome of the state-created or state-sponsored vulnerability that has forced people to choose between 'leaving the country by crossing the border' and 'receiving definite death' (Uddin 2017).

The slow-burning state-led campaign shows that the state has adopted policies and plans designed to cause harm and destruction to the Rohingya in Myanmar (Zarni and Cowley, 2014). Therefore, the Rohingya refugees who experienced the decades-long systematic exploitation, and whose own country is unable or unwilling to ensure their most fundamental human right, are recent suspects towards modern-day slavery-like transnational trafficking, debt bondage and forced labour. Indeed, this sentence advocates the failure of a systematic and transparent government in Myanmar, now the time has come for the international governing bodies to put maximum pressure on the so-called military junta and resolve this crisis. As Myanmar is a member of the ASEAN, now ASEAN leaders must come up with new strategies to reduce the military authoritarian violence against its people.

These analyses led to my observation that the depression and chaos in refugee camps have created an ideal condition for human trafficking, as the gender-specific violence justified where the girls in their early teens are trafficked transnationally. Furthermore, the gendered lens of enquiring presents an analysis of the male victim who was the major victim of debt bondage and working as bonded labour in the Thai fishing industries. Moreover, I have also emphasized the fact that both the native land and hosting nations have failed to guarantee sufficient protection to the Rohingya children, as their parents frequently expressed their uncertain gloomy future.

Finally, statelessness continues to be a fundamental cause of discrimination, exploitation and forced displacement in all regions of the world, nevertheless statelessness is not an unsolvable problem. This study also offers steps to protect the stateless Rohingya effectively. For that, highly stringent efforts are required. The Rohingya who are commonly seen through the lenses of 'ethnic minorities', strategic effort from the international community and the transnational institutions are the immediate necessity. Also, the state should apply adequate mechanisms to protect people from abuses that particularly affect the stateless Rohingya minority.

References

Ahmed, Imtiaz. 2010. *The Plight of the Stateless Rohingyas: Responses of the State, Society & the International Community Migration and Citizenship Legal Practice.* Dhaka: The University Press Limited.

Ahmad, Imitiaz. 2020. 'Special issue on the Rohingya Crisis: From the Guest Editor's Desk.' *Asian Journal of Comparative Politics* 5(2): 85–88. Available at https://doi.org/10.1177/2057891120929570 (accessed on 16 September 2021).

Allchin, Joseph. 2009. 'Rohingya Children Groomed for a Life of Abuse. *DVB (Burmese Media).* Available at http://english.dvb.no/features-old/rohingya-children-groomed-for-a-life-of-abuse/3033 (accessed on 16 September 2021).

Amnesty International. 1997. 'Myanmar/Bangladesh Rohingyas - The Search for Safety.' Index Number: ASA 13/007/1997. Available at https://www.amnesty.org/en/documents/ASA13/007/1997/en/ (accessed on 18 August 2020).

———. 2004. 'Myanmar: The Rohingya Fundamental Rights Denied.' Index Number: ASA 16/005/2004. Available at https://www.amnesty.org/en/documents/ASA16/005/2004/en/ (accessed 2 August 2020).

Andersen, Garly. 1997. 'Analysis of the Livelihood Situation of the Muslim Population in Northern Rakhine State.' Consultant UNHCR.

Appadurai, A. 1991. 'Global Ethnoscapes: Notes and Queries for a Transnational Anthropology.' In *Interventions: Anthropologies of the Present*, edited by R. Fox, 191–210. Santa Fe, NM: School of American Research.

Arakan Project. 2016. *Key Issues Concerning the Situation of Stateless Rohingya Women and Girls in Rakine State, Myanmar.* Washington, DC: National Endowment for Democracy.

Arendt, Hannah. 1973. *The Origins of Totalitarianism.* New York, NY: Harcourt Brace & Company.

Banerjee Paula, Ansasua Chaudary, and Atig Ghosh. 2015. 'Words of Law, Worlds of Loss: The Stateless People of the Indo-Bangladesh Enclaves.' In *The State of Being Stateless: An Account of South Asia*, edited by Banerjee Paula, Chaudary Ansasua, and Ghosh Atig. Hyderabad: Orient Black Swan.

Beech, Hannah. 2020. 'Hundreds of Rohingya Refugees Stuck at Sea With 'Zero Hope'.' *The New York Times.* Available at https://www.nytimes.com/2020/05/01/world/asia/rohingya-muslim-refugee-crisis.html (accessed on 16 September 2021).

Benhabib, S. 2004. *The Rights of Others: Aliens, Residents, and Citizens.* Cambridge: Cambridge University Press.

Berlie, Jean A. 2008. *Burmanization of Myanmar's Muslims.* Bangkok: White Lotus Press.

Bernstein, Richard J. 2005. 'Hannah Arendt on the Stateless.' *Parallax* 11, no. 1: 46–60. Available at https://doi.org/10.1080/1353464052000321092 (accessed on 16 September 2021).

Bhabha, Jacqueline. 2010. 'From Citizen to Migration: The Scope of Child Statelessness in Twenty First Century.' In *Children without a State: A Global Human Rights Challenge*, edited by Bhabha Jacqueline. Cambridge, MA: Massachusetts Institute of Technology.

Blitz, Brad K. 2009. *Forced Migration Policy Briefing 3: Statelessness, Protection and Equality*. Oxford: University of Oxford.

———. 2011. 'Kashmiris in the United Kingdom, Slovenia, Banyamulenge in the Democratic Republic of the Congo, Rohingya in Myanmar and Bangladesh.' In *Children without a State: A Global Human Rights Challenge*, edited by Bhabha Jacqueline, 43–67. Cambridge, MA: Massachusetts Institute of Technology.

Boniak, K. 2000. 'Citizenship Denationalized (the State of Citizenship Symposium).' *Indiana Journal of Global Legal Studies* 7, no. 2: 6–23.

Chatterji, Joya. 2012. 'South Asian Histories of Citizenship, 1946–1970.' *The Historical Journal* 55, no. 4: 1049–1071.

Chowdhory, Nasreen. 2018. *Refugees, Citizenship and Belonging in South Asia: Contested Terrains*. Singapore: Springer Nature.

Constituent Assembly of Burma. 1947. *The Constitution of the Union of Burma*. Available at https://www.ilo.org/dyn/natlex/docs/ELECTRONIC/79573/85699/F1436085708/MMR79573.pdf (accessed on 9 August 2021).

Equal Right Trust in Partnership with the Institute of Human Rights and Peace Studies, Mahidol University. 2014. *Equal Only in Name: The Human Right of Stateless Rohingya in Thailand*. Salaya: Equal Right Trust in Partnership with the Institute of Human Rights and Peace Studies, Mahidol University.

European Parliament. 2017. 'Statelessness in South and Southeast Asia.' Committee on Foreign Affairs. Available at https://www.europarl.europa.eu/doceo/document/TA-8-2017-0247_EN.html (accessed on 10 August 2020).

Farzana, Kazi. 2017. *Memories of Burmese Rohingya Refugees: Contested Identity and Belonging*. New York, NY: Palgrave Macmillan.

Frelick, B., and M. Lynch. 2005. 'Statelessness: A Forgotten Human Rights Crisis.' *Forced Migration Review* 24: 65–66. Available at http://www.fmreview.org/text/FMR/24/39.doc (accessed on 9 August 2021).

Frelick, B., and M. Lynch. 2015. 'Statelessness: A Forgotten Human Rights Crisis. Forced Migration Review' *Oxford Refugee Studies Center*. Available at https://www.fmreview.org/sudan/frelick-lynch (accessed on 16 September 2021).

Gerth, H. H., and D. Mills Wright. 1948. *From Max Weber: Essay in Sociology*. London: Routledge.

Goldberg, Mark Leon. 2015. 'Thai Fishing Industry Uses Rohingya Slaves.' Available at https://www.undispatch.com/thai-fishing-industry-uses-rohingya-slaves/ (accessed on 23 September 2020).

Gowen, Annle. 2017. 'Blood Flowed in the Streets: Refugees from One Rohingya Hamlet Recount Days of Horror.' *The Washington Post*. Available at https://www.washingtonpost.com/world/asia_pacific/blood-flowed-in-the-streets-refugees-from-one-rohingya-village-recount-days-of-horror/20

17/09/15/34059ecc-9735-11e7-af6a-6555caaeb8dc_story.html (accessed on 16 September 2021).

Hammadi, Saad. 2020. 'Why Bangladesh Must Let the Rohingya Speak for Themselves: Any Durable Solution for the Rohingya Will Not Come through More Restrictions on their Lives. *The Diplomat.* Available at https://thediplomat.com/2020/10/why-bangladesh-must-let-the-rohingya-speak-for-themselves/ (accessed on 16 September 2021).

Human Rights Watch. 2009. 'Perilous Plight: Burma's Rohingya Take to the Seas.' Available at https://www.hrw.org/report/2009/05/26/perilous-plight/burmas-rohingya-take-seas (accessed on 24 September 2020).

———. 2019. 'Are We Not Human? Denial of Education for Rohingya Refugee Children in Bangladesh.' Human Rights Watch.

———. 2020. 'ASEAN: Overhaul Regional Response to Rohingya Crisis: Protect Asylum Seekers, Press Myanmar to End Persecution.' Available at https://www.hrw.org/news/2020/06/26/asean-overhaul-regional-response-rohingya-crisis (accessed on 26 September 2020).

Institute on Statelessness and Inclusion Analysis. 2018. *Statelessness in Numbers, 2018: An Overview and Analysis of Global Statistics.* Tilburg: Tilburg University.

International Federation of Human Rights Leagues. 2000. 'Report on International Mission of Inquiry, Burma: Repression, Discrimination and Ethnic Cleansing in Arakan, Myanmar.' Available at https://www.refworld.org/docid/46f146120.html (accessed on 18 August 2020).

Ismail, Maizura. 2018. 'The Future of the Stateless.' The ASEAN Post. Available at https://theaseanpost.com/article/future-stateless (accessed on 9 August 2021).

Kara, Siddhartha. 2010. *Sex Trafficking Inside the Business of Modern Slavery.* New York, NY: Columbia University Press.

Kingston, Jeff. 2019. *The Politics of Religion, Nationalism, and Identity in Asia.* New York, NY: Rowman & Littlefield.

Lego, Jera. 2017. 'Why ASEAN Can't Ignore the Rohingya Crisis: The Rohingya Crisis is Not Just an Issue for Myanmar; It Will Impact Security and Economic Trends Throughout the Region. *The Diplomat.* Available at https://thediplomat.com/2017/05/why-asean-cant-ignore-the-rohingya-crisis/ (accessed on 16 September 2021).

Lewa, C. 2003. 'Rohingya Refuges in Bangladesh are Facing a New Drive of Involuntary Repatriation. Bangkok: Report of Asian Forum for Human Rights and Development (FORUM-ASIA).

Lori, N. A. 2017. 'Statelessness, in-between; Statuses, and Precarious Citizenship.' In *Oxford Handbook of Citizenship*, edited by A. Shachar, R. Baubock, I. Blomermraad, and M. Vink, 743–767. Oxford: Oxford University Press.

Lynch, M. 2005. *Lives on Hold: The Human Cost of Statelessness.* Washington DC: Refugees International. Available at https://www.refworld.org/docid/47a6eba00.html (accessed on 9 August 2021).

Maung, Z., and A. Cowley. 2014. 'The Slow Burning Genocide of Myanmar's Rohingya.' *Washington International Law Journal* 23, no. 3, 683–753.

Available at https://digitalcommons.law.uw.edu/wilj/vol23/iss3/8 (accessed on 16 September 2021).

Naik, Sagarika. 2021a. 'Forced Displacement Modern Slavery, and Human Right Challenges in South East Asia: A Revisit on Rohingya Refugee Crisis in the Changing World.' *Journal of Modern Slavery* (manuscript under review).

Naik, Sagarika. 2021b. 'Voiceless Rohingya: From Refugee to Modern Slaves.' In *Human Trafficking: Global History and Global Perspective*, edited by Elisha Jasper Dung and Avwunudiogba Augustine. New York, NY: Lexington Books, Rowman & Littlefield.

Razzaq, A., and Haque Mahfuzul. 1995. *A Tale of Refugee: Rohingya in Bangladesh*. Dhaka: Centre for Human Rights.

Sharma, Angel. 2017. How South Asia is Failing its Rohingya Challenge: Regional States Must Provide More Realistic and Comprehensive Solutions to Avert Instability in the Subcontinent.' *The Diplomat*. Available at https://thediplomat.com/2017/12/how-south-asia-is-failing-its-rohingya-challenge/ (accessed on 16 September 2021).

Thant, Myint-U. 2021. *The Hidden History of Burma: A Crisis of Race and Capitalism*. London: Atlantic Books.

The Daily Star. 2004, 21 November. '24 Rohingyas Sent to Jail.' Web Edition 5 (176). Available at http://www.thedailystar.net/2004/11/21/d4112101.htm (accessed on 9 August 2021).

The Irrawaddy. 2009, 16 October. 'Bangladesh Expels Rohingyas.' Available at https://www2.irrawaddy.com/article.php?art_id=17009 (accessed on 9 August 2021).

Uddin, Nasir. 2017. 'State of Stateless People: The Plight of Rohingya Refugees in Bangladesh.' In *Human Rights to Citizens: A Slippery Concept*, edited by Rhoda Howard-Hassmann and Margaret Walton-Roberts. Philadelphia, PA: The University of Pennsylvania Press.

———. 2019. 'The State, Transborder Movements, and Deterritorialised Identity in South Asia.' In *Deterritorialised Identity and Transborder Movement in South Asia*, edited by Uddin Nasir and Chowdhory Nasrin. Singapore: Springer Nature.

UNHCR. 1945. *Convention Relating to the States of Stateless Persons*. Geneva: UNHCR.

———. 2014. 'Global Action Plan to End Statelessness: 2014–2024.' Available at http://www.unhcr.org/en-us/protection/statelessness/54621bf49/global-action-plan-end-statelessness-2014-2024.html (accessed on 9 August 2021).

———. 2019. 'Refugee Movements in South East Asia: Searching for Safety.' Available at https://www.unhcr.org/news/briefing/2019/10/5d930fa94/refugee-movements-south-east-asia-decrease-threats-journey-rise.html (accessed on 9 August 2021).

———. 2020. 'New York Declaration for Refugees and Migrants, United States.' https://www.unhcr.org/en-us/new-york-declaration-for-refugees-and-migrants.html (accessed on 23 September 2020).

US State Department. 2018. 'Trafficking in Person Report.' Available at https://www.state.gov/reports/2018-trafficking-in-persons-report/ (accessed on 24 September 2020).

———. 2019. 'Trafficking in Persons Report.' Available at https://www.state.gov/reports/2019-trafficking-in- persons-report/ (accessed on 2 October 2020).

———. 2020. 'Trafficking in Persons Report.' Available at https://www.state.gov/reports/2020-trafficking-in- persons-report/ (accessed on 29 September 2020).

Walk Free Foundation. 2018. 'The Global Slavery Index.' Available at https://www.globalslaveryindex.org/ (accessed on 5 August 2020).

Weiner, Myron. 1993. 'Rejected Peoples and Unwanted Migrants in South Asia.' *Economic & Political Weekly* 28, no. 34.

Zarni, Maung, and A. Cowley. 2014. 'The Slow-burning Genocide of Myanmar's Rohingya.' *Pacific Rim Law & Policy Journal Association* 23, no. 3: 1–71.

CHAPTER 6

The Politics of 'Hate'
Anti-Rohingya Campaigns in Hyderabad and Jammu
Manas Dutta

6.1. Introduction

It has been historically true that the presence of the Rohingya along
with other communities is visible in India, Bangladesh and Myanmar
since the colonial times. Besides, Malaysia and Thailand also provide
shelter for the Rohingya, who are categorized now as 'nowhere-nation
precariat' (Alam 2020, 127) and 'Asia's new boat people' (Basu Ray
Chaudhury and Samaddar 2018, 4). They are widely known as the
world's most persecuted ethnic minority and often identified with
Muslim religion. Hundreds of thousands of Rohingya have been
fleeing to other countries for refuge since the 1960s while Myanmar
proves to be vulnerable for them. It has been estimated that the largest migrations of this community took place in 1978 and 1991–1992,
when diverse episodes of brutal suppression by the security forces of
Myanmar pointed towards the 723,000 Rohingya and compelled them
to seek refuge in neighbouring countries like Bangladesh and India,
which are within the border states of South Asia. Under such conditions, the Rohingya crossed the border to India mainly via Bangladesh

mainly in search of security and better livelihood and for employment opportunity. This chapter tries to explain the Rohingya's statelessness, or 'nowhere-nation' (Alam 2020, 127) condition and their consequent 'precarious' (Standing 2011, 23) and uncharted life in order to analyse their geopolitical significance in recent times. It also focuses on the various forms of rights and livelihood conditions of the Rohingya in India. Following this, the chapter engages with their relocation and negotiation as illegal immigrants or 'security threat' in India in the larger backdrop of the anti-Rohingya campaigns in Hyderabad and Jammu. In the context of the border politics, forced migration, refugee and stateless people and its intricate developments in South Asia at large, this chapter reflects on the recent debates on India's response to the Rohingya issue and its various stages of policy formulations to resolve the issue.

6.2. The Rohingya in India: Right to Have Rights and Livelihood

It is often believed that the contemporary political contexts and cultural obligations are crucial for highlighting the condition of the state, which provides shelter for its citizens but complicates the ground for refugee movements. Geo-strategic location, demographic negotiations and the question of statistical mechanism are also somewhat responsible with the refugee issues as well. The so-called immigration of the Rohingya had started towards India after the 2012 brutal Rakhine State riots and inhuman military atrocities in Myanmar. It is noteworthy that eight Indian states, namely Jammu and Kashmir, Delhi, Uttar Pradesh, Haryana, West Bengal, Tamil Nadu, Punjab and Telangana (Hyderabad) provided favourable shelter for the Rohingya refugees. Media reports have also suggested that the Rohingya took shelter in Rajasthan as well. International organizations namely the United Nations High Commissioner for Refugees (UNHCR) even confirms that there are an estimated 18,000 Rohingya asylum seekers and refugees registered in India. According to Kiren Rijiju, the Minister of State in the Ministry of Minority Affairs, there are about 40,000 Rohingya living illegally in the country. In this context, he has also informed that the state has denied giving the Rohingya the status of refugees and would like to portray them as 'illegal immigrants' (*The Hindu* 2017).

As refugees, the Rohingya have not been able to receive any favourable environment in India, though it has been clearly mentioned in the 1951 Refugee Convention by the UN that refugees should have fundamental rights such as non-discrimination (Article 3), freedom of religion (Article 4), right to work (Article 17) and right to education (Article 22). Now, one could argue in favour of the notion that those basic rights have not been availed by them subsequently. Besides, Indian government announced to deport seven Rohingya back to Myanmar and consequently announced the plans to deport all illegal foreign nationals including the Rohingya people who are registered with the UNHCR. UNHCR recently distributed around 16,500 refugee identity cards to the Rohingya. Despite having this initiative, they are repeatedly categorized as 'illegal immigrants' by the government officials of India (Human Rights Watch 2017). Historically, it has been observed that India used to be a natural choice for immigrants, mainly from neighbouring countries like Bangladesh and other South Asian countries (Pasricha 2018). In fact, it has been opined by Meenakshi Ganguly that the Indian government has disregarded its long tradition of protecting those seeking refuge within its borders in recent times in order to fulfil its some complex and aggravated agendas (Ganguly 2018).

Moreover, the 1954 UN Convention relating to the Status of Stateless Persons or the 1961 UN Convention on the reduction of statelessness has not been thoroughly maintained in India. India has ratified such international bodies as the International Convention on Civil and Political Rights, 1966 (ICCPR) in 1979; the Convention on the Elimination of Racial Discrimination, 1965 (CERD) in 1968 and the Universal Declaration of Human Rights (UDHR), which India participated in drafting and also acceded in 1979 to the International Covenant on Economic, Social and Cultural Rights, 1966 (ICESCR) that seek to provide and guarantee certain social, economic and cultural rights to asylum seekers and refugees in particular. India has also allowed cooperation with the UNHCR, which provides Refugee Status Determination (RSD) cards to the refugees to ensure various protections and rights for them in India (Basu Ray Chaudhury and Samaddar 2018, 42). It has been claimed that nearly 1,300 people from almost 300 families fled to neighbouring Bangladesh for asylum after receiving ill-treatment, including deportation. It has been argued that such incidents could definitely smear the image of that country among the international community which affects subsequently the country's relationships with others in the global order. Thus, one could argue that the expulsion of seven Rohingya from India to Myanmar is understood as a flagrant denunciation of their right to protection, violation of the principle of 'non-refoulement' and basic international human rights and provides a justifiable ground for the non-acceptance and non-consideration. Despite having such sense of annulments, Indian government has announced more than 98 long-term visas (LTV) especially for the Rohingya and a few for the Afghan refugees on December 2015.

6.3. The Rohingya in India: 'Illegal Immigrants' or 'Security Threat'?

After witnessing the susceptible conditions of the Rohingya in India, they have been viewed primarily from two opposite perspectives, namely as 'illegal immigrants' and 'security threat'. The precarious condition in the camps in Bangladesh and lack of employment opportunities along with the question of livelihood as well as increasing hostility and the hate speech towards them by the Awami League government in Bangladesh make them hysterical to cross the border of the northeastern part of India, often with the help of human traffickers. Yet, the reality shows something unbearable as their desperate perilous journeys end in slums and unauthorized make-shift colonies, with no access to proper sanitation, food, medicine and shelter (Alam 2020, 136), and the notions of vulnerability targeted towards them further amplify the obtuse attitudes of the host country. The various separatist yet powerful groups like Al-Qaeda's offshoot, Aqa Mul Mujahideen or Arakan Rohingya Salvation Army (ARSA), Jaish-e-Mohammed (JeM) and Lashkar-e-Taiba (LeT) and their anticipated solidarity in favour of Rohingya create a paradigm of the question of identity and interrogating their lived experiences in India. On the other hand, the government of India provided necessary allocations of evidence against the Rohingya to show them as 'illegal immigrants' and 'threat to the national security'. This atmosphere has been further intensified after the much talked-about and media-circulated incidents of Bodh Gaya (Bihar) blasts of 2013 and Khagragarh (Burdwan, West Bengal) blasts of 2015.

The stance and function of the UNHCR are indeed crucial here in India since 1982. It intends to offer favourable protection and proper inclusion of refugees so that they can avail national services like health and education in particular. However, it is trying to create ground ready for giving identity cards/certificate to Rohingya in India so that it helps them to get national services and tries to offer minimum resources for livelihood as their lived experience here fore-ground agony and misery in a larger scale. Moreover, the state of abject poverty, health inconvenience and lack of employment issues cause further worries for them. Due to not having any legal framework and national refugee status determination system in India, UNHCR has been adopting exertions to claim refugee status for the hitherto 'illegal immigrants' in India. UNHCR office at India has registered 25,865 Rohingya as refugees in 2014 and tried to provide with the RSD card (Chakraborty 2015). Yet the whole process remains to be opulent in several occasions.

Historically, it is quite acceptable that the splendid and vibrant Indian history is full of migration events and examples of offering basic hospitality to migrants since the dawn of civilization. As an example, we can cite the incident of the partition of India in 1947, which had led to ingenuous demographic upheavals causing migratory flow of more than 10 million people. Thus, India's journey as a postcolonial phenomenon had started with hosting those displaced refugee people and formulating policies for their assimilation and conciliation.

Various reasons could be instrumental in making the Rohingya a potential threat to the national security of India. To believe or to move towards this attitude, there are several catalysts one can identify, involved directly or indirectly, that lead to considering the refugees as stigmatization (Islamophobia for Rohingya as example), segregation, alienation and marginalization. While framing Rohingya as 'illegal', or 'terrorist' it may also lead radical groups to express their resentment against the Indian state and this has been further interrogated by the political sociologists. Now, the feeling of 'us' and 'them' is the preliminary boundary to make a distinction between peoples which often causes the distance between two communities and segregate them from each other and would rather start to believe each other common enemy of their respective community (Yhome 2018). Thus, it is often argued that the government policies of the possible exclusion of the refugees in the society, media's overenthusiastic reporting of refugee issues, sometimes worst treatment of refugees and less assistance often work as a catalyst for refugees and further charts the painful inconsistency of their lived experience in an alien land.

6.4. Anti-Rohingya Campaign in Hyderabad

It has been quite evident that hundreds of Rohingya Muslims escaped from Myanmar due to discriminatory violent activities and castigatory responses from the government of that state. Eventually, they had been able to reach Hyderabad through the possible routes of Bangladesh and West Bengal mainly for better employment and livelihood and to avoid state-sponsored carnages. Due to the substantial Muslim presence, the Rohingya decided to move to Hyderabad at the very outset. The environment and standard of living condition in Hyderabad proved to be initially worrisome for them. Even their failure to learn Urdu and Telegu languages makes it difficult for them to land jobs and several other employment opportunities (Khan 2013). It has been argued that nearly 1,500 Rohingya have settled down in the areas called Hafeebabanagar, Pahadeshareef, Balapur, Mir Momin Pahadi, Kishanbagh, Babanagar, Sainagar, Chandrayaanautta in Hyderabad (Nanjappa 2013).

Personalities like Mazher Hussain, executive director of Hyderabad-based NGO, Confederation of Voluntary Associations (COVA) exemplified how the process of influx of Rohingya Muslims has been deepened over the past five or six years.[1] His NGO has been working in partnership with UNHCR in Hyderabad for providing basic amenities and employment opportunities for the Rohingya refugees. According to Hussain, Hyderabad received around 100 refugees in 2010. He adds that in early 2011 there were about 150 settlers, and the number of Rohingya Muslims currently residing in the city stands at a rough estimate that ranges between 1,400 and 2,000 based on the COVA data.[2] According to UNHCR there are 8,836 Rohingya refugees and 2,434 Rohingya asylum seekers registered with them in India. Of these, nearly 1,400 persons are residing in Hyderabad.[3]

While visiting those makeshift Rohingya ghettos, it can be seen that they are living in a very miserable condition. The plight of the Rohingya can be highlighted through the lived experience of Fatima Khatoun (age: 30) and her son Md Farzan (age: 14) who are living in Kiskanabagh as Rohingya refugee. The reason for their flight to Hyderabad was her husband's death in the riots in Myanmar. She said that her husband was beaten to death in front of her eyes and the entire inhuman incident traumatized her and further goaded her feeling of helplessness and being a destitute. Under such conditions, she decided to migrate to Hyderabad along with her fellow travellers. Though, she had been in a state of difficulty in finding a job and also a place to stay (Velath and Chopra 2015). This is one of the many incidents continuously happening with the immigrant Rohingya in Hyderabad.

[1] COVA is a Hyderabad-based national network of over 700 organizations working for communal harmony, peace and social justice primarily at Hyderabad and 12 other states in India. It was initiated in 1995 and since then has been providing support to refugees for livelihood, health, education and monthly ration. It is also working with the UNHCR from 2011 to facilitate registration of refugees as per UNHCR norms. Available at covanetwork.org (accessed on 10 September 2020).

[2] Personal correspondence held with the author on 12 September 2020 through mail.

[3] Figures received from UNHCR Office in New Delhi. Available at https://www.unhcr.org/india.html (accessed on 20 August 2020).

6.5. Issues of Law and Order and Police Persecution

Initially, Hyderabad provided basic amenities to the Rohingya. Yet, one must understand that citing the law-and-order issue, it is repeatedly argued that the Rohingya in Hyderabad particularly have been a cause of worry for both the administration and the police in many occasions at different points of time. The finger of suspicion invariably falls on them whenever a Hindu or a Buddhist structure faces attack and this subsequently paves the way for police interrogation, which arguably makes it even vulnerable for them (Vickey 2015). Despite such an environment prevailing in Hyderabad, hundreds of Rohingya refugees have been able to consider the city as their own. The state of suspicion started to amplify further only when a Rohingya Muslim from Myanmar, Khalid Mohammad was arrested by the National Investigating Agency (NIA) for his purported links to the blast in Khagrgar of Burdwan district in West Bengal and the media has been constantly telecasting it for public attention.[4]

According to the reports of the intelligence officials Khalid had received large amounts of funds from the Rohingya who are based in Karachi (Pakistan) and Saudi Arabia. It has been found that Khalid had meetings with other Rohingya refugees in Delhi, Lucknow and Jammu, before setting up a base in Hyderabad, and has acted as one of the prime agents for conducting such blasts in India. Now, the government of India and its officials by pointing out this incident has cast the entire Rohingya community under the shadow of suspicion and subsequently public outrage engulfed, which went against them. Even, the Intelligence Bureau of India went one step ahead and identified that terror groups like Jamaat-ul-Mujahideen Bangladesh (JMB) and the Al-Qaeda have managed to permeate their trained men into the camps of Rohingya refugees in India in order to conduct blasts or other unlawful activities that can shake the government in India (Pagadala 2013). According to Malla

---

[4] Rohingya Muslim Refugees in Hyderabad. Available at http://mattersindia. com/rohingya-muslim-refugees- in-hyderabad (accessed on 10 September 2020).

Reddy, Joint Commissioner of Police, Special Branch, Hyderabad, many Rohingya started to stay in Hyderabad while Delhi, Aligarh, Mathura, Kolkata prove to be places where they had decided to reside with their fellow folks (Pagadala 2013). It has also been revealed that after the Burdwan blast, the Rohingya in Hyderabad experience tight surveillance and harsh interrogations from the police and often face severe harassment (Gupta 2014). Therefore, public opinion against them was reinforced and the communally driven groups used this as anti-national sensation, which gave birth to huge public outcry against the Rohingya. Thus, this calculated hate campaign against the Rohingya actually restrains from the notion of anti-Muslim identity issue. Eventually, it has been able to attract a large section of people to generate an unhealthy atmosphere (Basin 2019).

6.6. Local Political Discourse and Conflicting Sensibilities

While the forced displacement and the statelessness conditions compelled Rohingya to settle in various areas of Hyderabad for livelihood, local-level political parties which follow the Hindutva ideology/politics made their lives miserable as they openly criticized their stay in these places (Mohammed 2013). In the backdrop of the publication of the final draft of the historic and controversial National Register of Citizens (NRC) and Citizenship Amendment Act, 2019 (CAA), India faced serious civil and political challenges across the country and Hyderabad is not an exception in this regard. The immediate corollary seems to be directed towards the Rohingya as the government has recapped its plans to deport them to their native country, Myanmar. Ram Madhav of the Bharatiya Janata Party (BJP) at this atypical juncture, made the comment that the Rohingya will be deported as per the rules and regulations (Mathew 2018). The situation started to be even noxious after the release of the NRC list, Raja Singh, a BJP member of the Telangana Legislative Assembly asked the government to 'shoot Bangladeshi and Rohingyas if they refuse to leave' (Cockburn 2018). The continuation of projecting Rohingya as 'threat to national security' is also in the foreground to create the atmosphere of committing violence against them.

Furthermore, the ruling BJP and its allies is hoping to make electoral gains by doing such acts and trying to project that it has been here to protect a 'Hindu' nation from the threat of 'radical Muslim Rohingyas' and this automatically gains currency among the radical Hindutva force and some bizarre groups (Mudasir 2018). It is generally believed that the Rohingya are primarily Muslims; yet one must understand that there are Hindu Rohingya as well. The right-wing fundamentalists perhaps do not know this and their arbitrary decision to label them as 'terrorists' makes the situation even troublesome for the Rohingya to stay at various places in Hyderabad (Verma 2017).

Thus, it is clear that local politics and regional sensibilities along with right-wing fundamentalism collectively have provided a ground for the Rohingya which is uncompromising in nature and bears fruits of hate and antipathy exclusively for them. This entire episode has made the situation dangerous for the Rohingya to live in Hyderabad ever since their arrival.

6.7. Anti-Rohingya Campaign in Jammu

While it has been seen that the lived experiences of the Rohingya in Hyderabad proved to be dangerous, Jammu as another option of taking refuge produced more pain and sufferings in subsequent times. Jammu being the Hindu majority division has a more turbulent past that dates back to the time of Partition of India in 1947 and the course of Indian history has been shaped and reshaped due to its existence since then. The state forces of Maharaja Hari Singh, with the active support of right-wing Hindu forces, kept the Muslims under control and later categorized them as minority (Naqvi 2016, 2). The atrocities conducted by Hari Singh also led to the killing of more than 200,000 Muslims, while an equal number had fled to Pakistan for shelter (Chaudhary 2008, 56). Currently, Muslim population constitutes 31 per cent of the total population of Jammu. Yet, one can see the domination of Muslims in places like Rajouri, Poonch, Doda of Jammu (Chaudhury 2008, 57).

In current times, a substantial number (highest as compared to other places) of the Rohingya have settled in the outskirts of Jammu, where Muslim population is prevalent. Their influx in Jammu had started since 2012. Jammu and Kashmir has been a deliberate and natural choice for them as the majority of population in these regions are Muslims. After spending some years in Jammu, the Rohingya have now realized the ground reality in the state and the internal dynamics at play in the region against the sentiments towards them. Most of the Rohingya have not been able to understand the division of Kashmir and Jammu at the initial level and later Jammu turned to be hostile for them while the cold weather of Kashmir was at the same time excruciatingly long (Amin 2018).

6.8. Local Political Parties and Anti-Rohingya Activism

After their stay in these regions for quite some time, Jammu-based local political parties with narrow political goals, right-wing intolerant groups and other fundamentalist stakeholders and vigilantes have collectively organized anti-Rohingya expulsion campaign, which instantly gained malevolent momentum at a time while the Indian government's plan to deport the Rohingya and the statements made by the local leaders and members of the Chambers of Commerce, Jammu in this direction further worsened the situation especially for the Rohingya. Furthermore, the so-called/stereotyped Muslim identity of Rohingya has been brought to the forefront in the highly polarized society of Jammu. Besides, National Panthers Party (NPP), on the other hand, sponsored billboards at different places, asking the 'Rohingyas and Bangladeshis' to quit Jammu in early 2017. They even launched slogans like 'Chodho Humara Jammu Pradesh, Rohingya jaao Bangladesh' (Move away from Jammu, Oh! Rohingya return to Bangladesh; Amin 2018). Rohingya were labelled as a 'ticking time bomb' and a 'threat to communal harmony' in Jammu. Spearheading campaigns like this, the NPP invokes Article 370[5] of the Constitution

---

[5] It has been said that Article 370 of the XXI Schedule of the Indian Constitution grants special status to the State of Jammu and Kashmir and allows them to form a constitution of its own within the Indian Union and restricts Indian Parliament's Legislative power of the state.

as the justification for their 'protect Jammu Campaign'.[6] The same views were articulated by Rakesh Gupta, President, Chambers of Commerce, Jammu, who opined that the Article 370 makes it distinctively clear that the Rohingya cannot live in Jammu under any circumstances (Amin 2018).

Furthermore, the Chambers of Commerce, Jammu during its 2017 eviction campaign issued a one-month ultimatum to deport all Rohingya from Jammu. They were threatened to 'catch and kill' if they did not return to Bangladesh. Moreover, organized hate crime and targeted violent activism were continued against them at regular basis. For example, we can cite a few incidents and one among them happened in the first week of April 2017, when a group of Rohingya women and children collecting scrap in Jammu's Patta Bohri area were attacked by some masked men, who could not be identified when they were caught later (Kandhari 2017). Moreover, some 78 Rohingya families living in Jammu's Bhagwati Nagar area had to shift to other places after a mysterious fire gutted their shelters and the reason behind this also remains unknown (Kandhari 2017).

6.9. BJP and the Hate Campaigns against the Rohingya

Despite having the local political parties and their anti-Rohingya campaigns, the BJP has also been trying to pursue a persistent campaign to criminalize the Rohingya by describing them as 'terrorists'. On 10 February 2018, the Indian Army base camp in Sunjuwan, Jammu was attacked, and the then Speaker of the Jammu and Kashmir assembly, Kavinder Gupta instantly blamed the Rohingya for it, though it was not yet investigated then (Khajuria 2018). Gupta later withdrew his statement following much opposition to his pejorative remarks. Several ingenuities have been taken up to project the Rohingya to be identified with monstrous crimes such as rustling of narcotics, human trafficking, child abductions, beggary

[6] In an interview, Bhim Singh, the NPP Party supremo, asserted that allowing the Rohingyas to stay in Jammu was a violation of Article 370 of the Constitution of India (cited in Amin 2018).

and even engendering communal tensions along with establishing atrocious 'terrorist links'. However, those had not been sustained by the official documents like that of the Jammu and Kashmir police records. Further, the then state Chief Minister, Mehbooba Mufti, had thoroughly rebutted the assertion that the Rohingya were a threat to Jammu and Kashmir on the floor of the assembly based on the available police records. Communally driven groups in Jammu have been given a momentous ground to generates public opinion against the Rohingya as 'criminal' and 'threat to the people'. This spherical hate against the Rohingya actually fomented from the anti-Muslim discourse that is prevalent here and this has further complicated the scenario against the Rohingya and their livelihood in India (Alam 2020, 139).

Additionally, the BJP's election manifesto in 2014 under the sub-heading of *foreign relations, nation first, universal brotherhood* clearly indicated that India shall remain a natural choice for the persecuted Hindus and they shall be welcomed to seek refuge here (Bharatiya Janata Party 2014). Favouring the Hindus and largely argued for the majoritarian community, BJP and its right-wing supports have been trying to make India as homogenized society leaving behind its secular fabric (Ganguly 2015, 26).

6.10. Investigative Journalism and the Strategies of Anti-Rohingya Stance

Independent press reports and the forms of digitally driven investigative journalism by some of the media houses such as AajTak and Republic TV and several social media on Rohingya and their 'illegal presence' in Jammu have further provided a ground of stiff contest among the various political parties. Without considering much on Mufti's statement, the anti-Rohingya propaganda has continued in various forms. Under such annoying situations, three Jammu-based TV reporters associated with Republic TV and AajTak alleged that they were beaten up by a group of 100–150 Rohingya Muslims from the Narwal camp during a reporting assignment in the area. Subsequently, a video was circulated, where it has been depicted that the Rohingya were responsible for the attack and calling them the 'biggest threat to people' of Jammu. The Jammu and Kashmir police rushed to that camp and later it was clarified that no Rohingya was involved. While the independent digital news agency, News Click started its investigative journalism regarding this issue, it was found that the local youth and the reporters had been in an argument over an issue of parking space and the alleged incident had nothing to do with the Rohingya at all.

The situation of the Rohingya became more deteriorated when the rape and murder of an eight-year-old Muslim girl from Kathua was wrongly reported by some influential media houses like Zee News, Republic TV, AajTak, Dainik Jagran (Ayush 2019). Immediately after the broadcast, several Jammu-based fanatical right-wing groups started to denunciate the Rohingya for committing the crime, while the Jammu and Kashmir police had established that it was calculatedly committed by Hindu extremists with an intention to drive away a Muslim Gujjar community from the region. The rumours were further propagated by right-wing sympathizer/intellectual Madhu Kishwar. In a tweet, Kishwar (2018, cited in Amin 2018) wrote:

> Very likely that family accused of rape have been scapegoated. Murder of #Asifa suspected to be handiwork of jehadi #Rohingyas settled by PDP in Jammu region. Since Jammu people angry at settling criminal Rohingya in Hindu areas, Mehbooba used this murder as counterblast strategy.

Therefore, it is quite evident from the facts that anti-Rohingya activism in extreme measures has been driven across Jammu to percolate its stance among the people. The BJP and its local right-wing supporters have been proved strategically crucial for organizing campaigns against the Rohingya. Popular mobilization has been initiated and the majoritarian agenda pursued by the current regime rendered the issue of expulsion of the Rohingya along with the illegal migrants from other South and Southeast Asian countries caught the media's attention and garnering electoral dividend for the general elections in April and May 2019 (Kaveri 2020, 72; Uddin 2020, 4).

6.11. Understanding India's Response to Rohingya Crisis: Stand or 'No Stand' Policy

The Indian subcontinent is arguably a natural choice for those seeking refuge from Tibet and other countries from South Asian countries like Pakistan, Bangladesh, Afghanistan, Sri Lanka and even from the Far East. This has been further affirmed by historical documents as well. Though the Rohingya crisis has deepened in recent time, India's position remains the same because of Myanmar's strategic importance for economic, political, land and counter-Chinese influence. Thus, India's congenial relation with Myanmar in many respects especially geopolitical and economic respect kept it close to Myanmar. Even, India's hatred and direct competition with the Chinese investment in Myanmar have kept India's leadership away from making statements condemning Myanmar. The 1,360 km highway, a joint venture by India, Myanmar and Thailand and that eventually ropes in Laos, Cambodia and Vietnam, is seen by experts like C. Raja Mohan, Srikant Kondapalli and Happymoon Jacob as a counter to China's belt and road initiative and is said to give leverage to India as an economic driver in the region and also provided genesis in the geopolitical aspects. Despite having acknowledged globally, the crisis has not received anything substantive and Bangladesh is still in flux. India has taken initiative in September 2017 and as humanitarian aid a consignment of 53 metric tonnes comprising relief materials in the form of rice, pulses, sugar, salt, cooking oil, milk powder, dried fish, baby food, tea, ready-to-eat noodles, biscuits, mosquito nets, raincoats and gumboots amongst other things was sent to Rohingya in Bangladesh. Again, in May 2018, India sent a second 373-tonne consignment containing necessary items to aid the Rohingya in Bangladesh through the initiative of *Operation Insaniyat.*

Now, it has been perceptible that the Rohingya Muslims and the treatment towards them by the current government is complex in nature compared to other migrant groups and their projected treatment. Implementing forceful repatriation programme for the Rohingya who are already in India is clearly a departure from the manner in which previous Indian governments dealt with refugees.

Political strategists like Pratap Bhanu Mehta's remarks and media reports revealed the notion that India has initiated various humanitarian assistance for the Rohingya of Bangladesh while India's exiled Rohingya have not caught the sympathetic attention of the current government (Haider 2017). Now, the humanitarian concerns have been replaced by the strategies of realpolitik. Now, it could be argued that India's approach towards the Rohingya crisis has been viewed as contradicting its traditional position on refugees. It is even argued that there is still a lot that India can do to facilitate finding long-term solutions as a regional economic and political power by delivering altruistic attitudes towards the Rohingya. Actions towards them will be key in determining India's regional and geopolitical notions (Yhome 2018).

Thus, it has been observed that a combination of factors seemed to have shaped India's approach towards the Rohingya issue. In the first phase, the geopolitics, security interests and humanitarian concerns were key in moulding India's Rohingya response. The growing security concerns and the need for diplomatic balancing between Bangladesh and Myanmar could place alternative for the Rohingya. India also urged that the international community should take up initiatives to assist developmental efforts in Rakhine on urgent priority basis as only such developmental projects would perhaps solve the statelessness conditions of the Rohingya in the future.

6.12. Concluding Remarks

The innumerable anti-Rohingya campaigns projected against the Rohingya since their arrival in different parts of India have proved to be some of the glaring moments under the current regime. The majoritarian tendencies of the current government in India have further convoluted the atmosphere and raised the slogan of hate and apathy against them. Their statelessness and broadly refugee-hood tendency make their situation all the more worsened in India as they are not properly welcomed due to their marked identity. The 'subhuman life' (Uddin 2020) of the Rohingya therefore requires to have a policy of inclusion rather than political exclusion. Though India has offered development aid in Myanmar in the form of the Rakhine Development Programme, it has never taken up any initiative on the issue of Rohingya citizenship and its possible corollary with the Myanmar government. Some argue that instead of forced repatriation, the Indian government could use its compassionate nature and nonviolent attitudes to request the Myanmar government to mend the excruciating attitudes towards the Rohingya and then mediate a solution of political relegation and the question of citizenship. India could take an altruistic effort for the dignified repatriation of the Rohingya. There is a need for a more holistic understanding and further deepen and expand its engagements in resolving the Rohingya crisis. Despite aggressive and vindictive state policies, anti-Rohingya stance against this 'homeless', 'de-territorialized' (Uddin and Chowdhory 2018) people, India could manage to destabilize such hostilities and offer an issue of reconciliation as it would further strengthen its responsibilities and provide a life of dignity for the Rohingya in particular and other vulnerable communities in general.

References

Alam, Murshed. 2020. 'Violence and Perilous Trans-borderal Journeys: The Rohingyas as the Nowhere-nation Precariat.' In *Violence in South Asia: Contemporary Perspectives*, edited by Pavan Kumar Malreddy, Anindya Sekhar Purakayastha, and Birte Heidemann. New York, NY: Routledge.

Amin, M. 2018. '"Nobody's Children, Owners of Nothing:" Analysing the Indian State's Policy Response to the Rohingya Refugee Crisis.' Policy Report No. 24. The Hindu Centre for Politics and Public Policy, Chennai.

Arendt, Hannah. 1976. *The Origins of Totalitarianism*. San Diego, CA: Harcourt Brace & Company.

Ayush, T. 2019, 12 June. 'The Kathua False News Hall of Fame.' *Criticles, News Laundry*, New Delhi.

Bharatiya Janata Party. 2014. 'Bharatiya Janata Party Election Manifesto 2014.' Available at http://cdn.narendramodi.in/wp-content/uploads/2014/04/Manifesto2014highlights.pdf (accessed on 10 August 2021).

Basin, Anuradha. 2019, 7 February. 'Refugees Twice Over: Why Rohingya Who Had Found Shelter in Jammu Are Fleeing Again.' The Scroll, New Delhi.

Basu Ray Chaudhury, Sabyasachi, and Ranabir Samaddar, eds. 2018. *The Rohingya in South Asia: People without a State*. New York, NY: Routledge.

Chakraborty, Madhura. 2015. 'Stateless and Suspect: Rohingyas in Myanmar, Bangladesh and India.' In *Rohingyas in India: Birth of a Stateless Community*, edited by S. Majumder, Priyanca Mathur Velath, and Kriti Chopra. Kolkata: Mahanirban Calcutta Research Group.

Chaudhury, Zafar. 2008. 'Being Muslim in Jammu.' *Economic & Political Weekly* 43, no. 34.

Cockburn, H. 2018, 31 July. 'Shoot Bangladeshi and Rohingya Immigrants Who Won't Leave', Says Indian Politician.' *The Independent*, New Delhi.

Ganguly, Meenakshi. 2018. 'Rohingya Deported to Myanmar.' Available at https://www.hrw.org/news/2018/10/04/india-7-rohingya-deported-myanmar (accessed on 28 September 2020).

Ganguly, Sumit. 2015, 30 June. 'Hindu Nationalism and the Foreign Policy of India's Bharatiya Janata Party.' Transatlantic Academy Paper Series No. 2, Transatlantic Academy, Washington DC.

Gupta, Jayanta. 2014, 24 June. 'Khalid's Arrest Sparks-off Debate on Rohingyas in India.' *The Times of India*, New Delhi.

Haider, Suhasini. 2017, 30 November. 'Such a Strange Silence: India's Stand on the Rohingya Crisis.' *The Hindu*, New Delhi.

Human Rights Watch. 2017. 'India: Don't Forcibly Return Rohingya Refugees.' Available at https://www.hrw.org/news/2017/08/17/india-dont-forcibly-return-rohingya-refugees (accessed on 10 August 2021).

Jain, Bharti. 2018, 4 June. 'Confine Illegal Rohingya to Designated Camps: Centre to States.' *The Times of India*, New Delhi. Available at https://timesofindia.indiatimes.com/india/confine-illegal-rohingya-to-designated-camps-centre-to states/articleshow/64441862.cms (accessed on 10 August 2021).

Kandhari, M. 2017, 15 April. 'Shelter of Rohingyas Gutted in Mysterious Fire.' *The Pioneer*.

Kaveri. 2020. 'The Politics of Marginalization and Statelessness of the Rohingyas in India.' In *Citizenship, Nationalism and Refugeehood of Rohingyas in Southern Asia*, edited by N. Chowdhury and B. Mohanty. Singapore: Springer.

Khajuria, R. K. 2018, 10 February. 'Not the First Attack on Sunjuwan Army Camp: Militants Had Stormed Base in 2003.' *The Hindustan Times*, New Delhi.

Khan, Yar Asif. 2013, 30 June. 'Hyderabad's Rohingya Refugees Fight Language Barriers.' *The Hindu*, Hyderabad.

Mathew, L. 2018, 2 August. 'Ram Madhav: NRC Limited to Assam, but All Rohingya Will Be Deported.' *The Indian Express*.

Mohammed, S. 2013, 9 July. 'Rohingyas in Hyderabad Live in Fear.' *The Times of India*. New Delhi.

Nanjappa, Vicky. 2013. 'Around 1500 Rohingya Muslims Take Refuge in Hyderabad.' *Radiff News*, Hyderabad.

Naqvi, S. 2016, 10 July. 'The Killing Fields of Jammu: How Muslims Become a Majority in the Region.' The Scroll, New Delhi.

Pagadala, Tejaswini. 2013, 12 August. 'Seeking New Homes in Hyderabad.' *India Together*, New Delhi.

Pasricha, A. 2018, 14 October. 'Rohingya Refugees in India Rattled after First-ever Deportations.' VOA News. Available at https://www.voanews.com/

south-central-asia/rohingya-refugees-india-rattled-after-first-ever-deporta-tions (accessed on 10 August 2021).

Standing, Guy. 2011. *The Precariat: The New Dangerous Class*. London: Bloomsbury.

The Hindu. 2017. '"No Plan yet to Deport Rohingya," says Kiren Rijiju.' Available at http://www.thehindu.com/news/national/no-plan-yet-to-deport-rohingya-says-rijiju/article19664225.ece (accessed on 10 August 2021).

Uddin, Nasir. 2020. *The Rohingya: An Ethnography of 'Subhuman' Life*. New York, NY: Oxford University Press.

Uddin, Nasir, and Nasreen Chowdhury, eds. 2019. *Deterritortialised Identity and Transborder Movement in South Asia*. Singapore: Springer.

Velath, Priyanca Mathur, and K. Chopra. 2015. 'The Stateless People: Rohingyas in Hyderabad, India.' In *Rohingyas in India: Birth of a Stateless Community*, edited by S. Majumder, Priyanca Mathur Velath, and Kriti Chopra. Kolkata: Mahanirban Calcutta Research Group.

Verma, S. 2017. Why Is India Turning Its Back on Rohingya Refugees? The Wire.

Vickey. 2015. 'Rohingya Muslims: Worry ahead for India.' One India.

Yhome, K. 2018. 'Examining India's Stance on the Rohingya Crisis.' Issue Brief No. 247. Observer Research Foundation, New Delhi.

CHAPTER 7

Situating the Rohingya in India's Citizenship Conundrum

Parvin Sultana

7.1. Introduction

The Indian subcontinent underwent the plight of partition on two occasions; first in 1947, when two nations were formed—India and Pakistan—based on the two-nation theory which subscribed religion as the basis of a nation state; second in 1971, when East Pakistan broke away to form the new state of Bangladesh. The second partition foregrounded language and culture as the basis of the nation state, and the new state of Bangladesh was carved out of erstwhile East Pakistan. The newly formed Bangladesh and India shared multifaceted sociocultural and economic commonalities owing to geographical and cultural continuity. The region has also witnessed mobility of people for social practices, travelling and resettlement. However, the landscape started changing with the colonial expansion, demarcation and categorization of the territory (Sonowal 2018). In both instances of partition, people belonging to similar cultural and communal stock were randomly divided. People became aliens in their own homes overnight. The newly drawn boundary was so absurd that led to precarious situations for many, such as to move about from one's living room to the kitchen, one had to cross an international boundary within their houses. It also created peculiarities like enclaves, which were pockets of land belonging to Bangladesh but landlocked within the boundaries of India and vice versa, putting people in a situation of legal limbo when it came to citizenship. It was solved as late as 2015 with the signing of the Land Boundary Agreement between India and Bangladesh (Banerjee, Guha, and Choudhury 2017). The historical event of partition also led to the movement of people on a large scale from one country to another. It not only divided territory but lives as well. Urvashi Butalia's *Other Side of Silence* (1998) is an account of the many lives taken, divided and created by partition.

Migration or movement of people is a fact of the human race. People have moved from one place to another since forever. This movement is forced at times, but mostly it is voluntary. Migration is induced both by *push* and *pull* factors. Armed conflict, poverty, political turmoil, etc. tend to work as push factors and lead to forced displacement of people fleeing to a safer haven. On the one hand, large-scale migrations, particularly involuntary ones induced by war and political strife, have been a constant feature in world history and were often accentuated by the excesses of the Cold War. On the other hand, the presence of better job opportunities in the host country works as pull factors. Globalization and softening of national borders have also accentuated migration across countries. In the past 30 years, the numbers of international migrants have doubled. The vast majorities are economic migrants who move for better livelihood. However, involuntary movements, which occur under extraordinary circumstances such as wars, partition and ethnic/religious strife comprise the movement of a large number of people in a very short period, are difficult to understand. According to the World Migration Report of 2020, the number of global migrants stands at about 272 million with two-thirds being labour migrants (WMR 2020). Migration in the Indian subcontinent has also been there for a long time. The partition of India in 1947 saw an estimated 14.5 million people migrating within four years. People who were used to migrate to neighbouring states for a better livelihood could not comprehend the ramifications of crossing an international border. Overnight, areas became legally inaccessible. A complete halt to migration was hence difficult to implement. The nature of the border which was maritime in some places also made it difficult to regulate movement.

Migration discourse continues to shape the idea of citizenship in India. The north-eastern region of India which shares an international border with several neighbouring countries like Nepal, Bhutan, Bangladesh, Myanmar and China often becomes the reference point for statements about alleged illegal immigration to the country. The ex-Governor of Assam S. K. Sinha had claimed in 1998 through a report that the region has been inundated by illegal immigrants who needed to be deported (Choudhury 2019). To understand migration and mobility in the Indian subcontinent one needs to go back to the colonial days when migration was encouraged and endorsed on a massive scale.

7.2. Migration to Northeast India

The partition of newly independent India into two countries caused some subsequent problems. While the partition in the western front can be considered complete, the same was not the case on the eastern front. The randomly drawn border divided both lives and land along the Indo-Bangladesh border. With no proper fence and a long maritime border, the trans-border movement did not completely stop. This region also saw back and forth movement of people because of the Nehru–Liaquat Pact which was signed on 8 April 1950. Jawaharlal Nehru and the then Prime Minister of Pakistan Liaquat Ali Khan signed an agreement at the backdrop of large-scale migration of people belonging to minority communities of both the countries—Hindus from East Bengal and Muslims from West Bengal. This pact aimed at allowing the people to return to their countries to safely dispose of their property, it further confirmed minority rights and made provisions for the return of looted property and abducted women (Dutta 2019).

While the Northeast region of India has seen multiple waves of migration, the migrants started figuring as a prominent issue in the region's politics towards the end of the colonial rule. Sir Edward Gait in *A History of Assam* gives a detailed account of the conquest of the Ahoms and their glorious rule which lasted for almost 600 years (Gait 1906). The region has witnessed the movement of people from time to time. The second big wave of migration to the region was initiated by the British after the discovery of tea in Assam. Looking at the history of plantation work, Nitin Varma points out how it was difficult to persuade tea plantation labourers from Chhota Nagpur to cross over to the valley of Assam. Assam at that time was perceived as a lost world. The sense of loss associated with Assam tea plantation also became a part of *Jhumur* songs. This perplexed the British who needed cheap coolie labour to ensure a steady and good profit from the tea plantation (Varma 2014). The changing revenue system and its monetization did not encourage the Assamese locals to make agriculture profitable. Assamese agriculture was about self-subsistence. Amalendu Guha in *Planter Raj to Swaraj* ([1977] 2006) talks about how the Assamese economy during the colonial period was nurtured as a plantation economy and this was done at the cost of agriculture. Jayeeta Sharma in her *Empire's Garden* (2011) called Assam an empire's garden and how every development of the state revolved around it being a tea plantation economy. However, despite the reluctance, the British recruiters often succeeded in getting workers for the plantation by using fear, force as well as deceit.

Gorky Chakraborty (2009) gives a detailed account of immigration during the colonial rule. In his book *Assam's Hinterland* he points out that the British brought the first contingent of immigrants to serve the emerging plantation sector in 1858–1859. But as plantation improved at the cost of agriculture, the second batch of immigrants was brought from East Bengal to transform the agrarian scenario of the state. These people transformed Assam's uncultivated wasteland including forests into revenue-yielding fields. During this period, the char areas of the Brahmaputra region were also transformed from natural habitats to areas of human habitation. (Chakraborty 2009).

The Muslim peasants of East Bengal origin changed the agricultural scenario of Assam. They introduced the cultivation of jute in Assam. Along with the changing agrarian scenario, immigration from densely populated districts of East Bengal changed the demographic scenario of Assam. The census report of 1871 recorded major changes in the districts of Assam such as Goalpara, Nowgong, Darrang and Kamrup. The erstwhile scantily populated state now had a much higher density of population. Initially, the Assamese middle class of the Brahmaputra valley region welcomed this migration as it ensured the availability of cheap labour. But slowly the attitude towards immigrants changed. The earlier local inhabitants fearing minoritization wanted some kind of safeguard mechanism to ensure their cultural dominance. Such immigration posed a threat to the tribal population as well. This was acknowledged in 1947 when tribal belts were created by an amendment to The Assam Land and Revenues Regulation of 1886. It also allowed resettling people affected by natural calamities. Bengali Muslims from East Bengal who settled in river islands or *chars* and *chaporis* (i.e., low-lying areas) were also beneficiaries of this policy. Working on similar lines, the British government introduced the Line System in 1916 which was implemented in 1920 (Sattwakar 2013). This demarcated certain areas for settlement of immigrants and tried to check their indiscriminate settlement in the state. The aim was to segregate the indigenous population from the immigrants by making interaction minimal. The Line System tried to ensure that the immigrants did not work for the local population and the immigrants did not buy lands of indigenous people. But the Assamese population did often use the cheap labour of these immigrants and there was a breach of the Line System. The immigrants also bought lands from the indigenous people and hence made homes in areas earmarked for the local population.

At the backdrop of partition, which saw the country being divided in the lines of religion, the migration issue in the region also undertook a communal tone. Eventually, the Muslim peasant was earmarked as the problematic other. This was the reason for conducting the first National Register of Citizens (NRC) in Assam in 1951 which was subsequently upgraded in 2019 to differentiate between citizens and non-citizens.

The Citizenship issue in India has been mired in controversy owing to the alleged continued illegal migration of people from

Bangladesh. Migration to the north-eastern region is often cited for the need for more stringent rules of citizenship to keep suspicious people away. The north-eastern state of Assam is the only state where categories such as 'Doubtful Citizen' and 'Doubtful Voter' were included to keep people whose citizenship is under doubt from availing rights like the right to vote (Siddiqui 2019). Hannah Arendt (1951) coined the phrase 'right to have rights' arguing that stateless people suffer in the absence of this very right, that is, citizenship. She was critical of the discourse of modern human rights because it was based more on the principle of humanitarianism than legal rights. Also, human rights and their implementations are often at the mercy of nation states that implement them arbitrarily.

7.3. Migrants, Refugees and Citizens

Liberal democracies which are multicultural in nature often grapple with the question of who belongs and who is an outsider. Social democrats like Iris Marion Young, Anne Philips and others recognize this possibility and emphasize the need to make state institutions more inclusive to counter systematic exclusion of different groups. The liberal framework of citizenship emphasizes individual rights (Marshall 1950, 14, cited in Yuval-Davis 1997, 69) overriding group rights. However, this has been critiqued by scholars who point out the mediated and multi-layered nature of citizenship. Many individuals' relationships with the state are mediated through the groups of which they are members. Marshall is of the view that citizenship is a relationship between the individual and the state. On the other hand, such an understanding turns a blind eye to group-based differences derived from gender, ethnicity, class, etc. (Yuval-Davis 1997).

The question of citizenship in the post-colonial nation state of India has been a contested one. The figure of the citizen emerged as a legal and political sovereign being entitled to rights. But this figure also produced 'constitutive outsiders' into the code of citizenship (Balibar 2003, cited in Mezzadra 2006). This otherness is not a relationship of 'simple opposition' and the outsider is present discursively and constitutively in delineations of citizenship (Roy 2008). The outsider is indispensable for the identification of the citizen. The citizen is identified on his/her difference from the other.

Policies related to migration and repatriation in the post-independent era in India ripened an atmosphere in which identities of who is an Indian and who is an 'outsider' got rigidified. For certain communities, coming back to India was seen as homecoming (*ghar wapsi*), while others who have never left the country came to be viewed as foreigners or aliens because the religion they followed originated somewhere else. The religious identity of these people became the deciding factors. In fact, in the subsequent amendments to the Citizenship Act, religion came to be mentioned explicitly and it was done so in the 2004 amendment. While subsequently, laws of becoming a citizen became stringent, those who are left out became further marginalized. India has no rule pertaining to refugees. In fact, the very word refugee is not used in official discourse to describe entrants to the country's territory who have fled their home country.

Refugees and migrants are treated as foreigners in India who have entered the country illegally. This puts them in a precarious situation. The absence of clear categorization ensures that the migrants are also denied of basic rights and amenities. Most migrants who fled their home country due to armed conflicts barely end up officially as refugees. They are neither seen as rights-bearing citizens in their own country nor are they given the right to move to another country. In the process, they are reduced to 'bare life' (Agamben 1998). Refugees are determined through the prism of national security. The absence of clear laws means that refugees are dependent on the laws of the host country. In India, most of the refugees are looked after by the Indian state and the United Nations High Commissioner for Refugees (UNHCR). Denied any legal status, they are provided some basic rights by the Indian Constitution such as the right to equality (Article 14), right to personal life and liberty (Article 21; Chowdhury 2019).

In post-colonial Asia, the formation of nation states has turned out to be an exclusionary process as identity and its many narrow markers became a deciding factor. In most cases, the states have accelerated exodus by systematic othering of different ethnic communities. As a result, South Asian states have seen trans border movement not only owing to the prospect of a better future but also escaping vulnerability in their home countries (Banerjee, Anasua, and Atig 2016). This vulnerability is often produced by nation states (Uddin 2019) and further accentuated by the host country. The Rohingya have faced something similar in Myanmar. The state has produced such extreme forms of vulnerability for the Rohingya especially post 2017. The United Nations (UN) termed it as 'a textbook example of ethnic cleansing' and many acclaimed media outlets termed it as 'genocide'. Fleeing persecution, the Rohingya found themselves in different neighbouring countries such as Bangladesh, India, Thailand, Malaysia and Indonesia. The response of these states has been anything but welcoming. While some states have closed their borders and denied entry creating the category of the 'Boat people', others have forced the community to live in the margins.

7.4. The Rohingya in India

India has been home to a large number of people who have fled their home countries fearing persecution. The human displacement in South Asia, to a major extent, is a legacy of colonialism —be it the partition or the nation-building that followed. Tibetans who started entering India in 1959 are considered as a well-managed refugee group in Asia. With the birth of Bangladesh, an estimated 10 million people fled to India, but most of them were repatriated with the help of UNHCR (2000). The region has also seen Tamils fleeing from Sri Lanka to India, Afghans fleeing to Pakistan, Chakmas fleeing the Chittagong hill tracts of Bangladesh and Burmese ethnic groups fleeing to different neighbouring countries owing to increased ethnic strife.

Rohingya Muslims comprise a substantial number of the refugees who fled Myanmar. They have also entered India while fleeing persecution in Myanmar. For decades, Myanmar has witnessed ethnic strife amongst major ethnic groups. The military rule that followed Myanmar's independence in 1948 did not change the power equation. Certain majoritarian Burmese groups have been propagating majoritarian politics and this has further entrenched ethnic conflicts. Subsequent government policies have further fuelled the problems.

Systematic discrimination and persecution of the Rohingya led to their expulsion from Myanmar. The military government of Myanmar brought subsequent legislations which rendered even document-bearing Rohingya illegal. In 1982, Ne Win's military government officially authorized 135 ethnic groups as Myanmarese nationals and the Rohingya were excluded from this list. The Rohingya were treated as illegal immigrants from Bangladesh unless they could prove that their ancestors lived in the country before 1823 (Kaveri 2017). The very definition of citizenship was given an exclusionary tone with the Citizenship Act of 1982 of Myanmar, which did not recognize the Rohingya as one of the ethnic communities of Myanmar.

The 1982 Act put in place different categories of citizens and a hierarchical set-up in Myanmar. Certain groups like the Kachin, Kayah, Karen, Chin, Burman, Mon, Rakhine or Shan were recognized as full citizens and pink cardholders. There were other groups which could apply for citizenship under the category of associated citizenship and will be regarded as blue cardholders, but these people will have to produce proof of habitation in the country before 1983. The third category comprises green cardholders or naturalized citizens. Through this system, citizenship can be granted to ethnic communities not considered indigenous (Haque 2017). The Rohingya were required to apply for citizenship through the third system as they were disqualified from the other two categories. This put them in a precarious situation as it would mean accepting their foreign origins.

The Rohingya fleeing the country later recounted their plight. Habibur Rahman in his autobiographical account elaborated how not only the Rohingya but other ethnic minorities were also at the receiving end of the majoritarian Buddhist chauvinism. He also gives a detailed account of the harrowing experience of the Rohingya in Myanmar and how eventually their identity came into crisis. A large number of laws have been passed by the government which aims at regulating every aspect of the life of the Rohingya including the number of children they can have, the areas they can access and even the education that they can receive (Rahman 2019).

Since the late 1970s, the Rohingya have been present in large numbers in Bangladesh's Cox's Bazar area across the Naff River which separates Rakhine State from Bangladesh. From Bangladesh, it is believed that the Rohingya crossed over to India through its north-eastern region. Seeking a safe haven, these refugees made repeated demands of humanitarian assistance in India. However, even in India their claims have been repudiated time and again based on illegality and security threat. Subir Bhaumik points out that the focus on Rohingya shifted when a boatload of 109 Rohingya was intercepted in Northern Andaman in 2013. The latest wave of exodus followed the persecution of the Rohingya in 2012. A large number of the Rohingya are languishing in various jails in India.

The latest exodus post-2017 of Rohingya Muslims was initiated after retaliation by the Myanmar government against an attack by Arakan Rohingya Salvation Army (ARSA). While Bangladesh government has been struggling with the pressure of the Rohingya refugees, India has had a very mixed approach to the crisis. India has on the one hand stopped the entry of these refugees fleeing persecution and at the same time have decided to deport the refugees. In India also, the condition of the Rohingya is pathetic. Their Muslim identity further accentuates their continued persecution in this host country. The Rohingya in India struggle to get access to basic amenities. The living conditions in the camps are squalid, with very poor access to basic necessities such as clean water, sanitation and healthcare. Accommodation is provided in canvas tents (Amin 2018). As reported in *Malnutrition Daily*, pregnant mothers and newborn children are denied basic medical benefits provided by the Pradhan Mantri Maternity Scheme (PMMS; Dixit 2018).

India is not a signatory to any international policy aimed at providing protection to refugees and safeguarding their rights. India did not sign the 1951 UN Convention on Refugees, 1967 Protocol Relating to the Status of Refugees, 1954 Convention relating to the Status of Stateless Persons and 1961 Convention on the Reduction of Statelessness stating that the refugee problem is a by-product of the Cold War and the policies are Eurocentric. India has also no specific law in place to counter the refugee question. India continues to house a large number of refugees and despite not being a signatory to the 1951 Protocol, it largely respects the principle of non-refoulement.

But there is a discrepancy as to how the country tackles the problems of refugees. India has had a different approach to different groups of refugees.

7.5. NRC and the Citizenship Question

The question of citizenship in the post-colonial nation state of India has been a contested one. The figure of the citizen emerged as a legal and political sovereign being entitled to rights. But this figure also produced 'constitutive outsiders' into the code of citizenship (Balibar 2003, cited in Mezzadra 2006). This otherness is not a relationship of 'simple opposition' and the outsider is present discursively and constitutively in delineations of citizenship (Roy 2008). The outsider is indispensable for the identification of the citizen. The citizen is identified on his/her difference from the other.

The concept of citizenship in India has evolved through certain historical moments. Roy (2008) pinpoints moments like the commencement of independence when the newly formed state found itself on the verge of emerging on a democratic ride and the subsequent amendments to the Citizenship Act of 1955, first in response to the Assam Movement and the Accord that followed and then to the Amendment in 2003. The citizenship as envisaged in India has been further complicated by the Citizenship Amendment Act, 2019 which redefined categories of illegal migrants and rendered leniency to some while applying for inclusion as citizens.

The demarcation of who is a citizen and who is not has been largely a response to the context of partition. Articles 5–7 of the Indian constitution discuss the modalities of deciding the citizenship question of people migrating between the two countries India and Pakistan between 1 March 1947 and 26 January 1950. Coming to the second crucial moment, the Assam Accord was a result of the long-drawn sociopolitical movement that went on for six years from 1979 to 1985. The movement was aimed at safeguarding the rights and interests of the people of Assam and ensuring all-around development (Hussain 1993). The Accord broadly promised 'constitutional, legislative and administrative safeguards ... to protect, preserve and promote the cultural, social, linguistic identity and heritage of the Assamese people' (Assam Accord, Clause 6). In the case of migrants, the accord stated that those who entered between 1966 and 1971 should be disenfranchised for 10 years and those who entered after 1971 should be deported. Interestingly, the Indira–Mujib pact on the aftermath of the creation of Bangladesh did not provide any scope for inclusion of people who entered India from erstwhile East Pakistan. As a result, Assam had to accept all those who entered before 1971.

Eventually, Article 6A was included in the Citizenship Act. The category of migrant has been a point of reference even at this moment. While the earlier construction of citizenship has been more inclusive and generous, its scope narrowed with time. Migrants also started giving a connotation of illegality. As a category, it entered the Citizenship Act through an amendment in 1986 and again later in 2003 and 2005 to ensure the inclusion of Overseas Citizens of India. Unlike the Citizenship Act of 1955, in the latter two amendments of the Citizenship Act, the word migration was explicitly associated with illegality, where migrants were seen as a threat and 'others' (Roy 2010).

The question of citizenship has also changed its purview over time especially in Assam. From *bohiragoto* (outsiders to the state) to *bideshi* (foreigner) to *oboidho Bangladeshi* (illegal Bangladeshi migrant), the other continued to be defined and redefined. In fact, owing to different points in history, this connotation at times ambiguously donated a communal feature. Muslims of East Bengal origin found themselves at violent crossroads and often as being the primary suspect when it came to finding out the illegal immigrants.

Assamese nationalism vis-a-vis Bengali nationalism goes back to as early as 1838 when Assam was incorporated into the Bengal Presidency. The imposition of the language Bengali and its use as the official language tilted the balance in favour of Bengalis who were also more educated and had a better shot at jobs. It was as late as 1912 that Assam was reconstituted as a separate province, but the inclusion of Bengali-speaking Sylhet again created the problem. All this fuelled a fear in the Assamese-speaking people of the region who believed that eventually they will be rendered minority (Kar 1990). Moreover, defining who is indigenous and who is an outsider in a state like Assam is a challenge because it has seen multiple waves of migration.

Owing to this challenge, the Assam Accord fixed the date of entry to determine citizenship. However, the state which shares a border with the neighbouring country of Bangladesh had to take into account the Indira–Mujib pact. The pact did not make any provision for taking in the migrants who have entered Assam and India from East Pakistan. As a result, the cut-off year was decided as 1971, the year the new state of Bangladesh was formed. The Assam Accord stated that those who entered the state between 1 January 1966 and 24 March 1971 will be disenfranchised for 10 years from the date of detection. And those who entered thereafter will be deported. Illegal Immigration Determination by Tribunals Act (IMDT) 1983 was enacted to protect genuine Indian citizens from unnecessary harassment. Under this act, the onus was on the authority to prove that the person accused was indeed an illegal immigrant (Barbora 2019).

The IMDT was seen as a failure in Assam as the number of 'foreigners' detected under it was too few. It was eventually scrapped in 2005. And in 2013, the Supreme Court of India took cognizance of two writ petitions filed by non-governmental organizations (NGOs) from Assam and ordered the state and central governments to update the NRC adhering to the Citizenship Act of 1955 and the (amended) Citizenship Rules of 2003 (Barbora 2019). The National Register of Citizens was aimed at updating the NRC of 1951 and preparing a Register of Citizens instead of finding out who are foreigners. Those who are left out of the Register will be required to prove their citizenship through Foreigners' Tribunals—quasi-judicial bodies which will decide on the citizenship question of individuals.

The NRC was to be updated based on documents submitted by individuals to support their claims and these documents included: (a) land tenancy records, (b) citizenship certificate, (c) permanent residential certificate, (d) refugee registration certificate, (e) passport, (f) LIC policy, (g) government-issued licence, (h) government service/ employment certificate, (i) bank/post office account, (j) birth certificate, (k) board/university educational certificate, (l) court records/ processes, among others. But a preliminary look at these documents shows an inherent middle-class bias. Documents such as LIC, birth certificate, even landowning documents are not available to all. This tyranny of documents was more visible in the case of women who are systematically left out of land ownership in patriarchal societies.

An essentially technocratic and bureaucratic exercise, the NRC-updating procedure left out people who were already marginalized in the society. Floods, land erosion, etc. ensured people moved from place to place, encroached upon protected lands and had no documents to prove any kind of ownership. Many incidents came up which showed victims of river erosion were settled on government lands by locals in exchange for a huge amount of money. But they were later evicted creating another crisis (Saikia 2017).

The very procedure showed how people had to go through systematic harassment. False and flimsy accusations were made against people who were asked to go for verification again (Saikia 2019). People were made to travel to distant unknown places for verification on very short notice. Accidents happened, people were hospitalized. This was also a time when civil society and NGOs stepped in a very big way to help these people. Even then the final document of NRC left out 1.9 million people. While for right-wing political populists, this was not enough, others also felt that the list is far from perfect as it left out a large number of genuine Indians. Interestingly, a larger number of Hindus were left out owing to the discrepancy in documents and to correct this, it was felt that the Citizenship Amendment Act (CAA) was inevitable.

The CAA would violate the cut-off date set in Assam Accord as it would pave the way for people who entered the country till 2014 to claim citizenship. The state of Assam has demanded that all those who entered the state after 1971 irrespective of religion be deported. Unlike other parts of India, the protests in the state of Assam were slightly different. While people of Assam despite difficulties and discrepancies cooperated in the process of NRC updation, they are opposed to CAA because it subverts the accord (ET Online 2019). On the other hand, the people outside Assam opposed both NRC, which will only create more problems, and the CAA, because of its inherent communal nature which explicitly makes religion a marker of citizenship.

7.6. Citizenship Conundrum: Locating the Rohingya

Defining categories of citizens means earmarking certain groups who do not qualify as citizens. They are allowed some basic rights and made to live in the margins. Their existence is mired in illegality which is seen as a threat. The very presence of a large number of refugees, migrants and aliens on the soil of a particular state is perceived as a security threat and added pressure on the limited resources. They are often pitted against citizens and seen as a problem that needs to be resolved (Choudhury 2019).

India's response to the Rohingya crisis has undergone three phases. In the first phase that saw an exodus in 2012, India considered it an internal matter of Myanmar and instead of intervening and speaking against the attacks on Rohingya, it was more sympathetic to the Myanmar government. The then-external Minister Salman Khurshid also visited Myanmar and pledged a relief package of US$1 million (Ministry of External Affairs 2013).

The second phase seems to have begun sometime in 2017. It saw a hostile attitude in the government towards the Rohingya and there was a declaration to deport the Rohingya who have settled in different parts of India. Kiren Rijiju, while answering a question in the Parliament, stated that the Rohingya will be deported because they are 'illegal immigrants'. This shift became clearer when the ARSA staged attacks on police outposts in Myanmar and this was followed by a visit to Myanmar by Indian Prime Minister Narendra Modi. A joint statement issued with the Myanmarese government condemned the terrorist attacks but kept silent on the persecution of Rohingya.

The second phase is also a reiteration of the BJP government's declaration in its 2014 election manifesto—of dealing with infiltration and illegal immigrants in the north-eastern region on a priority basis. Interestingly, while India refers to the Rohingya in Bangladesh as 'displaced persons', the Rohingya in India are considered illegal immigrants (Yhome 2018). But international diplomacy also compelled India to take a long-term view on the issue and the need to maintain working relationships with both Myanmar and Bangladesh.

Following this, India supported the need for all-round development in the Arakan region and a subsequent return of the refugees. India also saw the opportunity of greater economic engagement in the region.

The third phase saw a reaction to China's approach to the Rohingya crisis. China forwarded a 'three-step' solution to the Rohingya crisis (Yhome 2018). This was followed by a signing of the repatriation agreement between Bangladesh and Myanmar. India believed that it should play a bigger role in the solution of the crisis. In May 2018, India was also a part of the United Nations Security Council (UNSC) delegation along with Laos, Thailand and China that visited Myanmar. The then External Affairs Minister Sushma Swaraj stressed the need to create a feasible environment for the speedy and safe return of the displaced persons to the Rakhine State.

While India's stance on the Rohingya immigrants has changed over time and is not at par with how India tackled the refugees coming from other countries, the use of the spectre of Rohingya as illegal immigrants and a security threat figured prominently in the country's citizenship discourse. The CAA has faced criticism from multiple fronts for being arbitrary on many counts. It limits its purview to only three neighbouring states of India—Bangladesh, Pakistan and Afghanistan, while it leaves out other neighbouring countries turning a blind eye to the persecution of religious minorities in those countries.

While Hindus of Bangladesh and Pakistan have been included, Shias have been excluded. Similarly, Myanmar and hence the Rohingya have been kept out of the act's purview. On the one hand, the Rohingya are presented as elements that need to be weeded out of the nation state—Muslim terrorists who are a security threat, on the other hand, are absent as the history of their persecution is overlooked. While persecuted Buddhists can claim asylum and eventual citizenship in India, persecuted Rohingya have been denied the same right.

The CAA makes two classifications of migrants who are eligible for Indian citizenship—one based on religion—only Hindus, Sikhs, Jains, Buddhists, Christians and Parsis are granted protection from being convicted as illegal immigrants even if they enter the country without a valid passport. Two, the act classifies on the basis of the country of origin—migrants coming from Pakistan, Afghanistan and Bangladesh are considered eligible for citizenship through naturalization under relaxed conditions. This act for the first time distinguishes immigrants based on religion (Ghosh 2019). The Rohingya are left out of this despite being a persecuted minority. Even Myanmar is left out of the purview despite the fact that people from Myanmar entered India fleeing persecution. Myanmar saw the latest surge of exodus owing to the military coup and Burmese nationals entered India afresh.

The Rohingya who have lived in India for almost a decade started figuring prominently when Indian government issued notices for their deportation, calling them illegal immigrants and a threat to national security. There was also a discrepancy between the figures presented by the Indian government and the UNHCR. While the Indian government claimed that there were 40,000 Rohingya, UNHCR claimed that it had issued registration cards to around 16,000 Rohingya. While the number is much smaller than the million present in Bangladesh, in India, their presence resulted in a 'legal, diplomatic and political slugfest' (Khandekar 2017).

The BJP's 2014 election manifesto stated that India shall remain a natural home for persecuted Hindus and they shall be welcome to seek refuge in the country. The CAA is a step towards fulfilling this vision. The other side of the vision is reflected in the urge to find out non-citizens and alienate them and eventually deport them. The notice to deport the Rohingya was followed by a portrayal of the Rohingya as the 'enemy other'. The Rohingya's Muslim identity fitted in this discourse neatly and the alleged terror links of the Rohingya were used to justify the government's act of leaving them out while including other persecuted minorities.

The presence of the Rohingya in India is portrayed as a problem. In fact, there are instances when the Rohingya have been described as terrorists and accused of having links with organizations like ISIS. This according to Ravi Nair is a part of the 'Islamophobic terrorist threat campaign' that is gathering momentum. This helps in also justifying the arbitrariness of the CAA in leaving out persecuted Muslims.

The Rohingya are both present and absent in the citizenship discourse of India. They are present as a threat to national security and hence India not only closed its borders to the Rohingya but also decided to deport them. But the Rohingya are absent amongst the persecuted minorities who are promised protection in India. The activity of the group ARSA is used to further reiterate the dangers of allowing entry to the Rohingya. In fact, claims are made about how Cox's Bazar is connected to the activities of ARSA. This is often upheld as a lesson for India to be cautious about (Bhattacharya 2017).

7.7. Conclusion

The Indian chapter of the Rohingya crisis adds another tragic example of how a persecuted minority continues to be marginalized and denied basic rights in other liberal countries. In India, the Rohingya find themselves in a precarious situation because India's domestic politics is undergoing crucial shifts. The CAA has been seen by many as a marker of a majoritarian shift. In such a situation, the Rohingya and their alleged antisocial activities are used to justify the arbitrary character of the act. On the other hand, the Rohingya and their saga of persecution continue to be overlooked. Such a stance of the Indian state has raised concerns about the impact on India's geopolitical relationship with neighbouring countries. Acts like the CAA presume that minorities are persecuted in India's neighbouring countries and put pressure on bilateral politics. (Sufian 2020). Similarly, it also implies that majoritarian domestic policies are influencing India's foreign policies (Ikwanek 2018). While India's stance might have changed slightly on the Rohingya question, it is intertwined with shifts in India's domestic politics. Electoral politics and polarization will ensure a continued marginalization and demonization of the Rohingya as the 'dangerous other'. And this image will be used to justify an exclusionary idea of Indian citizenship. India's decision to deport the Rohingya back to a country which is again on the cusp of a civil war will set a dangerous precedent.

References

Agamben, G. 1998. *Homo Sacer: Sovereignty and Bare Life.* Translated by D. Heller Roazen. Stanford, CA: Stanford University Press.

Amin, M. '"Nobody's Children, Owners of Nothing:" Analysing the Indian State's Policy Response to the Rohingya Refugee Crisis.' Policy Report No 24. The Hindu Centre for Politics and Public Policy, Chennai.

Arendt, H. 1951. *The Origins of Totalitarianism*. New York, NY: Harcourt Books.

Banerjee, P., C. Anasua, and G. Atig, eds. 2016. *The State of Being Stateless: An Account of South Asia*. New Delhi: Orient BlackSwan.

Banerjee, S., A. Guha, and A. Choudhury. 2017, July. 'The 2015 India–Bangladesh Land Boundary Agreement: Identifying Constraints and Exploring Possibilities in Cooch Behar.' ORF Occasional Paper. Observer Research Foundation, New Delhi.

Barbora, S. 2019. 'National Register of Citizens: Politics and Problems in Assam.' *Explorations* 3, no. 2: 3–28. Available at http://app.insoso.org/ISS_journal/Repository/Article_NRC.pdf (accessed on 25 September 2020).

Bhattacharya, R. 2017,10 November. 'How Bangladesh's Cox Bazar Contributed to ARSA's Movement in Myanmar's Rakhine.' The Wire. Available at https://thewire.in/external-affairs/bangladeshs-coxs-bazar-contributed-arsas-movement-myanmars-rakhine (accessed on 29 September 2020).

Butalia, U. 1998. *The Other Side of Silence*. New Delhi: Penguin Books India.

Chakraborty, G. 2009. *Assam's Hinterland: Society and Economy in the Char Areas*. New Delhi: Akanksha Publishing House.

Choudhury, A. 2019. 'Ex-Assam guv S. K. Sinha's Report on Illegal Immigration in State is Riddled with Contradiction, Dubious Data.' *Firstpost.com*, 25 July. Available at: https://www.firstpost.com/india/ex-assam-guv-sk-sinhas-report-on-illegal-immigration-in-state-is-riddled-with-contradictions-dubious-data-7057761.html (accessed on 30 September 2020).

Choudhury, N. 2019. 'Citizenship and Membership: Placing Refugees in India.' In *Deterritorialised Identity and Transborder Movement in South Asia*, edited by N. Uddin and N. Choudhury. Singapore: Springer.

Dixit, N. 2018, 2 February. 'Rohingya in India Seeking Basic Nutrition Services.' *News Deeply*. Available at https://deeply.thenewhumanitarian.org/malnutrition/articles/2018/02/02/india-blocking-rohingya-refugees-from-basic-nutrition-services (accessed on 25 September 2020).

Dutta, P. K. 2019, 10 December. 'What Is Nehru Liaquat Pact That Amit Shah Referred to Defend Citizenship Amendment Bill?' *India Today*. Available at https://www.indiatoday.in/news-analysis/story/nehru-liaquat-pact-that-amit-shah-referred-to-defend-citizenship-bill-1627036-2019-12-10 (accessed on 30 September 2020).

ET Online. 2019, 23 December. 'Understanding NRC: What It Is and If It Can Be Implemented across the Country.' *The Economic Times*. Available at economictimes.indiatimes.com/news/et-explains/is-a-pan-india-nrc-possible-the-lesson-from-assam/articleshow/72454225.cms?from=mdr (accessed on 30 September 2020).

Gait, Edward. (1906). 'A History of Assam.' Calcutta: Thacker, Spink & Co. Available at http://brahmaputra.ceh.vjf.cnrs.fr/bdd/IMG/pdf/Gait_historyassam.pdf (accessed on 16 September 2021).

Ghosh, A. 2019, 7 December. 'Why the Citizenship (Amendment) Bill Is Unconstitutional?' The Leaflet. Available at https://www.theleaflet.in/

why-the-citizenship-amendment-bill-2019-is-unconstitutional/# (accessed on 26 September 2020).

Guha, A. (1997) 2006. *Planter Raj to Swaraj: Freedom Struggle and Electoral Politics in Assam.* New Delhi: Tulika Books.

Haque, Md M. 2017. 'Rohingya Ethnic Muslim Minority and the 1982 Citizenship Law in Burma.' *Journal of Muslim Minority Affairs* 37, no. 4: 454–469. https://doi.org/10.1080/13602004.2017.1399600

Hussain, Monirul. 1993. *The Assam Movement: Class, Ideology and Identity.* New Delhi: Manak Publications.

Ikwanek, K. 2018. 'Interests before Ideas: Does Hindu Nationalism Influence India's Foreign Policy?' *Acta Asiatica Varsoviensia* 31: 97–113.

Kar, M. 1990. *Muslims in Assam Politics.* New Delhi: Omsons Publications.

Kaveri. 2017. 'Being Stateless and the Plight of Rohingyas.' *Peace Review* 29, no. 1: 31–39. https://doi.org/10.1080/10402659.2017.1272295

Khandekar, O. 2017, 15 October. 'How the Indian Government Is Keeping Rohingya Out?' *Economic Times.* Available at https://economictimes.indiatimes.com/news/politics-and-nation/how-the-indian-government-is-keeping-rohingya-out/articleshow/61082752.cms (accessed on 25 September 2020).

Mezzadra, S. 2006. 'Citizen and Subject: A Post Colonial Constitution for the European Union.' *Situations* 1, no. 2: 31–42. Research Direct. Available at http://ojs.gc.cuny.edu/index.php/situations/issue/view/3 (accessed on 30 September 2020).

Ministry of External Affairs. 2013. *Annual Report 2012–2013.* New Delhi: Ministry of External Affairs.

Rahman, Habibur & Ansel, Sophie. (2019). 'First They Erased Our Name: A Rohingya Speaks.' New Delhi: Penguin Viking.

Roy, A. 2008. 'Between Encompassment and Closure: The "Migrant" and the Citizen in India.' *Contributions to Indian Sociology* 42, no. 2: 219–248. https://doi.org/10.1177%2F006996670804200202

———. 2010. *Mapping Citizenship in India.* New Delhi: OUP.

Saikia, Arunabh. 2017, 11 December. 'In Assam's Sipajhar, Bengali Muslim Residents Claim They Were Targeted in Eviction Drive.' Scroll.in. Available at scroll.in/article/860841/did-an-eviction-drive-in-assams-sipajhar-target-bengali-muslim-residents (accessed on 28 September 2020).

———. 2019, 5 August. 'Panic in Assam as People Rush to NRC Re-verification Hearings on 24-hour Notice.' Scroll.in. Available at scroll.in/article/932815/panic-in-assam-as-people-rush-to-attend-nrc-hearings-on-24-hour-notice (accessed on 28 September 2020).

Sattwakar, B. 2013. 'The Immigration Issue, Line System and Legislative Politics in Colonial Assam (1927–1939): A Historical Study.' *IOSR Journal of Humanities and Social Science* 11, no. 4: 1–3. Available at http://iosrjournals.org/iosr-jhss/papers/Vol11-issue4/A01140103.pdf?id=6303 (accessed on 29 September 2020).

Sharma, J. 2011. *Empire's Garden: Assam and the Making of India.* New Delhi: Orient BlackSwan.

Siddiqui, N. 2019, 9 March. 'Discourse of Doubt: Understanding the Crisis of Citizenship in Assam.' *Economic & Political Weekly* 54, no. 10. Available at https://www.epw.in/journal/2019/10/perspectives/discourse-doubt.html (accessed on 25 September 2020).

Sonowal, B. 2018. 'Immigration in Assam during Colonial Rule: Its Impact on the Socio-economic and Demography in Assam.' *International Journal of Innovative Studies in Sociology and Humanities* 3, no. 2: 10–14.

Sufian, Abu. 2020. Geopolitics of the NRC-CAA in Assam: Impact on Bangladesh–India Relations. *Asian Ethnicity.* https://doi.org/10.1080/1463 1369.2020.1820854

Uddin, N. 2019a. 'The State, Transborder Movements and Deterritorialised Identity in South Asia.' In *Deterritorialised Identity and Transborder Movement in South Asia,* edited by N. Uddin and N. Choudhury. Singapore: Springer.

———. 2019b. 'The State, Vulnerability and Transborder Movements: The Rohingya People in Myanmar and Bangladesh.' In *Deterritorialised Identity and Transborder Movement in South Asia,* edited by N. Uddin and N. Choudhury. Singapore: Springer.

UNHCR. 2000. *The State of World Refugees 2000: Fifty Years of Humanitarian Action.* Geneva: UNHCR.

Varma, N. 2014. 'Unpopular Assam: Notions of Migrating and Working for Tea Gardens.' In *Towards a New History of Work,* edited by S. Bhattacharya, 227–244. New Delhi: Tulika Books.

World Migration Report, 2020. Available at https://www.un.org/sites/un2.un.org/files/wmr_2020.pdf (accessed on 5th August, 2020).

Yhome, K. 2018. 'Examining India's Stance on the Rohingya Crisis.' ORF Issue Brief No 247. Observer Research Foundation, New Delhi.

Yuval-Davis, N. 1997. 'Women, Citizenship and Difference.' *Feminist Review* 57: 4–7. https://doi.org/10.1080%2F014177897339632

Part III

The Rohingya
in Other Parts of
the World

CHAPTER 8

Knowledge-practices of the Collective Self
The Rohingya Social Movement in Canada
Yuriko Cowper-Smith

8.1. Introduction

They are the interpreters of their legacy. If they're not willing to share that knowledge, then it's gone in a generation. The youth said, we have to be the ones to bring this to light, or else it will disappear.

—RP35, 21 August 2018, interview in Cowper-Smith (2021)

Social movements engage in mentally challenging activities. Movement participants debate their roles, their vision and goals and the strategies used to achieve them. They also learn how to nurture opportunities, relationship-build and broadcast information. Although movement literature focuses on these activities, it has been slow to view them as intellectual labour. Indeed, '… empirical research on social movements has focused on their modus operandi through protest but left others of their activities understudied' (Della Porta and Pavan 2017, 303). Social movement scholarship usually focuses on movement activities, but just as important are movements' intellectual contributions to contemporary sociopolitical issues.

A recent vein of research has begun unpacking this approach (Arribas 2018; Casas-Cortes, Osterweil, and Powell 2008; Cox 2014; Chesters 2012; Choudry and Kapoor 2010; Della Porta and Pavan 2017; Eyerman and Jamison 1991; Hosseini 2010; Pavan and Felicetti 2019). Scholars from this perspective generally recognize social movements as sites where knowledge is generated, modified and mobilized (Casas-Cortes et al. 2008). Stemming from this idea, Della Porta and Pavan (2017) have conceptualized a repertoire of knowledge practices: collective self, political alternatives, the action network and transmission. This chapter focuses on the knowledge practices of the collective self, which are, as Della Porta and Pavan (2017, 305) describe,

> ...concerned with the construction of a critical collective subject, this practice of knowledge-production addresses, simultaneously, the cosmological and the organizational dimensions of a movement while providing the linchpin to the elaboration of its alternative epistemological approach.

Or as Pavan and Felicetti (2019, 3–4) define, they are 'the vision that grounds a collective endeavour as well as about the envisaged or actual practices that transform this vision into reality'. Using these definitions, I now turn to the case study of the Rohingya diaspora movement in Canada.

8.2. The Rohingya Diaspora Movement in Canada

Since 2017, the Rohingya diaspora movement in Canada has grown substantially, providing a timely occasion to study a budding social movement from this angle. Initiated by the recently arrived Rohingya community, the movement advocates for international justice and accountability concerning the genocide in Myanmar and the resulting refugee crisis in Bangladesh. This movement presents a vital case study to understand from this lens precisely because of the intellectual energy it has put into producing a specific understanding of their cause (Cowper-Smith 2021).

As written elsewhere in this edited volume, and also by numerous other scholars, since independence, successive military juntas have solidified control over Myanmar by persecuting numerous minority groups. The government has, in particular, severely oppressed the Rohingya community from northeastern Rakhine State (Aung 2017; Brinham 2012; Cheesman 2017; Huang 2013, 2016; Ninh and Arnold 2016; Nyein 2019, February 1; Uddin 2020; Ware and Laoutides 2019; Zarni and Cowley 2014). The government's actions are now widely recognized as a state-led and state-sanctioned genocide (Zarni and Cowley 2014). In August 2017, approximately 742,000 Rohingya people fled across the border into Cox's Bazar, Bangladesh (UNHCR 2020). Over the past four years, the Rohingya community has lived in what currently makes up the world's largest refugee settlement (UNHCR 2020). As written in this volume (Chapters 2–6, this volume, 2021) this sprawling settlement lacks adequate physical infrastructure, healthcare, education, employment opportunities and is prone to natural hazards (UNHCR 2020). Most Rohingya who were unable to leave Rakhine State were relocated to internally displaced persons (IDP) camps throughout the state (Human Rights Watch 2020).

The broader diaspora has mainly settled in Southeast Asia and the Middle East, as well as Europe and North America. Canada officially resettled Rohingya refugees from Cox's Bazar (UNHCR 2007) between 2006 and 2010. During that period, 295 Rohingya came as refugees to Canada, and most of them settled in Kitchener-Waterloo. As of 2019, research participants noted that the population consisted of approximately between 1,000 and 1,500 people across the country (Cowper-Smith 2021).[1]

Rohingya newcomers have founded several important grassroots organizations, such as the Canadian Burmese Rohingya Organization, the Canadian Rohingya Development Initiative, the Rohingya Association of Canada and the Rohingya Human Rights Network. These groups campaign for their cause by awareness-building and lobbying the Canadian government to acknowledge and respond to the two crises (Cowper-Smith 2021). Beginning in June 2015, Rohingya youth in Kitchener-Waterloo co-produced a play with InnerSpeak Media entitled *I Am Rohingya*, which eventually became an award-winning documentary topic of the same name. Between 2018 and

[1] This number is anecdotal.

2019, there were numerous documentary screenings across the country (Cowper-Smith 2021).

To better understand the knowledge practices of the movement, in this chapter, I pose the question, how does the Rohingya social movement in Canada make itself intelligible? I analyse a data set of interviews (n = 70) and participant observation of meetings, conferences, panel discussions, documentary screenings and other advocacy events to understand the knowledge practices of the collective self of the movement. Of the 70 people interviewed, 26 people had immigrated to Canada from Bangladesh and four were from other countries. As my main argument, I assert that the ethos and political visions of the movement constitute the knowledge practice of the collective self, and the collective self is a new type of knowledge that supports the movement in Canada. More specifically, the movement has developed an ethos around the collective feelings of responsibility, awareness and resolution. The movement has shaped its political visions against several challenges: Myanmar's geopolitical realities, difficulties in resettlement and Islamophobia in Canada, and difficulty with building representative bodies in the diaspora. In recognition of these structural obstacles, the movement's political vision is to raise awareness of the crisis to the Canadian public and reinstate the human rights and citizenship of the Rohingya people in Myanmar. The following section addresses these ideas and then discusses the significance of knowledge practices for broader studies of movements.

8.2.1. Creating a Movement's Ethos: Responsibility, Awareness and Resolve

As noted earlier, Pavan and Felicetti (2019, 3–4) describe knowledge practices of the collective self as 'the vision that grounds a collective endeavour as well as about the envisaged or actual practices that transform this vision into reality'. The term captures how the movement jointly conceptualizes and approaches the issues it faces (Pavan and Felicetti 2019). In the following section, I argue that the movement has developed an ethos around shared feelings of responsibility, awareness and resolve. Later, I show how the movement has shaped its political visions around various structural obstacles.

8.2.2. Responsibility

For the activists in my research, their early motivation to join the movement centred on their sense of responsibility towards friends and family in Myanmar and Bangladesh. One young Rohingya activist explained his sense of responsibility towards his community.

> Today, I see a strong social movement and commitment from Rohingya themselves demanding change and betterment of our people's life—surely not enough—but we've just begun our work.... Being voiceless at one point of my life, it is almost like a moral responsibility to use this newly gained voice to advocate for those who are still voiceless. Advocacy to me is using my voice to make the voice of the voiceless heard. I see advocacy as the forerunner and/or the engine behind some of the great laws with huge impacts on millions of lives and nature. It is advocacy that often helps develop and set the norm before the majority accepts it, often by refusing to accept the existing norm forcefully (if need be).
>
> (RP56[2], 18 January 2019, interview in Cowper-Smith 2021)

Or, as another young activist expressed:

> I am one of the most privileged Rohingya. I live in one of the most peaceful countries in the world, I am not targeted for extinction for my ethnicity, I can work, study, I always have a roof over my head, and I never have to worry about food.... I, therefore, have a responsibility to those who do not have these privileges.
>
> (RP60, 31 January 2019, interview, in Cowper-Smith 2021)

Another Rohingya activist explained how he became interested in politics and economics to learn more about what he could do for the cause. He said,

> ...it became more, survivor guilt. I am in a place of safety, so I'm responsible for those who are still in the cages, trying to survive

---

[2] RP refers to research participant. I used this naming system to anonymize the interviews.

the genocide. It's all the same [feeling] for Rohingyas who made it to a safe place.

> (RP56, 18 January 2019, interview in Cowper-Smith 2021)

Similarly, another Rohingya activist noted,

Human rights, freedom, it's my duty to represent my people.... My Rohingya people around the world, I'm proud to see what they are doing. Enough is enough. Our genocide has been through generations and decades. Come on, are we going to live this life? We have seen how beautiful life is. I feel responsible to have a decent life.

> (RP69, 10 May 2019, interview in Cowper-Smith 2021)

One participant voiced a related feeling of responsibility for those family and friends remaining in Myanmar and Bangladesh.

Several hundred Rohingya now call Canada home, but the oceans between do little to distance them from the suffering of family and friends. They only add to the sense of responsibility to speak up, to act and to hope their new home will embrace their old.

> (RP1, 13 May 2018, interview in Cowper-Smith 2021)

The aforementioned instances and other similar examples indicate how responsibility motivated activists to participate in the movement. Genocide and witnessing the suffering of friends and family triggered a sense of responsibility among their community. As will be explained further in the discussion, the sense of responsibility was developed on a personal basis, but it became a collective sentiment.

8.2.3. Awareness

Additionally, activists explained their subject positions as activists in the diaspora. The activists learnt about their subject positions within existing power relations in Canada and abroad by becoming involved in the movement. Activists and supporters critically interrogated the forces of domination in which Rohingya are implicated; indeed, activists discussed the process of learning more about the 'whole picture'. For instance, one activist who was a part of *I Am Rohingya* asserted:

> I didn't know my parents' past. I told my parents about the play and the history and my parents got interested. They supported me to do it. And then they started telling me the stories, and they supported me. Doing this play was a gift to them. I didn't know my background. I didn't know what my parents suffered to give us such a good life. At that moment, I said I'd raise my voice, and give something to my parents.
>
> (RP32, 2 August 2018, interview in Cowper-Smith 2021)

Another activist similarly noted, 'I started learning about my culture, my people, my parents, and the whole journey. I'm aware now. I know about myself more than I knew before. I felt like I wasn't living my life in the whole picture [before the play and documentary]' (RP39, 13 September 2018, interview in Cowper-Smith 2021). The youth involved in *I Am Rohingya* cultivated their resolve by listening to their parents' experience. Having recognized this growing awareness among the youth of *I Am Rohingya*, one of its directors stated:

> Their identity has changed. They felt disconnected from their identity. I can understand youth not wanting to be associated with their past and heritage. That changed for some of them. Telling their story. Learning about their parents' stories and their heritage. They now say, 'I saw myself as just Canadian and Rohingya-Canadian'.
>
> (RP33, 16 August 2018, interview in Cowper-Smith 2021)

As one research participant expressed, there is a 'real awakening of consciousness in the youth, shared destiny, common spirit' (RP47, 8 November 2018 in Cowper-Smith 2021). Rohingya activists interpret the reality on the ground in Myanmar, and they question what the international community and the Canadian government can do in this respect (Cowper-Smith 2021). In particular, those with lived experiences of the camps, detention or knowing of the violence inflicted on friends and family still living in Bangladesh or Myanmar, brought out this collective awareness. This sense of awareness is how, in one manner, participants developed their subject positions and shared conceptions of the world.

8.2.4. Resolve

With the sudden surge of new commentators and experts—many, not the Rohingya— Rohingya activists in the movement were determined to become the spokespeople of their cause. One activist ardently described how Rohingya voices need to be at the core of the social movement:

> We don't need people's money; we don't need their sentimental-izing. We aren't animals; I'm a human being with dignity and responsibility. It's time to act and show the people that we can represent ourselves. We don't need other people to represent us. We are more than three decades facing the same problem. We are still undocumented. I'm ashamed to say I'm stateless. I can't ignore the fact that I'm stateless.

> (RP69, 10 May 2019, interview in Cowper-Smith 2021)

One Rohingya activist shared his belief that those who have experienced marginalization and migration have a keen sense of what a resolution should entail. He explained his frustration about not being listened to as an authority:

> Rohingya, we can speak for ourselves. We are not considered to be decision-makers. We are the people who are suffering, they [the international community] are not. They are performing their duties, but they shouldn't neglect [us] like this. We have no right to speak. We have our right to express what we want, and they [the international community] should listen. They [the international community] are ignoring us.

> (RP59, 25 January 2018, interview in Cowper-Smith 2021)

An activist involved in *I Am Rohingya* noted, 'The voice of Rohingya children is powerful and global. We can tell the truth. When children are involved, it becomes obvious that these people [Rohingya] have done nothing wrong and don't deserve this suffering' (RP39,

13 September 2018, interview in Cowper-Smith 2021). As stated pithily, one Rohingya activist said, 'Rohingya know how to think why they are persecuted' (RP53, 8 December 2018, interview in Cowper-Smith 2021).

These statements highlight the resolve among activists to self-represent.

In summary, activists engendered responsibility, an in-depth perception of injustice and confidence in their role as spokespeople for the community. Participants created the ethos of the movement around responsibility, awareness and resolve. These collective sentiments formed the knowledge practices of the collective self.

8.3. Political Vision of the Movement: Experiences in Myanmar and Canada

Earlier, I examined how sentiments of responsibility, awareness and resolve are a part of the knowledge practices of collective self. The movement connects people to a common cause which engenders new knowledge regarding the ethos of the movement. The following section analyses the movement's political vision by contextualizing the specific structural obstacles that activists face. Participants identified their experiences and their families' experiences within Myanmar and Bangladesh, and their issues in resettlement while conducting activism. These issues include daily work–life balance and Islamophobia in resettlement and difficulty in creating representative bodies. Despite these obstacles, the movement has developed its vision of raising awareness of the crisis to the Canadian public and reinstating the human rights and citizenship of Rohingya people in Myanmar. I map out these challenges and demonstrate how they have shaped the movement's goals.

8.3.1. Genocide in Myanmar

Several participants discussed their lived experiences of the genocide in Myanmar and the refugee crisis in Bangladesh. A young Rohingya woman activist shared her experiences of the slow loss of legal status in Myanmar. She explained that the Rohingya were seen as less and less human by the Burmese government and society over time. She noted, 'we're not allowed to speak our language, our identity, be our people' (RP75, June 2019, interview in Cowper-Smith 2021). Another Rohingya activist recounted her family and friends' experiences:

> The conditions in Myanmar [are horrible]. There is an issue with the cards. Children are being detained in the police posts; 11–12 years old. Rakhine State is a prison. Women are being killed by medical professionals in the hospital, in Buthidaung. It became closer and closer to my problems. Just a couple of weeks ago, my family member, a female relative was beaten up, and others were beaten up at the hospital. She nearly died at the hospital while giving birth. [The military and government] want to strike fear in the community so that they leave.
>
> (RP75, June 2019, interview in Cowper-Smith 2021)

One Rohingya activist explained how the government stripped his family members of citizenship status and their associated rights:

> …My family came from an educated Rohingya family in Burma. We were sent to university…. My uncle is the registrar in the court, medical doctor, professionals in my family. One of my grandma's brothers was a banker in the national bank. Private and government. After restricting the citizenship of Rohingya, for example, my uncle can't practice medicine the next day, the pension of my grandpa was cut the next day because he wasn't recognized as a citizen anymore…. My mom and dad are in Yangon. My mom had her citizenship stripped. She had full citizenship before 1982. She was somehow able to keep a paper trail out of it. Also, we were not able to, me, and my siblings can't get actual degrees on paper. My brother studied business, my cousin is a medical doctor, but he can't practice because he wasn't able to get his degree conferred [due to lack of proof of citizenship]. If you don't have a degree, you can't get into the workforce. All I had were my transcripts from every year that I was able to show. Four of us siblings were university educated, but without citizenship, the degree wouldn't be conferred.
>
> (RP56, 18 January 2019, interview in Cowper-Smith 2021)

In narrating his relatives' experiences, he explained how their jobs and opportunities for future livelihoods were suddenly eliminated. Their educational credentials were abruptly no longer recognized due to the sharp shift in the law. An additional participant similarly raised the problem that healthcare, education, the right to marriage and freedom of movement were increasingly denied. Finally, another Rohingya activist described how the government took away their rights. She explained that the government justifies its actions by blaming the Rohingya for participating in domestic terrorism. However, the Rohingya rarely participate in violent protests; severe persecution over decades has decimated the community's ability to mount any organized insurgency. She stated:

> We don't use these sticks to go fight the government, but only as self-defense against the rape of our sisters and mothers, yet we are labelled the bad guys. They were raping girls as young as 8, 10, 11, 12, 13, even an 80-year-old woman they wouldn't spare. When we try to protect our families, we are called terrorists. When we try to speak to the world, they deny us the platform.

(RP26, 12 July 2018, interview in Cowper-Smith 2021)

These perspectives and experiences demonstrate the depth of Rohingya activists' insight into Burmese state violence and what it means to be rendered stateless. The process of losing citizenship is tied to many associated rights, such as opportunities for work, school, healthcare, marriage and freedom of movement (Cowper-Smith 2021). As one participant put eloquently, Rohingya activists have profound knowledge surrounding what it means to be persecuted. They recognize structural state violence for what it is. The movement collectively solidifies its vision of repatriation and reinstating citizenship by linking these experiences together.[3] As will be seen later, when discussing their political vision, interview participants identified two other main factors influencing their outlook: resettlement-related constraints, including Islamophobia, and difficulty creating representation/community building.

---

[3] Azeem Ibrahim (this volume, Chapter 13) and Paul Chaney (this volume, Chapter 14) cover the role of the international community and global civil society's views on how to address the Rohingya crisis.

8.3.2. Resettlement and Islamophobia

Rohingya activists explained how resettlement after displacement is beset with difficult choices. One Rohingya activist described the difficulties of her immigration experience, stating:

> With the grace of God and the Canadian government, we were able to move to Canada. But coming to Canada, we were not able to work, so we were on welfare. When we go to welfare, they tell us to work. And when we look for work, we have barriers due to language and lack of education. All we know is seeing someone get killed, getting burned. We don't have education and actual language. The country you're originally from is where you really feel at home. Here, I'm not able to work, I have kids, an elderly mother, and I need my husband's help. If I'm watching the baby, my husband needs to take care of my mother. We are forced to go to school to be able to take care of our home.

(RP26, 12 July 2018, interview in Cowper-Smith 2021)

Several other interview participants described the tension of trying to balance daily survival with activist pursuits. Those who undertake activist work are doing so beyond their other commitments. Additionally, Islamophobia produces fears of retribution in a resettlement context. Activists recognized undercurrents of discriminatory attitudes that dominate global debates on forced migration. One young Rohingya woman activist bluntly stated, 'Some people really care, but most don't. There are other people in Canada who think 'oh they're Muslims, so who cares' (RP39, 13 September 2018, interview in Cowper-Smith 2021). One Muslim activist asserted that activist life in Canada is shaped by paranoia and pessimism. He noted that it can be challenging to gather a group of Muslim supporters in this country to explicitly endorse a cause due to the added vulnerability caused by anti-Muslim and anti-immigration rhetoric. He shared that:

> Somehow, the way that the media works, and the way Muslims are portrayed, they're scared they'll be looked at differently, even though they are doing something completely legitimate. There's a

defensive outlook.... You'll be singled out if you talk about political issues and political activism.

(RP36, 30 August 2018, interview in Cowper-Smith 2021)

These examples illustrate how the movement recognizes that Islamophobia is a disincentive to activism in Canada. As the activists note, putting oneself in the public eye means risking anti-Muslim violence in this country. There are direct consequences for the activists themselves for being outspoken. The pursuit of activism needs to consider the dual structural obstacles of immigrant life coupled with Islamophobia, which affect how the movement approaches its goals in Canada.

8.3.3. Building Representation

Finally, the difficulty of developing representative bodies also weighs heavily on Rohingya activists' conscience and informs the political vision behind Canada's movement. This is an issue in Canada, but also in other countries. These comments were prevalent throughout the interviews. As activists and supporters recount, due to oppression and extreme persecution in Myanmar, Rohingya communities face significant hurdles to forming representative bodies. As a Rohingya activist noted, due to statelessness, lack of education, distrust and disharmony among the community, there is a worldwide leadership crisis. He said, 'The Rohingya became a broken community, with culture, professional standards, etc.' (RP1, 13 May 2018, interview in Cowper-Smith 2021). Another Rohingya activist echoed this sentiment. He noted that:

Rohingya don't have institutions.... So, in the future, what will these people be? Rohingya are designed to rot. Designed to fail. So, we are trying to make structures ... No one is thinking of durable solutions.... This nation needs a vision, these people need hope. If there's no plan, what will happen after 50 years? We will be lost. I'm trying to reconstruct the broken infrastructure that we have. We are physically stateless. If we don't become digital, we might become digitally stateless. So that the coming generation might have hope, survive rather than on handouts and live in a dignified way. Rebuilding the nation, rebuilding the hope....

(RP59, 25 January 2018, interview in Cowper-Smith 2021)

This activist elaborated on his plans to build institutions to preserve the Rohingya language and culture, while in parallel, underlining the difficulty of developing representative bodies. Two other Rohingya activists discussed how the historical colonial administration and successive military juntas have prevented the community from maintaining and practising their culture by various means. One participant said:

What we learned from the Burmese government, we only learned dictatorship. The mindset of the Rohingya became like our dictators. What our governments taught us is what we know ... No one is seen as constructive-minded ... If we compare with other communities, we are far away to reach our goal. May Allah protect our people by Rahmatullah (his mercy).

(RP1, 13 May 2018, interview in Cowper-Smith 2021)

One Rohingya activist explained that the political vision for the Rohingya community in Canada is different from that in Bangladesh and Myanmar by stating that:

The vision for the Rohingya community in different places will be different based on socio-economic and political barriers they face. While those in Canada are starting to settle down and become self-sufficient, those in Myanmar and Bangladesh are merely trying to survive day-to-day and meet their basic needs.

(RP56, 18 January 2019, interview in Cowper-Smith 2021)

However, he underlines that 'regardless of geography and the types of political punishments that Rohingya face in different parts of the world, a unified vision is to go back/live peacefully in our homeland' (RP56, 18 January 2019, interview in Cowper-Smith 2021). These quotes underline the significant obstacles that result in a lack of representative institutions in the diaspora. The interviewees indicate that there are pockets of leadership worldwide and prominent heads of organizations, but there remains a lack of cohesion and consensus on ways forward. The previous quote indicates that although there are several political visions and no prominent voice, there are at least two points that translate into a shared political vision of the movement: to bring a recognition of the crisis to the Canadian public and in doing so, influence and achieve the reinstatement of rights and citizenship of Rohingya people in Myanmar.

Ultimately, on this point, the movement is in the process of reconciling many perspectives to build institutions. Indeed, these extreme structural obstacles severely impede how the movement can effectively support the cause from abroad. The fragmentation across communities marginalized and persecuted by state forces are realities that the Rohingya face in the diaspora, which undergird the kinds of activism they undertake. Rohingya activists tangibly understand how their history in Myanmar has made it difficult for them to create new representative societies in the diaspora. The division sown deliberately by those who benefit from their division has contributed to forms of wariness and distrust, which follow Rohingya communities into the diaspora. The Rohingya community is keenly aware that disunity is politically advantageous for dominant groups. So, Rohingya groups in Canada are actively endeavouring to reconcile the forces that prevent them from working together through their political vision.

In summary, the participants have constructed an ethos and political vision of the movement. The ethos entails collective feelings of responsibility, awareness and resolve. Furthermore, they describe how in Canada, day-to-day obligations around work and family, issues stemming from Islamophobia and a lack of representative bodies have shaped their views. These issues in resettlement impact the visions of the movement. In appreciation of the international and local context in which they live and work, activists have reflected on these realities and put forward a long-term resolution to the cause; they have been able to build a powerful vision for their community. The creation of the ethos and vision can be interpreted as a part of the knowledge practices of the collective self. The movement has constructed their knowledge practice of collective self, a 'critical collective subject' (Della Porta and Pavan 2017).

8.4. Discussion

In this chapter, I suggest that the development of these practices is a part of the intellectual life of social movements. To reiterate, as Della Porta and Pavan (2017, 305) explain, knowledge practices of collective self are:

> ...particularly concerned with the construction of a critical collective subject, this practice of knowledge-production addresses, simultaneously, the cosmological and the organizational dimensions of a movement while providing the linchpin to the elaboration of its alternative epistemological approach.

Pavan and Felicetti (2019, 3–4) write, 'it is a type of knowledge that gives substance to this cosmology as personal experiences provide evidence of the actuality of collectively envisaged alternatives.' As Eyerman and Jamison (1991, 106) note, 'by spontaneously responding to new social problems, indeed often formulating those problems for society, social movements create spaces for new exploratory intellectual activities to become crystallized.' In other words, knowledge practices of collective self thus sustain the movement by articulating and manifesting the basic reasons behind why the movement exists. By developing the principles and vision forward, social movements are producing new knowledge; this intellectuality is one of the reasons why movements function the way they do.

The Rohingya movement in Canada established a new system of meaning through its ethos and political vision. Throughout this chapter, we saw that the Rohingya social movement's ethos centres around feelings of responsibility, awareness and resolve. And the movement developed a vision. The restoration of citizenship of the Rohingya remaining in Myanmar is critical. Without citizenship, the Rohingya community cannot safely return home nor live with basic human rights. These findings have several implications for enhancing the value of looking at knowledge creation within movements.

First, analysing the collective self-entails tracking how individual experiences and thought processes develop into a new and shared reason for coming together. The knowledge practices of collective self are about the spirit, principles and goals developed by and within the movement. As Della Porta and Pavan (2017, 306) describe, 'participants contribute to defining the very identity of the movement by bringing knowledge about their own experiences and visions.' Indeed, studying knowledge practices of collective self requires paying attention to how the movement treats self-articulation (Della Porta and Pavan 2017). Personal feelings engendered by participants are conjoined into a larger, collective whole. The process of recognizing oneself as being a part of a systemic process of marginalization is a substantial intellectual leap. Collective mental energy is required, and expended, through sharing experiences and perspectives, to recognize that persecution is structural rather than unintended and individual. The movement developed an understanding of itself, its principles and what it wants to strive for. In this case, the collective feelings of responsibility, awareness and resolve, which inform the ethos, as well as the political vision, are a brand-new type of knowledge. The movement puts forward a new interpretation of the Rohingya's plight and what can be done about it. To convey a community's principles in light of that persecution in a collaborative manner is a significant intellectual breakthrough. Following, to see responsibility, awareness and resolve, and the political vision, as a joint venture is to recognize the importance of the cognitive aspects of a movement. The originality of this knowledge cannot be overstated.

Second, the practices are a bridge between thought and action. The movement grew its ethos and political vision through being involved in advocacy work. There cannot be knowledge practices about the collective self without intention and action. Constant and continued interaction between the activists' selves, their supporters and their challengers feed into the knowledge practices of collective self. Again, these encounters demonstrate that this type of knowledge is not *a priori*; the movement forges knowledge practices of the collective self. This building of collective self, over time, provided the activists with a more nuanced view of themselves and the structural obstacles in Myanmar and elsewhere. This type of knowledge practice thus results from the strenuous effort of bridging and interpreting the Rohingya's experience with and understanding of the geopolitical realities in Bangladesh and Myanmar and the reality of activists' locally situated context in Canada. Indeed, Eyerman and Jamison (1991, 57) see continuous 'series of social encounters' as foundational to constructing movement knowledge. In other words, knowledge practices of collective self are a type of praxis. By being involved in the action, new understandings and interpretations emerge and are used to further the movement.

8.5. Revitalizing the Study of Knowledge Practices in Social Movement Literature

As written elsewhere in this volume, the Rohingya have suffered unimaginable persecution. From the discussion on 'bare life' in Chapter 3 (this volume) by Sayema Khatun to the treatment of statelessness in India in Chapter 9 (this volume) by Parvin Sultana, we recognize the plight of the Rohingya community in Myanmar, Bangladesh and other countries worldwide. To turn attention to the agency and resistance that the diaspora is mounting, in this chapter, I argued that a fundamental feature of the Rohingya social movement in Canada is its brainpower. To be a part of a movement is to create. In this case, it is the creation of a philosophy or spirit and a list of goals. The chapter described how the movement has built knowledge practices around collective self or the ontological purpose of coming together. By building a collective view of responsibility, awareness and resolve, the movement has packaged these sentiments into the ethos. Also, their interpretations of Myanmar's conditions and their experience in the Canadian contexts are bundled into the political vision of the movement. The movement wants to bring recognition of the crisis to the Canadian public, and in doing so, to reinstate the human rights and citizenship of the Rohingya people in Myanmar. The analysis of the knowledge practices reveals that a fundamental feature of movements is its ability to bring newfound knowledge to a topic—at the time—a topic that was not discussed at length or in depth in this country at the height of the crisis. Further recognition of knowledge practices in academia will go a long way in better understanding social movements.

References

Arribas, L. A. 2018. 'Knowledge Co-production with Social Movement Networks. Redefining Grassroots Politics, Rethinking Research.' *Social Movement Studies* 17, no. 4: 451–463.

Aung, K. 2017. 'The Colonial Roots of Myanmar's Rage against the Rohingya.' The Huffington Post, 19 December.

Brinham, N. 2012. 'The Conveniently Forgotten Human Rights of the Rohingya.' *Forced Migration Review* 41: 40–41.

Casas-Cortes, M., M. Osterweil, and D. Powell. 2008. 'Blurring Boundaries: Recognizing Knowledge-Practices in the Study of Social Movements.' *Anthropological Quarterly* 81, no. 1: 17–58.

Cheesman, N. 2017. 'How in Myanmar "National Races" Came to Surpass Citizenship and Exclude Rohingya.' *Journal of Contemporary Asia* 47, no. 3: 461–483. https://doi.org/10.1080/00472336.2017.1297476

Chesters, G. 2012. 'Social Movements and the Ethics of Knowledge Production.' *Social Movement Studies* 11, no. 2: 145–160.

Choudry, A., and D. Kapoor. 2010. *Learning from the Ground Up: Global Perspectives on Social Movements and Knowledge Production.* New York, NY: Palgrave Macmillan.

Cowper-Smith, Y. 2021. 'Social Movements That "Think": Knowledge-Practices of the Rohingya Canadian Social Movement.' Unpublished PhD thesis, Department of Political Science, University of Guelph, Guelph.

Cox, L. 2014. 'Movements Making Knowledge: A New Wave of Inspiration for Sociology?' *Sociology* 48, no. 5: 954–971.

Della Porta, D., and E. Pavan. 2017. 'Repertoires of Knowledge Practices: Social Movements in Times of Crisis.' *Qualitative Research in Organizations and Management: An International Journal* 12, no. 4: 297–314.

Eyerman, R., and A. Jamison. 1991. *Social Movements: A Cognitive Approach.* University Park, PA: Pennsylvania State University Press.

Hosseini, H. 2011. 'Activist Knowledge: Interrogating the Ideational Landscape of Social Movements.' *The International Journal of Interdisciplinary Social Sciences* 5: 339–357.

Huang, R. 2013. 'Re-thinking Myanmar's Political Regime: Military Rule in Myanmar and Implications for Current Reforms.' *Contemporary Politics* 19, no. 3: 247–261.

Huang, R. 2016. 'Myanmar's Way to Democracy and the Limits of the 2015 Elections.' *Asian Journal of Political Science* 25, no. 1: 25–44.

Human Rights Watch. 2020. '"An Open Prison without End" Myanmar's Mass Detention of Rohingya in Rakhine State.' Available at: https://www.hrw.org/report/2020/10/08/open-prison-without-end/myanmars-mass-detention-rohingya-rakhine-state (accessed on 11 August 2021).

Ninh, K., and M. Arnold. 2016. 'Decentralization in Myanmar: A Nascent and Evolving Process.' *Journal of Southeast Asian Economies* 33, no. 2: 224–225.

Nyein, N. 2019, 1 February. 'Timeline: 70 Years of Ethnic Armed Resistance Movements in Myanmar.' *Irrawaddy.*

Pavan, E., and A. Felicetti. 2019. 'Digital Media and Knowledge Production within Social Movements: Insights from the Transition Movement in Italy.' *Social Media + Society* 5, no. 4: 1–12.

Uddin, N. 2020. *The Rohingya: An Ethnography of 'Subhuman' Life.* Oxford: Oxford University Press.

UNHCR. 2007. 'Canada Is First Country to Resettle Rohingya Refugees from Bangladesh.' Available at http://www.unhcr.org/4628d83d4.html (accessed on 19 August 2020).

———. 2020. 'Rohingya Emergency.' Available at https://www.unhcr.org/rohingya-emergency.html (accessed on 19 August 2020).

Ware, A., and C. Laoutides. 2018. *Myanmar's 'Rohingya' Conflict.* Oxford: Oxford University Press.

Zarni, M., and A. Cowley. 2014. 'The Slow-burning Genocide of Myanmar's Rohingya.' *Pacific Rim Law & Policy Journal* 23, no. 3: 681–752.

CHAPTER 9

The Rohingya Crisis
Recent Bureaucratic Restructuring and Ethnic Politics in Myanmar
Syeda Naushin Parnini

9.1. Introduction

The Rohingya as a minority group in Myanmar are concentrated in the three townships of North Rakhine State, that is, Maungdaw, Buthidaung and Rathedaung. The population of the Rohingya, an ethnic minority in Rakhine State, has been estimated to be between 1 and 1.5 million. The existence of Rohingya in Myanmar can be traced back to the 15th century when Muslims had migrated to the Arakan Kingdom known today as the *Rakhine State* (Gamez 2017, 17). The Rohingya have thus lived in Northern Rakhine for centuries, and historically they have been identified as a distinct ethnic group with their own language and culture having a long-standing connection with Rakhine State (Human Rights Council 2016, 2).

The Rohingya have long historic ties with Rakhine State, as they claim their ancestors have stayed in this region for generations. The bone of contention is that the Rohingya are sometimes considered by the Myanmar government as illegal migrants from neighbouring countries called 'Bengali'; hence, the government of Myanmar refuses to recognize the Rohingya as one of the ethnic groups of that country. Ullah (2016, 289) argues that the Rohingya are deliberately excluded from being citizens of Myanmar to build a mono-religious nation, and as a result of being deprived of citizenship, the Rohingya are subject to state-sponsored violence. Frequent systematic state-supported persecution of the Rohingya has resulted in destruction of property and huge number of deaths. The Rohingya have been branded the most persecuted minority group in the world. Till date, the Rohingya have been deracinated from their homeland with many leaving Myanmar for taking refuge in Bangladesh and other countries; therefore, they have become scattered around the world. The Rohingya have been rendered stateless by the Myanmar government through various policies and bureaucratic procedures. Moreover, Myanmar launched various discriminatory policies against minority groups like the Rohingya focusing on their distinct Muslim identity, creed and race. These direct discriminatory laws always got them excluded from national developmental policies and hence the region (Rakhine) remains the least developed area. Therefore, the Rohingya are subject to acute poverty.

Historically, before 1900, the local ethnic groups in Burma started to suffer due to dominance and superiority of the British and the Indians. Hence, nationalism was infused with bureaucratic politics which were used against these groups and the Rohingya were also branded as Indians as their distinction was said to be blurred due to intermarriages with Indians in Arakan. University groups such as Young Men's Buddhist Association (YMBA, 1917) and the Do Ba Ma Asiayone ('Our Burman Association', 1930) stirred up national-ist sentiments (Marzilo 2015, 34), which had marked the beginning of Rohingyan ordeal before the attainment of independence. The situation worsened as the World War II precipitated; therefore, the Rohingya were persecuted (numbering more than 100,000 victims) and the survivors sought refuge in the territory of Bangladesh, which was under the British rule. This led to a war between two factions (Marzilo 2015, 34); on the one hand, there were the Japanese troops, together with the members of the BNA (Burmese National Army) and the Maghs; on the other hand, the Rohingya had no chance than joining forces with the British. This solidified the hatred towards the Rohingya, as they were known to have aided Burma's enemy during the British colonial era. Thus, the hatred and grudge towards the Rohingya were carried forward into independent Myanmar; however, it was the military rule that reinforced it, because initially, at independence, the civilian government sought national unity and inclusion of everyone into the society. Had all successive governments followed a positive approach towards unity and reconciliation, Myanmar might have had a different outcome regarding Rohingya issues, but the current situation is a result perpetrated by military rule and political ideologies towards the minority groups like Rohingya.

At independence, the Rohingya enjoyed full rights as they could be elected to political office, and they could take up any form of employment. The Rohingya had been recognized to be both as citizens and as an ethnic group by three successive governments—Sao Shew Thaik regime (1948–1952), Ba U regime (1952–1957) and Win Maung regime (1957–1962)—during the post-independence period of Myanmar (Zarni and Cowley 2014). This indicated that Aung San, the leader of the liberation movement, was assassinated by rivals a year before independence under the leadership of U Saw, but independence was achieved in 1948 under U Nu. U Nu became the first elected Prime Minister of Burma. In his speech on national radio in 1954, he announced that people living in Arakan 'were their brethren' and insisted that the Rohingya were part of the independent country along with other ethnic groups in Burma (Ullah 2017). Thus, the first Prime Minister of Burma had a democratic and human rights perspective which placed equality of all men at core and he wanted to build one nation without divisions or discrimination.

U Nu lost control of the state as domestic problems such as ethnic issues, insurgency, corruption, mismanagement ravaged the country, and most importantly, he failed to unite the fragile state. Thus, due to various socio-economic and political problems discontentment grew which led to the 1962 military coup under General Ne Win who overthrew the civilian government, and this marked the end of constitutional democracy in Myanmar (Barany 2016). Since then,

Myanmar had been under military rule for decades which shaped the political system and nature of control in the country. When the military replaced the civilian government it also replaced people with members of its own organization in strategic positions, eventually democracy was dismantled. Afterwards, the military clearly saw itself as being the most effective governor and protector of the state having historically evolved from its earlier role resisting colonial and Japanese forces to become active builders of the Myanmar state. The military has clung to power for so long and has largely remained in control. The beginning of military rule changed everything as the Rohingya were derecognized as citizens and hence denied the legal status and other national benefits which they had enjoyed prior to the military rule in 1962. In 1982, a new Citizenship Law was passed effectively rendering the Rohingya stateless. After the promulgation of the Citizenship Law, each Rohingya needed to show proof that they had lived in Myanmar before 1948, such paperwork was unavailable to the Rohingya since they were denied of these since independence. Therefore, the Rohingya have been made stateless through the tools of a sovereign state such as census and elections (Frewer 2015). The 'Burmese Way to Socialism' led to severe economic doldrums, which forced Ne Win to resign in 1988. However, the military cracked down and contained pro-democracy demonstrations in August 1988 killing several thousand protesters.

9.2. Conceptual Framework: Contractualism

The research for this chapter/study is premised on contractualism propounded by T. M. Scanlon. Contractualism is a theoretical perspective based on morals and ethical principles that can be used in societies to limit atrocities and misdeeds through subscribing to values that no reasonable person can object. These rules and principles are anticipated to have been set and mutually agreed upon by all members of the society. Thus, Russell (2016) said, 'we are required to be moral on the basis of the justifiability of our actions, and the relationship of "mutual recognition" that all inherently seek to stand in along with others.' As an entity in international relations, Myanmar is a signatory to various international statutes on International Bill of Human

Rights, which include Protection from Torture, Ill Treatment and Disappearance, Prevention of Discrimination on the Basis of Race, Religion, or Belief and Protection of Minorities, which must be adhered by Myanmar as these are all international legal obligations to follow and honour. Thus, genocidal tendencies and violation of human rights against the Rohingya have amounted to a violation of the aforementioned agreements and unjustifiable on any ground. Cohen in Estlund (2003) plausibly counters that 'we cannot expect outcomes that advance the common good unless people are looking for them.' Thus, to achieve common good in society, the initiative starts with collective will of the people to realize that virtue; lack of it can result to the hobessian state of nature, a condition which has brought minority groups to suffer a lot like the case of the Rohingya in Myanmar. In this regard, Stanford University elaborates that 'wrongness consists in unjustifiability: wrongness *is* the property of being unjustifiable.' Hence, the activities of the government to cover up the truth of what happened and blocking off international journalists and observers prove the unjustifiability of the actions of the government of Myanmar. Suikkanen (2007, 8) articulates,

> The main question to which Scanlon wants contractualism to provide an answer is when we claim that an action is wrong, what kind of judgment are we making (WWO1)? Or, in other words, how should we characterise the subject matter of judgments about right and wrong?

Thus, contractualism is not premised on individual beliefs, but the procedure on how we characterize an act as wrong or right is the essence of Scanlon's moral theory. Premising this study on such a theory vividly excavates the sanctity of life and the moral thinking and ideological paradigms that influenced the creation of humanitarian law. Carlson (2008, 246) poses a very good question on how to judge a question as right or wrong, 'Should We Kill to Avoid Headaches?' Russel (2016, 39) concludes that 'fairly clear' that 'life for headaches' is fundamentally unconvincing, and therefore unjustifiable. Thus, even if someone breaches the law, contractualism provides an alternative way of explaining the limits of punishment and its justifiability (Scanlon 2008a, 2). Thus, no matter what the allegations being levelled against the Rohingya, Myanmar government's moral limits to punishments should be taken into consideration.

However, due to the nature of subjectivity on the issue of moral values it is difficult for one to come to an objective conclusion of what is wrong. Scanlon fails to validate on what constitute practical reasons and from what dimension can we judge that this is practical reason and vice versa. Even though these are some limitations and critiques that can be levelled against the use of contractualism, there is no one theory we can juxtapose with contractualist ideology which justifies or supports Myanmar government's behaviour on the Rohingyan atrocities which in itself validates the moral dimension of the use of contractualism.

To clarify the issue of practical reasons, Suikkanen J. (2007) notes that the considerations about practical reasons are supposed to belong to an ordinary ontological class. What is significant about reasons is that considerations are reasons but rather what it is for these things to have the status of being reason. Scanlon (2008a, 2) points out that many people believe that in war it can be permissible to bomb a military target even though this will cause the deaths of some non-combatants living nearby, but it would not be permissible to bomb the same number of non-combatants in order to hasten the end of the war by demoralizing the population. Thus, the law of double effect does not give room or any justification whatsoever to open live ammunition deliberately targeting civilian population. '*Moral reaction responsibility* is relevant when we ask certain positive or negative moral reactions to a person –such as blame, resentment, praise, or gratitude – are appropriate' (Stanford University 2018). Thus, indiscriminate killing of innocent people which resulted in forced migration from Rakhine to Bangladesh and various other countries is a breach of international law, and such actions of the Myanmar government cannot be justified under any circumstances.

9.3. Methodology

This study made use of a qualitative methodology in soliciting relevant data. In essence since this research is qualitative in nature, it is therefore more concerned about understanding, explaining and clarifying situations, attitudes, beliefs, perceptions and experiences of minority groups in Myanmar focusing primarily on the Rohingya. To excavate important issues, the research made use of documentary analysis. Gibson and Brown (2009, 66) assert that 'documentary research refers to the process of using documents as a means of social investigation and involves exploring the records that individuals and organizations produce.' Thus data are collected from various sources such as from individuals, governments and organizations to limit the level of biasness; hence, measures were taken to ensure validity and reliability of the results. Neuman (2006) asserts that there are five research paradigms that underlie social science research, namely positivist social science (PSS), interpretive social science (ISS), critical social science (CSS), feminism and postmodernism. This research is interpretivist in nature which is strongly inclined to idealism and hence knits neatly with the theoretical underpinnings in this study. Hence, through a detailed analysis of various sources, meaning was created which helped to situate this research and cover an existing knowledge gap. This research is qualitative in nature and is more concerned with describing and interpreting phenomenon in its social setting.

9.4. Bureaucratization in Myanmar and the Rohingya Problem

From 1990, incitement and hatred towards the Rohingya were spearheaded by extremist groups; violence, torture, rape and an array of atrocities have continued with the most recent major outbreak of violent attacks on the Rohingya occurring in June and in October 2012 which led to hundreds of cases of injury and death, the destruction of property and the displacement of about 140,000 people. Human Rights Council (2016) in 2017 stated that this kind of atrocities would threaten to push the Rohingya out of the country with no possibility of return. Systematic use of violence against the Rohingya did not start recently, but this could be traced back to 1948 with the independence of Burma from the British rule; this was escalated at a massive scale in 1978, 1984 and 2012 and later in 2017. After decades of military control, democratic reforms had started in 2011.

The reforms culminated in historic elections on 8 November 2015, and the transfer of power to a civilian government in 2016. Human Rights Council (2016) posited that in April 2016, State Counsellor Aung San Suu Kyi had reiterated the importance of national reconciliation and the rule of law for all citizens. Steps taken by Aung San Suu Kyi's government included the establishment of a Ministry of Ethnic Affairs and the transformation of the Myanmar Peace Centre into the National Reconciliation and Peace Centre. However, this peace process had involved only those groups defined as indigenous peoples under the terms of the controversial, military-inspired 1982 Citizenship Act. The minority groups such as Kachin, Karen, Chin, Shan had been included into the peace process, but the Rohingya were excluded, which seemed to be contrary to the assertion by the democratically elected government of Myanmar as it had stated that the situation in Rakhine State is one of its highest priorities. Thus, despite the political restructuring and giant steps taken by the Aung San Suu Kyi's government towards democratization in Myanmar (post-2010 period), systematic alienation of the Rohingya from political processes had rendered realization of their minority rights murky. Bureau pathologies coupled with resentment towards minority groups (Rohingya) raised questions on the prospects of the democratization process. However, the military seized control again of the state through military coup in February 2021 following a general election which Aung San Suu Kyi's NLD party had won by a landslide. The military had backed the opposition, who were demanding a rerun of the vote, claiming widespread fraud. The coup took place as a new session of parliament was set to open and after taking over the military rulers declared a year-long state of emergency.[1] Therefore, the situation of the Rohingya has become more vulnerable as military government came back to power again in Myanmar.

The bureaucracy has contributed and aggravated Rohingya's misery and sufferings immensely, a matter warranting this research. A lot of scholarly work tends to concentrate more on the physical

---

[1] https://www.bbc.com/news/world-asia-55902070, visited 28 April 2021.

torment and brutality brought forth by the military, the police and the Buddhist community against the Rohingya, focusing more on the physical violence, rape, torture and other atrocities. But the complications of their day-to-day living emanate from discriminatory bureaucratic limitations and procedures, which make life unbearable in peaceful times which have not been effectively documented. The existing citizenship rules, derived from the 1982 law as discussed earlier, have largely fostered the concept of citizenship based on ethnic grounds, which is highly subjective and in contradiction to international law practices particularly to Article 15 of the Universal Declaration of Human Rights (UDHR).

The Citizenship Law in Myanmar put heavy emphasis on ethnicity which has led minority groups like the Rohingya to call it discriminatory. It has also been enforced haphazardly and selectively, with multiple layers of bureaucracy and endemic corruption adding to the confusion (Wallace 2016). The citizenship process as the core mechanism of Myanmar's bureaucracy has been in shambles at least since the military took power in 1962 (Ronan Lee, in Wallace 2016). Thus, the process of citizenship is shrouded in controversy as such perils have arisen from the bureaucratic processes in an era where human rights have become an important scholarly concept. This issue has become too vital to ignore. Dahm (2018) posits that decades of military rule have also left a legacy of risk aversion. As reflected in the saying there is no bad news for the king because the government officials are more concerned about being wrong by angering superiors and alienating other agencies than being excited to develop better operating models or piloting new initiatives. This has led to limited bureaucratic flexibility, initiatives and capacity to develop and execute any meaningful reforms towards the Rohingyan issue in the new political dispensation as they too fear victimization. It is an irony that one can easily be persecuted just for being a Rohingya and it happened even during the democratic Myanmar under Suu Kyi. The recent coup and the current military administrative set-up are heavily dominated by military control, producing bureau-pathologies that are militating against the ongoing efforts towards national reconciliation and cooperation with the Rohingya as a minority group in Myanmar.

9.5. Political Restructuring and the Rohingya Crisis

Myanmar's new president Htin Kyaw has set up a large-sounding, good-for-nothing committee, which has failed the Rohingya. The Central Committee for Implementation of Peace and Development in Rakhine State consists of 27 officials, including the members of the Cabinet and representatives of the Rakhine State government chaired by Aung San Suu Kyi herself. But the Rohingya fear that this is merely a bureaucratic device meant to postpone taking any firm decisions, and they also worry that they may not even have any input to the committee. Such fears hold water, because as it stands, the bulk of the Rohingya are at refugee camps in Bangladesh, so the question arises as how is it possible for this committee to deliberate with the said population when no efforts have been taken to consult the Rohingya who are at refugee camps in Bangladesh. The bureaucracy must provide the backbone for any transformation; however, all processes are designed in a precise, deliberate way to ensure that staff rely only on instructions coming from the top to execute tasks. These underlying rules reinforce the power of the Tatmadaw and have a crippling effect on reform efforts (Dahm 2018). Such constraints act as a deliberate mechanism to limit the effectiveness of the bureaucracy in general, since it relies on instructions from the army, acts as an extension of the army and hence an instrument to further the systematic alienation of the Rohingya. The new political dispensation itself therefore is still crippled by military domination in realizing its mandate, that is, to holistically realize democracy and inclusion of all minority groups into one unified Myanmar society. Lowenstein (2015) posits that 'Throughout 2011 and 2012, the government continued to restrict Rohingyas' travel by requiring them to obtain permission to travel outside of their home villages.' The movements of Rohingya are heavily constrained, they have to apply for bureaucratic approval to travel outside and within the Rakhine State, worse still, '"denial" [limited] access to health care facilities' is also a major problem (Green, MacManus, and Venning 2015), and they need bureaucratic clearance for hospital transfer, which might take longer and inappropriate in cases of emergency. After enacting citizenship law in 1982, a strong restriction was imposed on the movement of Rohingya people and they need authority's permission before travelling even within Rakhine state. Thus, Rohingya movements are not only restricted when one wants to go beyond the Rakhine State but within Rakhine itself (from one township to another).

9.6. Impact of Discriminatory Laws on Myanmar Rohingya

The Rohingya in Rakhine region must first obtain permission in order to travel between townships or outside of the state. This process seems notoriously bureaucratic as the approval is rarely given in practice and this comes with a price that few Rohingya can readily afford (Lowenstein 2015). The Rohingya have to register their arrival with authorities of the new township. These are archaic discriminatory laws that were used by apartheid regimes during colonial times, but this discriminatory law is still being applied in the 21st century against the Rohingya in Myanmar. Failure to notify immigration authorities is considered a crime. The Border Region Immigration Control Headquarters and the Township Peace and Development Council of Maungdaw issued population control policies in 1993 and 2005, respectively, which state that the Rohingya is reproducing faster than the 'international standards' of population increase. Moreover, the Myanmar governmental organogram entrenches the bureaucratic system, which is very much active in Rakhine to strictly control the Rohingya.

The administrative authorities in Rakhine State issued a policy document in 2008 titled 'Population Control Activities' clearly stating how law enforcement officials in Rakhine State should literally force people to 'use pills, injections and condoms for birth control at every [NaSaKa] regional clinic, township hospitals, and their own regional hospitals' (Lowenstein 2015). Hence, localized bureaucratic systems are used to monitor, control and implement repressive laws and systems against the Rohingya. In this case forcing discriminatory birth control systems are implemented against only the Rohingya, which seems to be against sexual and reproductive rights. Besides lack of political will, this is to prove the impact of bureaucracy on constraining the change which the new democratic government tries to bring, (Reed 2017) at the central and state government levels (Reed 2017). However, Aung San Suu Kyi was saddled with a legacy of bureaucrats who served the old regime, the pace of economic reform has suffered because the executive leadership seems weak and the bureaucracy is loyal to the former military government. This bureaucracy is corrupt, reckless and also aligned to the military, which still holds a lot of power in the state apparatus. To reflect how corrupt the bureaucracy is, Lowenstein (2015) states that the Rohingya can informally obtain permission to travel to Yangon by transferring payment of up to 1.5 million Kyats (US$1,167), an impossibly high sum for average Rohingya to a 'middleman' who in turn pays to authorities. The essence of paying through an agent is to hide the identity of the bureaucrats being involved in these rent-seeking activities just to sanction travels out of Rakhine for a short period. Wallace (2016) states that some people reported paying bribes of up to 500,000 Kyat (around US$390) for initiating citizenship processes.

9.7. Government in Myanmar and the Rohingya

The government of Myanmar has carried out various processes such as citizenship verification and validation and census, but all these programmes have negatively affected the Rohingya. The process of citizenship validation stripped the Rohingya of their identity cards from those who had acquired them after independence and Hay (2015) believes that the last census in Myanmar 'was an orderly affair, [and that] it was also a subtly weaponized bureaucratic tool'. Hay (2015) has added that the last census also allowed the government to perpetuate their relentless campaign to clean the nation by excluding ethnic Muslim minority like the Rohingya without publicly lifting a gun.

Thus, all the bureaucratic processes in Myanmar have a single aim, which is to get rid of the Rohingya from the Myanmar state and history by deliberately alienating them from national activities. This systematic process of alienation therefore relies on the use of soft power, which does not call for violence but that has an equal impact with primitive means on ethnic groups who were rendered unwanted. The fundamental feature of modern democratic state is cultural pluralism and hence the issues of ethnicity and identity have become important phenomena in modern state system. Thus, the instability in Myanmar reflects an imbalance in interest aggregation and historiographical trajectories on the nature of the problems since the issues have been taking place for years. The confrontation in Myanmar also reinforced this fragile state's incomplete democratic transition under Aung San Suu Kyi's regime, which left the military with three key ministries, which constitute a quarter of seats in parliament having control over the army and police (Reed 2017).

Many democrats all over the world had expressed disappointment with Aung San Suu Kyi for failure to ease the plight of the Rohingya despite her reputation as a fighter for human rights. However, despite some of these critiques labelled against Aung San Suu Ky's administration she deserved credit for strides taken so far to democratize Myanmar, though her handling of the Rohingyan crisis somewhat reflected her limitations and her fear of the military administration. As we know the military seized control of the state in Myanmar again through a coup d'état in February 2021 following a general election which Aung San Suu Kyi's NLD party won by a landslide. Therefore, the situation of the Rohingya has been getting worse as the military government is always harsh against them. The basic logic from the foregoing analysis is that since there has been systematic sidelining of minority groups, the people in power and in control of the bureaucracy are the Buddhist majority, most of whom fuel hatred and resentment towards the Muslim minority like Rohingya.

The Rohingya do not have any representation in political circles and hence the bureaucracy at the directive of the government is contributing to repression and degradation of the dignity of the Rohingya. In addition to a high level of cooperation between the military and state bureaucracy, the participation and complicity of the majority of the local population is a necessary prerequisite for genocide (Green et al. 2015, 22). Though a lot of research has been documented on the Rohingyan ordeal, there is only limited academic, peer-reviewed writing on the bureaucratic system and its technicalities used as tools to propagate the systematic alienation of minority groups like Rohingya in Myanmar. Hence, this research seeks to contribute to the distant voices on discriminatory bureaucratic tendencies in Myanmar.

There is basic literature on Rohingyian crisis by various organiza-tions, individuals and academic institutes. Amnesty International (2018) and Green et al. (2015) for instance focused on the violence against the Rohingya and the participation of local population. Unlike Amnesty International (2018), Green et al. (2015) traces the develop-ment of the problem and how the Myanmar state has effectively plot-ted and implemented policies to completely remove the Rohingya from the state, which is an effort started with the withdrawal of citizenship until the violence of 2012 and 2017. Marzoli (2015) concentrates on the role of the international community in protecting the Rohingyan human rights. Report of the Prime Minister's Special Envoy has high-lighted the situation on the Rohingyan humanitarian crisis in detail and also focused on the pragmatic ways of dealing with the situation after the 2017 violence. Nick Cheesman (2015) discussed Burma's 1982 Citizenship Law and its effect on those identifying Rohingya as the worst victim of human rights violation in Myanmar. But none of these sources have effectively analysed how acts emanating from soft power, mainly through bureaucratic initiatives, have contributed to effective alienation and inhuman treatment of the Rohingya.

9.8. Research Findings and Recommendations

In the case of Gamez (2017), there is a particular focus on how human rights commission of the ASEAN Intergovernmental Organization (regional organization) can protect rights of the Rohingya. Thus, this chapter has contributed immensely to the research work about Rohingya as it is centred on bureaucratic politics that has not yet been effectively examined. Though Dahm (2018) has discussed criti-cal issues on bureaucratic issues in Myanmar, he has done this in a generalized manner of bureaucratic functions. Yet, this chapter has gone an extra mile to trace how the bureaucratic system is actually impacting the political restructuring and national healing to facilitate reconciliation process aimed to unite and assimilate all the minority groups with the rest of Myanmar's majority groups as a nation. The Rohingya have been branded the most persecuted minority group in the world; yet no military intervention has ever been carried out to save them from the scourge of state-perpetrated violence.

Despite various waves of violence against the Rohingya in the past decades no interventionism has ever been carried out. States have only denounced the acts of violence and tried to help the survivors who are scattered around the world. Selective application of rules and procedures within the United Nations (UN) has largely remained a major barrier in the realization of global peace and security. States tend to react only in areas where their national interests are embedded and little is done where economic benefits tend to be low regardless of the level of sufferings for which the Rohingya's lives are still at stake. The double standards within international relations discourse are a cause of concern and has rendered the UN weak and ineffective. As threats are constantly evolving, there is a need to create a government of governments with full political power with its own separate arm to provide cheques and balances. Separation of power (SOP) should not be restrained by any archaic principles such as the principle of sovereignty. This would ensure compliance of international law as there would be legal authority to police abidance. Thus, the way state's policies are created and implemented should be in line with global standards and this would help avert manipulation of administrative functions by politicians who seek to achieve their unethical politics of racialism and ethnicity which has proved not only to be inhuman and degrading but overall destructive in nature.

9.9. Conclusion

This chapter concludes that there is a need to improve the systems of supranational or global governance and scrap away principles such as that of sovereignty to some extent in some cases which has tended to be the chief principle used by repressive regimes to justify their activities and shy away from international intervention. In some instances, as the one under discussion, thousands have perished while the UN pays lip service to human rights violations. This research is motivated by giving voice to the voiceless; in which case it is not only the Rohingya, but it uses the Rohingya as a classic case of persecution of civilians by their governments. This process will continue unabated as authoritarian regimes seek to cling to power indefinitely and do away with opponents, until drastic measures are taken and unless perpetrators of such acts are severely punished. The Rohingya crisis could be seen as an example for others and unless drastic measures are taken, such atrocities and human rights violations would continue to affect generations globally. The Rohingyian ordeal presents a long-term unpunished international crime and there are a lot of lessons to be learnt from it to avoid repetition of such activities in the world, but this is only possible if right resolutions and amendments are done and implemented at supranational level in some cases, creating a global authority with responsive government of governments along with full political power to regulate and control state practices domestically and internationally in a standardized and fair manner using a global constitution.

References

Amnesty International. 2018. 'Remaking Rakhine State.' Available at https://www.amnesty.org.au/wpcontent/uploads/2018/.../Remaking-Rakhine-State.pdf (accessed on 27 April 2018).

Barany, Zoltan. 2016. 'Armed Forces and Democratization in Myanmar: Why the U.S. Military Should Engage the Tatmadaw.' Available at https://www.csis.org/analysis/armedforces-and-democratization-myanmar-why-us-military-should-engage-tatmadaw (accessed on 11 August 2021).

Carlson, Eric. 2008. 'Aggregating Harms: Should We Kill to Avoid Headaches?' *Theoria* 66, no. 3: 246–255.

Cheesman, Nick. 2015. 'Opposing the Rule of Law.' Available at https://books.google.co.za/books?isbn=1107083184 (accessed on 19 July 2020).

Dahm, H. 2018. 'Who says Myanmar's bureaucracy can't change?' Frontier Myanmar.

Estlund, David. 2003. 'The Democracy/Contractualism Analogy.' Available at https://www.brown.edu/academics/philosophy/sites/brown.edu.academics.philosophy/file s/uploads/DemocracyContractualismAnalogy.pdf (accessed on 11 August 2021).

Frewer, Tim. 2015. 'A Love of Sovereignty: Borders, Bureaucracy and the Rohingya Crisis—Analysis.' Available at https://www.eurasiareview.com/22122015-a-love-of-sovereignty-borders-bureaucracy-and-the-rohingya-crisis-analysis/ (accessed on 11 August 2021).

Gamez, Kimberly Ramos. 2017. 'Examining the ASEAN Intergovernmental Commission on Human Rights (AICHR): The Case Study of the Rohingya Crisis.' Available at arno.uvt.nl/show.cgi?fid=142893. (accessed on 19 April 2020).

Gibson, William J., and Andrew Brown. 2009. *Working with Qualitative Data.* London: SAGE Publications.

Green, Penny, T. MacManus, and A. D. L. C. Venning. 2015. 'Count Down to Annihilation Genocide in Myanmar'. Available at https://qmro.qmul.ac.uk/xmlui/handle/123456789/25375 (accessed on 13 June 2020).

Hay, Mark. 2015. 'An Unlikely Bureaucratic Tool for Ethnic Cleansing.' Available at http://www.rohingyablogger.com/2015/03/an-unlikely-bureaucratic-tool-for.html (accessed on 27 April 2020).

Human Rights Council. 2016. 'Situation of Human Rights of Rohingya Muslims and Other Minorities in Myanmar.' Report of the United Nations High Commissioner for Human Rights. Available at http://www.globalr2p.org/media/files/hchr-reportrohingya.pdf (accessed on 3 February 2020).

Lowenstein Allard, K. 2015. *Persecution of the Rohingya Muslims: Is Genocide Occurring in Myanmar's Rakhine State? A Legal Analysis*. New Haven, CT: Yale *Law* School.

Marzoli, Riccardo. 2015. 'The Protection of Human Rights of Rohingya in Myanmar: The Role of the International Community.' Available at https://tesi.luiss.it/14877/7/marzoli-riccardo-sintesi-2015.pdf (accessed on 12 June 2020).

Neuman, W. Lawrance. 2006. *Social Research Methods: Qualitative and Quantitative Approaches*. 4th ed. Boston, MA: Allyn and Bacon.

Reed, John. 2017. 'Myanmar's New Regime Flounders Over Rohingya Crisis'. Available at: https://www.ft.com/content/36542620-a2ad-11e7-b797-b61809486fe2. [accessed on 27April 2020].

Russell, Bruno Reginald. 2016. 'Contractualism, Consequentialism and the Moral Landscape: A New Pro-contractualist Picture of Ethical Theory.' Available at https://www.researchgate.net/publication/313946817 (accessed on 21 September 2020).

Suikkanen, J. 2007. 'Ethics of Justification a Defence of Contractualism.' Available at https://helda.helsinki.fi/bitstream/handle/10138/21756/ethicsof.pdf?sequence=2 (accessed on 27 April 2018).

Ullah, A. K. M. Ahsan. 2016. 'Rohingya Crisis in Myanmar: Seeking Justice for the "Stateless."' *Journal of Contemporary Criminal Justice* 32, no. 3: 285–301.

———. 2017. 'Rohingya Migration: Is It a Function of Persecution.' Available at http://web.isanet.org/Web/Conferences/HKU2017-s/Archive/dd088865-65b9-4133-8f49-525700574b98.pdf (accessed on 11 August 2021).

Wallace, Julia. 2016. 'Bribes and Bureaucracy: Myanmar's Chaotic Citizenship System.' Available at https://www.irinnews.org/feature/2016/10/31/bribes-and-bureaucracymyanmar%E2%80%99s-chaotic-citizenship system (accessed on 27 April 2020).

World Atlas. 2018. 'Religious Beliefs in Myanmar (Burma).' Available at https://www.worldatlas.com/articles/religious-beliefs-in-myanmar-burma.html (accessed on 27 April 2020).

Zarni, Maung, and Alice Cowley. 2014. 'The Slow-burning Genocide of Myanmar's Rohingya.' *Pacific Rim Law & Policy Journal* 23, no. 3: 683.

CHAPTER 10

Myanmar's Muslim Communities Unbound
The Rohingya and Beyond
Matteo Fumagalli

10.1. Introduction

The Rohingya are a community on the cusp. Deported and cleansed over several waves of violence, they have mostly been removed from the territory they call home. Located at the political, legal and cultural margins of both Myanmar and Bangladesh, this ethnic community of just over two million people[1] belongs to neither and is othered by both states, as its members unsettle the two countries' respective nation-building projects. Over time, and particularly from 1962 onwards,

---

[1] There are no exact figures on this. This is both the result of Myanmar's politics of counting (the political and ideologically driven census taking), whereby Rohingya have repeatedly been refused the possibility to use this ethnonym in the local censuses and the consequence of the many waves of dispersals over the decades. For the use of census during colonial times, see Candier (2019); on more contemporary debates, see Ferguson (2015) and for debates specific to Myanmar Muslims, see Crouch (2014). For an excellent critique of the use of colonial-era sources (census and census categories) for studying the present, see Frydenlund (2020).

the Myanmar[2] authorities have disenfranchised and later persecuted this group, which has for very long been indigenous to the territory of Arakan/Rakhine. It has done so through a combined discourse of national unity centred around 'Myanmafication' (or Burmanization) and the Bengalization of the country's Muslims. While immigration of both Muslims and Hindus has in fact increased from India—including Bengal—during British colonial rule, bundling all Muslims into one undistinguished, bounded and—the argument goes—illegal immigrant group, this claim is used to justify the marginalization, even expulsion of a large portion of Myanmar's society. A 'purified', coherent and cohesive Myanmar society could then emerge, no longer under siege from an alien other, and built around Burman ethnicity and the Buddhist faith.

This chapter is concerned with interrogating and debunking the discourses of unity prevalent in certain periods of Burma/Myanmar's political life. Privileging 'Myanmafication' and collapsing ethnicity, race and religion all in one, the Rohingya, and the country's various—and varied—Muslim communities have been bundled into a single meta-group, in fact a 'meta-other'. In contemporary Myanmar at least, the Rohingya's 'alterity is perceived as inassimilable and irrefragable' (Frydelund 2020, 238).[3] Increasingly, this has become the case for many other Muslim communities too.

Whether this is driven by Myanmar nationalists (for a Rakhine nationalist take on history, see Tha Hla 2004), academics who do not seem to appreciate the Muslim input into the mixed and complex historical and cultural heritage of Arakan (Aye Chan 2005;

---

[2] I use the name Myanmar to refer to the country after independence. It does not mean endorsing the authorities' political stance, but this is now the country's official name. I use the term Burma for the colonial and pre-colonial period. I tend to use the term Arakan for the pre-independence period and Rakhine for the post-1948 era, although Rakhine State as a separate administrative unit was only established in 1974.

[3] There are some initial and timid signs that this might be changing as a result of the 1 February 2021 coup, when many members of the majority Bamar group, including former government officials, are reconsidering their past attitudes towards their Rohingya and, more broadly, their views of the group as 'part of the nation' (Bloomberg 2021; Myo Min 2021; Reuters 2021).

Leider 2014, 2018), political claim-making by Rohingya political entrepreneurs (Islam 2018; Ba Tha 1963; Yunus 1994) or even well-meaning advocacy groups, such an essentialist bias does not stand up to empirical scrutiny.

The chapter takes issue with such tendencies to essentialize and reify the Rohingya and more generally Myanmar's Muslim experiences. To do so, it draws on the insights of constructivist (Brubaker 2002, 2009) and more critical, anti-essentialist literature on trans-border identities and diasporic conditions (Appadurai 1996; Anthias 1998; Clifford 1994; Fumagalli 2021) and, empirically, the more nuanced anthropological studies of the Rohingya (Uddin 2019; Uddin and Chowdhory 2019) and Myanmar's Kamans (Nyi Nyi Kyaw 2016). By doing so, this chapter aims to shed light on this diversity by offering a more nuanced view on Myanmar's Muslims and contribute to the de-essentialization and a more fluid understanding of Myanmar's 'Muslim mosaic' (Crouch 2016). Due to space constraints, this chapter can provide only a bird's eye view of the topic under discussion. Also, compared to other more empirically grounded chapters in this volume, this is a more exploratory investigation into a much broader topic, and thus the chapter serves as an invitation to further in-depth research.

The contribution embeds the case of the Rohingya in a comparative perspective on Myanmar's Muslims, focusing especially on the Kaman, the Panthay (Chinese Muslims), Burmese Muslims and the Malay (Pashu) Muslims.[4] The chapter details the heterogeneity of Myanmar's Muslim communities by considering variation in size, region of settlement, historical patterns of settlement and status in today's Myanmar.

Two caveats are required before proceeding further. By critiquing the groupism and groupness biases in the literature and seeking to move past the notion of the Rohingya and other Muslim communities as timeless and unchanging bounded collectivities, I do not mean to suggest that ethnicity or ethnic groups do not exist. People should

---

[4] This list is of course limited and does not include the case of smaller Muslim communities among the Mon or the Karen or the Indian Muslims, which is well covered in the literature (Berlie 2008; Bowser 2020; Chakravarti 1971; Yegar 1972).

be referred to by what they decide and should be referred to with that name. Just like other ethnic groups, the Rohingya are an imagined, not imaginary community. The Rohingya are who *they* say they are. Also on 1 February 2021, the Myanmar military deposed the government led by the National League for Democracy (NLD) and arrested the country's leading civilian authorities, installing direct military rule. At the time of this writing in Summer 2021, the stand-off between the military and the pro-democracy protesters is unfolding, with no clear outcome in sight apart from an increase in military violence. While an analysis of the fallout of the 1 February coup lies outside the scope of this chapter, the events add a new layer of complexity and uncertainty to the position of the Rohingya in the country, given that the new ruler, Commander-in-Chief Min Aung Hlaing, was in charge of the 2017 'clearance operations' in Rakhine State.

The chapter is structured as follows. First, I briefly review the key themes in the scholarship on the Rohingya. Next, I embed the case study in a broader critique of the study of ethnicity and nations in a substantialist and essentialist manner and advance the case for anti-essentialism and a greater appreciation of hybridity and change. I subsequently detail the similarities and differences between Myanmar's various Muslim communities before concluding.

10.2. What's in a Name?

Rohingya identity and their very existence are shaped by mobility across recently established state borders. This trans-border community may not pose a military threat to either of the two main states where its members currently live, but it surely appears to pose a 'symbolic and an ideological one' to them (Bjornberg 2016, 148). This is because

> historical mobility threatens the coherence of the modern states of Myanmar and Bangladesh. The Rohingya represent a history that the national states of Myanmar and Bangladesh seek to obliterate. Their existence calls to mind historical mobilities and cultural exchange that undermine contemporary constructions of nationalism.

In other words, they unsettle their national projects. This is especially the case of Myanmar, a country which, under British colonial rule (1824–1948),[5] saw the flattening of the hierarchical social structure typical of Buddhist polities in Southeast Asia, Buddhism marginalized, the social role of the monkhood (*sangha*) undermined and its ethnic Bamar population marginalized (Bjornberg 2016), with colonial authorities elevating non-Burmese groups in the periphery in the army and an immigrant population from India in the administration and trade. Independence, achieved in 1948, did not bring peace but rather some of the world's longest running ethnic armed insurgencies along Burma's borderlands.

After decades of neglect by academia and the international community, the Rohingya and their quest for recognition have attracted growing interest in recent years. However, Rohingya history written by Rohingya authors is scant in number. The works of Tahir Ba Tha (1963)[6], Mohammad Yunus (1994) and Nurul Islam (2018) provide useful insights into what Rohingya authors consider important to their identity formation, focusing on the ancient histories of a Muslim presence in Arakan. Non-Rohingya historians have also focused on the early origins of a Muslim cultural and political presence in Arakan and the establishment of connections across Bengal and the interactions of peoples of different faiths on the territory of Arakan (Leider 2014, 2018), with others focusing more on the first half of the 20th century, detailing the rise of Burmese nationalism and the anti-Indian riots of 1936–1938 (Bowser 2020) and the inter-communal violence in Arakan during World War II, especially during the 1942–1945 period or the rise in militancy in the late 1940s (Selth 1986).

Scholars working on the Rohingya living in Bangladesh have focused on the effects of marginalization, exclusion and violence experienced in Myanmar and the current conditions of vulnerability. They have shed light on the dynamics of ethnic cleansing and

[5] The British Empire annexed Burma as a result of three Anglo-Burman wars. During the first (1824–1826), it annexed, among others, the territory of today's Rakhine State (Arakan).

[6] Ba Tha's work (1963) focuses on Rohingya and Kaman, the text—with the exception of a couple of pages—is actually predominantly about the Rohingya.

genocide (Ibrahim 2016; Uddin 2019), statelessness and refugeehood (Chowdhory and Mohanty 2020; Farzana 2015, 2017; Uddin 2012, 2019; Uddin and Chowdhory 2019). This cross-border mobility has led to a process of de- and re-territorialization of their identities, where state policies and boundaries have led to a heightened condition of vulnerability within the community insightfully detailed by Uddin and Chowdhory (2019). In a somewhat specular manner, the Myanmar scholarship has explored the origins of such processes. This includes a detailed historical and political theoretical exploration of Burmese political thought and nationalism (Min Zin 2015; Walton 2017a), the failures of Myanmar nation-building (Walton 2017b), the marginalization of ethnic minorities (Thant Myint-U 2020), the various waves of ethnic cleansing (Fumagalli 2018, 2019; Wade 2019; Ware and Laoutides 2018) and, inevitably, the question of denied citizenship (Cheesman 2017; Holliday 2015). However, within the scholarship on pre-colonial Burma and post-independence Myanmar, the literature on the emergence of a Muslim presence is scant. Seminal work on the topic includes the monographs of Yegar (1972) and Berlie (2008) and the edited collection on Islam and the state by Crouch (2016). The first two texts are empirically rich and detailed (if by now a bit dated) especially as regards the study of Muslim organizations in pre- and post-independent Burma by Yegar and an overview of the different extents of Burmanization of the country's Muslims (Berlie 2008). The contributions to Crouch's volume detail the colonial origins of the current relationship between Muslims and the Myanmar state, including the effects of British colonial policy, the rise of Islamophobia, Muslim political activity and much else.

Three related issues have received particular attention in the literature: the contested ethnonym, the group's claim to indigeneity and its denied citizenship. One of the central problems in the scholarship of the Rohingya 'is the question of the group's political identity and hence its belonging' (Farzana 2017, 2). This is not surprising because the denial of the Rohingya's existence constitutes the basis of its expulsion from Myanmar's social fabric, the citizenry and the state as a whole. The term Rohingya, as is widely known, is mentioned in Francis Buchanan's study when in his discussion of the languages spoken in the old royal capital of Amarapura (near Mandalay, in central Myanmar), he reports that one of them was spoken by 'Mohammedans, who have long settled in Arakan, and who call themselves Rooinga, or natives of Arakan' (Buchanan 1799). What follows, though, is a hiatus in local historical sources (including though not exclusively the censuses conducted in colonial times[7]), also widely noted in the literature (Leider 2018), where the label Rohingya does not reappear until the 1950s (Leider 2014) and comes in greater usage after 1978 (Farzana 2017, 54). On this basis, according to Myanmar's official narrative, there is no such a thing as a Rohingya ethnicity and that Rakhine's Muslims can only be illegal Bengali immigrants.[8] As noted earlier, immigration has taken place over centuries in both directions (Barua 2020; De Mersan 2019; Prasse-Freeman and Mausert 2020), although it is only from the British colonial period onwards that this becomes a mass-scale phenomenon (Nyi Nyi Kyaw 2016). The issue of legality is of course debatable as Burma was formally part of British India, and there was no border nor a separate immigration regime until 1937 when a separate administration was established in Burma under the Government of Burma Act of 1935.[9] The authorities' denial of existence led to a number of consequences, amongst which is the exclusion of this category from the national census, including the latest one conducted in 2014. Thus, the Rohingya faced a rather unpalatable choice: refusing to be counted out of insistence on the ethnonym of choice or be counted and classified as Bengalis. Since the term Bengali in Myanmar implies illegal immigration from Bangladesh/East Pakistan/British India, this would have exposed them to the risk of deportation.[10] Thus, the Rohingya have refused, consistently,

[7] For an insightful critique of the use of census and other colonial area as sources and forms of knowledge production, see Frydenlund (2020).

[8] There is, of course, a fundamental contradiction in Myanmar's own position here, as I discuss later. The Kaman are an officially recognized ethnic group; they are Muslim, speak Rakhine, are full citizens and are recognized as one of the national races of Myanmar, so it is pretty obvious that there is a Muslim presence in Rakhine State.

[9] The rise of Burmese nationalism and growing hostility to Indian immigration provide the context for the separation of Burma from India (Bowser 2020; Walton 2017b).

[10] Crouch (2014) notes that this was not just a problem exclusive to the Rohingya community, but rather all of Myanmar Muslims vigorously debated the issue of the census category and what the members should tick in the census.

to be registered as Bengali, 'resisting state-imposed definitions and manipulations of ethnicity and thus [the] criteria of belonging' (Oh 2013, 36). They were not counted in the official census, only appearing as a 'non-enumerated population' (Ministry of Immigration, Labour and Population 2016).

A related debate concerns the notion of national races (*thaing yin tha* in Burmese). The term refers to the groups (race here is used as coterminous with ethnic group, whereas *lumyo* refers to a more general category of 'people', Candier 2019; Parnini, this volume 2021) that are—as per official rhetoric—supposedly all indigenous to Myanmar. The list currently encompasses 135 groups and the Rohingya are not included, as is well known, despite their attempts to be. Because they are not listed they cannot be recognized as indigenous, though the number itself is arbitrary and has changed, repeatedly, over the course of the 20th century (Cheesman 2017), so there is no compelling reason why there should not be 136 or 134 groups listed. Who is and is not included matters because 'race' is both central to understanding the Rohingya's struggle for political group rights and the process through which they have been excluded from Myanmar's citizenry. In reality, as Cheesman compellingly shows, a genealogy of the concept reveals a complex history that elides a unified stable definition of category of national belonging (Cheesman 2017). In other words, the concept is mutable and has been so throughout Myanmar's history, so is the list and what is done with it. Yet, following the 1982 citizenship law, which *de facto* deprived the Rohingya of citizenship, ethnicity—not residence or even ancestry—being recognized as one of the national races becomes the basis for claiming Myanmar citizenship. Had residence been the criterion actually used for establishing eligibility this would have not been a problem, despite the Myanmar authorities' intent to look back to 1823, a year before the first Anglo-Burman War, as the time when ancestry in Burma had to be proven.

As mentioned earlier, in order to other and render the Rohingya population alien, the Myanmar authorities, particularly from 1962 when General Ne Win took over and politics took on an increasingly nationalistic tone, references to Bengali immigration have become commonplace. In my frequent visits to Myanmar since 2013, the term was preferred to the use of the ethnonym Rohingya, which the local population continues to be reluctant to use. In the media and public discourse, another term that is also used is *kala*. The term, which could be translated as 'foreigner' (primarily coming from the west, primarily with reference to those native of the Indian subcontinent), is used in a derogatory way to refer to the Muslim population (who reject its use as applied to them), and at times all the communities supposedly of Indian origins, although this was not always so. The term actually refers to a broader category of non-Burmese, or foreigners, and historically was not exclusively applied to the local Muslim population (Nyi Nyi Kyaw 2018).

Research into how the Rohingya themselves make sense of categories that are either the product of the colonial era (though they continue to be used in the post-colonial period) or actually refer to other sets of people is still in an embryonic stage. We still know very little of intra-group dynamics and change within the Rohingya community (Nursyazwani and Prasse-Freeman 2020), particularly of how forms of ethnic and religious identification work in practice for ordinary people and the conditions under which they opt for one form of identification or another, privileging religion, ethnicity or territory. In sum, although recent scholarly work has contributed tremendously by shedding light on the origins and consequences of the Rohingya predicament, our understanding has been shaped by the (unintended) convergent effects of a homogenizing discourse within Myanmar and an assumption of bounded-ness of both Myanmar's Muslims as a whole and the Rohingya in particular.

10.3. Against Essentialism

As Bourdieu aptly put it, '*we continue to be inclined to think the social world in a substantialist manner*' (Bourdieu and Wacquant 1992, 228, italics mine). Despite claims about the socially constructed nature of identities, their fluidity and hyphenization, there continues to be a tendency in the scholarly literature, media and policy community to 'represent the social and cultural world as a multi-chrome mosaic of monochrome ethnic, racial and cultural blocs' (Brubaker 2002, 164). This is because, as Rogers Brubaker explains, 'much work on ethnicity, race and nationalism continues to be informed by groupism', or 'the tendency to treat various categories of people as if they were internally homogenous externally bounded groups, even unitary collective actors with common purposes' (Brubaker 2009, 28). Consequently, much of the literature regards ethnic groups as 'constituents of social life, chief protagonists of social conflicts, and fundamental units of social analysis' (Brubaker 2009, 28). Such an approach not only reifies and essentializes groups but leaves those very groups mired in an eternal and unchanging present. Consequently, therefore, Rohingya—or the Rakhine or Bamar, for that matter—either 'are and have always been' an unchanging ethnic community, or 'aren't and will never be one'. The possibility of change or that individuals may, depending on the context, decide to enter or exit a group is not contemplated.

Instead of seeing substantial entities and treating ethnic groups as such, we should attend to the evolving role of 'ethnicity, race and nationhood as a single integrated family of forms of cultural understanding, social organization and political contestation' (Brubaker 2009, 22). *Neither eternal nor invented*, ethnic groups would then be seen and analysed as 'vague vernacular terms whose meaning varies considerably over place and time' (Brubaker 2009, 267). Thus, the Rohingya are neither a recent construction/invention nor the direct descendants of 9th-century Arab tradesmen shipwrecked on the coasts of east Bengal, Arakan and lower Burma, as if nothing—such as cross-cultural fertilization among the various communities of Arakan—had happened between then and now. 'Grasping ethnicity as something that happens' (Brubaker 2002, 29), as an occurrence that may happen at times but not others, more intense in certain historical phases, for example, during the inter-communal violence of 1942–1945 (Selth 1986), the debates over secession in the late 1940s (Yegar 1972), the quest for territorial autonomy that led to the short-lived instance of territorial autonomy of the early 1960s (Yegar 1972) or everyday resistance following ethnic cleansing (Farzana 2017). Conflicts harden identities, crystallize them, but identities are then reshaped and change again. This is not a challenge to the existence of the group, of course. As Brubaker (2002, 168) argues:

[T]o rethink ethnicity, race and nationhood along these lines is no way to dispute their reality, minimise their power or discount their significance. It is to construct their reality, power and significance in a different way [focusing on] racial idioms, ideologies, narratives, categories and systems of classification and racialised ways of seeing, thinking, talking and framing claims [that] are real and consequential, especially when they are embedded in powerful organizations.

Trans-border communities such as the Rohingya provide an excellent illustration of Appadurai's view that 'the notion of diaspora denotes the transnational moment and ties in with arguments around globalisation and the growth of non-nation-based solidarities' (Appadurai 1996). Although I am not suggesting that the Rohingya should be referred to as diasporas in the traditional sense, the de- and re-territorialization of identities as they move across borders examined by Uddin and Chowdhory (2019) is an especially insightful example of novel ways of thinking about identities and groups in this context. The group's mobility across boundaries (Farzana 2015) provides a crucial formative moment in their identity formation and transformation. Yet, there seems to be a hiatus between the opportunities for fruitful conceptual innovation offered by the liminality of Rohingya's position as a trans-border mobility of over two million people, whose identity has been shaped by border-crossing, conflicts as well as adaptation and coexistence with other communities and a reality of essentialism and reification. This timelessness of Rohingya-ness is problematic because it does not stand up to empirical scrutiny and ultimately does little to advance the rights of the community or enhance our understanding of the members of the group, let alone contribute to an improvement of their conditions. The study of the Rohingya would benefit from a more explicit appreciation of change within the community, interactions with other and mutual influence and exchange (Uddin, this volume 2021). Rethinking Rohingya identity (trans-)formation, accepting its hybridities and change would mean, in practice, de-exceptionalizing their study and more closely aligning the scholarship on Rohingya identity (trans-)formation to more recent reflections on ethnicity, race and nations. This would also pave the way to fruitful comparative conversations, highlighting commonalities in their experience as well as, whenever applicable, the distinctive traits of identity-making among the Rohingya. Admittedly, primary access to members of the community has been hampered in Myanmar by restricted access to the relevant locations in northern Rakhine State due to the political sensitivity of the topic and the fact that the Tatmadaw (Myanmar military) directly runs border affairs.

10.4. Minorities, Not Minority

During a visit to Mandalay in June 2018, a local young Muslim student I was meeting on the university campus lamented the marginality of Myanmar's Muslim community: 'We are invisible. We cannot speak up. Yet, the state knows we exist and treats us a second-class people.'[11] A Muslim woman in her late thirties, originally from the city of Mawlamyine in Mon state but now living in Yangon, emphasized how she felt 'Muslim and proud to be so,' while stressing that she also saw herself as 'culturally Myanmar'[12] (Burmese/Bamar).

Invisibility and marginality manifest themselves differently across the country. (In)visibility means different things to individual Muslims in the country. Some, mostly Rohingya and some ethnic Kaman too, experience socio-spatial segregation in the camps in North Rakhine State. Others, such as Chinese Muslims (Panthay) tend to live compactly in the Chinese neighbourhoods of Mandalay, where both Muslim and non-Muslim Chinese from Yunnan were allowed to settle in the late 19th century. The presence of a local vibrant Muslim presence is much more visible in the cityscape of the city of Mawlamyine in the south-east of the country, as the slow train from Yangon makes its way into the city after passing the long bridge on the Salween River and its many mosques on either side of the railway mark the landscape, next to churches and Buddhist temples. With its mosques and Hindu temples, the area near Sule Street and Bogyoke Aung San Street in downtown Yangon is a reminder of both the mixed Hindu–Muslim heritage of colonial Burma and the sheer diversity of today's Islam, with Shi'a and Sunni mosques in close proximity and Sunni mosques of different traditions.

[11] Interview, Mandalay, 16 June 2018.
[12] Interview, Yangon, 12 May 2019.

In this section I primarily focus on the Kaman, the Chinese, Burmese and Malay Muslims, although of course Myanmar's Muslim mosaic includes other communities. The main point I make here is that, in agreement with Nyi Nyi Kyaw (2018) there is not a single Muslim minority in the country. Myanmar's Muslims differ from each other in a number of crucial respects. A note of caution before proceeding further. As I offer a cursory overview of Myanmar's 'Muslim mosaic' (Crouch 2016), I do not intend to represent or reproduce the same rigidities that I am seeking to critique and unpack in this chapter. What follows is therefore nothing more than a snapshot. Neither of the groups examined in the following pages speaks with one voice or experiences life in today's Myanmar in the same guise.

10.4.1. Size

According to the 2014 census (conducted over 30 years since the previous one of 1983), Myanmar is home to about 51 million people. Of these, 50,728,900 'count' officially, whereas approximately 1.2 million are considered 'non-enumerated' (Ministry of Immigration, Labour and Population 2016, 2). The figure includes 69,753 persons living in Kayin state, 46,600 in Kachin and a whopping 1,090,000 persons living in Rakhine State. The report does not mention the term Rohingya a single time, but it hints at the fact that these 'non-enumerated persons' are Muslims (the same report states that 'they belong to one religious faith'). So, taking that into account, the overall figure of the population totals 51,486,253 (Ministry of Immigration, Labour and Population 2016, 2). Officially, Muslims make up 2.3 per cent of the population, but once the 'non-numerated' are added, the figure adds up to 4.6 per cent. Due to their politically sensitive nature, the breakdown by ethnicity and religion was released two years after the census was conducted. Since then, the forced removal of a large part of the Rohingya population from Rakhine State took place in August–September 2017 (Fumagalli 2017; 2018). About 650,000 Rohingya fled killings and persecution and found refuge in neighbouring Bangladesh, leaving just under half a million of them in Myanmar, and the total Muslim population in the country at just above 1.6 million (3.2% of the total). The Rohingya make up just a quarter of that. Getting an accurate picture is of course difficult for a number of reasons, not least because the Rohingya were not allowed to use this ethnonym for self-identification. There are debates among the population as to whether Muslim refers to an ethnic category or a religion, although in practice the two have all but fused in today's Myanmar. The Kaman are estimated to be less than 50,000 (Nyi Nyi Kyaw 2016), mostly settled in southern Rakhine State (there are 28,000 Muslims living in Rakhine according to the 2014 census, although it is not implausible that some Rohingya may be identifying as Kaman as this provides them with a pathway to citizenship; see the following), with others settled in Yangon and the area of Mandalay, where some Kaman resettled during the King Mindon era during 1853–1878 (Nyi Nyi Kyaw 2015). Other areas with a strong Muslim presence include Yangon, historically home to very large Indian Muslim presence, now at 345,612 and just under 5 per cent of the population, Mandalay and Mon state with less than 200,000 each. There are 72,074 persons who identify as Muslims in the Tanintharyi region and although many of these will be Burmese Muslims, some are likely to be Pashu or Malay Muslims, estimated to be around 30,000 (Kotwal 2018). The census does not allow us to know how many people identify as either Chinese or Burmese Muslims.

10.4.2. Region of Settlement

The Rohingya are primarily settled in three townships of North Rakhine State, namely Maungdaw, Buthidaung and (west) Rothedaung (alongside a minuscule presence in Yangon), whereas the Kaman are primarily settled in South Rakhine State, as well as in central Myanmar, where some of them resettled in the 17th century, in the areas of Mandalay, Meiktila and Myedu (Nyi Nyi Kyaw 2016, 289). Burmese Muslims are essentially spread out across the country and primarily in the central plains and the seven regions. Chinese Muslims are primarily concentrated in central and upper Myanmar, in the Mandalay division. Lastly, the Malay Muslims (Pashu) are settled in the Tanintharyi division in south-eastern

Myanmar, bordering Thailand, especially in the Kawthaung and Bokpyin townships and a few islands in the southern part of the Mergui archipelago.

10.4.3. Status

The status, or the lack of status, of the Rohingya is widely known. Although according to the 1948 constitution they were eligible to receive Burmese citizenship (Nyi Nyi Kyaw 2016), the 1982 law *de facto* rendered them stateless. The Rakhine-speaking Kaman are the only officially recognized Muslim ethnic group in the country. They are recognized in virtue of their separate ethnicity, not religion, as this does not—officially—form the basis for recognition, although in practice the concepts of ethnicity, race and religion tend to blend into one another. In terms of classification in today's Myanmar, the Kaman are regarded as part of the Rakhine 'meta-group' together with seven other groups (including the Rakhine, confusingly), which makes the Kaman one of the country's 135 national races. As such, the Kaman are eligible for full citizenship by birth. This type of citizenship is discussed by Cheesman (2017); Holliday (2015) and Nyi Nyi Kyaw. Although some Muslims report difficulties with applying for citizenship, especially in cases of mixed heritage, the only group without any pathway to citizenship is the Rohingya.

10.4.4. Territorial Autonomy

Administratively, Myanmar is structured around seven states (areas of more compact settlement by ethnic minority groups), seven regions (Bamar-majority areas) and the capital, Nay Pyi Taw. In today's Myanmar, as they are not recognized as ethnic groups, Muslims do not enjoy any form of territorial autonomy in areas where they are compactly settled. This was not always so. In recognition of and possibly in order to appease the fight by Rohingya groups during the late 1940s and 1950s, Prime Minister U Nu conceded a form of territorial autonomy—the Mayu Frontier District—for the territory of present-day Northern Rakhine (Maungdaw), an area predominantly populated with Rohingya. The autonomy was short-lived, though, lasting only from 1961 to 1964, when it was abolished during the Ne Win era (Leider 2020).

10.4.5. Historical Patterns of Settlement in Burma/Myanmar

This is perhaps where the heterogeneity of Myanmar's 'Muslim mosaic' stands out more vividly and where the discourse over the Bengalization of Myanmar Muslims is exposed for being so remote from reality.

To recall, the Rohingya trace their origins back to a presence established by Arab traders in the 9th century in the coastal regions of today's Myanmar, a presence consolidated in the intervening centuries (De Mersan 2019; Prasse-Freeman and Mausert 2020). According to the only known account of Kaman history (written incidentally by a Buddhist monk, but accepted by the community nonetheless), Kaman history dates back to the retreat of the Moghul prince Shah Shuja in 1660, when they permanently settled (Yegar 1972). At the same time, Rakhine sources (Le Way 2005, cited in Nyi Nyi Kyaw 2018, 287–288) trace the history of the Kaman to the Rakhine kings of 13th century. While the origins of both Kaman and Rohingya, both Rakhine-based Muslims, have to be understood in the centuries-old patterns of ship trade from the Middle East to Southeast Asia via India and Bengal, the Panthay originally came from southern China in more recent times. Their arrival on the territory of colonial Burma is much more recent and dates back to the collapse of the Sultanate in the Yunnan province of Qing China (Berlie 2008; Chang 2014; Forbes 1986; Yegar 1966, 1972). The Panthays are Chinese Muslims from Yunnan, where they are not known as such, but use the ethnonym Hui (or Huihui as an alternative). In 1856, a sultanate was established in Yunnan, adjacent to what was already British-ruled Burma. The Hui people who left China would later settle around the towns of Tangyab, Maymyo, Mandalay, the Tanunggyi area and Shan states (Berlie 2008; Yegar 1972).

The heyday of the sultanate was between 1860 and 1868, after which power declined rapidly. The polity held friendly relations with the British Empire, but the latter would not intervene in its support given that relations with China were a bigger strategic priority. The sultanate eventually collapsed in 1872–1875. The Burmese Muslims are descendants of mixed families, typically with a Burmese mother and an Indian Muslim father. Although mixed heritage poses its own distinct challenges to the population, Burmese Muslims are culturally and linguistically Burmese who happen to be Muslims and therefore, their indigeneity is less frequently questioned compared to that of other Muslim communities in the country.

10.4.6. Ethnic and Religious Affiliation

It may sound odd to speak of this issue when discussing Muslim communities. At the same time, in some cases, ethnicity trumps religion as the main source of affiliation. This actually is the case of the Rohingya themselves, among whom—despite the fact that the whole community is widely regarded as almost exclusively Muslim—includes some Hindus and Christians too, though very little is known of them (and more research should be carried out in this regard). Language is another area in which there is considerable variation. While the Rohingya speak Rohingya (and not Bengali as is commonly and erroneously believed in Myanmar), the Kaman speak Rakhine, a language that is partly related to Burmese (some would consider it a dialect although there are clear differences in vocabulary). For other Myanmar Muslims, such as the Chinese, Burmese and Malay Muslims, Burmese is their native tongue.

10.4.7. Conflict and Violence

Although rampant Buddhist Bamar (and Rakhine) nationalism has affected many Muslims in recent years (Nyi Nyi Kyaw 2016), it is the Rohingya and the Kaman who have suffered disproportionately over several waves of conflict in 1978, 1991, 2012, 2015, 2016 and recently, 2017. The Kaman have been in some cases confined to camps in Rakhine State, despite the fact that the authorities had imposed confinement only to the undocumented Rohingya. The Kaman were also affected during the June and October 2012 violence, although their deaths went unregistered/unrecognized as the state commission distinguished only between Rakhine Muslim victims, thus bundling Rohingya and Kaman deaths, despite the fact that some Kaman-majority villages were also directly affected during the clashes. This was also despite the fact that the government enquiry commission on violence in Rakhine State fails to mention them or the Rohingya, breaking down figures into Rakhine (Buddhist) and Muslims (Nyi Nyi Kyaw 2018, 284). According to figures provided by the National Democratic Party for Development (a Kaman political party), 500 Muslims were killed, including in towns and villages in Kyaukphyu, Mrauk-U, Thandwe and Myebon, which are in Kaman-populated areas (Niy Nyi Kyaw 2016, 286). In the following years, 4,000 Kaman were confined to camps as of July 2015 (Nyi Nyi Kyaw 2018, 286). The military coup of 1 February 2021 not only unleashed both mass protests unseen since 1988 and a brutal response in return but also has led to a reassessment of the relations between the majority group (those opposing the military intervention) and ethnic minorities (International Crisis Group 2021).

10.4.8. Relationship with the Rohingya

Although the Rohingya have typically supported the National League for Democracy (Ali 2021), only to be severely disappointed from the mid-2010s onwards, no political organization—including Muslim groups or parties—in contemporary Myanmar would want to be perceived as pro-Rohingya, since this would amount to committing political suicide. Furthermore, some Kaman have resented—and rejected—Rohingya attempts to claim to be Kaman in order to take up Myanmar citizenship (Nyi Nyi Kyaw 2018). The coup is a potential game-changer in this respect. Former NLD government officials and spokespersons of the new parallel government have publicly expressed regretted over their previous positions and silences on the Rohingya issue, including the 2017 events (the Committee for Representing Pydaungsu Hluttaw, CRPH; Bloomberg 2021). Myanmar is also experiencing the new reality of Bamars (and others) marching alongside the Rohingya against the military (Myo Min 2021; Jap 2021).

It is far too soon to speculate whether a radical change of course, and the position of ethnic and religious minorities, is especially vulnerable in the face of a military driven by Buddhist Bamar nationalism, but across society as a whole, new relations might be taking shape at last.

As this section has shown, there is an urgent need for greater nuance in discussions of Myanmar's Muslim communities. Islamophobia has been rampant in the country and has been manifested with all its virulence since political liberalization began in 2011. Inter-communal violence too has flared up across the country. Because of the scale of violence in Rakhine State and the intractability of that conflict, the attention of the international community, but also media and academia, has primarily focused on that experience, *de facto* subsuming the conditions and experiences of Myanmar's Muslims into one.

10.5. Conclusion

Alongside being home to an ancient and rich Buddhist past dating back to the 1st century of the common era, Myanmar is also a Muslim country, home to an old, diverse and complex Islamic heritage, whose origins also go back several centuries, a product of multiple connections to the west (the Indian subcontinent and the Middle East), the north (Yunnan and China) and the east (the Malay archipelago).[13] The discussion in the chapter has sought to add some nuance to the study of the Rohingya and other Muslim communities in Myanmar, leading to two main conclusions. First, Myanmar's Muslim community is no monolith. Quite the contrary, Myanmar is home to a variety of heterogeneous Muslim minorities, and for some, religion is the main source of identification, while for others it is ethnicity. Their present is shaped by different and distinct spatial and historical geographies. They currently experience different relations with the state and other ethnic groups in the country. Also different are the patterns of settlement, professions, role in society, status (citizenship) and degrees of integration/exclusion

---

[13] On cross-Bengal connections, see Barua (2020), Chakravarti (1971), Egreteau (2011), Elverskog (2019), Ghosh (2016). For movements in the opposite directions, with Buddhist Rakhine moving westwards, see Pum Khan Pau (2020) and Thant Myint-U (2004).

in Myanmar's society. De-essentializing the Rohingya may be quite novel in the scholarship on the group, but such an approach is entirely consistent with some of the most insightful empirically grounded scholarship on Myanmar's minorities, such as the Karens (Harriden 2002; South 2007; Thawnghmung 2008), Mons (South 2003), Kachins (Sadan 2013), Chin (Sakhong 2003) and Shans (Sai 2008). Second, and related to this, the history of Arakan/Rakhine, Burma's coastline and East Bengal is a history of mobility, border-crossings, mutual influence and coexistence—and conflict as well. The borderlands of different kingdoms and empires have seen the circulation of goods, peoples and ideas. The Rohingya currently embody the liminality but also the hybridity of these Asian borderlands (Van Schendel 2005).

To conclude, there is still much we do not know about the Rohingya and other Muslim communities in Myanmar. Future research should draw on the important work on the complexity and changing understandings of Rohingya identity (Farzana 2017; Uddin 2020, 2021 forthcoming) and explore intra-Rohingya heterogeneity in greater detail (Frydenlund 2020; Nusyazwani and Prasse-Freeman 2020) by looking, for example, at how different religious subgroups (Hindu, Christian, Muslim) embrace and articulate their self-identification as Rohingya or, when and how groups privilege other identities. In due course, it might also be possible to see how the 2021 military coup has reshaped some inter-group relations. Further, we should think more comparatively and regionally, with more comparative work across generations (pre-/post-violence in the 2010s) and localities (Rakhine, Yangon, Bangladesh and elsewhere such as in Malaysia, Pakistan or Saudi Arabia), so that a richer, more nuanced and diverse picture of this beleaguered community can emerge. We also know little of the Rohingya's interactions with the Kaman in Rakhine State. Finally, future research should also look past an exclusive focus on conflict and violence and revisit stories of coexistence and efforts at peace-building and reconciliation so that pathways out of the current hostilities can be identified from the local communities' own experiences and tell the stories of the relations between different Muslim groups (especially between the Rohingya and the Kaman) and also with other ethnic communities. In sum, while the Rohingya's conditions of statelessness, refugeehood and persecution are exceptional, their study should not be.

Acknowledgement

The author gratefully acknowledges the support of the UK's Arts and Humanities Research Council for its support of research related to this chapter (AH/S00405X/1).

References

Ali, Mayyu. 2021, 18 February. 'Where Do the Rohingya Go after the Coup in Myanmar?' *New York Times*.

Anthias, F. 1998. 'Evaluating "Diaspora": Beyond Ethnicity?' *Sociology* 32, no. 3: 1–24.

Appadurai, A. 1996. *Modernity at Large: Cultural Dimensions of Globalization*. Minneapolis, MN: University of Minnesota Press.

Aye, Chan. 2005. 'The Development of a Muslim Enclave in Arakan (Rakhine) State of Burma (Myanmar).' *SOAS Bulletin of Burma Research* 3, no. 2: 396–420.

Ba Tha, M. A. Tahir. 1963. *A Short History of Rohingya and Kamans of Burma*. Available at https://www.burmalibrary.org/sites/burmalibrary.org/files/obl/docs21/Ba_Tha-Kaladan-News%26Network-Myanmar-2007-09-13-A_Short_History_of_Rohingya_and_Kamans_of_Burma-en.pdf (accessed on 16 September 2021).

Barua, D. M. 2020. 'Arakanese Chittagong Became Mughal Islamabad: Buddhist–Muslim Relationship in Chittagong (Chottogram), Bangladesh.' In *Buddhist–Muslim Relations in a Theravada World*, edited by I. Frydenlund and M. Jerryson, 227–260. New York, NY: Springer.

Berlie, J. A. 2008. *The Burmanization of Myanmar's Muslims*. Bangkok: White Lotus.

Bjornberg, A. 2016. 'Rohingya Territoriality in Myanmar and Bangladesh: Humanitarian Crisis and National Disordering.' In *Myanmar's Mountain and Maritime Borderscapes. Local Practices, Boundary-making and Figured Worlds*, edited by S. A. Oh, 146–168. Cambridge: Cambridge University Press.

Bloomberg News. 2021, 29 March. 'Suu Kyi Ally Wants Equal Rights for Persecuted Myanmar Muslims.' Bloomberg News.

Bowser, M. J. 2020. 'Partners in Empire? Co-colonialism and the Rise of Anti-Indian Nationalism in Burma, 1930–1938.' *Journal of Imperial and Commonwealth History*. https://doi.org/10.1080/03086534.2020.1783113

Bourdieu, P., and L. J. D. Wacquant. 1992. *An Invitation to Reflexive Sociology*. Chicago, IL: The University of Chicago Press.

Brubaker, R. 2002. 'Ethnicity without Groups.' *Archives Européenes de Sociologi e XLIII*, no. 2: 163–189.

———. 2009. 'Ethnicity, Race and Nationalism.' *Annual Review of Sociology*. 35: 21–42.

Buchanan, F. 1799. 'A Comparative Vocabulary of Some of the Languages Spoken in the Burma Empire.' *Asiatic Researches* 5: L219–240.

Candier, A. 2019. 'Mapping Ethnicity in Nineteenth-century Burma: When "Categories of People" (*Lumyo*) Became "Nations."' *Journal of Southeast Asian Studies* 50, no. 3: 347–364.

Chakravarti, N. R. 1971. *The Indian Minority in Burma: The Rise and Decline of an Immigrant Community*. London: Oxford University Press.

Chang, W. C. 2014. *Beyond Borders: Stories of Yunnanese Chinese Migrants of Burma*. Ithaca, NY: Cornell University Press.

Cheesman, Nick. 2017. 'How in Myanmar "National Races" Came to Surpass Citizenship and Exclude Rohingya.' *Journal of Contemporary Asia* 47, no. 3: 461–483.

Chowdhory, N., and B. Mohanty, eds. 2020. *Citizenship, Nationalism and Refugeehood of Rohingyas in Southern Asia*. New York, NY: Springer.

Clifford, J. 1994. 'Diaspora.' *Cultural Anthropology* 9, no. 3: 302–338.

Crouch, M. 2014, 4 November. 'Myanmar's Muslim Mosaic and the Politics of Belonging.' New Mandala.

———, ed. 2016. *Islam and the State in Myanmar: Muslim–Buddhist Relations and the Politics of Belonging*. Oxford: Oxford University Press.

De Marsan, A. 2019. 'How Muslims in Arakan Became Arakan's Foreigners.' In *Current Myanmar Studies. Aung San Suu Kyi, Muslims in Arakan, and Economic Insecurity*, edited by G. Winterberger and E. Tenberg, 59–98. Newcastle: Cambridge Scholars Publishing.

Egreteau, R. 2011. 'Burmese Indians in Contemporary Burma: Heritage, Influence, and Perceptions since 1988.' *Asian Ethnicity* 12, no. 1: 33–54.

Elverskog, J. 2019. Buddhist and Muslim interactions in Asian History. *Oxford Research Encyclopaedia of Asian History*. http://dx.doi.org/10.1093/acrefore/9780190277727.013.418

Farzana, K. F. 2015. 'Boundaries in Shaping the Rohingya Identity and the Shifting Context of Borderland Politics.' *Studies in Ethnicity and Nationalism* 15, no. 2: 292–314.

———. 2017. *Memories of Burmese Rohingya Refugees. Contested Identity and Belonging*. New York, NY: Springer.

Ferguson, J. M. 2015. Who's Counting: Ethnicity, Belonging and the National Census in Burma/Myanmar. *Bijdragen tot de Taal-, Land- en Volkenkunde* 171: 1–28.

Forbes, A. D. W. 1986. 'The "Panthay" (Yunnanese Chinese) Muslims of Burma.' *Journal of Muslim Minority Affairs* 7, no. 2: 384–394.

Frydenlund, S. A. 2020. 'Motherhood, Home, and the Political Economy of Rohingya Women's Labor.' In *Unraveling Myanmar's Transition. Progress, Retrenchment and Ambiguity amidst Liberalization*, edited by P. Chachavalpongpun, E. Prasse-Freeman, and P. Strefford, 235–260. Kyoto: Kyoto University Press.

Fumagalli, M. 2017, 21 September. 'How Geopolitics Helped Create the Latest Rohingya Crisis.' *The Conversation*.

Fumagalli, M. 2018. 'Myanmar 2017: The Rohingya Crisis between Radicalisation and Ethnic Cleansing.' *Asia Maior* XXVIII: 227–243.

———. 2019. 'Myanmar 2018: Botched Transition and Repatriation Plan.' *Asia Maior* XXIX: 233–246.

———. 2021. '"Identity through Difference": Liminal Diasporism and Generational Change among the Koryo Saram in Bishkek, Kyrgyzstan.' *European Journal of Korean Studies* 20, no. 1: 35–70.

Ghosh, D. 2016. 'Burma–Bengal Crossings: Intercolonial Connections in Pre-independence India.' *Asian Studies Review* 40, no. 2: 156–172.

Harriden, J. 2002. 'Making a Name for Themselves: Karen Identity and the Politicization of Ethnicity in Burma.' *Journal of Burma Studies* 7: 84–144.

Holliday, I. 2015. 'Addressing Myanmar's Citizenship Crisis.' *Journal of Contemporary Asia* 4, no. 3: 404–421.

Ibrahim, A. 2016. *The Rohingyas. Inside Myanmar's Hidden Genocide*. London: Hurst & Co.

International Crisis Group. 2021, 1 April. 'The Cost of the Coup: Myanmar Edges toward State Collapse.' *Asia Briefing* 167.

Islam, N. 2018. 'Rohingya and Nationality Status in Myanmar.' In *Citizenship in Myanmar. Ways of being in and from Burma*, edited by A. South and M. Lall, 264–278. Singapore: ISEAS.

Jap, Jangai. 2021, 22 March. 'Protesters and Bystanders: Ethnic Minorities in the Pro-democracy Revolution.' *Tea Circle Oxford*.

Kotwal, H. 2018, 8 February. 'A Story Rarely Told.' *New Straits Times*.

Leider, J. P. 2014. 'Rohingya: The Name, the Movement, the Quest for Identity.' In *Nation Building in Myanmar*, 204–255. Yangon: Myanmar EGRESS/ Myanmar Peace Center.

———. 2018. 'Rohingya: The History of a Muslim Identity in Myanmar.' *Oxford Research Encyclopaedia of Asian History*. https://doi.org/10.1093/ acrefore/9780190277727.013.115

———. 2020. 'Rohingya: The Foundational Years.' *TOAEP* 123: 1–4.

Maung Min Zin. 2015. 'Anti-Muslim Violence in Burma: Why Now?' *Social Research: An International Quarterly* 82, no. 2: 375–397.

Ministry of Labour, Immigration and Population. 2016, July. *The 2014 Myanmar Population and Housing Census. The Union Report: Religion. Census Report Volume 2-C*. Nay Pyi Taw: Ministry of Labour, Immigration and Population.

Myo Min. 2021, 25 March. 'Equality or Animosity: Where Will the Democratic Uprising Take the Rohingya?' Tea Circle Oxford.

Nursyazwani, and E. Prasse-Freeman. 2020, 12 June. 'The Hidden Heterogeneity of Rohingya Refugees.' *New Mandala*.

Nyi Nyi Kyaw. 2015, 24–25 July. 'Muslim Minorities in Transitional Societies. Different Myanmar Muslims Groups' Different Experiences in Transition.' International Conference on Burma/Myanmar Studies, Chiang Mai University, Chiang Mai.

Nyi Nyi Kyaw. 2016. 'Islamophobia in Buddhist Myanmar: The 969 Movement and Anti-Muslim Violence.' In *Islam and the State in Myanmar: Muslim-Buddhist Relations and the Politics of Belonging*, edited by M. Crouch, 184–210. Oxford: Oxford University Press.

———. 2018. 'Myanmar's Other Muslims: The Case of the Kaman.' In *Citizenship in Myanmar. Ways of Being in and from Burma*, edited by A. South and M. Lall, 279–300. Singapore: ISEAS.

Oh, Su-Ann. 2013. 'Rohingya or Bengali? Revisiting the Politics of Labelling.' *IIAS Newsletter* 66: 36.

Prasse-Freeman, E., and K. Mausert. 2020. 'Two Sides of the Same Arakanese Coin: "Rakhine" and "Rohingya," and Ethnogenesis as Schismogenesis.' In *Unraveling Myanmar: Progress, Retrenchment and Ambiguity amidst Liberalization*, edited by P. Chachavalpongpun, E. Prasse-Freeman, and P. Strefford, 261–289. Chicago, IL: University of Chicago Press.

Pau, Pum Khan. 2020. 'Transborder People, Connected History: Border and Relationships in the Indo-Burma Borderlands.' *Journal of Borderland Studies* 35, no. 4: 619–639.

Reuters. 2021, 24 March. 'Myanmar Junta's Civilian Rivals Promise Justice for Rohingya.' Reuters.

Sadan, M. 2013. *Being and Becoming Kachin: Histories beyond the State in the Borderworlds of Burma*. Oxford: Oxford University Press.

Sai Aung Tun. 2008. *History of the Shan State: From Its Origin to 1962*. Chiang Mai: Silkworm Books.

Sakhong, L. H. 2003. *In Search of Chin Identity: A Study in Religion, Politics and Ethnic Identity in Burma*. Richmond: NIAS Press.

Selth, A. 1986. 'Race and Resistance in Burma, 1942–1945.' *Modern Asian Studies* 20, no. 3: 483–507.

South, A. 2003. *Mon Nationalism and Civil War in Burma: The Golden Sheldrake*. Richmond: Routledge Curzon.

———. 2007. 'Karen Nationalist Communities: The "Problem" of Diversity.' *Contemporary Southeast Asia* 29, no. 1: 55–76.

Tha Hla, Maung. 2004. *The Rakhaing*. New York, NY: The Buddhist Rakhaing Cultural Association.

Thant, Myint-U. 2004. *The Making of Modern Burma*. Cambridge: Cambridge University Press.

———. 2020. *The Hidden History of Burma. Race, Capitalism, and the Crisis of Democracy in the 21st Century*. New York, NY: W.W. Norton & Company.

Thawnghmung, A. M. 2008. *The Karen Revolution in Burma: Diverse Voices, Uncertain Ends*. Washington, DC: East–West Center.

Uddin, N., ed. 2012. *To Host or to Hurt: Counter Narratives on Rohingya Refugee Issue in Bangladesh*. Dhaka: Institute for Culture and Development Research.

———. 2019. 'Ethnic Cleansing of the Rohingya People.' *Palgrave Handbook of Ethnicity*, 1–7. New York, NY: Springer.

Uddin, N., ed. 2020. *Rohingya. An Ethnography of 'Subhuman' Life*. Delhi: Oxford University Press.

Uddin, N., and N. Chowdhory, eds. 2019. *Deterritorialised Identity and Transborder Movement in South Asia*. New York, NY: Springer.

Van Schendel, W. 2005. *The Bengal Borderland. Beyond State and Nation in South Asia*. London: Anthem Press.

Wade, F. 2019. *Myanmar's Enemy Within. Buddhist Violence and the Making of a Muslim 'Other'*. London: ZED Books.

Walton, M. J. 2017a. 'Nation-building.' In *Routledge Handbook of Contemporary Myanmar*, edited by A. Simpson, N. Farrelly, and I. Holliday, 393–403. London: Routledge.

———. 2017b. *Buddhism, Politics and Political Thought in Myanmar*. Cambridge: Cambridge University Press.

Ware, A., and C. Laoutides. 2018. *Myanmar's 'Rohingya' Conflict*. London: Hurst & Co.

Yegar, M. 1972. *The Muslims of Burma. A Study of a Minority Group*. Wiesbaden: Otto Harassowitz.

———. 1966. 'The Panthay (Chinese Muslims) of Burma and Yunnan.' *Journal of Southeast Asian History* 7, no. 1: 73–85.

Yunus, M. 1994. *A History of Arakan. Past and Present*. Chittagong: Magenta Colour.

The Rohingya Crisis: Policy Issues, Global Justice and Responsibilities Sharing

Part IV

The Rohingya
Crisis
Policy Issues,
Global Justice and
Responsibilities
Sharing

CHAPTER 11

Roles of the International Community to Redress the Rohingya Crisis

Azeem Ibrahim

11.1. Introduction

So far, the international community has paid relatively little attention to either the human rights abuses endemic in Burma/Myanmar[1] since the early 1960s or the specific persecution of the Rohingya. One reason is its self-chosen isolation but also first the perceived difficulty of influencing the military regime and then, since 2010, a view that to place undue pressure on the government would undermine the gradual moves towards democracy. Equally, there has been a fear that to place too many demands on the Myanmar government would simply make them more reliant on Chinese backing. That would remove any incentive towards improving human rights, link Myanmar firmly to China's emerging economic zone and possibly give China a naval base on the Indian Ocean.

---

[1] For convenience, in this chapter the modern names of Myanmar (Burma) and Rakhine (Arakan) are used except where the original name is useful to place historical changes into their context.

This lack of clear sanctions for ongoing human rights abuses has effectively created the space in which the government of Myanmar has expelled one million of the estimated 1.6 million Rohingya still living in Myanmar in 2017–2018 with no significant sanctions or structured response. Those Rohingya still in Myanmar have been described in a judgement by the International Court of Justice (ICJ) as being 'extremely vulnerable' (Rosenberg 2020) to persecution and genocide.

The Rohingya are an ethnically distinct Muslim community that has lived in western Myanmar (in the region once known as Arakan and now as Rakhine province) for centuries (Ibrahim 2016). However, a key part of the narrative constructed first by the Burmese military regime and now widely shared across the majority Buddhist Burmese population is that the Rohingya are 'Bengalis' who arrived after British rule was imposed in 1826. That this is both false (Baxter 1941) and utterly irrelevant (Al Jazeera 2013) has not stopped it being spread by the military, by the Buddhist Monks (International Crisis Group 2013) and by the pro-democracy National League for Democracy (NLD; Global Post 2013). However, it is used to deny them citizenship in their own country and forms the basic justification used by the regime for their persecution and expulsion.

This prejudice has meant that while Myanmar has notionally moved from military rule to some form of democracy in the period 2010–2020, the Rohingya have faced ongoing persecution. Ethnic attacks in 2012 and 2013 set in train a wider refugee crisis and saw many forced into internal camps (United Nations 2013). The military attacks in the period 2017–2018 led to thousands of deaths and the expulsion of around one million Rohingya into Bangladesh (the remainder, some 600,000 live in isolated camps inside Myanmar to which access is controlled by the military; UNHCR 2018).

Against this background, the traditional attitudes of the United Nations (UN) and the wider Western community have to change. Myanmar is not enduring some problems on the bumpy road to democracy, it is ruled by an elite that have a shared hatred of its Muslim minority and now face charges of genocide at the ICJ (UN News 2019). The government of Myanmar has had almost 10 months to respond to a demand that it show how it will protect the Rohingya still in Rakhine and has conspicuously failed to do so (Rosenberg 2020) while being prepared to deny charges of human rights abuses at the ICJ (UN News 2019).

11.2. Persecution of the Rohingya

11.2.1. Background

All the limited linguistic, ethnic and written records tend to point to the Rohingya arriving in Arakan around 2,000 years ago (Gutman 1976) as the region was more accessible across the Bay of Bengal than through the mountains that separate it from the Irrawaddy valley. After 1000 CE, the Burman-related ethnic group, the Rakhine, moved into the region as Burmese power spread from Tibet into the Irrawaddy region. The next eight centuries saw Arakan (modern-day Rakhine) as part of the Burmese state, independent or dominated by Bengal. A resurgent Burma conquered the region in the 1780s with the intent on protecting the Buddhist Rakhine and protecting Buddhism from other religious influences. The resulting violence led to some 30,000 Muslims fleeing to Bengal. However, the gains were short-lived as Burmese expansion brought it into conflict with the British who conquered Arakan in 1826 (Paton 1826).

The immediate effect was the return of most of those Muslims who had fled, but the region retained its Buddhists Rakhine majority throughout the period of British rule (Baxter 1941). Under normal discussions an analysis of a modern-day genocide would need to take little account of the partial records indicating who lived where in the early 19th century. Unfortunately, the myth that the Rohingya are really 'Bengalis' who arrived during British rule is assiduously promoted by the Myanmar regime to justify their modern-day persecution and readily repeated by their apologists (see Leider 2012; Tonkin 2014, 2019).

Upon independence the Rohingya were initially given a status less than full citizenship but were acknowledged as part of the new Burmese nation (in contrast to the treatment of those seen as Indian nationals; Citizenship Election Officer 1948). In practice, the democratic government, which ruled up to 1962, treated them as any other ethnic group but this changed after the military coup. The military regime sought scapegoats for its increasingly failing economic policies (Ibrahim 2016). They were steadily stripped of their rights and from the mid-1970s faced systemic persecution (that in turn provoked regular refugee crises with Bangladesh; Sharples 2003).

The brief period of relative democracy from 1989 to 1992 saw little change. The nascent NLD formed an electoral alliance with the Rakhine-ethnic Arakan League for Democracy (which was calling for the Rohingya to be expelled; National League for Democracy 2003) and subsequently challenged the right to have votes, and be in the parliament, of the few ethnic Rohingya who had won seats. In effect, the NLD differed from the military as to who should be in charge and the direction of the country, but they fully shared the prejudices against the Rohingya (Lubina 2019).

11.2.2. Since 2010

The return of relative democracy in 2010 (United Nations 2011) also saw a return of the electoral alliance between the NLD and the Rakhine extremists. Thus, local politics in the region continued to exclude the Rohingya and they faced ongoing discrimination and violence. This led to communal violence in 2012 mainly between the Rakhine and the Rohingya though in places the military joined in the attacks (Human Rights Watch 2012). A subsequent investigation by the Myanmar authorities was to blame the Rohingya for harming the good name of Myanmar among the international community (Rakhine Investigation Committee 2013). Far worse attacks followed in 2013, this time carefully orchestrated (not least via Facebook; Al Jazeera 2014) with the goal of forcing the Rohingya to live away from the Rakhine (Human Rights Council 2014). Again, the authorities initially denied any state involvement (United Nations 2013) despite overwhelming evidence to the contrary (Quintana 2014).

This period of persecution ended with the majority of the Rohingya driven from their homes and forced to live in internal camps. Here, they were denied work, education and healthcare and were effectively segregated from the Rakhine majority. One response was to try and escape, mostly by sea, to Malaysia, Indonesia and Thailand in search of work and refuge. This escalated in 2015 when those countries closed their borders stranding many Rohingya at sea. In the end, Myanmar was forced to take the refugees back, but many families had paid smugglers with their final assets leaving them even more impoverished.

Ongoing persecution and disappointment that the NLD continued to ignore the Rohingya after its electoral victory in 2015 led to the emergence of a small-scale military response. The Arakan Rohingya Solidarity Army (ARSA) appeared in October 2016, when it attacked three police outposts and killed nine police officers. It carried out more attacks in 2017. The emergence of ARSA fitted neatly into the preferred narrative of the Myanmar state that it faces a sustained terrorist threat to its very existence due to the presence of the Rohingya (ICC 2019). The origins of ARSA are obscure, but they most likely were funded by the small Rohingya diaspora in Saudi Arabia and Pakistan (International Crisis Group 2016) and the extent they have links to the wider international jihadi movements is limited. This has not stopped the Myanmar authorities seeing their emergence as proof of their long-repeated claims about links between the Rohingya community and Al-Qaeda (Ibrahim 2016).

The practical implication of ARSA's attacks was that the violence against the Rohingya that followed in the period 2017–2018 was led by the army even if it also involved local Rakhine groups. In the violence of 2012–2013, the army had played an ambiguous role, sometimes leading the attacks, in others making some attempt to protect the Rohingya. This time it led and organized a genocidal onslaught, burning villages and using murder and rape to force the Rohingya to flee. By August 2017, some 150,000 had fled to Bangladesh, by the end of the year around one million were living in, or near, the refugee camps at Cox's Bazar.

In August 2020, the Electoral Commission disqualified six Rohingya candidates, including Kyaw Min who had been first elected in the 1990 elections (in support of the military USDP). The reason was the claim that the candidates were unable to prove that their parents were citizens of Burma at the time of their birth as per the openly discriminatory 1982 Citizenship regulations (UNHCR 1982).

11.3. International Involvement

11.3.1. The Wider International Community

Upon independence from Britain in 1948, Burma opted not to remain part of the wider British Commonwealth and turned down much of the financial aid the British offered to most of their former colonies (Charney 2009). However, the new Burmese regime did join the UN (Steinberg 2010) and became one of the main players in the emerging Non-aligned Movement (Abraham 2008). This relative engagement with the outside world ended with the military coup in 1962. Despite its claim to be a socialist regime it had relatively little contact either with the USSR or China (Busczynski 1986), even though it later found a more congenial ally in North Korea (with whom it traded food for weaponry; *Asia Times* 2013). In general, the regime was dismissive of foreign involvement and any external pressure over human rights.

From 2007 onwards, it had growing commercial links with China (OilPrice 2010) as it sought external investment. With the return to relative democracy in 2010, Myanmar looked for more external investment (Reuters 2014a) and generally gained political support from the USA, the UK and the European Union (EU; Dosch and Sidhu 2015). The underlying logic was that all these powers wished to support moves to what they hoped would be a full democracy and, possibly equally important, prevent Myanmar becoming too closely aligned with China (*Myanmar Times* 2015). Equally, the regime was prepared to use the threat of having to rely on China to force concessions from its neighbours, notably during the 2015 refugee crisis (*The Atlantic* 2015), when it was under pressure from other ASEAN states.

It is possible to characterize the approach of the EU, the US and the UK as broadly seeking to not pressure the NLD to act in a manner that might have provoked a backlash from the military and to reduce the risk that Myanmar would turn to China for support (Hurst 2017). In effect, this reflected a combination of the power rivalries between the US and China and a willingness to see internal violence and unrest as part of the process of moving from authoritarian to democratic rule. At its worst, this mindset saw the EU praise the regime for its restraint (*The Guardian* 2014) in how it handled the ethnic cleansing of the Rohingya in 2013. Even after the government banned outside agencies such as Médecins Sans Frontières (MSF) from working in Rakhine, the twin desires to minimize Chinese influence and to support the NLD meant there was little systemic criticism of Myanmar's actions (*New York Times* 2017).

11.3.2. The UN and Its Agencies

The UN and its related bodies (UNHCR 2001) such as the International Labour Organization (1998) have long been aware of systemic human rights abuses in Burma. During the military rule, the UN struggled to bring effective pressure on the regime, but it had to also deal with the regular refugee crises that erupted when the Rohingya were driven into Bangladesh as well as refugees fleeing the various border wars into Thailand and Cambodia. Here, the UN became complicit in Bangladesh's enduring focus on returning the Rohingya to Burma even if they then faced further persecution (Sharples 2003). This error was repeated at each turn of the persecution of the Rohingya (ViceNews 2016).

The military violence of 2017–2018 shifted some of these attitudes (UNHCR 2018) and led to a systemic reappraisal of the UN's historical approach to the Rohingya (Rosenthal 2019). In effect, historically, the UN felt it had to try to remain engaged to mitigate the worst effects and this led to compromises both with Myanmar and Bangladesh. However, in doing so, it understated just how deep-seated the prejudice against the Rohingya is and that this was widely shared by the NLD and its leader, Aung San Suu Kyi (McPherson 2016). As a consequence, Myanmar has faced very few sanctions until Gambia brought a charge of genocide to the ICJ in 2018 (Venkatraman and Jordana 2020).

11.4. Bangladesh and the Immediate Neighbours

As noted earlier, Bangladesh is probably the one state most affected by the persecution of the Rohingya. The simple geography of the state has made it the preferred location of majority of refugees every time there has been violence in Myanmar. The first wave occurred in the mid-1970s and this set a dynamic that has been repeated. At that time, Bangladesh was struggling to recover from its war with Pakistan and lacked resources to cope with a large refugee population. It had no desire to also reward the Burmese military for their ethnic cleansing (Médecins Sans Frontières 2002), and this has led to a dual policy of denying the Rohingya refugee status and collaborating with Burma/Myanmar to force them to return.

Myanmar's other neighbours have been less directly affected (Alternative ASEAN Network on Burma 2009) by the persecution of the Rohingya. The two regional Muslim-majority states (Indonesia and Malaysia) have generally been unwilling to directly criticize the domestic actions of another member state of the ASEAN grouping. This briefly changed during the period after 2013 when both states (along with Thailand) faced substantial numbers of refugees fleeing by sea (*The Observer* 2015). This led to them blocking the refugees from landing in 2015 and tried to force Myanmar to both repatriate the refugees and stop the persecution of the Rohingya. During this crisis, Myanmar quite deliberately indicated that if it was criticized (*New York Times* 2015), then it would become more reliant on China in response. Equally, the Myanmar regime was more worried that the Rohingya were only using that name in the hope of gaining international sympathy (*The Guardian* 2015a) while at the same time announcing that there was to be 'no change in the government's policy toward the Bengalis'.

Overall, ASEAN states have expressed concern about Myanmar's actions towards the Rohingya especially when the refugee crises have threatened to destabilize the region. A further deterrence to action is the perception that Myanmar is now closely aligned with China, and ASEAN tends to avoid any conflict with China due to the wider dynamics across Southeast Asia.

11.4.1. Next Steps

11.4.1.1. *The Current Refugee Crisis*

Since late 2017, the United Nations High Commissioner for Refugees (UNHCR) has officially recorded almost 750,000 Rohingya refugees in Bangladesh, mostly near to the border around Cox's Bazar (UNHCR 2019), and it is estimated the true number is closer to one million. In effect, the Cox's Bazar region has become the biggest refugee camp in the world. Of these, 53 per cent are under the age of 17. These young people often act as heads of families, lack access to educational opportunities and are suffering from mental health problems (Riley et al. 2017) as many family units were disrupted during their flight (and often their parents were murdered; Reliefweb 2018; UNHCR 2017).

This has represented a major challenge to the authorities in Bangladesh, especially as historically they have been unwilling to accept Rohingya refugees and regularly try to send them back to Myanmar (Médecins Sans Frontières 2002) and to reject the racist dialogue of many Myanmar politicians that the Rohingya are really 'Bengalis'. Equally, it has been prepared to use the Rohingya in its other disputes with Myanmar, seeing them as useful for embarrassing Myanmar in front of the international community. However, Bangladesh is also denying the refugees the right to work, trying to relocate them to islands in the Bay of Bengal and return them to Myanmar. The result is the situation in the camps is dire, and the Bangladeshi authorities have started to accuse the refugees of engaging in criminal acts while denying them the ability to work to earn a living.

At the moment, if the Rohingya do go back to Myanmar the most likely fate is to be placed in the internal camps which have been widely criticized as lacking basic amenities. There is also a widespread fear that such camps are an easy target if the Myanmar regime decides on outright genocide (Early Warning Project 2015). What is not on offer from Myanmar is the ability to return to the lands the Rohingya were driven from in 2017, especially as many villages have been burnt to the ground. As noted, to change this will mean sustained pressure on

Suu Kyi and the NLD to reverse their own collusion with 40 years of systemic denigration of the Rohingya and the denial of their rights to live in Myanmar.

11.5. The Charge of Genocide

Genocide never starts with mass murder, most commonly it starts with the denial of basic shared human rights and the exclusion of an identifiable group from the wider polity. If this is combined with a wider social attitude that a given group has no rights and an elite that reflects only one ethnic, political or confessional group, then there are few internal breaks on the situation escalating. The US-based Holocaust Memorial Museum (Rosenberg 2020) places particular weight on the first two (citizenship and inclusion in civic life) as precursors to genocide and the Rohingya have been denied both for over 50 years in Myanmar.

Even so genocide has a particular meaning defined in the UN Convention on the Prevention and Punishment of the Crime of Genocide adopted in 1951 (United Nations 1951). A key part to the convention is that genocide includes the 'intent to destroy, in whole or in part, a national, ethnical, racial or religious group'. Culpability is established not just by the act of genocide but by conspiracy to do so, incitement to do so, attempts to do so and complicity. So, the test is substantial, not only must an identifiable group face destruction (at least in a given location), the regime must be complicit and actively engaged. Inter-communal violence, however bad, will fail this second test.

This interpretation has been used consistently at the ICJ (Rosenberg 2020), where, in the case of Serb aggression in Bosnia, a key concept was when should the Serbian regime have known of the existence of a serious risk of genocide will be committed as that represents the moment where the regime failed to abide by the need to prevent genocide. Myanmar ratified the 1948 Convention on the Prevention and Punishment of the Crime of Genocide and so shares the obligation to prevent and punish genocide.

There have been several attempts to bring a charge of genocide to the ICJ, but these have historically been rejected as not being backed by another signatory state. Gambia is also a signatory to the Convention and has invoked its right that the ICJ must rule on the following charges (Wes Rist 2020):

1. Myanmar has violated the provisions of the Genocide Convention.
2. Myanmar must cease any acts that violate the Convention (in effect, stop committing genocide) but also to implement its obligation to prevent genocide.
3. Myanmar must hold individuals who committed acts in violation of the Genocide Convention criminally accountable within its domestic legal system.
4. Myanmar must pay reparations to the Rohingya, including allowing them to return to Myanmar, reinstating their citizenship and undertaking protection of the group's human rights.
5. Myanmar must demonstrate its intent to not commit further violations of the Genocide Convention.

In addition, Gambia asked for provisional measures to prevent any further acts of genocide while these charges are being considered. In February 2020, the ICJ agreed to this and ordered Myanmar to:

1. immediately stop all acts that could possibly be construed as violations of the Genocide Convention;
2. exert control over any non-state actors (like militias or paramilitary groups) that might also be committing such acts;
3. preserve evidence (and explicitly forbid it from destroying evidence) which might relate to genocidal acts;
4. cooperate with the UN and any of its bodies that might seek to investigate ongoing violence related to the case.

Myanmar, so far, has not responded to show how it will protect those Rohingya still in Rakhine (Rosenberg 2020) nor has it reported back to the ICJ. Since Suu Kyi refused to consider that human rights abuses had taken place in 2017 (BBC 2019) or to use the word Rohingya in her evidence, this suggests they intend to ignore the ICJ ruling and do anything to protect the remaining Rohingya.

11.6. The Need to Force Myanmar to Act

Suu Kyi and the NLD face no domestic pressure to respond or stop the persecution of the Rohingya. It is a prejudice widely spread among the population, shared with the Buddhist monks who give them much of their popular support and sees them aligned with the mindset of the military leaders. Even if they wanted to act, local politics in Rakhine are dominated by the latest incarnation of the ethnic Rakhine party that has long called for the expulsion of the Rohingya and was behind the 2012–2013 violence.

In preparation for the 2020 elections, they intend to use the same census (Ferguson 2015), and it seems the NLD is confident enough of a large majority as it no longer raises the problem that the military retain 25 per cent of the seats for its own nominees. If in 2015, the NLD was complicit in refusing to let the Rohingya vote, in 2020 it has overseen a situation where one million Rohingya are refugees in Bangladesh. Unfortunately, the EU is also complicit in this process. For the period 2017–2020 it has given Myanmar almost 700 million euros for projects including providing 'access to justice and legal aid for the poor and vulnerable'. This is despite no progress on human rights since 2015 and the mass-murder and expulsion of the Rohingya in 2017. The EU's documentation follows that of Myanmar's census, and, coyly, fails to mention the Rohingya, merely reflecting on problems in Rakhine State. Having illusions about Suu Kyi and the NLD was understandable (if wrong) in 2012–2015, given their record in power, funding them and failing to name their victims are tantamount to endorsement of genocide.

This lack of pressure matters. The Rohingya diaspora is poor, in most places they have long been denied refugee status, so there is little scope for them to place external pressure on Myanmar. The NLD faces no real domestic pressure to change its policy and as long as international bodies see this as a technical problem to be managed, they will ignore all requests. At some stage the 600,000 Rohingya still in the camps in Rakhine will become the next victims.

The Gambia called on the UN Security Council 'to fulfill its role in ensuring compliance with the Court's Order' (Rosenberg 2020).

However, China has already threatened a veto in the UN Security Council to prevent discussion on the situation in Myanmar suggesting that the UN will be unable to act due to this veto.

If so, then the regime faces no domestic pressure to stop the persecution, has a powerful external backer and continues to enjoy a degree of tolerance due to a view that Suu Kyi is committed to human rights (Lubina 2019). The ICJ ruling matters not in terms of really protecting the Rohingya still in Myanmar but in making it clear that any further attacks will meet the definition of genocide. Myanmar knows what its policies will lead to.

The military coup in 2021 is irrelevant to the persecution of the Rohingya. As noted, the NLD shares the same prejudices as the military and was prepared to go to the Hague to justify the 2017 violence. At the same time, while Bangladesh was trying to repatriate the Rohingya, and ensure they are isolated in refugee camps, the coup again makes little practical difference. The NLD was unable and unwilling to arrange for a safe return, and the same generals who organized the 2017 expulsion are not going to enable the return of the Rohingya.

At one level, the coup presents the international community with a stark choice. It cannot assume that a democratic government, constrained by domestic politics, is acting in good faith towards the Rohingya. In many ways, the coup simply confirms what was already the case, that between 2010 and 2017, the government of Myanmar carried out an act of genocide. If there is a positive side, there are some suggestions that some of the population of Myanmar now recognize what happened to the Rohingya and that the Rohingya are offering support and trying to build links with the opposition.

11.7. Conclusion

The current situation of the Rohingya is intolerable. Many are scattered across the wider region working with no rights in low-wage work (and that is where they avoid conditions of slavery on Thai fishing boats; Environmental Justice Foundation 2014; Equal Rights Trust

2014; *The Guardian* 2015b) and with no refugee status. Those in India have become caught up in Modi's ongoing anti-Muslim campaigns and face expulsion. The bulk are now in refugee camps in Cox's Bazar denied the chance to work and at the mercy of a host government that wishes them gone. A significant minority remain in internal camps in Myanmar at the whim of a government that carried out mass murder and rape and burnt Rohingya villages in 2017.

In effect, they run the risk of the fate of the Palestinians. Their new host countries are very unwilling to accept them as part of the population, even though many are descendants of those who fled in 1948. As such, they can neither integrate into their host nations nor return to their homes. But their plight is readily used by Islamists and Arab nationalists who wish to challenge Israel. Some of this is reflected in how Bangladesh acts, it does not want the Rohingya, it does not wish to accept the outcomes of Myanmar's ethnic cleansing, but the Rohingya are a ready means to criticize and challenge Myanmar in terms of regional disputes and politics.

This presents a practical challenge to the world. Even if what happened in 2017 is found to be not genocide at the ICJ, it was clearly a crime against humanity and the Myanmar military are guilty of gross human rights abuses. So, the challenge is basically what can be done and what has to change to allow the Rohingya to go home.

First, there can be no illusion of voluntary domestic reform in Myanmar. In 2015, some in the NLD were calling for an acknowledgement that continued verbal attacks would inevitably lead to violence (*Sydney Morning Herald* 2015), but this was rejected by Suu Kyi who consistently refused to speak up for the Rohingya (Sacirbey 2013; Winn 2013) and has been accused of systemic anti-Muslim bias (*The Telegraph* 2016). For the NLD there is no domestic reason to alter course. It shares and promotes the narrative that the Rohingya do not belong in Myanmar (McPherson 2016) and its leader is content to justify actions that forced one million people to flee for their lives (BBC 2019). Such prejudices now fit well with the beliefs of the Burman and Rakhine Buddhist majority in Myanmar. Equally, the NLD seems to have come to an electoral duopoly with the military regime (at least in terms of the votes of the Buddhist majority) and has nothing to gain and much to lose (in terms of internal politics) by breaking the consensus on the Rohingya.

Internationally there are two problems.

First, Myanmar has expelled many NGOs and limits the scope of the UN, especially in Rakhine (UNHCR 2018). Linked to this is the enduring view of organizations such as the EU that Myanmar is on a democratic path and it would be unwise to push the NLD into conflict with the military (Reuters 2012). It is time to put this hope to rest, there is no reason why the NLD will come into conflict with the military. More importantly, the NLD will not stop the persecution of the Rohingya and no degree of careful use of words will alter this. However, the ICJ statement of early 2020 (Venkatraman and Jordana 2020) is very useful. Due to its wording, if anything happens to the remaining Rohingya in Myanmar, then a charge of genocide can be sustained as this time the regime cannot argue they were unaware of the consequences of their policies.

Second, as elsewhere, China has emerged a major backer. ASEAN traditionally avoids conflict with China limiting the scope for a regional response. In addition, China has tried to ensure that the UN Security Council will not discuss human rights abuses in Myanmar. However, while China gives Myanmar a degree of security, this comes at a price. If Myanmar becomes too reliant on China, then China will expect to dominate both domestic politics and the local economy. In addition, while China is still powerful, more states are prepared to challenge its actions than previously. This wider, and welcome, shift of Western attitudes may place Myanmar in a difficult position. So far, it has managed to combine closer ties with China with other international links and sources of external investment. This relative independence is something that Burma has prized since 1948, and it may be less content to become a Chinese satellite than it implies.

On the one hand, we are faced with a classic problem. We have a state that has genocidal policies towards a minority and over which it appears we have little influence. If so, we have nothing to gain from pandering to the regime and can assert some basic principles in our dealing with Myanmar. The Rohingya must be given full citizenship of the state of their birth (Gibson, James, and Falvey 2016; Rosenberg 2020), and this demand should be raised in every instance. Equally, there should be no accommodation to Myanmar's sensitivities about using the name Rohingya. On the other hand, we should demand the full return of the refugees, to their villages, with full protection and compensation. This will be uncomfortable as it means challenging 60 years of ingrained prejudice in Myanmar, but unless we do this, then the Rohingya remain stateless, persecuted and isolated.

Finally, it is worth stressing the regime is not impervious to pressure. The ICJ ruling means that any more violence against the Rohingya will sustain a charge of genocide. It remains possible that the current case by the Gambia might lead to this, but the grounds are less secure. This will concentrate minds in the NLD as to the practical consequences of their actions. Also, while China can act as a protector in some forums, it is unlikely that the Myanmar authorities wish to become fully reliant on China. In effect, they may well wish to seek a counterbalance to Chinese control, and the price of this has to be the rights of the Rohingya. Both these are tasks that the international community can, and should, carry out.

References

Abraham, Itty. 2008. 'From Bandung to Nam: Non-alignment and Indian Foreign Policy, 1947–65.' *Commonwealth & Comparative Politics* 46, no. 2: 195–219.

Al Jazeera. 2013, 18 October. 'No Place for Islam? Buddhist Nationalism in Myanmar.' Al Jazeera. Available at http://www.aljazeera.com/ indepth/opinion/2013/10/no-place-islam-buddhist-nationalism-myan-mar-2013101710411233906.html (accessed on 26 February 2014).

———. 2014, 14 June. 'Facebook in Myanmar: Amplifying Hate Speech?' Available at http://www.aljazeera.com/indepth/features/2014/06/facebook-myanmar-rohingya-amplifying-hate-speech-2014612112834290144.html (accessed on 19 February 2015).

Alternative ASEAN Network on Burma. 2009. *Rohingya, Asylum Seekers and Migrants from Burma: A Human Security Priority for ASEAN*. Bangkok: Alternative ASEAN Network on Burma.

Asia Times. 2013, 5 September. 'Myanmar, North Korea Stay Brothers in Arms.' *Asia Times*. Available at http://www.atimes.com/atimes/Southeast_Asia/ SEA-01-050913.html (accessed on 27 June 2015).

Baxter, James. 1941. *Report on Indian Immigration*. Calcutta: Rabgoon, Superintendent Government Printing and Stationery.

BBC. 2019, 12 December. 'Myanmar Rohingya: Suu Kyi Accused of "Silence" in Genocide Trial.' BBC. Available at https://www.bbc.co.uk/news/world-asia-50763180 (accessed on 7 January 2020).

Busczynski, Leszek. 1986. *Soviet Foreign Policy and Southeast Asia.* London: Routledge.

Charney, Michael W. 2009. *A History of Modern Burma.* Cambridge: Cambridge University Press.

Citizenship Election Officer. 1948. 'Indigenous Race Recognition.' Available at https://www.burmalibrary.org/sites/burmalibrary.org/files/obl/docs/Union_Citizenship_%28Election%29_Act-1948.htm?__cf_chl_jschl_tk__=pmd_TfL2BCI2l3mVEocpVJXLp1bt0zYdH5TzYL0z_CT4OGg-1631564089-0-gqNtZGzNAjujcnBszQel (accessed on 10 September, 2021).

Dosch, Jörn, and Jatswan S. Sidhu. 2015. 'The European Union's Myanmar Policy: Focused or Directionless?' *Journal of Current Southeast Asian Affairs* 34, no. 2: 85–112.

Early Warning Project. 2015. 'Risk of Mass Atrocities and Policies of Persecution in Burma.' Available at http://www.earlywarningproject.com/2015/07/16/policies-of-persecution-in-burma (accessed on 15 October 2015).

Environmental Justice Foundation. 2014. 'Slavery at Sea: The Continued Plight of Trafficked Migrants in Thailand's Fishing Industry.' Environmental Justice Foundation. Available at http://ejfoundation.org/sites/default/files/public/EJF_Slavery-at-Sea_report_2014_web-ok.pdf (accessed on)

Equal Rights Trust. 2014. 'The Human Rights of the Stateless Rohingya in Thailand.' Equal Rights Trust. Available at http://www.equalrightstrust.org/ertdocumentbank/The%20Human%20Rights%20of%20Stateless%20Rohingya%20in%20Thailand%28small%29.pdf (accessed on 12 August 2021).

Ferguson, Jane M. 2015. 'Who's Counting? Ethnicity, Belonging and the National Census in Burma/Myanmar.' *Bijdragen Tot de Taal, Lad en Volkenkunde* 171: 1–28. https://doi.org/doi: 10.1163/22134379-17101022

Gibson, Trevor, H. James, and L. Falvey. 2016. *Rohingyas: Insecurity and Citizenship in Myanmar.* Songkhla: Thaksin University Press.

Global Post. 2013, 2 May. 'Suu Kyi Spokesman: "There Is No Rohingya."' Available at http://www.globalpost.com/dispatch/news/regions/asia-pacific/myanmar/130501/suu-kyi-no-rohingya (accessed on 26 February 2014).

Gutman, Pamela. 1976. 'Ancient Arakan.' PhD diss., Department of Asian Civilisations, The Australian National University, Canberra.

Human Rights Council. 2014. *Hear Our Screams.* Geneva: Human Rights Council.

Human Rights Watch. 2012. *The Government Should Have Stopped This.* New York, NY: Human Rights Watch.

Hurst. 2017, 11 September. 'Why the U.S. Cannot Ignore the Rohingya.' Available at https://www.hurstpublishers.com/u-s-cannot-ignore-rohingya/ (accessed on 1 July 2019).

Ibrahim, Azeem. 2016. *The Rohingyas: Inside Myanmar's Hidden Genocide.* Oxford: Oxford University Press.

ICC. 2019, 28 January. 'Myanmar: Humanitarian Crisis and Armed Escalation.' Available at https://www.crisisgroup.org/asia/south-east-asia/myanmar/myanmar-humanitarian-crisis-and-armed-escalation (accessed on 15 December 2019).

ILO. 1998, 2 July. 'Forced Labour in Myanmar (Burma).' Available at http://www.ilo.org/public/english/standards/relm/gb/docs/gb273/myanmar3.htm (accessed on 1 March 2014).

International Crisis Group. 2013. 'The Dark Side of Transition: Violence against Muslims in Myanmar.' Available at http://www.crisisgroup.org/~/media/Files/asia/south-east-asia/burma-myanmar/251-the-dark-side-of-transition-violence-against-muslims-in-myanmar (accessed on 12 August 2021).

———. 2016. 'Myanmar: A New Muslim Insurgency in Rakhine State.' International Crisis Group. Available at https://www.crisisgroup.org/asia/south-east-asia/myanmar/283-myanmar-new-muslim-insurgency-rakhine-state (accessed on 12 August 2021).

Leider, Jacques P. 2012. '"Rohingya," Rakhaing and the Recent Outbreak of Violence—A Note.' *Burma Studies* 89/90: 8–12.

Lubina, Michał. 2019. *The Moral Democracy: The Political Thought of Aung San Suu Kyi.* Warsaw: Scholar.

McPherson, P. 2016, 23 May. '"No Muslims Allowed": How Nationalism Is Rising in Aung San Suu Kyi's Myanmar.' *The Guardian.* Available at http://www.theguardian.com/world/2016/may/23/no-muslims-allowed-how-nationalism-is-rising-in-aung-san-suu-kyis-myanmar?CMP=Share_AndroidApp_Tweet (accessed on 23 May 2016).

Médecins Sans Frontières. 2002. *10 Years for the Rohingya Refugees in Bangladesh: Past, Present and Future.* Geneva: Médecins Sans Frontières.

Myanmar Times. 2015, 8 July. 'On China, the Lady Has No Choice.' *Myanmar Times.* Available at http://asiapacific.anu.edu.au/newmandala/2015/07/08/on-china-the-lady-has-no-choice/ (accessed on 20 August 2015).

National League for Democracy. 2003, 1 February. '1990 Multi Party Democracy: General Elections.' National League for Democracy. Available at http://www.ibiblio.org/obl/docs/1990_elections.htm (accessed on 2 July 2015).

New York Times. 2015, 21 May. 'In Reversal, Myanmar Agrees to Attend Meeting on Migrant Crisis.' *New York Times.* Available at http://www.nytimes.com/2015/05/22/world/asia/myanmar-rohingya-migrant-crisis-malaysia-thailand-indonesia.html?_r=0 (accessed on 15 June 2015).

———. 2017, 18 September. 'Aung San Suu Kyi, a Much-changed Icon, Evades Rohingya Accusations.' Available at https://www.nytimes.com/2017/09/18/world/asia/aung-san-suu-kyi-speech-rohingya.html (accessed on 10 October 2017).

OilPrice. 2010, 15 September. 'China Backs Burma's Junta Leaders.' Available at http://oilprice.com/Geopolitics/Asia/China-Backs-Burmas-Junta-Leaders.html (accessed on 1 July 2015).

Paton, Charles. 1826. *A Short Report on Arakan.* London: Colonial Office.
Quintana, Tomás Ojea. 2014. *Report of the Special Rapporteur on the Situation of Human Rights in Myanmar.* Geneva: United Nations General Assembly.
Rakhine Investigation Committee. 2013. 'Summary of Recommendations. Government of Myanmar.' Available at https://docs.google.com/file/d/0B6-RIYkUW0vjR0ZqOU1xc3k2SnM/edit?pli=1 (accessed on 12 August 2021).
Reliefweb. 2018, 22 January. 'Psychological Support for Refugee Children of Myanmar in Bangladesh.' Available at https://reliefweb.int/report/bangladesh/psychological-support-refugee-children-myanmar-bangladesh (accessed on 4 April 2018).
Reuters. 11 June 2012. 'Eu Welcomes "Measured" Myanmar Response to Rioting.' Available at http://uk.reuters.com/article/2012/06/11/us-myanmar-violence-idUSBRE85A01C20120611 (accessed on 18 June 2015).
———. 2014a, 16 September. 'Myanmar Sees Foreign Investment Topping $5 Bln in 2014-15.' Available at http://www.reuters.com/article/2014/09/16/myanmar-investment-idUSL3N0RH3EZ20140916 (accessed on 20 April 2015).
———. 2014b. 27 August. 'Will the Rohingya, Driven from Their Homes, Spend the Rest of Their Lives Segregated in Ghettoes?' Available at http://www.trust.org/item/20140827082155-p627d/ (accessed on 20 July 2015).
Riley, A., A. Varner, P. Ventevogel, M. M. Taimur Hasan, and C. Welton-Mitchell. 2017. 'Daily Stressors, Trauma Exposure, and Mental Health among Stateless Rohingya Refugees in Bangladesh.' *Transcultural Psychiatry* 54, no. 3: 304–331. Available at https://www.ncbi.nlm.nih.gov/pubmed/28540768 (accessed on 12 August 2021).
Rosenberg, Erin. 2020. *Practical Prevention: How the Genocide Convention's Obligation to Prevent Applies to Myanmar.* Washington, DC: United States Holocaust Memorial Museum. Available at https://www.ushmm.org/m/pdfs/Practical_Prevention_Report_2.pdf (accessed on 12 August 2021).
Rosenthal, Gert. 2019. *A Brief and Independent Inquiry into the Involvement of the United Nations in Myanmar from 2010 to 2018.* New York, NY: UN. Available at https://www.un.org/sg/sites/www.un.org.sg/files/atoms/files/Myanmar%20Report%20-%20May%202019.pdf (accessed on 12 August 2021).
Sacirbey, Muhamed. 2013. 'Aung San Suu Kyi -- Silence to Genocide?' Huffington Post. Available at http://www.huffingtonpost.com/ambassador-muhamed-sacirbey/aung-san-suu-kyi-silence-_b_3032958.html (accessed on 25 February 2014).
Sharples, R. 2003. 'Repatriating the Rohingya.' *Burma Issues* 13, no. 3: 1–3.
Steinberg, David I. 'The United States and Myanmar: A "Boutique Issue?"' *International Affairs* 86, no. 1: 175–194.
Sydney Morning Herald. 2015, 20 May. '"They Are Humans": Myanmar Opposition Says Rohingya People Have Rights.' Available at http://www.smh.com.au/world/they-are-humans-myanmar-opposition-says-rohingya-

people-have-rights-20150519-gh4q8m.html (accessed on 23 September 2015).

The Atlantic. 2015, 12 June. 'Burma Doesn't Want the Rohingya but Insists on Keeping Them.' The Atlantic. Available at http://www.theatlantic.com/ international/archive/2015/06/burma-rohingya-migration-ban/395729/ (accessed on 15 June 2015).

The Guardian. 2014, 28 February. 'Burma Tells Medécins Sans Frontières to Leave State Hit by Sectarian Violence.' Available at http://www.theguardian.com/ world/2014/feb/28/burma-medecins-sans-frontieres-rakhine-state (accessed on 1 March 2014).

———. 2015a, 22 May. 'Burma Military Chief Claims Refugees Pretending to Be Rohingya to Get Aid.' Available at http://www.theguardian.com/world/2015/ may/22/burma-military-chief-claims-refugees-pretending-to-be-rohingya-to-get-aid (accessed on 15 June 2015).

———. 2015b, 20 July. 'Revealed: How the Thai Fishing Industry Traffics, Imprisons and Enslaves.' Available at http://www.theguardian.com/global-development/2015/jul/20/thai-fishing-industry-implicated-enslavement-deaths-rohingya (accessed on 20 July 2015).

The Observer. 2015, 17 May. 'Burma's Boatpeople Faced Choice of Annihilation or Risking Their Lives at Sea.' *The Observer.* Available at http://www.theguardian.com/world/2015/may/17/rohingya-burma-refugees-boat-migrants (accessed on 15 June 2015).

The Telegraph. 2016, 25 March. 'Aung San Suu Kyi in Anti-Muslim Spat with BBC Presenter.' Available at http://www.telegraph.co.uk/news/2016/03/25/ aung-san-suu-kyi-in-anti-muslim-spat-with-bbc-presenter/ (accessed on 1 May 2016).

Tonkin, Derek. 2019. *Migration from Bengal to Arakan during British Rule 1826–1948.* Brussels: Torkel Opsahl Academic EPublisher.

———. 2014. *The 'Rohingya' Identity: British Experience in Arakan 1826–1948.* Rangoon: Network Myanmar.

UNHCR. 1982, 15 October. 'Burma Citizenship Law.' Available at http://www. refworld.org/docid/3ae6b4f71b.html (accessed on 28 February 2014).

———. 2001. *Oral Statements (Burma).* Geneva: UNHCR.

———. 2017, 26 October. 'Mental Health First Aid on the Frontlines of the Rohingya Crisis.' Available at http://www.unhcr.org/uk/news/ stories/2017/10/59de22951b/mental-health-first-aid-frontlines-rohingya-crisis.html (accessed on 4 April 2018).

———. 2018. *Report of the Detailed Findings of the Independent International Fact-Finding Mission on Myanmar.* New York, NY: United Nations Human Rights Council. Available at https://www.ohchr.org/en/hrbodies/hrc/myanmarFFM/ Pages/ReportoftheMyanmarFFM.aspx (accessed on 12 August 2021).

———. 2019, 31 May. 'Refugee Response in Bangladesh.' Available at https:// data2.unhcr.org/en/situations/myanmar_refugees (accessed on 15 June 2019).

UN News. 2019, 11 December. 'Aung San Suu Kyi Defends Myanmar from Accusations of Genocide, at Top Un Court.' Available at https://news.un.org/en/story/2019/12/1053221 (accessed on 9 January 2020).

United Nations. 1951. *Convention on the Prevention and Punishment of the Crime of Genocide.* New York, NY: United Nations. Available at https://treaties.un.org/doc/Publication/UNTS/Volume%2078/volume-78-I-1021-English.pdf (accessed on 12 August 2021).

———. 2011. *Burma's 2010 Elections: A Comprehensive Report.* New York, NY: Burma Fund UN Office. Available at http://www.burmalibrary.org/docs11/BurmaFund-Election_Report-text.pdf (accessed on 12 August 2021).

———. 2013. *Situation of Human Rights in Myanmar.* New York, NY: United Nations. Available at http://www.ohchr.org/Documents/Countries/MM/A-68-397_en.pdf (accessed on 12 August 2021).

Venkatraman, Prachiti, and Ashley Jordana. 2020, 4 October. 'Myanmar's Compliance with the Icj Provisional Measures Order & the Road Ahead.' UK Human Rights. Available at https://ukhumanrightsblog.com/2020/09/03/myanmars-compliance-with-the-icj-provisional-measures-order-the-road-ahead/ (accessed on 12 August 2021).

ViceNews. 2016, 22 May. 'Leaked Documents Show How the Un Failed to Protect Myanmar's Persecuted Rohingya.' Available at https://news.vice.com/article/how-the-un-failed-to-protect-myanmars-persecuted-rohingya (accessed on 23 May 2016).

Wes Rist, D. 'What Does the Icj Decision on the Gambia V. Myanmar Mean?' *ASIL Insights* 24, no. 2. Available at https://www.asil.org/insights/volume/24/issue/2/what-does-icj-decision-gambia-v-myanmar-mean (accessed on 12 August 2021).

Winn, P. 2013. 'Suu Kyi Spokesman: "There Is No Rohingya."' The World.

CHAPTER 12

'Situated Knowledge'

Exploring Global Civil Society Views on the Rohingya Crisis

Paul Chaney

12.1. Introduction

This chapter explores the crisis faced by an estimated one million Rohingya people (UNHCR 2020a), a Muslim minority group that fled persecution in Rakhine State, Myanmar and took shelter in Bangladesh. Yet, Myanmar has denied them citizenship and Bangladesh has denied them even refugee-hood. They have become subject to inhuman treatment, oppression and rights denial. This chapter addresses the question: how can the extensive data from three cycles of United Nations' Universal Periodic Review (UPR)—the five-yearly monitoring mechanism associated with UN human rights treaties—inform our understanding of the plight of the Rohingya in Bangladesh? It draws on the 'situated knowledge' (Stoetzler and Yuval-Davis 2002) of civil society organizations' daily experience of the emergency; specifically, the perspectives of non-governmental organizations (NGOs) working with the Rohingya refugees as set out in their UPR submissions to the United Nations (UN). These are contextualized by reference to the reports of the Government of Bangladesh (GoB) and the UN.

Whilst the GoB espouses a participatory approach to its rights obligations, for example,

> [I]t is widely acknowledged that policy and material support of the government have contributed greatly to the growth of the NGO sector…. Indeed, successes in areas of human rights, good governance and development are largely the outcome of complementary activities carried out by the government and NGOs at both national and local levels.
>
> (GoB 2009, 10, para 49)

[T]he following discussion questions such assertions. It reveals how official response of the GoB to the crisis is failing to address a broad range of rights breaches including violence, intimidation, access to healthcare and education and sex trafficking. The NGOs' accounts reveal how women, girls and disabled people fare badly. This chapter asserts that whilst the international community could do more to help, the GoB must end its growing repression of civil society and engage with NGOs and Rohingya people in order to shape an effective crisis response that ends their inhumane treatment.

12.2. Background

For around a thousand years, the people who have become known as the Rohingya resided in Arakan (Ahmed 2010). Following invasion by the Rakhine, the previously independent kingdom became a part of Burma in 1785. The Rakhine referred to the Rohingya as dark-skinned people—or Kula (Ware and Laoutides 2018). In the face of growing oppression, they took flight to northern Arakan in today's Myanmar and became known as Rohingya. The Rakhine and Rohingya coexisted, but ethnic tensions again flared up during the British colonial era. This continued over ensuing decades leading to a gradual Rohingya exodus from Myanmar to Bangladesh in the 1970s. A turning point was reached in 1982, when, under the administrative pretext that they were not able to prove that their forefathers settled in Burma before 1823, the Burmese government stripped the Rohingya people of their citizenship (Kyaw 2017).

A further exodus of 250,000 Rohingya to Bangladesh followed military operations in Myanmar during 1991–1992. Subsequently, in the next two decades, as part of a major exercise, many thousands of these refugees were repatriated to Myanmar. Tragically, state-sponsored persecution, discrimination and violence awaited many of those who returned to Rakhine State. Another crisis point was reached in 2017. As a UN report explains: 'the cornerstone of the oppression is lack of legal status. Successive laws and policies regulating citizenship and political rights have become increasingly exclusionary in their formulation, and arbitrary and discriminatory in their application' (UNHRC 2018, 6, para 21). In 2017, this led to the Arakan Rohingya Salvation Army (ARSA) attacking several police stations. As Ahsan (2018, 571) explains, 'the violence it let loose was precipitated by a continuing campaign of atrocities by the Myanmar authorities against the Rohingyas.' The Myanmar Armed Forces responded to these attacks with a 'widespread assault, ostensibly against the Rohingya armed group which they deem a terrorist organisation, but now demonstrably also against the civilian population of the region' (Beyrer and Kamarulzaman 2017, 1570). Amongst the casualties were 6,700 Rohingya civilians, including more than 700 children living in Rakhine (Friedrich 2018). In consequence, hundreds of thousands fled across the Bangladesh border. One account described,

> It is essentially a massive rural slum—and one of the worst slums imaginable. There are hardly any latrines so people have tried to rig up their own plastic sheeting around four bamboo poles, but there is nowhere for their waste to go except into the stream below. That is the same stream that, just 10 miles away, others are using to collect drinking water.
>
> (White 2017, 1947)

Others reported that, 'overall, the living conditions of Rohingya refugees inside the overcrowded camps remain dismal. Mental health is poor, proper hygiene conditions are lacking, malnutrition is endemic, and physical/sexual abuse is high' (Milton et al. 2017, 942). Writing a year after the mass exodus another observer concluded: 'It is unacceptable that watery diarrhoea remains one of the biggest health issues we see in the camps. The infrastructure to meet even the most basic needs of the population is still not in place' (Murphy 2018, 231). Recent research details their vulnerability. One study found that, 'even using conservative projections of somewhere between 15 to 18 per cent would place the likely number of Rohingya living with a disability in Bangladeshi displacement camps between 130,000 and 180,000 people' (Landry and Tupetz 2018, 99). Another concluded that '36 per cent of its participants had Post Traumatic Stress Disorder symptoms, while 89 per cent had depression symptoms' (Wali et al. 2018, 59). Thus, the welfare of persons with disabilities and the elderly is a particular concern. Yet, contemporary analysis shows they are 'not sufficiently being taken into account in the [emergency] response... the challenge is really about the NGOs' financial ability to deliver programming to meet enormous disability needs. Moreover, humanitarian funding agencies rarely prioritize disability before, during, or after complex emergencies' (Arbeiter Samariter-Bund, Centre for Disability Development in Bangladesh, and Aktion Deutschland 2017, 3). Before turning to this chapter's findings, we consider this study's data source, the UN's UPR.

12.3. The Universal Periodic Review

The United Nations Human Rights Council (UNHRC) was established in 2006, its remit is to complete five-yearly periodic reviews based on accurate data sources and full cooperation in order to assess how effective individual states are in meeting their human rights treaty obligations (United Nations General Assembly/Human Rights Council 2006). The reviews commenced in 2008 and apply to all member states. Annually, there are three UN Working Group sessions each of which assesses 14 countries.

There are three stages to the review process. In the first preparatory phase, civil society organizations can give their views and evidence on prevailing rights practice. In the second, the UN UPR Working Group examines the National Report compiled by the state under review, as well as a supplementary report by the Office of the High Commissioner for Human Rights (OHCHR) that includes a summary of the views of civil society organizations and other stakeholders.

Having assessed the evidence, the Working Group Report gives its assessment of human rights treaty compliance, including recommendations for improvements and remedial action.

The states under review then have a few months to provide the Working Group with their response to the report, setting out the actions that they propose to take—and whether they 'note' or 'support' the Working Group recommendations (they cannot ignore them). Subsequently, State-under-Review Reports are considered—and when there is agreement, they are adopted by the UNHRC. The third stage of the UPR process is voluntary, takes place half-way through the UPR cycle and constitutes an interim assessment of the ongoing implementation of the UN recommendations in the state concerned.

Till date, Bangladesh has completed three UPR cycles. Extant work shows it to be a useful monitoring mechanism (Chaney and Sahoo 2020; Chaney, Sahoo, and Sabur 2020). Observers also note that it is a rich, if often overlooked, data source for rights analysis, describing it as:

> A collaborative, participatory qualitative process [that] is much stronger than indicators in realising rights; firstly, because the reform/change is built into the process; it is produced at the time that violations are shared. And, secondly, because a hidden voice that needs change is revealed through the marginalised experiences of rights holders. (Ferrie and Hosie 2018, 18)

12.4. What Do the UPR Data Tell Us about the Growing Crisis?

We now turn to examine civil society views on the Rohingya crisis; the discussion is organized chronologically with attention to key issues emerging in successive UPRs.

12.4.1. First Cycle UPR, 2009

Bangladesh had approximately 28,000 stateless Rohingya refugees from Northern Rakhine. Since 1991, many of these refugees have been residing in camps in Nayapara and Kutupalong in the south-east of Cox's Bazar. In addition, it is estimated that a further 100,000 Rohingya who were not recognized as refugees were residents of Bangladesh. In its report to the 2009 UPR the GoB states that, it:

> ...Has been actively supporting the Myanmarese refugees by providing them with temporary shelter, food, and medical assistance. Mindful of the difficulties faced by them in refugee camps, the government has made special provisions for improving their living conditions in the camps. The government has allotted a total of 703 acres of land... for their residence.
>
> (GoB 2009, 17, para 95)

The government proceeds to note that

> A total of 20 schools have been set up to cater nearly 7,500 refugee children residing in the camps. Provisions have been made to generate self-help activities and skills development by the refugee population. The government has spent approximately Taka 100 million on providing administrative support to Myanmarese refugees.
>
> (GoB 2009, 18, para 96)

For its part, the UNHCR (2008) highlights several issues including the fact that the country has neither signed the Convention on Refugees (1951) nor its subsequent Protocol (1967). Furthermore, Bangladeshi legal code does not extend protection to refugees. However, limited support is provided by the Office of the Refugee Repatriation and Rehabilitation Commissioner (RRRC) in the Ministry of Food and Disaster Management. The UNHCR also notes that whilst Bangladesh has signed some international human rights treaties that indirectly offer protection to refugees, these are not enforceable by Bangladeshi courts of law.

The UN also notes that between 2007 and 2009 Bangladesh 'can be credited for improving the situation of the refugees significantly' (UNHCR 2008, 2). Yet it also highlights some ongoing and significant challenges including poor living conditions and prosecution for illegal entry of Rohingya residing outside the official camps—even if they are survivors of violence. More positively, it was noted that there had been improvements in healthcare provision for refugees in the camps because of the work of UN agencies and national and international NGOs. Reflecting these improvements, over a period of 24 months in the refugee camps, the proportion suffering from acute malnutrition declined from 16.8 per cent to 8.6 per cent. According to the First Cycle discourse, camp police were cooperating with the refugee community, and court cases involving refugees were generally fair and unhindered. Notwithstanding the issues and challenges, the period covered by the First Cycle UPR can be seen as a highpoint in the government response.

12.4.2. Second Cycle UPR 2013

At this juncture, estimates suggest that there are almost a third of a million unregistered Rohingya. For its part, in its second UPR report the GoB asserts 'Bangladesh is not a party to the 1951 Refugee Convention and its 1967 Protocol, and yet been hosting refugees from Myanmar for the last three decades with full respect to the international protection regime' (GoB 2012, 23, para 122). As the following reveals, this is an assertion that the NGOs take issue with. The government's UPR report proceeded to claim,

> Earlier the Government, in close consultation with the Myanmar Government had achieved, with support from the UNHCR, voluntary repatriation of 250,000 refugees to Myanmar during 1991–2005. During 2009–12, the present government took a number of initiatives to deepen dialogue with the Myanmar government to arrange voluntary repatriation of the remaining refugees.
>
> (GoB 2012, 23, para 122)

Again, the NGOs' second cycle UPR submissions take issue with this assertion. In addition, the GoB makes the following statement, 'Owing to its socio-economic, environmental and demographic challenges, Bangladesh is constrained to accept any further influx of Rohingyas from Myanmar' (GoB 2012, 23, para 122). This is noteworthy not only because the government is signalling that it has reached the limits of its capacity to cope with the crisis but also because it highlights the environmental impact of the emergency.

The denial of citizenship is a growing concern for NGOs in the second cycle UPR. NGOs note an increasing number of unregistered Rohingya who are in Bangladesh without any legal status. The discourse also records a shift in the GoB response, which, as one NGO noted:

> ...Exposed the Bangladesh Government's [Second Cycle UPR] assertions of respect for the Refugee Convention as false. Not only did Bangladesh push Rohingyas back at the border, it also began denying critical humanitarian assistance to its long-term Rohingya population in a bid to deter other refugees from entering.... Government officials began publicly labelling the Rohingya as 'intruders' and 'criminals'.
>
> (Human Rights Watch 2013, 9)

In consequence, others observed how only some of those in need receive minimal humanitarian assistance and all are at risk of arrest and prolonged detention. The second cycle UPR submissions highlight how women and girls are particularly vulnerable to sexual violence and trafficking. Moreover, core concerns are the refoulement of Rohingya fleeing a post-June 2012 upsurge in violence in Myanmar. For the first time, there is sustained NGO attention to how the presence of Rohingya refugees is taking its toll on the environment. The NGOs' discourse also provides powerful accounts of Rohingya fleeing violence in Myanmar. For example, one recalled that:

> Riots broke out at the night. We could not stay there anymore. The fishing boats were beached on the shore. Those boats belonged to Burmese people. There were more or less 100 people in the boat with all the kids and females. We sailed to the sea at night. I do not know what happened to the others. We were in the middle of the sea for three days. On the fourth day we beached on the shore. After that it started to rain. However, we were not allowed to take shelter in Bangladesh. They pushed us back to the sea. We were all on our own. And we had to swim for some time to reach Bangladesh.
>
> (Equal Rights Trust 2013, 11)

The discourse also highlights how GoB accession to the 1951 Refugee Convention could transform the situation and facilitate greater mobilization of international support and alleviate the burden primarily shouldered by Bangladesh.

For its part, the OHCHR (2013, 7, para 23) observed, 'The Special Rapporteur on extreme poverty noted that the situation of the most vulnerable groups ... She reiterated the need to actively tackle discrimination against those groups and ... adequate social protection, particularly the Rohingya refugees.' The vulnerability of women and girls repeatedly features in the NGO and UN discourse. For example, 'the UNHCR welcomed the ongoing work on a new anti-trafficking law, the Prevention of Oppression Against Women and Children Act (2000, amended 2003).'[1] Amongst the UN's second cycle UPR recommendations are that government should: 'Ensure free access and without constraints of the NGOs to the Rohingyas in the Cox's Bazaar district';[2] and 'Adopt measures to guarantee the rights of the Rohingya refugees who are in Bangladesh, applying the principle of non-refoulement and allow NGOs to carry out their work regarding refugees.'[3]

12.4.3. Third Cycle UPR 2018

As acknowledged in the GoB's UPR submission, by this point the scale of the crisis had been transformed:

> The realization of Bangladesh's human rights commitments faced setbacks in the face of sudden influx of nearly one million forcibly displaced Myanmar nationals (Rohingyas) to Bangladesh. Out of humanitarian consideration, Prime Minister Sheikh Hasina and the people of Bangladesh stood beside the displaced Rohingyas and opened their homes and hearts and shared the resources allocated for them with the Rohingyas.... Bangladesh remained committed to the obligations of putting its best efforts

[1] A/HRC/WG.6/16/BGD/2, p. 8, para 32.
[2] A/HRC/24/12/Add.1.
[3] A/HRC/24/12, para 129.

in implementing the recommendations accepted in the 2nd Cycle of UPR.

(GoB 2018, 2, para 3)

Reflecting the gravity of the unfolding humanitarian crisis the following discussion examines the key issues reported in civil society organizations' third cycle UPR discourse.

1. *Legal and International Treaty Failings*

A fundamental and enduring problem is Bangladesh's failure to sign the key international treaties on refugees. It was a shortcoming highlighted in the first cycle UPR back in 2009. The UNHCR had then underlined that:

> The lack of a legal framework to deal with refugees further provides for an *ad hoc* environment of cooperation with Government institutions which in turn provide an insecure and unpredictable protection environment for refugees.... There are a large number of refugees in Bangladesh without access to asylum procedures and refugee status determination.

(UNHCR 2009, 3)

The dire situation is exacerbated by the fact that the country does not have domestic laws guaranteeing the protection of stateless and refugee population (Yesmin 2016). Twelve years on from the first UPR, the latest cycle reveals that there has been no progress. In order to protect all stateless Rohingya refugees on Bangladesh territory, the civil society discourse urges the government to finally accede to—and fully implement—the 1954 and 1961 Statelessness Conventions and the Refugee Convention (1951). NGOs also call for greater cooperation from the international community, including negotiating resettlement programmes with third countries.

2. *The Right to Nationality*

The current failure of Bangladesh to grant citizenship rights is a breach of the country's obligations under Article 7 of the UN Convention on the Rights of the Child ('the child shall be registered immediately after birth and shall have the right from birth to a name, the right to acquire a nationality ...') (Chaney 2018). Thus, a key trope in the civil society discourse is the need to ensure that all those born in Bangladesh, or to a Bangladeshi parent, are guaranteed right to a nationality. Thus, NGOs demand that in the draft citizenship bill the GoB respond to issues of nationality, statelessness and discrimination (Abrar 2016). According to the UPR submissions the latter should comply with relevant international standards and allow for considered public debate and consultation.

3. Gender-based Oppression and Discrimination

The Rohingya women and girls suffer from trafficking, violence and sexual exploitation. This is a clear violation of Bangladesh's obligations under Article 6 of the Convention on the Elimination of Discrimination against Women (CEDAW, ratified in 1984). In the case of trafficking, one NGO referred to the 'continuous vulnerability of the Rohingya, being subject to human trafficking and smuggling under harsh conditions on boats to other countries in the region' (Institute on Statelessness and Inclusion 2017, 5). Others highlighted how children and young women were vulnerable to trafficking and organ trading. Other civil society voices attribute the failure to address these issues to government's lack of political will. NGOs were forthright in demanding that government implement recommendations that it noted and/or accepted at the last UPR (circa 2012). Recent studies support the third cycle discourse and underline the precarious position of women. One analysis of gender norms and freedom of movement found that in the refugee camps around a third of women said they would never go out alone (MSNA/ISCG 2019, 23). Yet this is just one aspect of the inequalities that women and girls face:

> As refugees, they are not allowed to find employment in Bangladesh. The mobility of refugee men is highly restricted by violence and intimidation, which forces refugee women into the role of the family's breadwinner. Despite this, the women's status has not improved in either the family or the community. On the contrary, the women are exposed to increased violence from their families, the refugee community and outsiders. Though all refugees suffer violence, women face it both inside and outside the home.

> (Akhter and Kusakabe 2014, 225)

4. *Suppression of Civil Society and Intimidation of Human Rights Defenders*

As noted in its submission to the previous UPR, the government claimed 'Bangladesh will ... continue to fully involve CSOs in promoting human rights at all levels' (GoB 2013, 18). Yet, in reality, the context for CSOs (Civil Society Organizations) in Bangladesh has worsened appreciably over recent years. In short, there is shrinking political space for civil society (Chaney and Sahoo 2020; Chaney et al. 2020; Chowdhury, Jahan, and Rahman 2017; Mohajan 2013; Saidul Islam 2011; Suykens 2016). However, in direct contradiction to a growing evidence base, the ruling administration claimed that it, 'is providing full access to all international partners and agencies, including [the] UN, INGOs, humanitarian actors, media and other civil society organizations to work in Cox's Bazar and support the Rohingyas' (GoB 2017, 5). Contesting this claim the UNHRC has registered its concern about limitations on the rights to freedom of opinion, expression and association—as well as intimidation and harassment of journalists, bloggers and human rights defenders (HRC 2018, 5). Underlining the lack of progress, such calls are a repetition of the UN's second cycle UPR report of 2012 that called on the government to allow NGOs to carry out their work regarding refugees and, to increase its efforts to ensure that human rights defenders are protected (UNHRC 2012, para 129). This concern is repeated in the civil society discourse. For example, one NGO asserted that the government should 'end any formal and informal restrictions preventing the UN and NGOs from providing aid to refugees' (Amnesty International 2018, 2).

5. *Forced 'Repatriation'*

Article 13 in the International Covenant on Civil and Political Rights (ICCPR, acceded to by Bangladesh in 2000) states,

> An alien lawfully in the territory of a State Party to the present Covenant may be expelled therefrom only in pursuance of a decision reached in accordance with law and shall, except where compelling reasons of national security otherwise require, be allowed to submit the reasons against his[/her] expulsion and to have his case reviewed by ... the competent authority.

In GoB's UPR submission it claimed that it supported the Rohingya's 'right to safe, dignified, voluntary return to their homes in Myanmar [based on] … voluntariness, non-criminalization, livelihood, resettlement, reintegration and other universal elements of human rights' (GoB 2018, para 32). However, the civil society discourse refers to a series of Article 13 violations. It notes how, following the violence in Myanmar in October 2016, Bangladesh Border Guards were instructed to push Rohingya refugees back across the border, reinforcing a longstanding and unlawful policy. The core NGO message in the UPR data is that government should respect the principle of non-refoulement and ensure an effective resettlement programme for Rohingya refugees. NGOs also demanded that UN peacekeeping forces be sent to Rakhine. However, when a memorandum of understanding with two UN agencies was signed by the Myanmar government (UNHRC 2018) to pave the way for Rohingya repatriation, the refugees were not consulted. As a result, in 2019, all those who were offered the choice of returning to Rakhine refused to go.

6. *Children's Rights*

Earlier research concluded that 30 years after ratification of the United Nations Convention on the Rights of the Child (CRC), breaches of children's rights are commonplace (Chaney 2018, 23). The situation is particularly acute in the case of refugee children. Thus, the civil society UPR discourse places significant attention on children's welfare rights. In their UPR submissions, NGOs speak of the urgent need to provide education for children and ensure that assistance reaches all vulnerable children in need. The reasons given are not just educational but are framed in terms of what one NGO refers to as refugee children's 'psycho-social healing'. The discourse also highlights how cultural attitudes deny girls' access to schooling as the mobility of post-pubescent girls is restricted by social norms. Thus, a recent study found that 34 per cent of girls attend temporary learning centres in the camps, compared to 54 per cent of boys (MSNA/ISCG 2019, 23).

In addition, a draft of CSO UPR submissions referred to the need to address breaches of Article 24 of the CRC ('combating disease and malnutrition'). These detailed how children commonly suffered from different types of malnutrition including iodine deficiency, wasting, low birth weight, stunting and anaemia. NGOs' clear message to the authorities was that children need extra support. Recent academic studies support this and outline the severity of the malnutrition problem. For example, Mahmood et al. (2017, 1845) observe,

> In Bangladesh, nearly 20 per cent of Rohingya children suffer from wasting ... stunting, or low height for age, [this] is caused by chronic malnutrition and exists among 60 per cent of Rohingya child refugees in Bangladesh, a rate 50 per cent higher than the rest of the Bangladesh population.

This has prompted calls for the crisis response to be improved including a significant increase in the distribution of supplemental fortified food (Leidman, Humphreys, and Cramer 2018). A further trope in the civil society discourse underlines the suffering of Rohingya mothers. Several NGOs expressed their fears that failure to improve shelter, healthcare and hygiene will lead to more infant deaths. Again, recent research supports these concerns. Thus, the maternal mortality rate exceeds 173 in 100,000 with a neonatal mortality rate of 17.1 in 1,000 (World Bank 2019). Another study underlined the scale of the problem.

> 40,000 Rohingya women are estimated to be pregnant, and ensuring emergency obstetric services in the difficult-to-access area is quite challenging and contributes to maternal morbidity and mortality ... the services provided during childbirth in the Rohingya community are inadequate. Facility delivery is low, at 22 per cent.
>
> (Hasan-Ul-Bari and Ahmed 2018, 2439)

7. Healthcare

In its national report to the third cycle UPR, the GoB says the goal of the National Health Policy of 2011 is to 'provide primary health care and emergency health facilities for all on equitable basis' (GoB 2018, 0, para 55). It also refers to increased government investment in healthcare and new rights and obligations for patients and the stakeholders in the Patient and the Health Care Service Provider (Protection) Bill of 2016. In contrast, and reflecting wider concerns (Mohiuddin 2020) in their UPR submissions, NGOs highlight unacceptable rates of mortality and morbidity in the refugee camps, as well as shortcomings in refugees' access to healthcare. For its part the UN said, 'it is further concerned about the very low level of public funding allocated to social services, including social security, health care and education' (UN Committee on Economic, Social and Cultural Rights 2018, 3, para 19). Although post-dating the third cycle UPR, the COVID-19 pandemic has compounded the health difficulties faced by the refugees. In the first months of 2020 the World Health Organization (WHO) reported over 4,760 confirmed cases of COVID-19 and several deaths in the 34 Rohingya refugee camps in Cox's Bazar (UNHCR 2020a, 1). Experts warn that:

> The COVID-19 pandemic is now a global crisis and the Rohingya refugees in Bangladesh are in the most vulnerable situation. Lack of access to services that are considered critical and life-saving such as food, drinkable water, and shelter, together with limited access to health services are turning an already serious crisis into a major human disaster.
>
> (Banik et al. 2020, 1578)

8. *Impact on Local People*

The growing tensions between the locals and the refugees are a further trope in the civil society discourse. In this regard, there is consistency over UPR cycles, as similar concerns were raised during the first cycle in 2009. At that time, as now, NGOs complained that the GoB is failing to engage with local people when seeking to address the refugee crisis and in consequence their needs are ignored. Over recent years, the tensions have led to some violent incidents. Notably, in 2017, when indigenous residents complained of the influx of refugees there were clashes and the houses of 70 indigenous residents were burnt to the ground.

The economic impact on the host communities is a further major problem owing to the spread of the camps. As the UN notes, 'it has also become increasingly clear that the response actors [i.e. NGO and state aid providers] will need to increase their focus on host community food security, particularly in hard-hit communities' (United Nations Office for the Coordination of Humanitarian Affairs 2019, 9). The UN also highlighted the impact of the crisis on local education, noting that, 'Bangladeshi para-teachers have left host community schools for higher paid work in the camps' learning facilities, increasing student–teacher ratios in the [local, indigenous] schools, and leading to [further] tensions over the impacts of the Rohingya influx' (United Nations Office for the Coordination of Humanitarian Affairs 2019, 35). A further issue is the impact of the crisis on local people's food security. According to one study, only a fifth of households had an acceptable level of food consumption (World Food Programme 2018, 3).

Recently, a number of factors have combined causing the law-and-order situation to deteriorate. The police have accused refugees of trafficking drugs (notably, methamphetamine) from Myanmar. Matters came to a head in 2019 when a refugee was shot dead following the earlier murder of a local official by suspected Rohingya criminals. The resulting civil unrest saw hundreds of local people blocking the road to a refugee camp, vandalizing shops and burning tyres. The Bangladesh government's response has been to establish additional police check posts and increase the number of enforcement officials and military personnel in Cox's Bazar (GoB 2017, 7). However, in the face of a rise in the number of criminal gangs, NGOs' UPR submissions claim the state response has been inadequate. Overall, the plight of the indigenous minority people of Bangladesh has become increasingly difficult in the wake of the influx of refugees. There is a likelihood of newcomers outnumbering the indigenous people—raising, as yet unanswered, questions about the extent to which the Bangladesh government will protect them.

9. Environmental Impact

The dire impact of the refugee crisis on the environment is also a major concern in NGOs' UPR submissions. As a recent study explained,

> The mass influx of Rohingya refugees has resulted in environmental degradation both within the refugee camps and in the surrounding areas. The expansion of existing campsites has led to more than 2,000 hectares of forest loss in the Cox's Bazar region... the remaining elephant habitat is under severe pressure from uncontrolled fuelwood collection in the forest.

(Mukul et al. 2019, 138)

The civil society discourse emphasizes how humanitarian aid in the refugee camps is hampered by environmental issues such as flooding and soil erosion. Over-collection of firewood, poor drainage and flooding associated with monsoon rains have a severe impact on vulnerable refugees, including the elderly and disabled people.

12.5. Conclusion

A decade ago, an analysis concluded that,

> There is an urgent need to create a refugee law that provides work permits, and even short-term dual citizenship to those refugees in the border region. Given its location, resources, and capability, Bangladesh, is in a position to create a refugee policy that will prevent long-term encampment of refugees, militarization of Rohingya camps, and consequently, avert potential conflict behaviour within its borders.
>
> (Rahman 2010, 233)

However, the current analysis of three cycles of UPR data shows why this has not happened. Drawing on the situated knowledge of NGOs, it reveals the huge increase in the scale of the emergency and how the government's response is marked by an inability and/or unwillingness to address the myriad issues facing refugees. From a historical perspective, the first cycle data show the government response at the time to be a highpoint; one that is cautious, yet generally backed by good intentions. Notwithstanding extensive shortcomings in access to services and poor living conditions, the civil society discourse shows how some Rohingya refugees were issued with permanent resident certificates, whilst others were included on the local electoral register. During this period there was also co-working between camp police and the refugee community. The NGO discourse also refers to court cases involving refugees being processed on an equal basis with other proceedings. Whilst it is important not to overstate things, a UN report of the time notes that between 2007 and 2009 Bangladesh 'can be credited for improving the situation of the refugees significantly' (UNHCR 2008, 2).

Subsequently, by the time of the second cycle UPR there are an estimated 300,000 unregistered Rohingya in Bangladesh. The growing influx of refugees combines with a political shift founded on government fears of losing control of a rapidly escalating situation, as well concerns over the potential for extremism undermining security on Bangladesh soil. Whilst international agencies and NGOs make great efforts, there is less state action to improve living conditions in the camps. Thus, in essence the official response is one of trying to deter future waves of refugees and containment based on notions of difference rather than the extension of citizenship and long-term integration of refugees into Bangladeshi society. This is reinforced by coverage in the popular media (Kasun 2019). The denial of citizenship is a growing concern in the NGOs' second cycle discourse. NGOs report how the Rohingya have routinely been called 'criminals' and 'intruders'. Trafficking and sexual violence pose a major threat to women and girls. The economic and social situation of the Rohingya has also deteriorated. A further major concern at this time is the refoulement of Rohingya fleeing a post-June 2012 upsurge in violence in Myanmar. The GOB's response is to seal the border and strengthen the presence of border guards. The UN and NGO discourse again highlights how signing the Refugee Convention of 1951 would likely lessen relief demands on the Bangladeshi by increasing the level of international support; yet, as in the past, the government is deaf to such entreaties.

By the time of the third cycle UPR, the crisis is spiralling out of control. Notwithstanding the work of NGOs and UN agencies, it is well beyond government's capacity to deal with. Official estimates suggest there are over one million forcibly displaced Rohingya. The government's response is shaped by fear of losing control and worries over rising extremism. The civil society of Bangladesh and NGOs continue to urge the government to accede to the 1954 and 1961 Statelessness Conventions and the Refugee Convention (1951). NGOs also call for greater cooperation from the international community, including negotiating resettlement programmes with third countries. NGOs express concern about state denial of freedom of expression and association—as well as intimidation and harassment of journalists, bloggers and human rights defenders. Civil society's core message in the Third Cycle discourse is that government should take measures to ensure that the Rohingya do not face obstruction or discrimination when applying for asylum. Gender-based violence, trafficking and sexual exploitation also remain key problems. In the wake of the Third Cycle UPR, the government's containment approach is vividly illustrated by its proposals to relocate 100,000 refugees to a tiny landmass in the Bay of Bengal called Bhasan Char. The civil society discourse is unified in its condemnation of this idea. For example,

> [F]or the Rohingya, Bangladesh's Bhasan Char will be like a prison … relocating refugees to unsafe island would risk lives and livelihoods … dumping a battered and traumatized people on Bhasan Char to face yet another threat to their survival is not a solution. Bangladesh should terminate the relocation plans.
>
> (Adams 2019)

As noted, the Rohingya crisis cannot be divorced from the wider issue of religious extremism and instability in the region (Chaney and Sahoo, 2020). This has also shaped the GoB's response to the crisis because a small minority of Rohingya refugees are linked with militant Islamic extremists such as Tehrek-Azadi Arakan, the Arakan Rohingya Islamic Front, the Rohingya Patriotic Front, Jamaat-e-Islami and the Rohingya Solidarity Organisation. Located on the border of Bangladesh and Myanmar, they are pressing for a new mode of citizenship that challenges established geopolitics, namely membership of a separate Islamic state. Thus, an earlier study notes, 'one consequence of the Rohingya's influx that struck Bangladesh in 1978 was the destabilization of the government following its inability to cope with the Rohingya intruders or migrants in its border areas' (Naushin Parnini 2013, 284). Accordingly, 'in public, the Jamaat is keeping a low profile, but that is hardly any reason to suppose it and some other Islamist groups will not mount surreptitious campaigns to recruit young Rohingyas in armed action against the Bangladesh state and government' (Ahsan 2018, 580).

As the UPR discourse underlines, an enduring answer to the Rohingya crisis must include the right to return to Myanmar: 'in order to avoid repeating the humanitarian crisis … Efforts to resettle Rohingya must also be continued by the UN's member nations … the durable solution for the Rohingya crisis lies within Myanmar ... parliament has the opportunity to end an historical suffering' (Mahmood et al. 2017, 389). Yet, this is a highly unlikely scenario owing to a broad range of factors, including the ongoing oppression of the Rohingya driven by Buddhist nationalists and the Myanmar military, the stifling of Aung San Suu Kyi and other erstwhile human rights champions and the 2019 failure of governments and international agencies to consult Rohingya people on an initial scheme of voluntary return to Rakhine, thereby further undermining their trust in government.

Notwithstanding ongoing human and citizenship rights violations of the Rohingya, the current analysis of the UPR data shows that the GoB is not exclusively responsible for the breaches. The Bangladesh state has been overwhelmed by the crisis and, as a resource-poor country it is in dire need of greater international support. The GoB has repeatedly pleaded for more international support at the UN and elsewhere (Dowd and McAdam 2017). Alongside this, the Association of Southeast Asian Nations (ASEAN) has been of little help, for it has proved largely ineffective in securing greater international cooperation (Petcharamesree 2016, 153). Contemporary civil society discourse recognizes this and calls for a 'redoubl[ing] of bilateral and multilateral diplomatic efforts through regional and international forums to ensure safe and speedy return of all Rohingya refugees to Myanmar' (Human Rights Forum, Bangladesh 2017, 8). A further obstacle preventing resolution of the growing crisis is the unwillingness of UN Security Council members China and Russia to invoke the legal obligation of the UN Charter and back a demand for Myanmar to allow the Rohingya to return to their villages and be legally recognized as citizens (Adams 2019).

All of this means that the plight of the Rohingya is an increasingly desperate one owing to political failure on the part of the international community. In the face of this intractability government proposals aimed at containment are becoming more extreme. This is not only illustrated by the Bhasan Char proposals but also Bangladesh's Parliamentary Standing Committee on Defence's recommendation that a wall be built around the Cox's Bazar camps. In short, the history of the Universal Periodic Reviews of Bangladesh is one that charts a growing humanitarian crisis that is being met by an increasingly repressive stance by the Bangladesh state; one fuelled by its fear of losing control of the situation, as well as its failure to embrace dialogue with NGOs, accede to the UN refugee conventions, end rights violations and empower—as well as extend citizenship rights to—the Rohingya people. Consequently, more effective future policies are needed from the GoB, the UN and the ASEAN, and crucially this needs to be accompanied by effective civil society advocacy and mobilization.

Acknowledgement

Grant funding by the Economic and Social Research Council (Award number ES/S012435/1) is gratefully acknowledged.

References

Abrar, C. R. 2016, 4 June. 'The Curious Contents of the Citizenship Law.' *Daily Star*. Available at https://www.thedailystar.net/op-ed/politics/the-curious-contents-the-citizenship-law-1233943 (accessed on 22 October 2020).

Adams, B. 2019, 14 March. 'For Rohingya, Bangladesh's Bhasan Char "Will Be Like a Prison" Relocating Refugees to Unsafe Island Would Risk Lives, Livelihoods.' Human Rights Watch. Available at https://www.hrw.org/news/2019/03/15/rohingya-bangladeshs-bhasan-char-will-be-prison (accessed on 22 November 2020).

Adams, S. 2019. 'The Responsibility to Protect and the Fate of the Rohingya.' *Global Responsibility to Protect* 11, no. 4: 435–450.

Ahmed, I., ed. 2010. *The Plight of the Stateless Rohingyas*. Dhaka: The University Press Limited.

Ahsan, S. B. 2018. 'The Rohingya Crisis: Why the World Must Act Decisively.' *Asian Affairs* 49, no. 4: 571–581.

Akhter, S., and K. Kusakabe. 2014. 'Gender-based Violence among Documented Rohingya Refugees in Bangladesh.' *Indian Journal of Gender Studies* 21, no. 2: 225–246.

Amnesty International. 2018. *Submission for the UN Universal Periodic Review 30th Session of the UPR Working Group, April–May 2018*. New York, NY: United Nations.

Arbeiter Samariter-Bund, Centre for Disability Development in Bangladesh, and Aktion Deutschland. 2017. *Rohingya Refugee Crisis in Bangladesh: Age and Disability Inclusion Rapid Assessment Report*. Available at https://www.humanitarianresponse.info/sites/www.humanitarianresponse.info/files/

assessments/asbcdd_rohingya_refugee_crisis_-_age_and_disability_inclu-sion_rapid_assessment_report.pdf (accessed on 12 October 2020).

Banik, R. Rahman, M. Hossain, Sikder T. Md., and D. Gozal. 2020. 'COVID-19 Pandemic and Rohingya Refugees in Bangladesh: What Are the Major Concerns?' *Global Public Health* 15, no. 10: 1578–1581.

Beyrer, C., and A. Kamarulzaman. 2017, 30 September. 'Ethnic Cleansing in Myanmar: The Rohingya Crisis and Human Rights.' *The Lancet* 390: 10102, 1570–1573.

Chaney, P. 2018. 'Limited Gains, Enduring Violations: Civil Society Perspectives on the Implementation of the United Nations' Convention on the Rights of the Child in Bangladesh.' *Journal of South Asian Development* 12, no. 3: 47–58.

Chaney, P., and S. Sahoo. 2020. 'Civil Society and the Contemporary Threat to Religious Freedom in Bangladesh.' *Journal of Civil Society* 16: 3, 191–215. https://doi.org/10.1080/17448689.2020.1787629

Chaney, P., S. Sahoo, and S. Sabur. 2020. 'Civil Society Organisations and LGBT+ Rights in Bangladesh: A Critical Analysis'. *Journal of South Asian Development*. https://doi.org/10.1177/0973174120950512

Chowdhury, M., F. Jahan, and R. Rahman R. 2017. 'Developing Urban Space: The Changing Role of NGOs in Bangladesh.' *Development in Practice* 27, no. 2: 82–97.

Dowd, J., and R. McAdam. 2017. 'International Cooperation and Responsibility Sharing to Protect Refugees: What, Why And How?' *International and Comparative Law Quarterly* 66, no. 4: 863–892.

Equal Rights Trust. 2013. 'NGO Submission to the Second Cycle UPR – Bangladesh.' Geneva: UN.

Ferrie, J., and A. Hosie. 2018. 'Methodological Challenges in Developing an Evidence Base, and Realising Rights.' *The International Journal of Human Rights* 22, no. 1: 5–21.

Friedrich, M. 2018. 'High Rates of Violent Death among Rohingya Refugees.' *Journal of the American Medical Association* 319, no. 7: 648.

Front Line Defenders. 2017. *NGO Submission to the Third Cycle UPR*. New York: United Nations.

GoB. 2009, 2–13 February. 'National Report Submitted in Accordance with Paragraph 5 of the Annex to Human Rights Council Resolution 16/21: Bangladesh.' Papers of Human Rights Council Working Group on the Universal Periodic Review, Fourth Session, A/HRC/WG.6/4/BGD/1, United Nations Human Rights Council, Geneva.

GoB. 2012. 'National Report Submitted in Accordance with Paragraph 5 of the Annex to Human Rights Council Resolution 16/21: Bangladesh.' Papers of Human Rights Council Working Group on the Universal Periodic Review, Sixteenth Session, A/HRC/WG.6/16/BGD/1, United Nations Human Rights Council, Geneva.

GoB. 2013, 22 April–3 May. 'National Report Submitted in Accordance with Paragraph 5 of the Annex to Human Rights Council Resolution 16/21: Bangladesh'. Papers of Human Rights Council Working Group on the

Universal Periodic Review, Sixteenth Session, Geneva, A/HRC/WG.6/16/BGD/1, United Nations Human Rights Council, Geneva.

GoB. 2017. 'National Report submitted in Accordance with Paragraph 5 of the Annex to Human Rights Council Resolution 16/21: Bangladesh.' Papers of Human Rights Council Working Group on the Universal Periodic Review, Sixteenth Session, A/HRC/WG.6/16/BGD/1, United Nations Human Rights Council, Geneva.

GoB. 2018. 'National Report Submitted in Accordance with Paragraph 5 of the Annex to Human Rights Council Resolution 16/21: Bangladesh.' A/HRC/WG.6/30/BGD/1, United Nations Human Rights Council, Geneva.

Hasan-Ul-Bari, S. M, and T. Ahmed. 2018. 'Ensuring Sexual and Reproductive Health and Rights of Rohingya Women and Girls.' *The Lancet* December 392, no. 10163: 2439–2440.

Human Rights Council. (2018). 'National Report Submitted in Accordance with Paragraph 5 of the Annex to Human Rights Council Resolution 16/21: Bangladesh. UN: Geneva.

Human Rights Forum, Bangladesh. 2017. *NGO Submission to the Third Cycle UPR.* New York, NY: United Nations.

Human Rights Watch. 2013. NGO Submission to the Second Cycle UPR – Bangladesh.' Geneva: UN.

Institute on Statelessness and Inclusion. 2017. *NGO Submission to the Third Cycle UPR.* New York, NY: United Nations.

Kasun, U. 2019. 'Framing Statelessness and "Belonging": Rohingya Refugees in Bangladesh's The Daily Star Newspaper.' *Pacific Journalism Review* 25, no. 1–2: 260–275.

Kyaw, N. N. 2017. 'Unpacking the Presumed Statelessness of Rohingyas.' *Journal of Immigrant & Refugee Studies* 15, no. 3: 79–91.

Landry, M., and A. Tupetz. 2018. 'Disability and the Rohingya Displacement Crisis: A Humanitarian Priority.' *Archives of Physical Medicine and Rehabilitation* 99: 2122–2124.

Leidman E., A. Humphreys, and B. Greene Cramer. 2018. Acute Malnutrition and Anemia among Rohingya Children in Kutupalong Camp, Bangladesh. *JAMA* 319, no. 14: 1505–1506.

MSNA/ISCG. 2019, October. *Joint Multi-Sector Needs Assessment—Key Findings: Refugees and Host Communities.* Geneva: MSNA/ISCG.

Mahmood, S., E. Wroe, A. Fuller, and J. Leaning. 2017. 'The Rohingya People of Myanmar: Health, Human Rights, and Identity.' *Lancet* 389: 1841–1850.

Milton, A. H., M. Rahman, S. Hussain, and C. Jindal. 2017. 'Trapped in Statelessness: Rohingya Refugees in Bangladesh.' *International Journal of Environmental Resources and Public Health* 14: 942.

Mohajan, H. 2014. 'Child Rights in Bangladesh.' *Journal of Social Welfare and Human Rights* 2, no. 1: 207–238.

Mohiuddin, A. K. 2020. 'An Extensive Review of Patient Satisfaction with Healthcare Services in Bangladesh.' *Patient Experience Journal* 7, no. 2: 59–71.

Mukul, S., S. Huq, J. Herbohn, A. Nishat, A. Rahman, R. Amin, and F. Ahmed. 2019, April. 'Rohingya Refugees and the Environment.' *Science* 364, no. 6436: 138.

Murphy, D. 2018. 'Stateless: The Rohingya Refugees One Year On.' *British Medical Journal* 29: 362.

Naushin Parnini, S. (2013) 'The Crisis of the Rohingya as a Muslim Minority in Myanmar and Bilateral Relations with Bangladesh.' *Journal of Muslim Minority Affairs* 33, no. 2: 281--297. doi: 0.1080/13602004.2013.826453

Office of the High Commissioner for Human Rights. 2013. Compilation Prepared by the Office of the High Commissioner for Human Rights in Accordance with Paragraph 5 of the Annex to Human Rights Council Resolution 16/21: Bangladesh. Geneva: OHCHR.

Petcharamesree, S. 2016. 'ASEAN Human Rights Regime and Mainstreaming the Responsibility to Protect: Challenges and Prospects.' *Global Responsibility to Protect* 8, no. 2–3: 133–157.

Rahman, U. 2010. 'The Rohingya Refugee: A Security Dilemma for Bangladesh.' *Journal of Immigrant & Refugee Studies* 8, no. 2: 233–239.

Saidul Islam, M. 2011. 'Minority Islam in Muslim Majority Bangladesh: The Violent Road to a New Brand of Secularism.' *Journal of Muslim Minority Affairs* 31, no. 1: 43–55.

Stoetzler, M., and N. Yuval-Davis. 2002. 'Standpoint Theory, Situated Knowledge & The Situated Imagination.' *Feminist Theory* 3, no. 3: 315–333.

Suykens, B. 2018. 'A Hundred per cent Good Man Cannot Do Politics: Violent Self-sacrifice, Student Authority, and Party-State Integration in Bangladesh.' *Modern Asian Studies* 52, no. 3: 883–916.

UNHCR. 2008. 'Input Provided by the United Nations High Commissioner for Refugees into the Office of the High Commissioner for Human Rights.' Compilation Report for the Universal Periodic Review of the Peoples Republic of Bangladesh, Protection Operation and Legal Advice Section, Division of International Protection Services, UNHCR, Geneva.

UNHCR. 2009. 'Input Provided by the United Nations High Commissioner for Refugees into the Office of the High Commissioner for Human Rights.' Compilation Report for the Universal Periodic Review of The Peoples Republic of Bangladesh. Geneva: OHCHR.

———. 2018, 6 June. 'UNHCR and UNDP Sign a Memorandum of Understanding (MOU) with Myanmar to Support the Creation of Conditions for the Return of Refugees from Bangladesh.' Joint UNHCR/UNDP Press Release. Available at https://www.unhcr.org/news/press/2018/6/5b1787e64/unhcr-undp-sign-memorandum-understanding-mou-myanmar-support-creation-conditions.html (accessed on 12 August 2021).

———. 2020. 'Latest Update—Bangladesh.' Available at https://reporting.unhcr.org/bangladesh#:~:text=some%20900%2C000%20stateless%20Rohingya%20refugees,in%20previous%20waves%20of%20displacement (accessed on 22 October 2020).

UNHRC. 2012. *Bangladesh Second Cycle UPR Report*. A/HRC/24/12. New York, NY: United Nations.

———. 2018. *Report of the Independent International Fact-finding Mission on Myanmar*. A/HRC/39/64. New York, NY: United Nations.

United Nations Committee on Economic, Social and Cultural Rights. 2018. *Concluding Observations on the Initial Report of Bangladesh*. E/C.12/BGD/CO/1. New York, NY: United Nations.

United Nations General Assembly/Human Rights Council. 2006, 3 April. *Resolution Adopted by the General Assembly–60/251*. A/60/L.48. Geneva: UN General Assembly/Human Rights Council.

United Nations Office for the Coordination of Humanitarian Affairs. 2019. *2019 Joint Response Plan for Rohingya Humanitarian Crisis*. Geneva: OCHA.

Wali, N., C. Wen, L. Rawal, A. S. M. Amanullah, and A. Renzaho. 2018. 'Integrating Human Rights Approaches into Public Health Practices and Policies to Address Health Needs amongst Rohingya Refugees in Bangladesh: A Systematic Review and Meta-ethnographic Analysis.' *Archives of Public Health* 76, no. 2: 34–41.

Ware, A., and C. Laoutides. 2018. 'The Rohingya "Origin" Narrative.' In *Myanmar's 'Rohingya' Conflict*, edited by Anthony Ware and Costas Laoutides, 35–43. Oxford Scholarship Online.

White, K. 2017. 'Rohingya in Bangladesh: An Unfolding Public Health Emergency.' *The Lancet* 390, no. 10106: 1947.

World Bank. 2019. 'World Bank Data. Mortality Rate, Neonatal (per 1000 Live Births) – Bangladesh.' Available at https://data.worldbank.org/indicator/SH.DYN.NMRT?locations=BD (accessed on 15 October 2020).

World Food Programme. 2018, December. *Rohingya Refugee Emergency—Food Security Update*. Rome: World Food Programme.

Yesmin, S. 2016. 'Policy towards Rohingya Refugees: A Comparative Analysis of Bangladesh, Malaysia and Thailand.' *Journal of the Asiatic Society of Bangladesh* 61, no. 1: 71–100.

CHAPTER 13

Sustainable Rohingya Repatriation in Myanmar
Some Criteria to Follow

**Bayes Ahmed, Md. Touhidul Islam,
Peter Sammonds, S. M. R. Arfanul Alam,
Mohammad Shaheenur Alam,
Anurug Chakma, Fahima Durrat and
Obayedul Hoque Patwary**

13.1. Introduction

On 25 August 2017, the Myanmar Army (Tatmadaw) started a brutal crackdown on the non-armed Rohingya civilians in Northern Rakhine; the military in uniform was accompanied by the local Rakhines (the local Buddhist majority communities in Rakhine) who took part in the attack with machetes and wooden sticks (Human Rights Watch 2017). The Médecins Sans Frontières (MSF) estimated that at least 9,400 people lost their lives (6,700 due to violence) in Myanmar between 25 August and 24 September 2017, and at least 730 of them were children under the age of five. Experiences of violence have ranged from gunshots and burns to sexual violence and rape, especially against women and girls (MSF 2018).

The United Nations (UN) termed this brutality as a textbook example of ethnic cleansing and the gravest of crimes against humanity (UN 2017). To flee the persecution, the Rohingya migrated to the nearby Muslim-majority country, Bangladesh by crossing the Naf River. From a humanitarian perspective, the Government of Bangladesh (GoB) opened its borders for the Rohingya and provided basic life-saving assistance—food, healthcare and makeshift shelters. The local Bengali host communities also welcomed them wholeheartedly. Various international organizations responded immediately to support the Rohingya.

With more than 1.3 million Rohingya refugees in total (Uddin 2020), Bangladesh now has the world's largest refugee camp located in Cox's Bazar district (Figure 13.1). As of 31 March 2021, the United Nations High Commissioner for Refugees (UNHCR) has registered 884,000 Rohingya who are living in 190,000 households/shelters and identified more than 733,350 Rohingya who arrived after 25 August 2017 (UNHCR 2021). The rest of them are unlawfully staying outside the official camps in Bangladesh as undocumented individuals (Ahmed 2010; Uddin 2020).

Bangladesh hosted Rohingya refugees in the past too, and they were repatriated in Myanmar once in 1978 and again in 1991–1992 (Human Rights Watch 2000). Although both the governments of Bangladesh and Myanmar signed an agreement for the repatriation in November 2017 following the exodus, two consecutive attempts failed to execute voluntary repatriation due to the Rohingya's mistrust in the process and fear of recurrence of the persecution all over again (Uddin 2020). Consequently, safe, dignified, voluntary and sustainable repatriation necessitates a thorough understanding of the refugees' perspective.

The Rohingya unquestionably want to go back to their 'homeland' in Myanmar (Uddin 2020) but only after their criteria for repatriation are fulfilled. What are those criteria and how far are they feasible given the current mindset of Myanmar towards them? This chapter focuses on the criteria set by the Rohingya refugees and critically analyses the challenges of fulfilling them. In doing so, it also depicts the life of the Rohingya in Myanmar that has been accompanied by

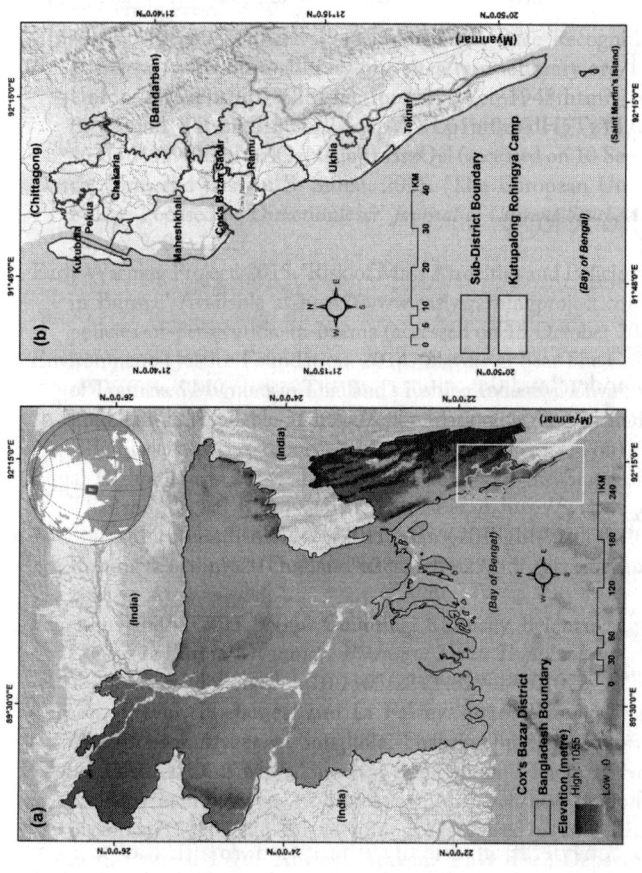

Figure 13.1 Location of (a) Cox's Bazar District in Bangladesh (b) Kutupalong Rohingya Camp in Cox's Bazar

Disclaimer: This figure has been redrawn and is not to scale. It does not represent any authentic national or international boundaries and is used for illustrative purposes only.

Source: Bayes Ahmed, 2021.

systemic oppression and targeted violence against them. Unlike other discourses of repatriation from state actors' point of view, this chapter sees the process from the perspective of a non-state actor, in this case, the Rohingya refugees.

To reach the objective, 600 Rohingya were randomly surveyed in their shelters in the Kutupalong Rohingya camp in Cox's Bazar, Bangladesh (Figure 13.1) and three focus group discussions (FGDs) were conducted with Rohingya refugees in Bangladesh between September and November 2018.

13.2. Methodology

A mixed-methods research technique (qualitative and quantitative) was applied for the research based on which this chapter has been prepared. A series of activities were undertaken to develop tools and techniques to understand the criteria for successful voluntary repatriation from a Rohingya refugee perspective. The research was funded by the British Academy (Award Reference: IC2\100178) under its 'The Humanities and Social Sciences: Tackling the UK's International Challenges Programme 2017'.

First, a scenario workshop titled 'Rohingya Health and Disaster Simulation' was organized at University College London on 30 November 2017. Second, a questionnaire development workshop was held on 6 August 2018 at the University of Dhaka, where journalists, academicians, development/non-governmental organization workers and security sector actors with ground-level experience in their respective fields evaluated the pre-prepared draft questionnaire and made recommendations taking the ethical, security and the field-level contexts into consideration. Finally, the questionnaire was revised incorporating some of the feedback by the experts and was tested by the project team in the Rohingya camps from 9–18 August 2018. The questionnaire was translated to Bangla. All the research assistants and local volunteers/translators were adequately trained.

All sorts of ethical approvals and fieldwork permissions were taken from the concerned authorities: the Ministry of Foreign Affairs,

Bangladesh; the Ministry of Disaster Management and Relief, Bangladesh; and the Office of the Refugee Relief and Repatriation Commissioner, Cox's Bazar. All the essential guidelines and research ethics were strictly maintained during the fieldwork. Nothing untoward regarding ethics, safety and security occurred during this project.

13.2.1. Qualitative FGDs

For the qualitative survey, three FGDs were conducted with 'Rohingya men' in the no man's land between Myanmar and Bangladesh in Tumbru, Naikhongchari, Bandarban district, and with 'Rohingya elderly persons' and 'women only' in the Kutupalong Rohingya camp (Figure 13.1) in Cox's Bazar, Bangladesh in September 2018. All the qualitative interview narratives were transcribed, translated into the English language and later systematically analysed.

13.2.2. Quantitative Survey

The sample size was determined through a stratified random sampling method (Krejcie and Morgan 1970; Lavrakas 2008). The data collection phase started in September and continued till November 2018. All the enumerators were trained and introduced to the research instruments (code of conduct, ethics, safeguarding and fieldwork-related risks). This study covered *Kutupalong* (202 respondents), *Lambashia* (121 respondents), *Modhurchora* (159 respondents) and *Tanzimar Khola* (118 respondents) areas. Finally, in total, 600 Rohingya refugees were surveyed in their respective shelters. A Statistical Package for the Social Sciences (SPSS) database was prepared from the survey.

13.3. Results

The quantitative results of the survey have been generated from the analysis of the SPSS database, while the FGDs have been analysed for the qualitative part. It should be noted that the Rohingya are referred to as Forcibly Displaced Myanmar Nationals by authorities in Bangladesh.

Table 13.1 *Age Distribution of the Rohingya Respondents*

Age Group[a] (Years)	Frequency	Frequency (%)	Valid (%)
Youth (18-24)	91	15.2	15.4
Primary working (25-54)	422	70.3	71.3
Mature working (55-64)	57	9.5	9.6

Source: Fieldwork in Cox's Bazar, September-November 2018.
Note: [a] The age group was classified as per the definition set by Index Mundi, https://www.indexmundi.com/burma/age_structure.html (accessed on 24 April 2021).

13.3.1. Demographic Information

The respondents were primarily male (62%) and aged between 25 years and 54 years (71%). No children and vulnerable people were interviewed (Table 13.1). All of them were Muslims, born in Myanmar (97% from Maungdaw Township), and they speak the Rohingya language. Among them, 94 per cent were married, and 74 per cent of them had never entered Bangladesh before the 2017 exodus.

13.3.2. Life in Myanmar

The primary occupation of male respondents in Myanmar was farming (40%), business (20%) and day labour (10%). Farming activities included crop cultivation and raising cattle and poultry. Businesses mainly included running small grocery shops and tea stalls. The women were mostly involved in non-income generating activities like that of housewives (75%). However, 20 per cent of women were involved in agricultural activities (Figure 13.2). About 62 per cent of the respondents lived below the poverty line and 25 per cent had no land in Myanmar. The average household poverty line was calculated considering the mean household size of 4.8 persons in Sittwe Township (UNFPA Myanmar 2014) and the threshold of 1,241 Myanmar Kyat[1] in per capita terms (The World Bank Myanmar 2017).

[1] 1 US Dollar ($) = 1,025 Myanmar Kyat on 1 January 2015.

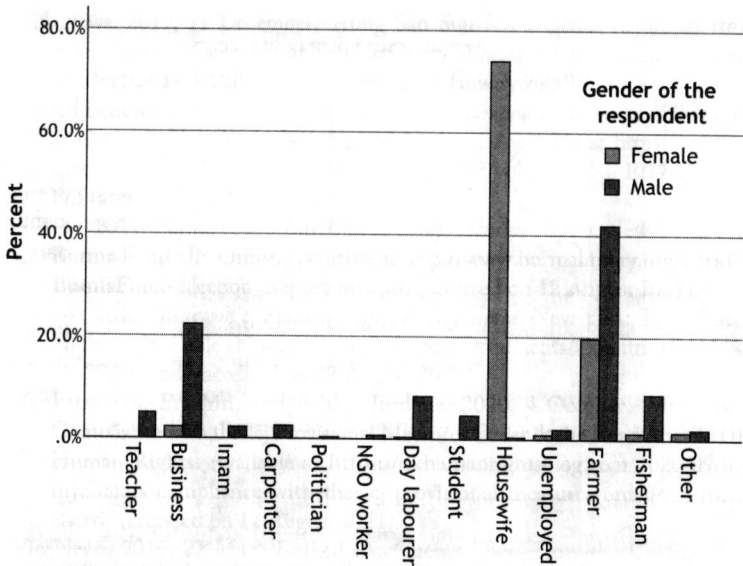

Figure 13.2 *Profession of the Respondents in Myanmar by Gender*

Source: Fieldwork in Cox's Bazar, September–November 2018.

13.3.3. Gender-based Violence and Torture

Women respondents from households living below the poverty line were found to be the most vulnerable. For example, about 65 per cent of women in Myanmar did not enjoy the right to gender equality (Figure 13.3a); 45 per cent of them left Myanmar because of sexual violence (Figure 13.3b); 72 per cent faced physical torture (Figure 13.3c); 78 per cent did not enjoy the right to free speech (Figure 13.4a); 62 per cent had no job opportunities/income-generating activities (Figure 13.4b) and approximately 55 per cent women from low-income households in Myanmar had no freedom of movement (Figure 13.4c).

The qualitative narratives depict the type of violence and the tools and techniques used by the Myanmar Army and the local Rakhines/Moghs against the Rohingya women. Though no children and vulnerable people were interviewed, the adults in the FGD groups described the horrific

(a)

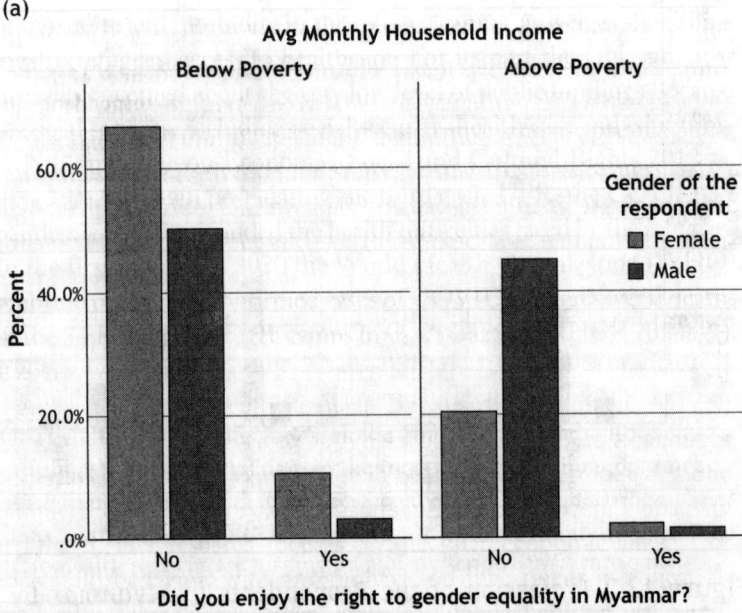

Did you enjoy the right to gender equality in Myanmar?

(b)

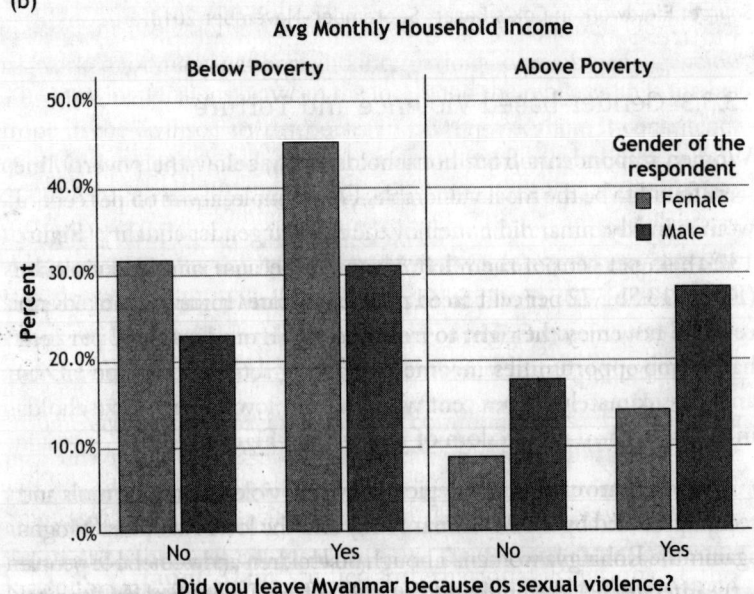

Did you leave Myanmar because os sexual violence?

(Figure 13.3 Continued)

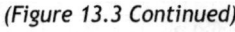

(Figure 13.3 Continued)

(c)

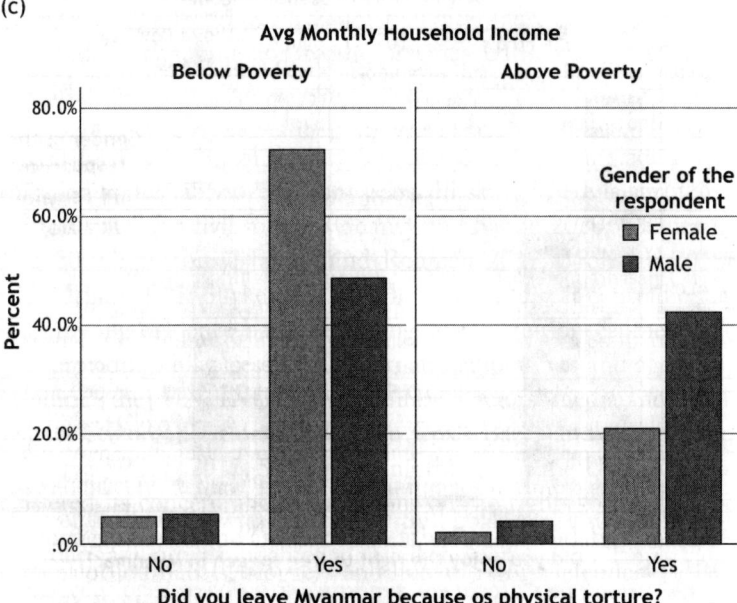

Figure 13.3 *Responses on (a) Gender Equality, (b) Sexual Violence and (c) Physical Torture by Gender and Income*

Source: Fieldwork in Cox's Bazar, September–November 2018.

scenario of torturing and killing of children and the elderly people too, especially in August 2017. During the attacks by the Myanmar Army and the local Rakhines, while youths and energetic ones were fleeing the persecution, children, the elderly and women fell behind. The women's group was asked to describe the violence. One participant said that she had two daughters, they were abducted, raped and shot dead.

Women were raped and killed, boys were shot dead or put in jails, the children were trodden to death and some of them were tossed in the fire. One of the common killing methods for youth and children was slaughtering. Many children died of hunger on the way to migrating to the Bangladesh border. One participant said that she had a baby boy who died on the way to Bangladesh border and she had no option but to leave it there in the jungles.

(a)

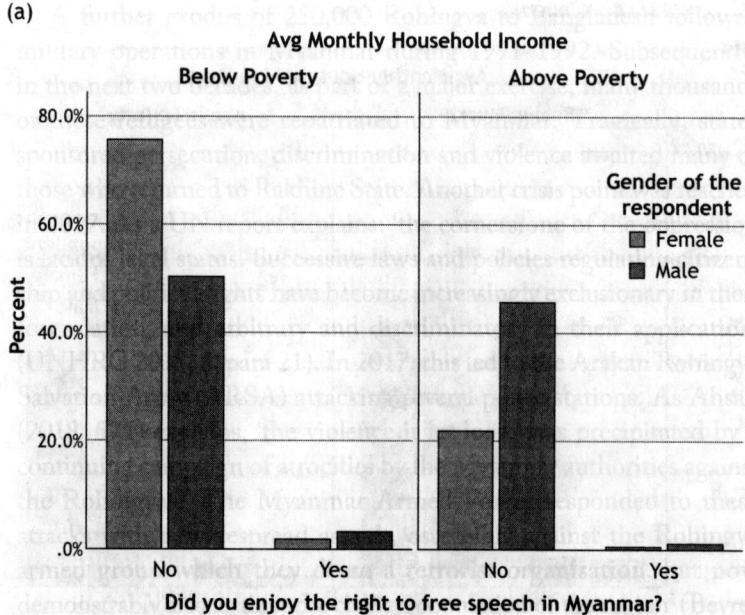

(b)

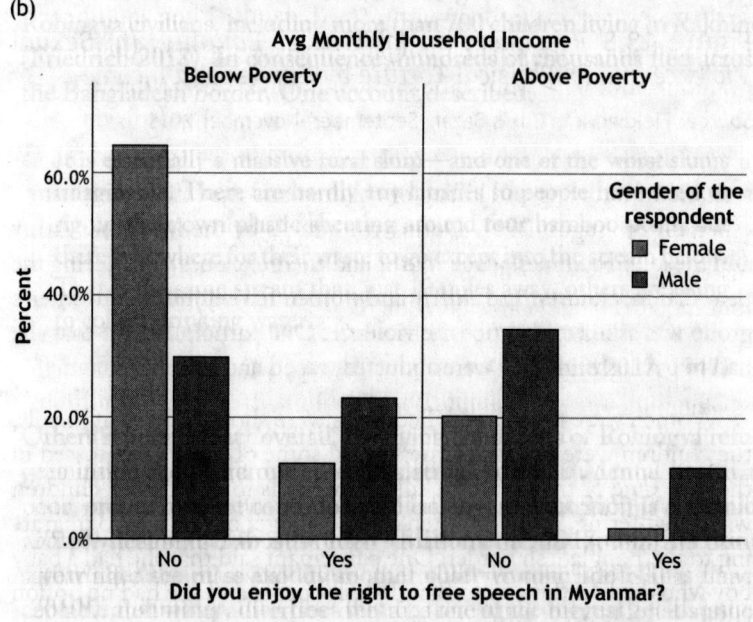

(Figure 13.4 Continued)

(Figure 13.4 Continued)

(c)

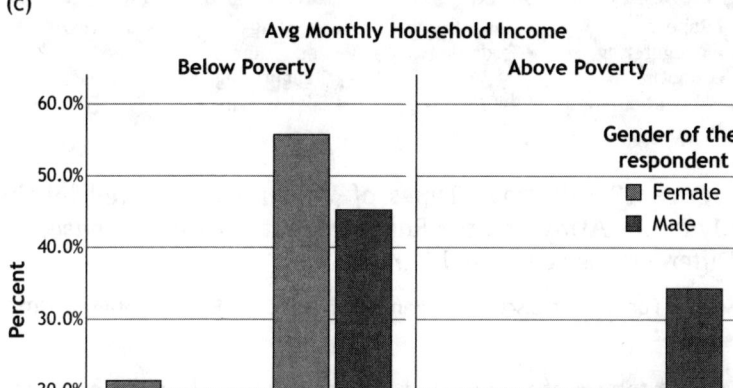

Figure 13.4 *Responses on (a) Free Speech, (b) Employment Opportunities and (c) Freedom of Movement by Gender and Income*

Source: Fieldwork in Cox's Bazar, September–November 2018.

'Enforced disappearance' had become a tool for the Myanmar army used especially against young boys and girls. Some of the youth were put in jail. To quote an elderly man,

> The Burmese Army came in a large group and cordoned our communities and then abducted young boys; we don't know where they are.

On the first night of the attack in August 2017, the local Rakhines and the military abducted many young girls from the villages. They were raped; some of them were spared alive and the rest were killed (Figure 13.5).

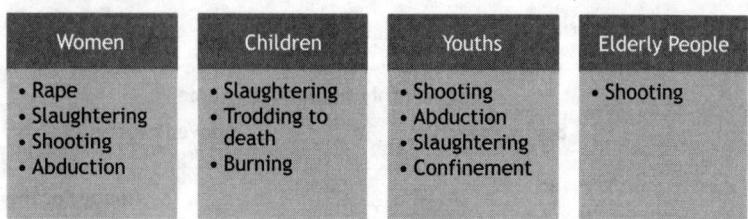

Figure 13.5 *Various Types of Violence Committed by the Myanmar Army and the Rakhines on the Rohingya based on Different Age Levels and Gender*

Source: Focus group discussions, Bandarban and Cox's Bazar, September 2018.

The torture of women and children by the Myanmar army and the local Rakhines proves that the violence towards Rohingya women and children was extremely severe in Myanmar. Besides women and children, 85 per cent of the male respondents were subject to physical torture.

13.3.4. The Long-run Cycle of Oppression

The criteria set by the Rohingya have a direct linkage with the long-run cycle of oppression against them. Men had no access to the formal job market, but they were involved in farming and fishing for survival. About 92 per cent of the male respondents had no freedom of speech, and 80 per cent of them were not allowed to move about freely in Myanmar. The Myanmar government imposed restrictions on going from one village to another. The Rohingya needed to bribe the police at various check posts, and sometimes, the personnel took away all their money while during security checks. What is more oppressing is that Rohingya could not take a seat if any local Rakhine was travelling in the same vehicle. Thus, they had to travel standing. The restrictions and harassment made it even more difficult to avail of the necessary services.

Both genders equally (80% of both male and female) faced restrictions on practising Islam in Myanmar (Figure 13.6). For Muslims, praying at the Mosques is a group activity. Especially, the prayers on Friday (*Jumu'ah*) necessitate members of the community to be together

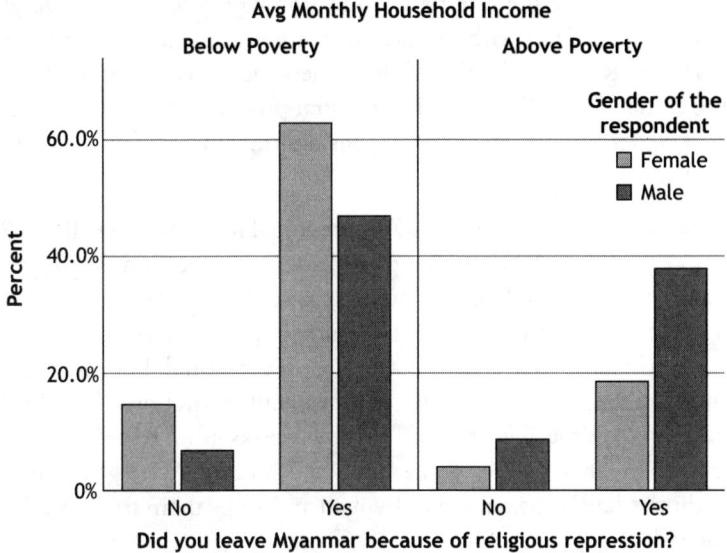

Figure 13.6 *Responses on Religious Oppression by Gender and Income*

Source: Fieldwork in Cox's Bazar, September–November 2018.

at the Mosques. But the Rohingya community cannot gather at the Mosques to perform prayers. The military banned gathering of more than five people in the Rohingya villages. The Mosques along with the madrasas (Islamic religious schools) were razed during the attacks in August 2017.

Among the respondents surveyed, 92 per cent had no citizenship right, 95 per cent had no right to identify themselves as Rohingya, 73 per cent had no right to marriage, 97 per cent had no right to justice and 77 per cent had no right to property. The situation became more difficult when the Myanmar government brought Moghs[2] from other

---

[2] The participants, Rohingya refugees used the term Mogh/Magh to refer to the local people in Rakhine who are by religion Buddhists. Their counterparts in Bangladesh are called Rakhines who fled the persecution by the Burmese ruler in their land in 1784; more than 100,000 of them still live in Ramu sub-district in Cox's Bazar as Bangladeshi citizens (Rashid 2019).

places and made them settle them in Rohingya villages. The Moghs grabbed their land with the help of the government authorities and made the Rohingya landless. The settlers took over the property and the cattle of the villagers. The ancestral property of the Rohingya is now under the ownership of Moghs and they have been isolated in captive villages.

Among the respondents, 47 per cent had no housing facilities, 34 per cent had no facilities for pure drinking water, and 56 per cent had no sanitary facilities. About 57 per cent of the respondents had no access to healthcare facilities. There were no healthcare facilities in the villages. At a distant place there is a hospital, but most often they could not visit it because of movement restrictions. One FGD participant described that if anyone sneaks into Bangladesh for treatment, they cannot come back to Myanmar. The government authority labels the person as Bengali and stops them from entering the village.

Education facilities were limited to the Rohingya population in Myanmar. Among the respondents of the quantitative survey, 58 per cent had no access to education. One of the male groups reported that children were allowed to study up to grade 10 and thereafter, the school authorities forbid the Rohingya students from attending the school. The women's group described that this restriction is even harder for girls—they can study up to grade four or five. At schools, children were taught Burmese and English. No one in the group ever had a chance to study at a university. Being asked by the interviewer if anyone in the group attended a university, one Rohingya participant replied, 'No, we cannot even go from one village to another. Forget about college, we cannot even go for an excursion'.

While all the other major ethnic groups in Myanmar can attend schools and universities, for the Rohingya community, education has remained a luxury that can even cost their life. Overall, both male and female respondents confronted different types of violence and tortures. They were deprived of basic human rights and community services and facilities in Myanmar, particularly respondents from low-income households (Figure 13.7).

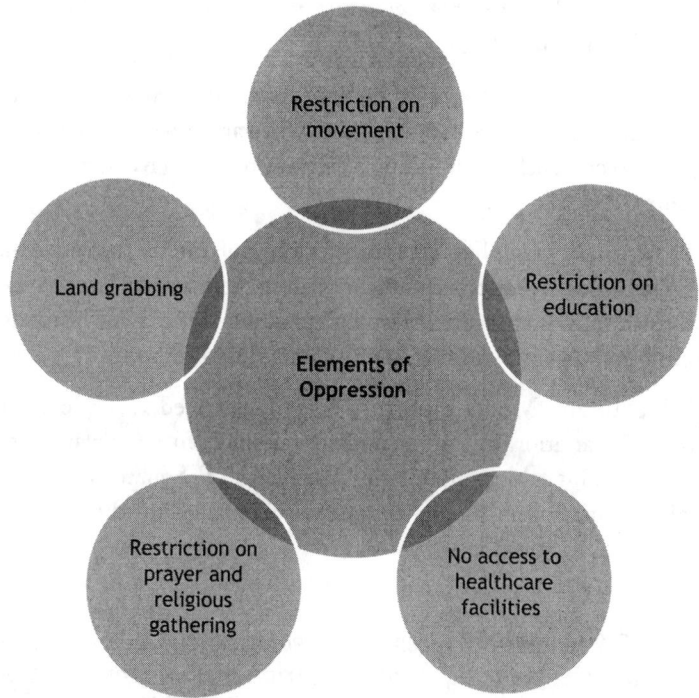

Figure 13.7 *Elements of Oppression used against the Rohingya Community by the Myanmar Authorities in Rakhine*

Source: FGDs, Bandarban and Cox's Bazar, September 2018.

13.3.5. Criteria for Sustainable Repatriation

This section deals with the criteria set by the Rohingya refugees for successful voluntary repatriation. To identify the criteria for successful repatriation in Myanmar, it is pertinent to understand the drivers that forced them to flee to Bangladesh. This section uses quantitative analysis first and then qualitative analysis for an explanatory purpose.

In the case of quantitative analysis, a binomial logistic regression model was applied on SPSS software (version 25). Before conducting the analysis, it was tested that all the observations were independent, the data did not show multicollinearity, there were no significant outliers and the categories of the dichotomous dependent variables and all independent variables were mutually exclusive and exhaustive (Field 2018; Pallant 2020).

A detailed interpretation of results obtained from the binomial logistic regression model for the dependent variable—'Do you think the right to citizenship is important for your return to Myanmar?'—is explained in Table 13.2.

Table 13.2a, 'Omnibus Tests of Model Coefficients', provides the overall statistical significance of the model (namely how well the model predicts categories compared to no independent variables). The model is found statistically significant ($p < 0.0005$; 'Sig.' column).

Table 13.2b, 'Model Summary' can be referred to understand how much variation in the dependent variable can be explained by the model. This table contains the Nagelkerke R Square value. The explained variation in the dependent variable based on the model is 22.3 per cent (Table 13.2b).

Table 13.2 *Logistic Regression Predicting the Likelihood of Ensuring Citizenship Rights for Repatriation in Myanmar Based on Household Income, Educational Facilities, Experience of Physical Torture and Availability of Jobs in Myanmar*

Table 13.2a Omnibus Tests of Model Coefficients (Model Fit)

		Chi-Square	df	Sig.
Step 1	Step	44.926	4	0.000
	Block	44.926	4	0.000
	Model	44.926	4	0.000

Table 13.2b Model Summary (Variance Explained)

Step	-2 Log Likelihood	Nagelkerke R Square
1	191.311[a]	0.223

Note: [a] Estimation terminated at iteration number 8 because parameter estimates changed by less than 0.001.

Table 13.2c Classification Table[a] (Category Prediction)

			Predicted		Percentage correct
			Do you think the right to citizenship is important for your return to Myanmar?		
	Observed		No	Yes	
Step 1	Do you think the right to citizenship is important for your return to Myanmar?	No	0	30	0.0
		Yes	0	551	100.0
	Overall percentage				94.8

Note: [a] The cut value is 0.500.

Table 13.2d Independent Variables in the Equation

		B	S.E.	Wald	df	Sig.	Exp(B)
Step 1[a]	Avg. monthly household income (1)	0.921	0.407	5.122	1	0.024	2.512
	Did you enjoy educational facilities in Myanmar? (1)	2.169	0.748	8.411	1	0.004	8.750
	Did you leave Myanmar because of physical torture? (1)	1.862	0.472	15.562	1	0.000	6.437
	Did you enjoy employment opportunities in Myanmar?	1.447	0.756	3.666	1	0.056	4.251
	Constant	0.204	0.453	0.202	1	0.653	1.226

Note: [a] Variable(s) entered in step 1: avg. monthly household income, did you enjoy educational facilities in Myanmar? Did you leave Myanmar because of physical torture? Did you enjoy employment opportunities in Myanmar?

After determining the model fit and explained variation, it is common practice to use the binomial logistic regression model to predict whether cases can be correctly classified (i.e., predicted) from the independent variables. Logistic regression estimates the probability of an event (in this case, the importance of the right to citizenship for repatriation) occurring. If the estimated probability of the event occurring is greater than or equal to 0.5 (better than even chance), SPSS Statistics classifies the event as occurring (e.g., 'yes' to citizenship rights as a repatriation criterion). If the probability is less than 0.5, SPSS Statistics classifies the event as not occurring (e.g., no for citizenship rights). The model correctly classifies 94.8 per cent of cases overall (see 'Overall Percentage' row in Table 13.2c).

Finally, one can assess the contribution of each independent variable to the model and its statistical significance using Table 13.2d. The Wald test ('Wald' column) is used to determine statistical significance for each of the independent variables. The statistical significance of the test is found in the 'Sig.' column. From these results, it is found that households from the low-income group (p = 0.024), without having access to educational facilities in Myanmar (p = 0.004), left Myanmar because of physical torture (p = 0.000) and did not enjoy formal employment opportunities in Myanmar (p = 0.056) added significantly to the model prediction (Table 13.2d).

The odds ratios of each of the independent variables in the 'Exp(B)' column inform the change in the odds for each increase in one unit of the independent variable. For example, for the educational facilities variable, an increase in one unit (i.e., a household not enjoying educational facilities in Myanmar) increases the odds by 8.750. What this means is that the odds of demanding the right to citizenship for repatriation in Myanmar ('yes' category) is 8.750 times more for households that did not have access to education as opposed to those who had access to educational facilities in Myanmar (Table 13.2d). In simple words, the results can be summarized as follows.

A binomial logistic regression model was performed to ascertain the effects of monthly household income, educational facilities, the experience of physical torture and availability of jobs in Myanmar on the likelihood that the Rohingya respondents will demand the right to citizenship for successful repatriation in Myanmar. The Logistic Regression model was statistically significant $\chi^2(4)$ = 44.926, p < 0.0005. The model explained 22 per cent (Nagelkerke R^2) of the variance in demanding citizenship rights and correctly classified

95 per cent of cases. Respondents from households who lived below the poverty line, who had no access to education, who fled Myanmar due to physical torture, and who had no jobs in Myanmar are consecutively 2.5, 8.8, 6.4 and 4.3 times more likely to support citizenship rights for repatriation in Myanmar (see Table 13.2).

Following Table 13.2, the binomial logistic regression model was applied for the remaining repatriation criteria as dependent variables (rights to decision making, Rohingya identity, gender equality, marriage right, religious freedom, free speech, justice, property, peaceful situation and other basic provisions) and their association with Rohingya living experiences in Myanmar as independent variables. The results are summarized in Table 13.3.

The independent variables were broadly classified into four groups: demographic and socio-economic, civic rights, community facilities and services and experiences of violence and torture. For each statistically significant association ($p < 0.005$), a tally was marked for an independent variable, and then it was summed up to calculate the overall priority. Later, the independent variables were labelled as high ($\Sigma > 5$), medium ($\Sigma = 3$–5), low ($\Sigma = 1$–2) and no-priority ($\Sigma = 0$) based on applying a random classification method (Table 13.3).

13.3.6. Demand for Socio-economic, Civil Rights and Community Services

According to the participants of the FGDs, the Rohingya have been living in the Rakhine state of Myanmar for hundreds of years and they are one among the numerous ethnic groups in Myanmar. The participants stated that though the history of Burmese oppression of the Rohingya is long, it reached a peak in 1982, when all their citizenship rights were taken away by the Myanmar government.

The participants also stated that their parents and grandparents had valid documents of citizenship, for example, an identity card and documents for owned properties. One participant insisted that they still have the identity card, but the government denies its validity since 1982. The refugees strongly believe that without citizenship rights, life will not be normal in Rakhine again. They will not be able

Table 13.3 Criteria for Safe and Dignified Repatriation of Rohingya in Myanmar

Parameters for Judgement		Rohingya Repatriation Criteria [p-value/Exp(B)]											Sum of Importance
		Citizenship	Decision-Making	Rohingya Identity	Gender Equality	Marriage Right	Religious Freedom	Free Speech	Justice	Property Right	Peaceful Situation	Basic Provisions	
Demographic and Socio-Economic	Age												0
	Gender					0.000 (2.068)						0.037 (2.174)	2
	Income Level/Poverty Status	0.024 (2.512)											1
	Employment/Profession											0.027 (2.374)	1
	Land Ownership			0.014 (2.145)					0.007 (1.835)	0.000 (2.481)	0.000 (2.897)	0.002 (2.100)	5
Civic Rights	Citizenship Right		0.003 (3.150)			0.001 (3.451)							2
	Decision Making												0
	Rohingya Identity				0.013 (3.616)				0.021 (2.681)		0.045 (4.500)		3
Life in Myanmar	Gender Equality												0
	Marriage Right							0.036 (1.633)					1

Life in Myanmar							
Civic Rights	Religious Freedom	0.000 (3.268)		0.000 (2.882)	0.000 (3.647)		3
	Free Speech						0
	Justice	0.003 (4.706)					1
	Property Right	0.005 (2.217)	0.001 (2.217)	0.006 (1.828)	0.005 (2.407)		4
Facilities and Services	Healthcare Facilities		0.036 (1.670)	0.000 (2.658)	0.000 (3.119)		3
	Educational Facilities	0.004 (8.750)	0.011 (1.799)				2
	Vaccination				0.007 (1.850)		1
	Housing	0.000 (4.591)					1
	Pure Drinking Water						0
	Sanitation Access						0
	Employment Opportunities	0.056 (4.251)	0.037 (1.688)				2

(Table 13.3 Continued)

(Table 13.3 Continued)

Parameters for Judgement		Rohingya Repatriation Criteria [p-value/Exp(B)]											Sum of Importance
		Citizenship	Decision-Making	Rohingya Identity	Gender Equality	Marriage Right	Religious Freedom	Free Speech	Justice	Property Right	Peaceful Situation	Basic Provisions	
Life in Myanmar	Physical Torture	0.000 (8.750)	0.002 (3.264)	0.001 (3.571)									3
	Burning Houses												0
	Military Attack					0.004 (2.704)		0.027 (2.430)					2
Violence and Torture	Restricted Movement		0.000 (4.566)	0.023 (2.032)	0.000 (4.999)	0.000 (2.877)	0.000 (2.606)	0.000 (6.908)	0.006 (1.942)		0.000 (2.925)	0.000 (2.468)	9
	Religious Repression		0.000 (3.716)		0.000 (2.976)	0.001 (2.464)	0.000 (3.372)	0.000 (3.481)	0.000 (3.176)	0.000 (3.373)	0.000 (15.138)	0.000 (6.304)	9
	Sexual Violence				0.000 (2.300)	0.000 (2.242)	0.000 (2.824)	0.000 (2.978)	0.000 (3.897)	0.000 (2.473)	0.001 (2.150)		7

Scale	Label (Sum)	No Priority (Σ = 0)	Low Priority (Σ = 1-2)	Medium Priority (Σ = 3-5)	High Priority (Σ > 5)
	Color Code				

to own property and will be stripped of all facilities and services that they need to lead a life. Also, if they return to Rakhine without proper and documented assurance of citizenship, they fear that they will face everything from exploitation to mass killing to rape to confinement to abduction all over again.

It is not only the citizenship, the Rohingya also want the associated elements under the citizenship rights. The elements stated in the FGDs are:

1. The guarantee of the availability of services like healthcare and education facilities. They want these services to be equally distributed the way all other ethnic groups in Myanmar enjoy them now.
2. The assurance of being treated equally like all other ethnic groups in Myanmar and for this to happen, they demand the recognition of the Rohingya as an ethnic group. They want the right to own property especially repossession of the property that was given away to the Rakhines/Moghs. Without the right to property, they will lose their livelihood.
3. National identity card is a documented form of citizenship. Like all other people in Myanmar, they want national identity cards.

13.3.7. Safety, Security and Justice for the Genocide

Safety and security were mentioned every time the participants talked about repatriation. In order to avoid further mass killing, the Rohingya want international protection while resettling in the Rakhine state. The FGD participants believe that it is not possible to repatriate in Myanmar without the protection of the international community. If the Rohingya refugees are sent back without the required protection, they will become the victims of mass killing again.

Being asked what should the international community do for the repatriation, the participants stated that all nations in the world should get united for a permanent solution to the Rohingya problem. They urged the international community to come forward to creating sustainable solutions for the refugee crises all over the world.

While talking about justice for genocidal violence, the participants mentioned that they want justice especially for killing their children.

The results show that the Rohingya are keen to repatriate subject to the Myanmar authority ensures their free movement, religious freedom and stop sexual violence towards women (high priority). They also demand rights to land and property ownership, healthcare facilities and recognizing their Rohingya identity (medium priority). Lastly, they require access to employment, education, marriage and citizenship rights, no military attack in their villages and bringing justice for them (low priority). No major influence of demography and socio-economic conditions (except land ownership) were found in their decision making. Overall, the Rohingya want protection from violence and torture followed by ensuring their civic rights and freedom to availing community facilities and services.

13.4. Discussion

This section discusses the results with a special focus on the criteria set by the Rohingya refugees and the challenges of the voluntary repatriation (UNHCR 1996) of them in Myanmar. By looking at the criteria set by the respondent Rohingya refugees, it can be inferred that they possess a deep sense of fear, mistrust and uncertainty.

The Rohingya are depicted as 'one of the most persecuted ethnic minorities in the world' (UN 2017), who are being forced to live a 'sub-human life' (Farzana 2017; Uddin 2020). It tells a part of the big story. Historically, the Rohingya have been tortured, killed and forcibly displaced at least five times—during the late 1700s and early 1800s, the 1940s, 1978, 1991–1992 (Human Rights Watch 2000) and in 2017. As the country 'Bangladesh' came into existence in 1971, the repatriations in 1978, 1991–1992, and the recent attempts are more relevant here. The repatriation processes in 1978 and 1991–1992 did not guarantee any sustainable solution to the Rohingya crisis. Even, the whole process is doubted as not a fair voluntary repatriation (Ahmed 2010; Ibrahim 2016). As a result, the Myanmar government and the local Rakhines/Moghs erupted in violence again and again in an attempt to drive the Rohingya out of the Rakhine state of Myanmar. Looking at the pattern of the violence in 2017 against the Rohingya, it can be said that it is a continuation of the previous ones.

Currently, more than a million Rohingya refugees are living in camps in Bangladesh (Uddin 2020). But they can neither stay for the rest of their life at the camps nor can they be assimilated in the host country because of Bangladesh's socio-economic conditions. Moreover, settlement in a third country is a long and complex process which in the case of Rohingya seem nearly impossible. The only viable solution to this crisis is repatriation to the country of origin. But the repatriation is not only 'going back home', it is a complex political process. The following is a discussion on the challenges of the criteria:

13.4.1. Stopping all Kinds of Violence and Oppression

According to the results, this criterion ranks high in priority. There is little or no possibility of voluntary repatriation of the Rohingya refugees without ensuring their safety and security in Myanmar. But Myanmar's denial of atrocities makes it complex to ensure their safety and security. Myanmar is criminalizing the victims while morally empowering the local Rakhines/Moghs and the army for the violence. Myanmar even failed to create a safe zone for the victims. Needless to say, this kind of action will give impetus for further violence in the region.

The Rohingya have been oppressed historically. Looking at the description and timeline of the oppression against the Rohingya, it can be deduced that it is systematic. Myanmar government put restrictions on education for the Rohingya community. If an ethnic group remains out of educational facilities for a longer period, they fall behind in every aspect of life. Thus, the Rohingya are not skilled enough for any formal job; they earn a livelihood through agricultural activities, day labour and small businesses such as owning a grocery shop within their community.

Restrictions on movement and communications (no internet, TV, radio, telephone, or mobile phone) made it even more difficult for them to be aware of the happenings in the outside world. This is how an entire ethnic group loses the ability to communicate with the international community, raise voice against oppression in a more political way, earn a standard livelihood and even understand the right method for asking for their rights. The history, approaches and the process of the oppression show that the oppression in Rakhine is planned, systematic and targeted at a specific ethnic group.

13.4.2. Ensuring Social and Civil Rights that come from Citizenship

While there is strong proof in various historic documents that the Rohingya are the nationals of Rakhine state (Karim 2016), the Myanmar authority labels them as 'illegal Bengali' and 'immigrants from Bangladesh' (Reuters 2018). This falsified labelling will keep the Rohingya alienated in the mindset of the Burmese and thus, there is hardly any chance that Myanmar will accept the proposal of granting them citizenship and/or recognizing them as one of the ethnic groups in Myanmar. Ironically, unless the Rohingya are granted citizenship, the existing social and civil rights will not be available for them in Myanmar.

The repatriation agreement signed between Bangladesh and Myanmar in November 2017 shows that the Myanmar government imposed some conditions for the process to complete. One of those conditions is presenting any document as proof of their residence in Myanmar. This condition is tricky. First, the Rohingya have been denied citizenship since 1982 that made it virtually impossible to prove their citizenship status (Ahluwalia and Miller 2018). Second, they left Rakhine to flee the persecution by the army and the local Moghs, and in a situation like that no one would stop and search for old citizenship documents when their houses were on fire, women were being dragged out of homes, children killed and elderly people shot. As most of the Rohingya houses were burnt down to ashes, it is highly unlikely that any of the documents, including that of residence, will have been spared.

13.4.3. Availability of Community Services and Facilities

The Rohingya are denied educational and health services in the Rakhine state of Myanmar. There is no hospital in the villages and children are not allowed to study after grade 10. Without health services and education facilities, life will not be normal in Rakhine. It is still not sure whether Myanmar will ensure these, though there is a mention of these services and facilities in the 2017 repatriation agreement.

13.4.4. Justice for the Genocide Victims

One of the major demands by the Rohingya among the criteria for repatriation is the justice for genocide victims through which the culprits will be meted out punishments and the Rohingya will get compensation for the loss of life of their near ones and property. The gateway to justice would be the recognition of the genocide in the first place. While Myanmar acknowledged that there have been war crimes in Rakhine (ICJ 2021), they have deliberately denied the act of genocide.

The mass killing, rape and torture intended to destroy the Rohingya minorities fall under the definition of genocide, according to Article 2 of the Convention on the Prevention and Punishment of the Crime of Genocide (ICJ 2021). But the description of the genocidal violence as a 'clearance operation' by Myanmar and 'ethnic cleansing' by the international community demeans the merit of the violence. Ahluwalia and Miller (2018) argue that despite the increased international commitment towards refugees in the last three decades, they failed the most vulnerable human beings miserably. They argue that the politics around the exclusivity of the term 'genocide' and terming the most inhuman brutality as 'mere ethnic cleansing' contributed to that failure (Ahluwalia and Miller 2018).

However, the International Court of Justice (ICJ), on the appeal of Gambia, ordered Myanmar six provisional measures including the prevention of further genocide and not to destroy the pieces of evidence of genocide which is the first step towards the desired justice for the Rohingya people (ICJ 2021). Rohingya need to wait for a few years to receive the complete verdict by the ICJ in the Gambia vs Myanmar case.

13.5. The Geopolitical Race

If the repatriation needs to be voluntary, there is no way other than eradicating the mistrust and fear from the minds of the Rohingya, and only Myanmar can do that. The geopolitical race in the region gives the Rohingya crisis a complex shape (Bose 2019).

Bose (2019) argues that both China and India are focusing more on the geopolitical position and the mineral resources of Myanmar. China has invested US\$7.3 billion in Rakhine. The geographic position of the state is important for the Belt and Road Initiative of China. During the economic sanction on Myanmar by the United States and Japan, China supported Myanmar's military and economy through trade and investment. On the other hand, Narendra Modi, the current Prime Minister of India, is a right-wing politician who along with the nationalist organization Rashtriya Swayamsevak Sangh spread Islamophobia among the Indian nationals that turned them against the 'Muslim Rohingyas'. Bose also argues that the Hindu–Buddhist peace zone is an attempt by Hindu nationalists to avoid the influence of the China–Pakistan axis. The United States did not do anything more than condemning the killing and assisting financially. While taking actions to protect human rights and establishing democracy in other parts of the world, the international community and the United States largely remained silent in the case of Rohingya.

However, China helped Bangladesh by influencing Myanmar in signing an agreement for the repatriation; Bose (2019) calls it 'the only tangible option' for Bangladesh. Another challenge for the repatriation and integration of the Rohingya in Myanmar is the internal political culture and religious practice. Wei and Yishuang (2019) suggest that the internal dimensions of Myanmar should be taken into consideration while thinking about the repatriation of the Rohingya. They argue that 80 per cent of Myanmar's citizens are Buddhists; for them, the Muslim Rohingya are a threat to the Buddhist culture and their national security for the image resulted due to the attacks of the Arakan Rohingya Salvation Army on Rakhine police posts. The politics of vote will not allow any political party to grant the Rohingya civil rights. The repatriation of the Rohingya and their assimilation in Myanmar might attract more Rohingya to the region.

Overall, historical disputes, religion, culture, national security and the domestic politics of Myanmar all together resist the granting of civil rights and repatriation of the Rohingya. Therefore, to create a safe and secure environment for the Rohingya in Myanmar, necessary steps should be taken to make the Rohingya acceptable to the Burmese people.

13.6. Recent Developments

In Bangladesh, the stateless Rohingya are currently living in dire humanitarian conditions inside overcrowded camps, where they are concurrently facing natural (cyclone/storms, flooding and landslides) and anthropogenic hazards (fire, human-trafficking, drugs), health hazards (mental stress and diseases) and COVID-19 pandemic (Ahmed 2021; Ahmed et al. 2018). To save them from natural disasters and ensure their better living standards, the GoB has started to relocate 100,000 of the most vulnerable Rohingya to Bhasan Char—a remote island in the Bay of Bengal (Zaman et al. 2020).

At present, there is a growing concern among the Rohingya and host community. The Rohingya crisis is adversely contributing to the rising price of daily essentials, creating job scarcity for labourers, challenging livelihood patterns of low-income families and reducing agricultural cultivation and production in Cox's Bazar. Local people perceived that the crisis in various ways distressed social fabrics adversely affected the education sector—both in the short and long terms—and degraded environmental balance through deforestation, hill cutting, losing biodiversity and generating competition over access to fresh drinking water (IRDR 2019).

Most recently, on 1 February 2021, the Myanmar military seized full control of authority following a coup and overthrew the country's ruling party and detained State Counsellor Aung San Suu Kyi. Civil resistance and demonstrations emerged in opposition to the coup, however, the security forces continued to kill hundreds of civilians and increase systematic attacks on peaceful protesters (UN News 2021). Regrettably, the Myanmar military chief Min Aung Hlaing, who is now in power, is also accused of war crimes and the genocide of Rohingya Muslims (ICJ 2021). The social-political-cultural context of Myanmar is complex, highly dynamic and changing rapidly in recent years (Ibrahim 2016). However, this sudden and unexpected transformation in Myanmar's internal political atmosphere will definitely shed uncertainty on the Rohingya repatriation process.

In addition, because of the ongoing global-level COVID-19 pandemic, most developed countries are struggling to keep their economic activities functional. For example, the UK government's borrowing has reached the highest level (£303 billion) since the end of the second World War. As a result, they have decided to cut the foreign aid budget from 0.7 per cent to 0.5 per cent of total national income and reduce humanitarian assistance by more than £500 million (BBC 2021). This kind of decision could be a major risk factor to the continuing humanitarian aid for the refugees in registered camp contexts.

Overall, regional geopolitics, internal tensions between the refugees and host communities, social-economic-cultural disparities, political instability in Myanmar, pre-existing vulnerabilities of the Rohingya and global recession due to the COVID-19 pandemic could jeopardize the achievements so far and bring a dearth of insecurities in the entire region. To overcome such limitations, regional and global-level cooperation for finding durable solutions for the Rohingya refugees is required straight away.

13.7. Conclusion and Way Forward

This chapter described the Rohingya refugees' criteria for their sustainable repatriation in Myanmar based on primary field-level research. It examined the linkages between the criteria and their experience of violence in the Rakhine state in Myanmar. It also critically evaluated the feasibility of meeting the demands of the Rohingya for successful voluntary repatriation. The repatriation process is not only about leaving the overly crowded camps in Bangladesh, but it is also about deciding a future for the Rohingya and the generations to come. While the existing literature discusses the Rohingya repatriation from a global and regional perspective, this chapter sheds light on how the Rohingya themselves want to shape their future and the challenges they face in doing so.

Two of the three UN-recognized methods used worldwide for the durable solution to the refugee crises—local integration and resettlement (UNHCR 2016)—seem nearly impossible in the case of the Rohingya refugees due to the economic and demographic condition of Bangladesh as the host country and lack of interest from a third country (Rashid 2019). The only option left is voluntary repatriation. For a successful and 'truly voluntary' repatriation process, it is important to understand what the refugees themselves think rather than explaining the process from the policymakers' perspectives. To do so, this chapter investigated the inside stories of the repatriation criteria from the Rohingya's perspective.

The short-term actions that would increase the chances of voluntary repatriation are (a) creating a safe zone in Rakhine for the Rohingya minority, (b) reaching out to the citizens of Myanmar through various programmes to alleviate the hatred against the Rohingya and (c) mediating among the parties involved in the geopolitical race in Myanmar. In order to increase the political and economic pressure on Myanmar to prevent the recurrence of the violence and ease the safe repatriation of the Rohingya, sanctions on all kinds of economic investments in Rakhine should be imposed on the condition of the peaceful settlement of the dispute. In the long term, the application of multiple mechanisms to create political will of Myanmar towards resolving the Rohingya crisis should be considered. This may include requesting the United Nations Security Council for deploying UN peacekeeping mission in Rakhine.

The Rohingya scenario can be described by saying that international powerhouses are busy with their calculation of investment in Rakhine, the geostrategic facilities and the political implications of supporting Myanmar. Bangladesh, being one of the densely populated and least developed countries, cannot afford to assimilate the refugees. The Burmese population in Myanmar do not consider the Rohingya as nationals of Myanmar and thus, the Tatmadaw and the local Rakhines/Moghs killed and systematically tortured the Rohingya.

It seems that the phrase, the most persecuted minority in the world, falls short to describe the plight of the stateless Rohingya. But this time, they want to go back to their 'homeland' with a durable solution. The international community and Myanmar cannot afford to fail again.

References

Ahluwalia, P., and T. Miller. 2018. 'The Rohingya Crisis: Another Failure of the International System'. *Social Identities* 24(3): 291–292.

Ahmed, B. 2021. 'The Root Causes of Landslide Vulnerability in Bangladesh'. *Landslides* 18 (5): 1707–1720.

Ahmed, B., M. Orcutt, P. Sammonds, R. Burns, R. Issa, I. Abubakar and D. Devakumar. 2018. 'Humanitarian Disaster for Rohingya Refugees: Impending Natural Hazards and Worsening Public Health Crises'. *The Lancet Global Health* 6 (5): e487–e488.

Ahmed, I., ed. 2010. *The Plight of the Stateless Rohingyas: Responses of the State, Society & the International Community*. Dhaka: The University Press Limited.

BBC. 2021. 'UK Aid Budget: Charities Call £500m Cut a Tragic Blow'. BBC News. Available at: https://www.bbc.co.uk/news/uk-politics-56836430. (accessed on 25 April 2021).

Bose, T. 2019. 'Rohingyas: Pawns in the Geopolitical Chessboard'. In *The Rohingya Refugee Crisis: Towards Sustainable Solutions*, edited by I. Ahmed. Dhaka: Centre for Genocide Studies, University of Dhaka.

Farzana, K. F. 2017. *Memories of Burmese Rohingya Refugees: Contested Identity and Belonging*. New York: Palgrave Macmillan.

Field, A. 2018. *Discovering Statistics using IBM SPSS Statistics*. London: SAGE Publications.

Human Rights Watch. 2000. Burmese Refugees in Bangladesh: Still No Durable Solution. Available at: https://www.hrw.org/reports/2000/burma/index.htm (accessed on 23 April 2021).

Human Rights Watch. 2017. Burma: Methodical Massacre at Rohingya Village. Available at: https://www.hrw.org/news/2017/12/19/burma-methodical-massacre-rohingya-village (Accessed on 23 April 2021).

Ibrahim, A. 2016. *The Rohingyas: Inside Myanmar's Genocide*. London: Hurst Publishers.

ICJ. 2021. Application of the Convention on the Prevention and Punishment of the Crime of Genocide (The Gambia v. Myanmar). International Court of Justice (ICJ), the Hague, Netherlands. Available at: https://www.icj-cij.org/en/case/178. (accessed on 23 April 2021).

IRDR. 2019. The Rohingya Exodus: Issues and Implications for Stability, Security and Peace in South Asia. Institute for Risk and Disaster Reduction (IRDR), University College London (UCL), UK. Available at: https://www.ucl.ac.uk/risk-disaster-reduction/sites/risk-disaster-reduction/files/final_report_ba.pdf. (accessed on 25 April 2021).

Karim, Abdul. 2016. *The Rohingyas: A Short Account of their History and Culture*. Dhaka: Jatiya Sahitya Prakash.

Krejcie, R. V., and D. W. Morgan. 1970. 'Determining Sample Size for Research Activities'. *Educational and Psychological Measurement* 30 (3): 607–610.

Lavrakas, P. J. 2008. *Encyclopedia of Survey Research Methods*. New Delhi: SAGE Publications.

MSF. 2018. *"No one was Left": Death and Violence Against the Rohingya in Rakhine State, Myanmar*. Geneva: Médecins Sans Frontières (MSF),. Available at: https://www.doctorswithoutborders.ca/sites/default/files/2018_-_03_-_no_one_was_left_-_advocacy_briefing_on_mortality_surveys.pdf. (accessed on 25 April 2021).

Pallant, J. 2020. *SPSS Survival Manual: A Step By Step Guide to Data Analysis using IBM SPSS*. New York: Routledge.

Rashid, S. R. 2020. Finding a Durable Solution to Bangladesh's Rohingya Refugee Problem: Policies, Prospects and Politics. *Asian Journal of Comparative Politics* 5 (2): 174–189.

Reuters. 2018. 'How Myanmar Forces Burned, Looted and Killed in a Remote Village'. Available at: https://www.reuters.com/investigates/special-report/myanmar-rakhine-events/. (accessed on 23 April 2021).

The World Bank Myanmar. 2017. 'An Analysis of Poverty in Myanmar. Part 02: Poverty Profile. The Government of Myanmar and the World Bank'. Yangon, Republic of the Union of Myanmar. Available at: http://documents.worldbank.org/curated/en/829581512375610375/pdf/121822-REVISED-PovertyReportPartEng.pdf. (accessed on 23 April 2021).

Uddin, N. 2020. *The Rohingya: An Ethnography of 'Subhuman' Life*. New Delhi: Oxford University Press.

UN News. 2021. 'Myanmar: "Significant Action" needed by Security Council to Prevent "Bloodbath." The United Nations'. Available at: https://news.un.org/en/story/2021/03/1088822 (accessed on 25 April 2021).

UN. 2017. 'UN Human Rights Chief Points to "Textbook Example of Ethnic Cleansing" in Myanmar. The United Nations (UN), the UN News'. Available at: https://news.un.org/en/story/2017/09/564622-un-human-rights-chief-points-textbook-example-ethnic-cleansing-myanmar (accessed on 23 April 2021).

UNFPA Myanmar. 2014. 'Sittway Township Report, Rakhine State, Sittway District. The 2014 Myanmar Population and Housing Census, Department of Population, Ministry of Labour, Immigration and Population, Office No.48, Nay Pyi Taw'. Available at: https://myanmar.unfpa.org/sites/default/files/resource-pdf/Rakhine_Sittway_en.pdf (accessed on 23 April 2021).

UNHCR. 1996. 'Handbook on Voluntary Repatriation: International Protection. The United Nations High Commissioner for Refugees (UNHCR)'. Available at: https://www.unhcr.org/uk/publications/legal/3bfe68d32/handbook-voluntary-repatriation-international-protection.html (accessed on 25 April 2021).

UNHCR. 2016. 'The 10-Point Plan in Action. Chapter 7: Solutions for Refugees. The United Nations High Commissioner for Refugees (UNHCR)'. Available at: https://www.unhcr.org/uk/publications/manuals/5846d10e7/10-point-plan-action-2016-update-chapter-7-solutions-refugees.html (accessed on 25 April 2021).

UNHCR. 2021. 'Refuge Response in Bangladesh. The United Nations High Commissioner for Refugees (UNHCR)'. Available at: https://data2.unhcr.org/en/situations/myanmar_refugees (accessed on 23 April 2021).

Wei, Liu, and Yang Yishuang. 2019. 'Rohingyas: Pawns in the Geopolitical Chessboard'. In *The Rohingya Refugee Crisis: Towards Sustainable Solutions*, edited by Imtiaz Ahmed. Dhaka: Centre for Genocide Studies, University of Dhaka, Bangladesh.

Zaman, S., P. Sammonds, B. Ahmed, T. Rahman. 2020. 'Disaster Risk Reduction in Conflict Contexts: Lessons Learned from the Lived Experiences of Rohingya Refugees in Cox's Bazar, Bangladesh'. *International Journal of Disaster Risk Reduction* 50, 101694.

CHAPTER 14

The 'Myth' of Repatriation

The Prolonged Sufferings of the Rohingya

Bulbul Siddiqi

14.1. Introduction

The Rohingya crisis is deeply rooted in history (Ullah 2011) with geo-political and economic interests of some vested groups than just religious and ethnic tensions (Bepler 2018). The persecution of the Rohingya was predicted by some academic and researchers, for example, Grundy-Warr and Wong (1997) and Prasse-Freeman (2017) observing the several previous episodes of the forced displacement of the Rohingya from Myanmar. Besides, since 2012, 130,000 Rohingya are living in inhuman conditions in detention in Rakhine state, which is a violation of their right to live (Human Rights Watch 2020). The Rohingya are like birds in a cage in North Arakan, which is an 'open prison' (Lewa 2009). Thus, a sustainable and lasting solution to the ongoing Rohingya crisis is nowhere in sight. Bangladesh has been facing the repeated influx of the Rohingya since the end of the 1970s (Ullah 2011). It was estimated that about 400,000–500,000 Rohingya were living in Bangladesh before the largest Rohingya influx took place in 2017; of these, only 33,131 were registered as refugees (Milton et al. 2017). In response to such repeated Rohingya influx, only a few initiatives were successful as far as repatriation is concerned, and a tiny portion of the Rohingya was repatriated to Myanmar in the past (Azad and Jasmin 2013). In contrast to this view, Myanmar continues to blame Bangladesh and shows no indication to resolve the crisis initiating the repatriation process of the Rohingya from Bangladesh.[1]

Repatriation as a method of resolving the refugee crisis is generally a lengthy process. Despite several repatriation attempts of the Rohingya in the past, the crisis has remained unresolved and continued with further complexity for several decades now. It was argued in the past that if Myanmar does not comply with providing protection and granting citizenship for the Rohingya, there will not be a durable solution to the crisis (Ullah 2011). The outcome of the Rohingya repatriation and sustainable resolution remained the same even after the largest Rohingya exodus in 2017. The Government of Bangladesh (GoB) has time and again emphasized that the resolution of this crisis is in the hands of Myanmar.[2] Moreover, since Bangladesh is not a signatory of the 1951 refugee convention, most of the Rohingya are not recognized as refugees by the GoB. Thus, they are denied the rights as refugees—denial of recognizing them as refugees acts as the major cause of prolonged vulnerabilities during the displacement. In addition, the recent military coup in Myanmar could worsen the situation of the Rohingya if the global communities do not take the necessary steps immediately (Musa 2021), and repatriation will be delayed further (Hasan, Hawksley and Georgeou 2021). The fear of torture among the Rohingya is also evident after the military coup in Myanmar (Westerman 2021). Thus, the discussion of putting an embargo against the military leaders is also in the proposal (Musa 2021).

This chapter will discuss the complex issues of repatriation from three different perspectives: civil society, humanitarian and the Rohingya community. Thus, it will give a comprehensive understanding of the difficulties of resolving the Rohingya crisis and, the chapter

[1] 'Myanmar blames Rohingya repatriation failure on Bangladesh'. Available at: https://www.dhakatribune.com/bangladesh/rohingya-crisis/2019/08/23/myanmar-blames-rohingya-repatriation-failure-on-bangladesh accessed on 14 October.

[2] 'Bangladesh "outraged" by Myanmar's Fabrication of Facts at UNGA'. Available at: https://www.thedailystar.net/bangladesh-outraged-myanmar-fabrication-facts-at-unga-1969981 accessed on 4 October 2020.

shows that the delay of repatriation and failure to ensure a sustainable resolution of the Rohingya crisis will increase the broader spectrum of sufferings for the Rohingya refugees in Bangladesh and Myanmar. The chapter is divided into three broad sections: the first section discusses the rhetoric of Rohingya repatriation, the second section brings out the perspectives from the humanitarian actors and the third section is based on the Rohingya understanding of the repatriation, which in many cases remain unheard and ignored.

14.2. The Rhetoric of Rohingya Repatriation: Past, Present and Future

The idea of repatriation is seen as a common yet complex resolution in the refugee context globally. The case of the Rohingya is not an exception; particularly, the crisis has become a complex one that constituted one of the largest displaced communities in the current time. Thus, the idea of safe, dignified and volunteer repatriation has been the priority for the sustainable resolution of the Rohingya crisis in Bangladesh. The idea of voluntary repatriation is the highest priority of the GoB in the current Rohingya crisis, as involuntary repatriation can be problematic (Faulkner and Schiffer 2019). The United Nations High Commissioner for Refugees (UNHCR) is also in agreement with the GoB on the idea of voluntary repatriation that has to be safe and dignified.[3] Although voluntary repatriation is seen as the most expected one (Rashid 2020), there remain risks of involuntary, forced and organized repatriations if the voluntary repatriation is delayed for an uncertain period (Toft 2007). While talking about repatriation, ensuring citizenship for the Rohingya is seen as the most durable solution for them (Robinson and Rahman 2012). However, granting citizenship alone without providing other human rights measures may not bring a positive change for the Rohingya. There should be an initiative to change the existing perception of seeing the Rohingya as outsiders and treating their religion as unsuited with the mainstream society (Prasse-Freeman 2017). The Rohingya in Myanmar are mainly

[3] 'UNHCR Statement on Voluntary Repatriation to Myanmar'. Available at: https://www.unhcr.org/news/press/2019/8/5d5e720a4/unhcr-statement-voluntary-repatriation-myanmar.html accessed on 15 October 2020.

seen as illegal migrants and a threat to national security (Farzana 2017; Haque 2020; Karim 2016).

Although the largest number of the Rohingya repatriation took place between 1992 and 1997, there was the claim of involuntary repatriation (Abrar 1996; Faulkner and Schiffer 2019; Grundy-Warr and Wong 1997). However, the notion of involuntary repatriation was favourable for many developing nations which find it difficult to host a large number of refugee communities (Chimni 2004). As an interim measure, the GoB has already developed a village for the Rohingya in a remote island called Bhashan Char, although it has a capacity for only 100,000 people. However, shifting a portion of them to a remote and low-lying island (Bhashan Char) in the Bay of Bengal can be a risky option (Ahmed et al. 2018). The government representatives took a group of Rohingya community leaders who are generally known as *majhi* on 5 September 2020 to observe the facilities at Bhashan Char and thereby to motivate the Rohingya community to relocate to Bhashan Char.[4] However, many Rohingya seem to be reluctant to accept the offer for a few reasons: one, the island is located in a remote area where they would not be able to move around for work and other necessities; two, there is a lack of necessary infrastructure for their safety from various natural disasters like cyclones; and the three, some Rohingya believe that such relocation may delay the process of repatriation. Despite such various concerns, the GoB shifted more than 1,000 Rohingya to the Bhashan Char on 3 December 2020[5] that created a huge media uproar. There also remains a concern by many rights groups including Amnesty International. Amnesty International particularly pointed out that relocation has to be carried out with informed consent of the population.[6] The same report also raised an

[4] '40 Rohingyas reach Bhashan Char to Visit Accommodation Project'. See more at https://www.thedailystar.net/40-rohingya-refugees-their-way-visit-bhashan-char-project-1956293 accessed on 15 October 2020.

[5] 'Bangladesh begins Rohingya Relocation Despite Rights Concerns'. Available at: https://www.aljazeera.com/news/2020/12/3/rights-groups-urge-bangladesh-to-halt-rohingya-relocation accessed on 5 December 2020.

[6] 'Bangladesh: Halt Relocation of Rohingya Refugees to Remote Island'. Available at https://www.amnesty.org/en/latest/news/2020/12/bangladesh-halt-relocation-of-rohingya-refugees-to-remote-island/ accessed on 5 December 2020.

issue of separation and isolation from the other family members of the Rohingya community if they are to be relocated to Bhashan Char.

In the context of the Rohingya refugees in Bangladesh, a high-level government official sees the potential of introducing various skill development training for the Rohingya community as an interim measure. The government official stated that skill development training is essential for many Rohingya so that they can work and survive once they get back to their country.[7] Some types of vocational training, including tailoring skills, mobile phone repair and the like are being provided in a few camps.[8] The introduction of the skill development training for the Rohingya shows a strong hope for the repatriation among authorities in the GoB. But the repatriation has still remained a dream as the previous efforts of the GoB show no immediate possibility for repatriation of the Rohingya. Here, it is also worthwhile to note that two earlier efforts at repatriation had failed since the exodus of 2017.[9] The situation has not improved even after the 2017 Rohingya exodus, where a single Rohingya was not repatriated, as Prime Minister Sheikh Hasina referred to it at the 75th UNGA speech. She mentioned,

> The problem [the Rohingya crisis] was created by Myanmar, and its solution must be found in Myanmar. I request the international community to play a more effective role for a solution to the crisis.
>
> [The honourable Prime Minister Sheikh Hasina in her 75th UNGA speech.[10]]

---

[7] The foreign secretary Mr Masud Bin Momen mentioned it in his speech in a webinar held on 24 August 2020, organized by the Center for Peace Studies at North South University, Bangladesh.

[8] 'Skills Training to Equip 8,400 Rohingya Adolescents with Hope for a Better Future' see at https://www.wvi.org/myanmar-%E2%80%93-bangladesh-refugee-crisis/article/skills-training-equip-8400-rohingya-adolescents-hope accessed on 5 December 2020.

[9] 'Rohingya Repatriation: No Third Attempt Without Confirming Success' see at https://www.dhakatribune.com/bangladesh/rohingya-crisis/2019/10/03/rohingya-repatriation-no-third-attempt-without-confirming-success accessed on 15 October 2020.

[10] 'Bangladesh 'Outraged' by Myanmar's Fabrication of Facts at UNGA' see at https://www.thedailystar.net/bangladesh-outraged-myanmar-fabrication-facts-at-unga-1969981 accessed on 4 October 2020.

In contrast, Myanmar continues to blame Bangladesh for lingering upon the crisis. This is why Prime Minister Sheikh Hasina mentioned that the solution lies with Myanmar. However, blaming Bangladesh for the Rohingya crisis would not bring any solution as another ex-government official said in a meeting.[11] He also referred that despite many bilateral initiatives between Bangladesh and Myanmar, and several attempts of the Rohingya repatriation made since the 2017 exodus, not a single Rohingya could return. The past experiences of the Rohingya repatriation were not entirely successful. Besides, a good number of Rohingya people have remained in Bangladesh, where many have already integrated into the broader community of Bangladesh.

The historical perspectives of the Rohingya repatriation show that it has never been successful for Bangladesh. A researcher and academic mentioned in an in-depth interview that

> Repatriation has never been successful in the past; thus, it won't be an easy task for Bangladesh even this time. It may not take place in the near future. The existence of a sporadic border between Bangladesh and Myanmar is an issue. If the Rohingyas do not feel secured and safe after their repatriation, there is a good chance for them to return to Bangladesh […] this is why I believe that integration is the only durable solution for this crisis.

> [An academic and researcher, the interview was taken on 28 August 2020 over Zoom platform.]

Although the interviewees emphasized local integration as the durable solution to the Rohingya crisis, the GoB continued to reject the idea of integration since the earlier phases of the crisis as mentioned by the top governmental official who repeatedly refers to the fact that Bangladesh is not in favour of local integration. In a webinar hosted by the Center for Peace Studies at NSU, foreign Secretary Masud Bin Momen has said that

> I must clarify that we would certainly not prefer investments, which will directly or indirectly prolong the refugee situation

---

[11] Mr Shahidul Haque the then-foreign secretary of Bangladesh mentioned it in his speech in a webinar held on 24 August 2020, organized by the Center for Peace Studies at North South University, Bangladesh.

by creating new and greater pull factors for the remaining Rohingyas inside Rakhine. The Government of Bangladesh rejects any notion of local integration.[12]

[The speech was delivered on 24 August 2020 over Zoom platform, Dhaka.]

There remains a challenge for long-term local integration as the host community attitude towards the Rohingya is mixed and sensitive. In addition, in many cases, people from the host community see the Rohingya as troublemakers, for example, they are seen as a social threat, sources for many social problems and environmental imbalances (Jerin and Mozumder 2019). If the crisis remains, and the repatriation does not happen, there is no doubt that the vulnerabilities of the Rohingya community will increase. In such cases, children, adolescent boys and girls will suffer the most. As one of my informants mentioned that

> Adolescents are not doing anything; they just roam around. They do not have any scope for education. Thus, their only motivation is to get married. They just wait for a good marriage to start a different life. Moreover, the temptation of drugs and engaging in various criminal activities are there, which can pose a security threat.
>
> [An academic and researcher, the interview was taken on 28 August 2020 over zoom platform.]

The solutions being considered to end the Rohingya crisis can be divided into three broad categories: one, adopting short-term measures to ensure the refugee rights of the Rohingyas in Bangladesh; two, adopting mid-term approaches to convert the huge refugee burden into a resource for Bangladesh, and three, ensuring permanent Burmese citizenship for the Rohingya as the sustainable solution of

---

[12] 'Bangladesh Rejects Local Integration of Rohingyas' see at https://www.dhakatribune.com/bangladesh/rohingya-crisis/2020/08/24/bangladesh-rejects-local-integration-of-rohingyas accessed on 2nd December 2020.

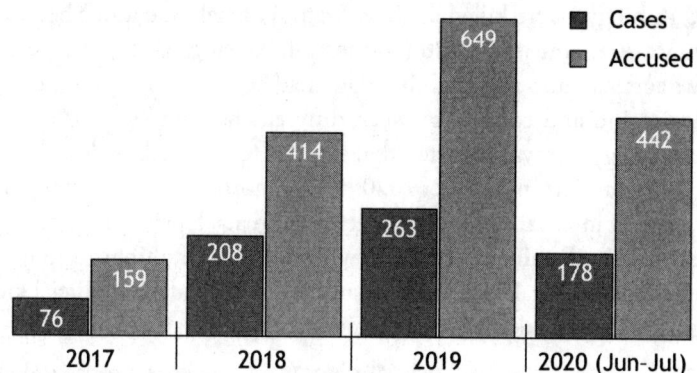

Figure 14.1 *Cases Against Rohingya*
Source: Khan (2020).

the problem (Robinson and Rahman 2012). Although this study was conducted a long time before the 2017 influx of the Rohingya in Bangladesh, it remains remarkably relevant for thinking about the potential solutions to the Rohingya crisis in the current context.

During my field visit in 2019 to one of the camps in Leda, I witnessed that NGO officials who were guiding me to the field suggested not to go inside the camp as a Rohingya leader was killed in a gunfight.[13] In this context of increasing criminal activities in the camp areas, a report by Khan (2020) shows that criminal cases are increasing very fast. He also shows that the number (see Figure 14.1) is only the tip of the iceberg as the actual number of illegal activities, including murder, abduction and sexual harassment in the camps, may be higher than this figure as most of them go unreported.

Moreover, the number of deaths among the Rohingya are increasing in the camps and neighbourhood due to various conflicts. A report published by Amnesty International claimed that more than

---

[13] 'Rohingya Leader Dies from Gunshot Wounds in Hospital' see https://www.dhakatribune.com/bangladesh/nation/2019/03/30/rohingya-leader-dies-from-gunshot-wounds-in-hospital last accessed on 11 October 2020.

100 Rohingya were killed in alleged extrajudicial executions between August 2017 and July 2020 (Amnesty International 2020). Various news agencies also reported that there had been increased and noticeable tension and conflict between different factional groups among the Rohingya. It was reported that several Rohingya died due to such internal conflicts in October 2020.[14] The unofficial number may vary. The risk of internal and regional security threats, tensions between the host and the Rohingya, conflicts within various Rohingya groups,[15] allegations of illegal drug and human trafficking and extrajudicial killings have been making the crisis more complex than ever.

Thus, the GoB neither could think of a formal integration as there is an apprehension of killing the existing minimum chances of repatriation nor put sufficient pressure on Myanmar for the repatriation. Since Bangladesh has to depend heavily on the international communities for sustainable and dignified solutions to the crisis, international communities failed to put pressure on Myanmar to resolve the crisis, which has been another concern for Bangladesh. Therefore, the concept of 'myth' of repatriation has been used as a metaphor to analyse the complexity of the Rohingya repatriation that has been delayed and left the Rohingya in uncertainties.

14.3. Perspectives of Humanitarian Actors in Cox's Bazar

Although the crisis started a few decades ago, there were not many humanitarian actors active in the past episodes of the Rohingya influx in Bangladesh as seen today. An estimate suggests that about 130

---

[14] 'Several killed in "Gang War" at Rohingya Camps in Bangladesh' see at https://www.aljazeera.com/news/2020/10/9/several-killed-in-gang-war-at-rohingya-camps-in-bangladesh?fbclid=IwAR3zWsxMZHXwocP84HPj3PXqz ZpOrP2y_0wG6UkEmBaUfW0B_8HJjujAkR0 accessed on 11 October 2020.

[15] In a violent conflict between different groups of the Rohingya eight people were dead in Kutupalong camp. Nearly 50 people were injured and the law enforcing agency arrested 16 people afterwards. See more at https://www.dhakatribune.com/bangladesh/nation/2020/10/10/16-arrested-over-clash-at-kutupalong-rohingya-camp accessed on 7 December 2020.

humanitarian actors have been working in makeshift camps for the Rohingya in Cox's Bazar since 2017 (Khan 2018). The exact number may be higher than this, as many humanitarian actors disclosed. It would have been a massive challenge for Bangladesh to manage the crisis without the support from the humanitarian actors. In a press conference, the Prime Minister mentioned that 'we took steps for their [Rohingya people] repatriation. However, a section of Rohingyas launched a movement against their return. Who instigated them? International volunteers do not want repatriation'.[16]

Furthermore, there is a report published in *the Daily Star*[17] about most part (about 75%) of the aid being spent to manage the increased staff of various organizations working on the Rohingya issues. Despite such allegations against the humanitarian actors, their roles are highly appreciated both at home and abroad. Insights from the humanitarian actors working on this displaced and marginalized group helped me enrich my understanding of the crisis. The humanitarian actors talked about the crisis based on their long experiences of working on the Rohingya response. Some started working after the 2017 Rohingya exodus, and some started working even long before 2017.

The first point that one of the humanitarian actors raised was the non-existence of a comprehensive and dedicated refugee management policy focusing on the Rohingya crisis. As Bangladesh has been mired in this problem since the end of the 1970s, a comprehensive policy would have been better to manage the Rohingya crisis. As he mentioned,

> The Rohingya crisis requires policy recommendations that could deal with the complex nature of repatriation. There should be a long-term policy of dealing with the Rohingyas in Bangladesh.

[16] 'Voluntary Organisations don't want Rohingya Repatriation: PM' see at https://en.prothomalo.com/bangladesh/news/196999/Voluntary-organisations-don%E2%80%99t-want-Rohingya; accessed on 24 June, 2019.

[17] '"Tk 150 crore Spent on Hotel Bills in 6 Months": *Minister Blasts Foreign Agencies Working for Rohingyas*'. see at https://www.thedailystar.net/city/news/tk-150-crore-spent-hotel-bills-6-months-1714909 accessed on 15 October 2020.

But we do not see appropriate levels of preparedness among the government agencies in formulating a firm policy on this. There remains a considerable gap in the readiness of a policy of the Rohingya crisis.

[A mid-level male humanitarian actor, the interview was conducted on 10 January 2020 at Cox's Bazar.]

This mid-level humanitarian actor also emphasized that there is no such integrated policy at the government level to deal with the complex phenomenon of the Rohingya crisis, which is multifaceted in many ways. Moreover, the lack of such policy contributes to the increased sufferings of the Rohingya, putting their lives in a limbo, which is frustrating for them. However, Bangladesh considers the entire Rohingya refugee issue from a disaster perspective; hence, the Ministry of Disaster Management has the core responsibilities to respond and manage the crisis, which many humanitarian actors consider as another limitation of dealing with the Rohingya crisis.

Defining and recognizing the displaced Rohingya population in Bangladesh is another complex phenomenon where the GoB is unwilling to recognize the Rohingya as refugees who entered Bangladesh during the exodus of 2017. The debate was there in the past, where academics also argued that Bangladesh should sign and ratify the 1951 Refugee Convention to comply with the international obligation of taking good care of the Rohingya community in Bangladesh (Robinson and Rahman 2012). However, the situation worsened after the exodus in 2017 as the number of Rohingya was very high. Thus, the GoB made it clear that the Rohingya should be treated and defined as Forcibly Displaced Myanmar Nationals (FDMNs).[18] In this context, another humanitarian actor expressed that such a stance of the GoB in determining the Rohingya as FDMNs may create challenges to formulate a long-term policy for the Rohingya in Bangladesh.

---

[18] 'GoB identifies the Rohingya as "Forcibly Displaced Myanmar Nationals" right after the 2017 Influx in Bangladesh' see at https://www.thedailystar.net/city/forcibly-displaced-myanmar-nationals-1469374 accessed on 20 November 2019.

The GoB sees the repatriation of the Rohingya as the only solution, which in a way is holding them back from formulating long-term and sustainable strategies for the Rohingya. As a humanitarian actor mentioned that

> To the government agencies, repatriation is the only solution. This is the official transcript, and they prefer to promote such of their views. This acts as the key barrier for developing a long-term plan. Thus, the approach so far, we could see is to adopt a short-term strategy, which is, in most cases, a yearly plan.
>
> [A mid-level humanitarian actor, male, the interview was conducted on 10 January 2020 at Cox's Bazar.]

In contrast to this view, there is a fear of not repatriating the Rohingya entirely if the GoB takes a long-term and sustainable approach for the Rohingya in Bangladesh. The actor further added that the agencies working at the ground level do not have much decision-making capabilities at the policy level. Thus, they are just continuing with meeting the essential daily needs of the Rohingya, following the instructions from their superiors. This is also a significant limitation in dealing with the Rohingya crisis in Bangladesh. Thus, they started to adapt to the local, social and economic sphere as one of the humanitarian actors mentioned based on his long working experience among the Rohingya in Ukhia.

Besides, there remains a concern to ensure the basic needs and rights of the Rohingya community in Bangladesh. It has already created added development challenges for Bangladesh, as the GoB has to bear the cost to manage the Rohingya in camps (Chowdhury 2018). Various studies show the adverse impacts of the Rohingya in Ukhia and Teknaf sub-districts of Cox's Bazar (Ahmed and Mohiuddin 2020; Ahmed et al. 2018; Bhatia et al. 2018; Bowden 2018; Kipgen 2014; Milton et al. 2017). These challenges have further aggravated by nearly one million Rohingya refugees (741,577 since August 2017) living in makeshift camps in Bangladesh (UNHCR 2019).

Apart from such development challenges of Bangladesh in dealing with the Rohingya crisis, the impact of the Rohingya settlement on the host communities is another concerning issue. Growing dissatisfaction among the host community is one of such effects. One of the reasons for the growing dissatisfaction of the host communities is the increased living expenses due to the huge Rohingya population in Ukhia and Teknaf. In this context, a humanitarian actor mentioned that

> The Rohingyas have started to find a way to work with a low wage rate outside of the camps. They can now move outside the camps using the remote and less explored roads to look for various working opportunities. In Ukhia (where I live), I have seen that many Rohingyas were working in a building construction area, where only one was from the host community. They are willing to work long hours without any extra money with a relatively lower wage rate than the host community. It has an impact on the local labour market and acts as the primary reason for tension between the Rohingyas and host communities.
>
> [A male humanitarian actor, the interview was conducted on 30 September 2020 over the phone from Dhaka.]

His statement points towards the informal and spontaneous pattern of integration of the Rohingya in the local economic sphere. However, the government initiatives of relocating them to Bhashan Char may bring the debate whether this would be the first official phase of the integration of the Rohingya or would it be seen as an example of isolating some of the Rohingya with increased environmental vulnerabilities.

In this context, the GoB needs to be very clear in negotiating with the external authorities to facilitate the Rohingya crisis as another person referred. He mentioned that

> GoB is very vulnerable in forcing international communities. Their position, in some cases, is not very clear. Thus, there remains a lack of coordination within different governmental agencies at the ground level. In addition to this, there is also a lack of coordination between NGOs, INGOs, the UN and the GoB.
>
> [A mid-level male humanitarian actor, the interview was conducted on 10 January 2020 at Cox's Bazar.]

The matter of coordination is an important factor that requires urgent attention of the central coordinating unit. The lack of trust between the government agencies and NGOs (both national and international) is also evident. In many cases, the government representatives repeatedly claim that some NGOs misguide the Rohingya to not return to their homeland.[19] Humanitarian actors, in many cases, were very critical of the roles and approaches of the government agencies in dealing with the Rohingya crisis. Thus, the lack of coordination, the inexistence of a long-term plan and blaming the humanitarian actors would make the lives of the Rohingyas further complicated and vulnerable. Finally, the knowledge gap in understanding the crisis from the very beginning is a severe concern that contributes not to formulate an effective strategic plan to resolve the crisis. Although Bangladesh has witnessed a regular Rohingya influx since the end of the 1970s, there were no reflections of learning from the past episodes of the Rohingya inflows, which frustrate most stakeholders in the Rohingya response.

14.4. Voices of the Rohingya

The Rohingya influx in 2017 sympathized the people of Bangladesh when thousands of Rohingya started crossing the border to enter Bangladesh. The entire country stood up to support and give shelter to the Rohingya. The crisis was managed with strong coordination by the state, which helped to also create a narrative of national generosity and religious piety (Lewis 2019). I have also witnessed several initiatives where local political leaders, students and many other people initiated donations to support the Rohingya. The emotional statement of Prime Minister Sheikh Hasina, 'if needed we will eat a full meal once a day and share the rest with them'[20] helped enormously to mobilize the sentiments of the mass of Bangladesh to stand for the Rohingya. However, this well-grown, sympathized emotion towards

---

[19] 'Bangladesh says "Some NGOs Impeding" Rohingya Repatriation by "Misguiding" them' see at https://bdnews24.com/bangladesh/2019/08/22/bangladesh-says-some-ngos-impeding-rohingya-repatriation-by-misguiding-them last accessed on 7 December 2020.

[20] 'Bangladesh Vows to Support One Million Rohingya Muslims Fleeing Burma: "If Needed, We'll Eat a Full Meal Once a Day and Share the Rest with them"' see at https://www.independent.co.uk/news/world/asia/rohingya-muslims-bangladesh-latest-updates-flee-burma-million-food-shelter-a7987761.html accessed on 15 October 2020.

the Rohingya has already faded away for various reasons from many local people of Ukhia and Teknaf who have been facing the direct impact of the Rohingya crisis in their everyday lives in present time. Three main points can be identified at this stage: one, the access to the forest has been restricted for the local people as many of them were dependent on the forest for their livelihood; two, the local labour market is affected due to the influx of the Rohingya and three, there is a notion of increasing violent activities in the region. Thus, the fear of growing tension between the Rohingya and the host community is a significant concern (Ahmed and Mohiuddin 2020). Such fear of lack of cohesion and tension between the host and the Rohingya was there in the past (Crabtree 2010; Rahman 2010). Besides, various news on the extrajudicial killings of many Rohingya in connection with drug dealings and human trafficking started to be visible in the last three years (Amnesty International 2020). Such added problems are the outcome of delaying the Rohingya repatriation. The internal conflicts within many factional Rohingya groups are also on the rise.

In such a context, the possibilities of local integration of the Rohingya are also not there. Although my long field experience with the Rohingya shows that they are thankful to Bangladesh for providing them with shelter and fulfilling other basic needs from 2017, now they feel that they need to have a better living condition with extended social security. They have survived the violence and risk of being killed in 2017, and they need a permanent solution to the problem. The Rohingya are now looking for the active initiatives by the GoB to resolve the crisis. As a young man from camp 20 told me that

> We are thankful to Prime minister Sheikh Hasina for sheltering us. But internal and local dynamics in many camps have been changing very fast since 2017. Therefore, the issue of security and human trafficking have become concerning for us these days.

> [A 27-years-old Rohingya, male the interview was conducted on 4 April 2019 at Rohingya camp 20 at Cox's Bazar.]

Such concerns will increase if the repatriation does not take place soon. However, different perspectives can also be found when an older man living in Bangladesh for 35 years eagerly waits to return to his homeland. Despite the opportunity of getting the paperwork for citizenship in Bangladesh, he decided to live in the camp as a registered refugee. As he mentioned

> It is a matter of *iman* [good deed] to live in your country. This is why I am waiting to return to my homeland one day. I did not go for attaining the citizenship paperwork from Bangladesh.

> [The interview was taken on 6 April 2019 at a registered camp located at Shamlapur at Cox's Bazar.]

This was very common among the people who came to Bangladesh before the 2017 influx to get a national identification (NID) card and even a passport from Bangladesh. I met such a person in a camp who claimed that his entire family holds citizenship documentation from Bangladesh. He came to Bangladesh in 2001, and he has been living in the district of Bandarban (a neighbouring district of Cox's Bazar) since then. He can now speak the local Bengali dialect very well. He has travelled to many districts and worked in various places to support his family in Bangladesh. His elder daughter is preparing to sit for the Secondary School Certificate examination from a local school. He has started living in a newly established camp with other family members who took shelter in 2017. One reason for moving to a camp is to get relief goods and other essential services from the camp authority.

Such news was also reported from various camps that many Rohingya have already received the NID card from the local representatives with a bribe. A recent report claimed that such a tendency to receive NID cards has started right after the Rohingya influx in 2017, which shows the presence of an organized network.[21] Various

---

[21] 'টাকার বিনিময়ে ভো টার হচ্ছনে রো হিঙ্গিারা!' (The Rohingyas have become voter spending money) see at https://www.channel24bd.tv/special-news/art icle/152886/%E0%A6%9F%E0%A6%BE%E0%A6%95%E0%A6%BE%E 0%A6%B0-%E0%A6%AC%E0%A6%BF%E0%A6%A8%E0%A6%BF%E 0%A6%AE%E0%A7%9F%E0%A7%87-%E0%A6%AD%E0%A7%8B%E- 0%A6%9F%E0%A6%BE%E0%A6%B0-%E0%A6%B9%E0%A6%9A%E0%A 7%8D%E0%A6%9B%E0%A7%87%E0%A6%A8-%E0%A6%B0%E0%A7%8 B%E0%A6%B9%E0%A6%BF%E0%A6%99%E0%A7%8D%E0%A6%97%E 0%A6%BE%E0%A6%B0%E0%A6%BE accessed on 14 October 2020.

other news reports also show many failed attempts of availing passports by many Rohingya.[22] However, many Rohingya still believe that repatriation is the only solution for them, and they are eager to go back to their homeland. A 27-year-old Rohingya man mentioned that

> We want our citizenship status in Myanmar, and we do not want to live like this. We want to return to our homeland. I had a perfect wooden house in my village. I used to work as a carpenter there and earn good money back home.
>
> [The interview was conducted on 4 April 2019 at camp no 20E at Cox's Bazar.]

Although they have taken shelter in a makeshift camp with a very congested housing pattern on the hilly areas of Cox's Bazar, there are many dissatisfactions among the Rohingya. Among them, child education, legal work opportunity, a limited and fragmented social life and the lack of security make their lives vulnerable in camps. Despite the restriction on working in or outside the camps, many people have already found ways to get work. There is also a tendency to reject the offer to be a volunteer community leader in the camps as they could earn more by working in the local villages. It was also evident that many Rohingya engaged in various forms of income-generating activities in the past as part of their continuing adaptation strategy (Crabtree 2010), which is no different for many Rohingya under the current situation. Crabtree (2010) identified day labour, selling products in the local market, remittances, integrating with the local community, local employment, exploring education choices, working at the camps as the most common ways of their coping mechanisms. The occasions of unsafe migration have become another harsh reality as traffickers lure many Rohingya to take the risky journey to

---

[22] 'Syndicate helps Rohingyas get NID, Passports' see at https://www.thedailystar.net/frontpage/syndicate-helps-rohingyas-get-nid-passports-1796749 and '3 Rohingyas held with Bangladeshi passports, 4 with NIDs in Chattogram' see at https://tbsnews.net/bangladesh/3-rohingyas-held-bangladeshi-passports-4-nids-chattogram accessed on 14 October 2020.

move into another country.[23] While interviewing a police officer, I witnessed a situation in a police station in Teknaf, where a group of rescued Rohingya from a potential human trafficking initiative was kept in the police station.

Under such a complex situation, the GoB has taken the initiative to relocate a portion of the Rohingya to Bhashan Char to improve the living standards of the Rohingya. However, my observation suggests that many Rohingya have realized that the hope of repatriation is fading away as there is no progress; thus, staying in Cox's Bazar would give them a better chance to integrate locally than moving to Bhashan Char. While talking to many Rohingya in camps, I noticed their reluctant attitude towards moving to Bhashan Char. Some also raised the concern of climate disasters at Bhasan Char, which might bring a further devastating impact on the lives of the Rohingya. In this context, a Rohingya participant said that

> People will not go there. We will not go to Bhashan Char as it is a remote place. It would be challenging to live and stay in such a remote and disaster-prone area. Many people have relatives in camps. They believe that going to Bhashan Char would isolate them from their relatives.
>
> [A middle-aged Rohingya man, the interview was conducted on 24 March 2019 at camp nine at Cox's Bazar.]

They mainly see the entire issue of going to Bhashan Char from the perspectives of opportunity and benefits. However, if a good number of people do not agree to proceed, it would be a difficult task for the authority to motivate them to move. Moreover, many Rohingya see relocating to the remote island as detention that would be a violation of the Rohingya refugees' rights (Amnesty International 2020).

The long-stay of the Rohingya in Bangladesh has put the fate of their next generation in a vulnerable situation. Identity crisis is one of

---

[23] 'Taking on Traffickers at the World's Largest Refugee Site' see at https://www.unhcr.org/news/stories/2019/12/5ddbafa04/taking-traffickers-worlds-largest-refugee-site.html accessed on 14 October 2020.

them. They can neither consider Bangladesh as their homeland nor could they go back to Myanmar as the repatriation has not started yet. Moreover, most of them do not get the proper opportunity to receive education in Bangladesh. Thus, their children and the youth do not have much to do in the camps. However, the GoB has recently declared that the Rohingya children would be able to access education. The reality is a little different; even if anyone from the Rohingya community manages to go to a university, people start bullying him/her once he/she is exposed to the host community. In 2019, a Rohingya university student was temporarily expelled from a private university at Cox's Bazar. She was born in Kutupalong camp in the early 1990s.[24]

As the repatriation has been delayed for many years, the idea of third country relocation could be an option. In this context, a young Rohingya man born in a camp raised the question of why a third country settlement is not considered. As he mentioned that

We are a burden in Bangladesh for three decades. Although some countries welcome us, why does the GoB not allow us for resettlement in the country like Canada, Norway, the USA, and Australia? If we get the opportunity to live in a third country and get a higher education, we will be able to raise our voices and fight for our rights!

[A 25-year-old Rohingya man at a webinar in Zoom, organized by the Center for Peace Studies at North South University, Dhaka on 24 August 2020.]

The past scenarios of resettlement of the Rohingya in the third countries will not give us any hope because only 920 out of 1,997 requests were accepted in various countries between 2006 and 2010 (Azad and Jasmin 2013). Keeping this limited success in mind, it was also pointed out that the GoB should also push for third country resettlement for the Rohingya (Zaman 2017).

[24] 'Rohingya Student Faces Temporary Expulsion by a Cox's Bazar University' see at https://www.dhakatribune.com/bangladesh/rohingya-crisis/2019/09/12/rohingya-student-faces-temporary-expulsion-by-a-cox-s-bazar-university accessed on 4 October 2020.

It is imperative to note that the Rohingya should have their voice to raise awareness among the international platforms. Since the Rohingya crisis has been a decade's problem now, many Rohingya youth who have been living for many years in the United Kingdom, the United States, Canada, Australia and many more countries could be the ambassador to raise global awareness in support of their Rohingya community. They slowly have started creating a space for their voice in the international arena. The Rohingya diaspora could make a real difference by creating global consciousness about the rights of the Rohingya (Ahmed and Mohiuddin 2020). They have started to also organize themselves, forming Rohingya-centric international humanitarian organizations, which is a significant development. It would help to create an international pressure group that would keep mobilizing the government of Myanmar, as without involving Myanmar in the process of a sustainable and dignified resolution for the Rohingya, it would be entirely fruitless. Support from the international community in the name of only aid would not be enough. Also, meeting the day-to-day needs of the Rohingya will not bring any changes to the ill-fated life of the Rohingya in Bangladesh. The international community has to work on the return of the Rohingya to their home country; focusing only on the temporary fix of the Rohingya crisis would only prolong the sufferings of the Rohingya (Uddin 2020).

14.5. Conclusion and Way Forward

In conclusion, it can be said that repatriation is seen as the most sustainable resolution from the perspective of Bangladesh. However, past experiences of the Rohingya repatriation do not show much hope of a quick solution to the crisis. The inability to ensure the safety, security and citizenship of the Rohingya will not bring a sustainable resolution for them. Instead, it would create a vulnerable situation for the Rohingya. It is also imperative that the Rohingya will not return if they see the threat of such violence again in the Rakhine state of Myanmar. There remains a dilemma for Bangladesh to take interim and mid-term approaches to manage the Rohingya population better as there is a fear of further delaying the repatriation process. Therefore, the idea of local integration is also denied by the GoB. The only mid-term approach is to relocate a portion of the Rohingya to the remote island Bhashan Char, which most Rohingya do not appreciate. Since Bhashan Char cannot host the entire Rohingya population, what permanent solution would it bring by relocating only less than one-tenth of the Rohingya to Bhashan Char is a big question. However, it may give a wrong message to Myanmar that Bangladesh has started a slow process of containing the Rohingya population in Bangladesh and relocating to Bhashan Char is the first such step. Thus, it may push away the repatriation further, which is a grave concern for Bangladesh. Moreover, the recent military coup has brought the fear of delaying the repatriation again. Rohingya community leaders from various countries and many policymakers also see the military coup in Myanmar as another major barrier to sustainable and dignified resolution for the Rohingya.

There is a lack of a comprehensive approach to managing the Rohingya with a policy formulation of refugee management as Bangladesh is not a signatory of the 1951 refugee convention. There has to be a national plan of action to manage the refugees systematically following the best practices from the global refugee crises. The current situation of the Rohingya crisis suggests that it may take a few to several years to reach a sustainable solution to the crisis. Therefore, an interim measure has to be taken to ensure the rights and basic needs of this population, including practical approaches for the education of their children. Moreover, without seeing the Rohingya as a burden, they should be transformed into effective human resources by initiating different skills training. It was observed that many Rohingya have already started an informal process of integration, which is a natural process of survival mechanism for the refugees. In continuation of such a process, many Rohingya have found ways to work and assimilate with the local communities. Due to the symmetry of their language with the Chittagonninan dialect and Islamic identity, assimilation for many Rohingya would not be much difficult. Furthermore, adopting various unsafe modes of migration in the hope of a better future, many Rohingya have ended up either in bonded labour or in the trap of human trafficking. A generation without cultural roots and the inability to access better educational opportunities would act as the key facilitator for their vulnerabilities and sufferings in Bangladesh.

Some of the Rohingya who were raised in Bangladesh advocate the idea of third country relocation. Bangladesh should also push the international community to share the responsibilities by hosting some of the Rohingya, keeping the pressure on Myanmar, and continue mobilizing funding for the betterment of this marginalized, persecuted and displaced population. Apart from financial burden-sharing, accepting Rohingya refugees to be integrated into the third country could be an effective alternative. Above all, failing to bring about a sustainable and dignified resolution to the Rohingya crisis, that is, repatriation, would further increase their prolonged sufferings, and the idea of repatriation will remain as a 'myth'.

Acknowledgement

This study was funded by the Conference, Travel and Research Grants of North South University, Dhaka, Bangladesh.

References

Abrar, C. 1996. *Repatriation of* Rohingya *Refugees*. Dhaka: Refugee and Migratory Movements Research Unit.

Ahmed, A. 2018. 'Impacts of Vocational Training for Socio-economic Development of Afghan Refugees in Labor Markets of Host Societies in Baluchistan'. *Journal of International Migration and Integration* 20 (3). doi: 10.1007/s12134-018-0627-4.

Ahmed. B., M. Orcutt, P. Sammonds, et al. 2018. Humanitarian Disaster for Rohingya Refugees: Impending Natural Hazards and Worsening Public Health Crises'. *The Lancet Global Health* 6(5). [This is an Open Access article under the CC BY 4.0 license: e487–e488. DOI: 10.1016/S2214-109X(18)30125-6.]

Ahmed, K., and H. Mohiuddin. 2020. *The Rohingya Crisis: Analyses, Responses and Peacebuilding Avenues*. Maryland: Lexinton Books.

Amnesty International. 2020. *Let Us Speak for Our Rights: Human Rights Situation of Rohingya Refugees in Bangladesh*. London.

Azad, A., and F. Jasmin. 2013. 'Durable Solutions to the Protracted Refugee Situation'. *Journal of Indian Research* 1 (4): 25–35.

Bepler, S. 2018. 'The Rohingya Conflict: Genesis, Current Situation and Geopolitical Aspects'. *Pacific Geographies* 28 (50): 4–10. doi: 10.23791/500410.

Bhatia, A., A. Mahmud, A. Fuller, et al. 2018. 'The Rohingya in Cox's Bazar'. *Health and Human Rights* 20 (2): 105–122.

Bowden, M. 2018. 'The Current Context to the Rohingya Crisis in Bangladesh'. *Humanitarian Exchange* 8 (73): 5–6. doi: 10.1080/14631369.2017.1407236.

Chimni, B. 2004. 'From Resettlement to Involuntary Repatriation: Refugee Problems'. *Refugee Survey Quarterly* 23 (3): 55–73.

Chowdhury, M. 2018. 'Rohingya Refugees Remain a Heavy Burden on Bangladesh'. *The Conversation* (August 2017): 22–25. Available at: https://theconversation.com/rohingya-refugees-remain-a-heavy-burden-on-bangladesh-101570.

Crabtree, K. 2010. 'Economic Challenges and Coping Mechanisms in Protracted Displacement: A Case Study of the Rohingya Refugees in Bangladesh'. *Journal of Muslim Mental Health* 5 (1): 41–58. doi: 10.1080/15564901003610073.

Farzana, K. F. 2017. *Memories of Burmese Rohingya Refugees*. doi: 10.1057/978-1-137-58360-4.

Faulkner, C., and S. Schiffer. 2019. 'Unwelcomed? The Effects of Statelessness on Involuntary Refugee Repatriation in Bangladesh and Myanmar'. *Round Table* 108 (2): 145–158. DOI: 10.1080/00358533.2019.1591766. Routledge.

Grundy-Warr, C., and E. Wong. 1997. 'Sanctuary Under a Plastic Sheet—The Unresolved Problem of Rohingya Refugees'. *IBRU Boundary and Security Bulletin* 5: 79–91. Available at: https://www.dur.ac.uk/resources/ibru/publications/full/bsb5-3_grundy.pdf.

Haque, Mahbubul. 2020. 'A Future for the Rohingya in Myanmar'. In: *The Rohingya Crisis*, edited by N. Swazo, S. Haque, Md Haque, et al., 52–78. Routledge Focus. doi: 10.4324/9780429324109-3.

Human Rights Watch. 2020. 'Myanmar: Mass Detention of Rohingya in Squalid Camp: Camp "Closures" Entrench Confinement, Persecution'. Available at: https://www.hrw.org/news/2020/10/08/myanmar-mass-detention-rohingya-squalid-camps?fbclid=IwAR0HoSsjW3jB-_gYjo0Q77paC8gGTakBu2CjbI-ZhHcDjH90_nC8zgvpMlsQ (accessed on 11 October 2020).

Jerin, M. and M. Mozumder. 2019. 'Exploring Host Community Attitudes towards Rohingya Refugees in Bangladesh'. *Intervention* 17 (2): 169–173. doi: 10.4103/INTV.INTV_27_19.

Karim, D. A. 2016. *The Rohingyas: A Short Account of Their History and Culture*. Dhaka: Jaitya Sahitya Prakash.

Khan, M. 2018. 'The Coordination Conundrum'. *Life Goes On: As the World Watches, The Daily Star*. Dhaka, 2 September.

Khan, M. J. 2020. *Refugee Camps in Cox's Bazar: Rohingyas Tangled Up in Crimes. The Daily Star*. Dhaka, 27 August. Available at: https://www.thedailystar.net/frontpage/news/refugee-camps-coxs-bazar-rohingyas-tangled-crimes-1951517 (accessed on 24 April 2021).

Kipgen, N. 2014. 'Addressing the Rohingya Problem'. *Journal of Asian and African Studies* 49 (2): 234–247. doi: 10.1177/0021909613505269.

LetcHamanan, H. 2013. 'Myanmar's Rohingya refugees in Malaysia: education and the Way forward'. *Journal of International and Comparative Education* 2 (2): 86–97.

Lewa, C. 2009. North Arakan: 'An Open Prison for the Rohingya in Burma'. *Forced Migration Review* (32): 11–13. Available at: http://ezproxy.cul.columbia.edu/login?url=http://search.proquest.com/docview/2365167 19?accountid=10226%5Cnhttp://rd8hp6du2b.search.serialssolutions.

com/?ctx_ver=Z39.88-2004&ctx_enc=info:ofi/enc:UTF-8&rfr_id=info:sid/ ProQ:sociology&rft_val_fmt=info:ofi/fmt.

Lewis, D. 2019. 'Humanitarianism, Civil Society and the Rohingya refugee Crisis in Bangladesh'. *Third World Quarterly* 40 (10): 1884–1902. doi: 10.1080/01436597.2019.1652897. Routledge.

Milton A. H., M. Rahman, S. Hussain, et al. 2017. 'Trapped in Statelessness: Rohingya Refugees in Bangladesh'. *International Journal of Environmental Research and Public Health* 14 (8): 1–8. doi: 10.3390/ijerph14080942.

Mubashar, Hasan, Charles Hawksley, Nichole Georgeou, and AER. 2021. 'What Myanmar's Coup D'état means for the Rohingya Refugees and their Future'. Available at: https://www.abc.net.au/religion/myanmar-military-coup-and-the-future-of-the-rohingya-refugees/13180680 (accessed on 20 April 2021).

Musa, M. 2021. Panel Discuss Rohingya Future Following Myanmar Coup: Academics, Journalists, Politicians urge Sanctions, Embargo against Military Leaders.' Available at: https://www.aa.com.tr/en/asia-pacific/panel-discuss-roh-ingya-future-following-myanmar-coup/2166498# (accessed on 20 April 2021).

Prasse-Freeman, E. 2017. 'The Rohingya Crisis'. *Anthropology Today* 33 (6): 1–2. doi: 10.1111/1467-8322.12389.

Rahman, U., 2010. 'The Rohingya Refugee: A Security Dilemma for Bangladesh'. *Journal of Immigrant and Refugee Studies* 8 (2): 233–239. doi: 10.1080/15562941003792135.

Rashid, S. R. 2020. 'Finding a durable solution to Bangladesh's Rohingya Refugee Problem: Policies, Prospects and Politics'. *Asian Journal of Comparative Politics* 5 (2): 174–189. doi: 10.1177/2057891119883700.

Robinson, I. G., and I. S. Rahman. 2012. 'The Unknown Fate of the Stateless Rohingya'. *Oxford Monitor of Forces Migration* 2 (2): 16–20.

Toft, M. D. 2007. 'The Myth of the Borderless World: Refugees and Repatriation Policy'. *Conflict Management and Peace Science* 24 (2): 139–157. doi: 10.1080/07388940701257549.

Uddin, N. 2020. 'Pressuring Bangladesh to do more will not help the Rohingya'. Available at: https://www.aljazeera.com/opinions/2020/8/25/pressuring-bangla-desh-to-do-more-will-not-help-the-rohingya/ (accessed on 14 October 2020).

Ullah, A. A. 2011. 'Rohingya refugees to Bangladesh: Historical Exclusions and Contemporary Marginalization'. *Journal of Immigrant and Refugee Studies* 9 (2): 139–161. doi: 10.1080/15562948.2011.567149.

UNHCR. 2019. 'Operational Portal Refugee Situations: Refugee Responses in Bangladesh'. Available at: https://data2.unhcr.org/en/situations/myan-mar_refugees (accessed on 9 June 2019).

Westerman, A. 2021. 'What Myanmar's Coup Means For The Rohingya'. Available at: https://www.npr.org/2021/02/11/966923582/what-myanmars-coup-means-for-the-rohingya (accessed on 20 April).

Zaman, M. 2017. 'Is Third-Country Resettlement an Option?' *The Daily Star*. Dhaka. Available at: https://www.thedailystar.net/opinion/third-country-resettlement-option-1507387 (accessed on 12 October 2020).

Part V

New Developments

CHAPTER 15

Rohingya Relocation to Bhasan Char
Myths and Realities
Nasir Uddin

15.1. Introduction

Following two sequential failures of repatriation attempts,[1] Bangladesh finally brought in the option of 'relocation'[2] as part of the Rohingya refugee management policy. As per the policy, Bangladesh has meanwhile relocated around 18,500 Rohingya[3] beginning from 4 December 2020, from Ukhia and Teknaf refugee camps to Bhasan

---

[1] The first repatriation attempt was made on 15 November 2018 and the second one took place on 22 August 2019, but both the attempts failed. See for details, Uddin (2018).

[2] Relocation doesn't essentially mean migration of people from one place to another, but a plan of shift from one 'locale' to another. Rohingya relocation to Bhasan Char follows a couple of principles including the shift of location, basis of temporality, controlled mobility and execution of shipment not by themselves but the state machineries.

[3] 18,500 is a round figure counted until May 2021. See for details, Moinuddin (2021).

Char, a remote island in Noakhali District. The translocation of the first batch to Bhasan Char triggered huge attention among the general public and the international partners in Bangladesh (Abrar 2020). Many human rights organizations have expressed deep concerns (Bangladesh Amnesty International 2020) on the ground of human rights violations for alleged 'coercive relocation'; yet, Bangladesh denies this claim. Given the context, the chapter covers the recent development in the Rohingya crisis paying particular attention to the Rohingya relocation to Bhasan Char. The chapter examines the various forms of 'myths' and 'realities' regarding Bhasan Char as well as the merits and demerits of the 'relocation'. There is a serious dearth of knowledge about Bhasan Char among the international partners who have been actively involved in Rohingya refugee management in Cox's Bazar for years. Besides, the planning and outcome of the Rohingya relocation programme is not quite clear even among the general public in Bangladesh. Furthermore, the disapproval/concern among human rights organizations regarding Rohingya relocation to Bhasan Char holds ambiguity, suspicion and non-clarity. The chapter critically analyses the Government of Bangladesh's (GoB's) initiative to relocate the Rohingya to Bhasan Char while the United Nations, European Union (UN), the United States and some international human rights organizations have raised questions about the move. It also discusses the settings, preparation and management of Bhasan Char against the rumours about cyclones, floods, tidal surges and monsoon rains. It covers the perspectives of the Rohingya, the general people, the international community, media and some rights bodies about the relocation. The chapter based on ethnographic evidence and netnography[4] examines the claims and blames of the 'voluntary relocations' and 'coerced migrations' beneath the discourse of myths and realities regarding Bhasan Char.

[4] Netnography is a technique of data collection by using various net-based techniques and a specific approach to conducting ethnography on the internet by using Facebook Messenger, WhatsApp, email, Viber, Google Meet, Zoom, and many other interactive communicative apps, programmes, web portals and software. For details, see Kozinets (2010).

15.2. Relocation: An Alternative Model of Rohingya Management

There are three standard models of solutions to the refugee problems; social integration, voluntary repatriation and third country resettlements (UNHCR 2009). Bangladesh applied all three models before but failed due to the complexity of the Rohingya crisis and Myanmar's strategic stand over the Rohingya issue (Uddin 2017a). Fleeing stern persecution in then Burma, the first influx of about 200,000 Rohingya to Bangladesh occurred in 1978. And the second influx took place in 1991–1992 which brought about 250,000 Rohingya to Bangladesh. Amidst multiple sittings and negotiations, Myanmar agreed to take the Rohingya back (Uddin 2020a). Under the repatriation process, about 236,000 Rohingya went back to then Burma, but a majority of them returned to Bangladesh in different illegal ways (Uddin 2020a). They returned because Burma's situation remained unchanged and threatened the peaceful living of the Rohingya. That was the first and last repatriation attempt made by Bangladesh as since then not a single Rohingya has returned to Myanmar officially as part of repatriation. So, the repatriation as a widely known model of the solution to the refugee crisis did not work out for the Rohingya until 2017 and afterward.

The second solution to refugee crisis put forward by various actors is social integration[5] in the host society. In fact, social integration perhaps largely is 'attributed to voluntary repatriation being the globally preferred refugee policy' (Fielden 2008).

Jaff Crisp (2004, 01) wrote,

Local integration as a durable solution combines three dimensions. Firstly, it is a legal process, whereby refugees attain a wider range of rights in the host state. Secondly, it is an economic process of establishing sustainable livelihoods and a standard of living

---

[5] Integration means merging with the host society in various ways like marrying one from host society, getting citizenship through naturalization, managing legal documents in illegal ways as the permanent resident or citizens of the host country.

comparable to the host community. Thirdly, it is a social and cultural process of adaptation and acceptance that enables the refugees to contribute to the social life of the host country and live without fear of discrimination.

During 1978 and 1991–1992, many Rohingya socially integrated through marriage, managing Bangladeshi passport, building affinal[6] and consanguineal relations with the host society, involving in various business with local Bengalis, joining the job market, particularly in fishing, being day-labourers and labour in agricultural activities (Uddin 2012). This integration was not part of state policy but happened spontaneously (Uddin 2017b). From the Rohingya point, it was their necessity because they had no option left. Local people also initially accepted them because of their religious homogeneity and larger linguistic uniformity. But, after the following influxes in 2012, 2015, 2016 and 2017, the bilateral relation between the host society and the Rohingya refugees has been drastically transformed and declined (Uddin 2012). Therefore, there is hardly any space left for any sort of social integration for the Rohingya because the host society has become intolerant of the Rohingya presence in Bangladesh. There is a strong anti-Rohingya public discourse in Bangladesh emerging following the big influx in 2017 because their massive presence has been considered as the reason for increasing social, economic, political and security crises (Uddin 2020b). So, the second option could not be possible in the given situations though integration makes its way very slowly.

Bangladesh also tried the third option of 'third country resettlement', but it did not work out as well. According to the United Nations High Commissioner for Refugees (UNHCR), 'Resettlement under the auspices of the UNHCR involves the selection and transfer of refugees from a State in which they have sought protection to a third State that has agreed to admit them as refugees with permanent residence status' (UNHRC 2013). Under an agreement with the international partners, Bangladesh started sending Rohingya out to the third country, beyond

---

[6] Inter-ethnic marriage between Bengali and Rohingya took place on a regular basis in the South-eastern part of Bangladesh during the 1980s and 1990s.

the country of origin and of migration, which includes Canada, New Zealand, the United Kingdom, Australia, Ireland, Norway, Sweden and the United States (Uddin 2017a). The third country resettlement programme started in 2006 and ended in 2010 because it did not finally work out (Ahmed ed. 2010). After 2010, no country sincerely expressed their interests to shelter some Rohingya in their countries. Though we listened to Presidents and Prime Ministers of some countries that they wanted to take Rohingya to their countries (*The Daily Star* February 28, 2019), but we saw that all these promises turned into vain. Even after the big influx in 2017, no country showed any interest to take some Rohingya to their country though they expressed big sympathy and deep concerns for the Rohingya people (Uddin 2020b). So, finally, the third option of refugee settlement is not working at all and will not take any effective shape soon.

Having experienced failure of all three standard models, Bangladesh has brought in a new model through the relocation of Rohingya to Bhasan Char. This is neither a migration nor a transfer of refugees, but a relocation is what the GoB claims. Ideally, it means 'location' is shifted from Ukhia–Teknaf to Bhasan Char since their status, position and treatment will remain identical though facilities offered in Bhasan Char are much more than what they now receive. Since Bangladesh has no set rules on refugee management, no national refugee policy and no designated ministry to deal with refugees,[7] relocation could be considered as a new model of refugee management, though an experimental one. But, how the relocation of 100,000 Rohingya out of more than one million from Ukhia–Teknaf to Bhasan Char could contribute a solution to the Rohingya crisis remains still ambiguous. The GoB insists that this relocation is nothing but a temporary move to reduce crowding in the camp and the locality, which has received a little trust from the stakeholders. Therefore, it remains an unanswered question among the general public and some stakeholders about the outcome of this relocation process in the long run as far as the Rohingya crisis is concerned.

[7] Rohingya refugees are taken care of by the Ministry of Disaster Management and Relief since Bangladesh does not have a designated ministry to deal with refugee crises.

15.3. Bhasan Char: Known and Unknown Facts

Historically, sending people to a remote island represents a kind of punishment for the people who are reportedly criminals, social disorders and legally convicted in the eyes of authoritarian states. Karen Larkins explains why islands are built for exile, sending people there as punishment across time from ancient to modern periods 'to banish dissidents and criminals, these islands are known for their one-time prisoners, from Napoleon to Nelson Mandela' (Larkins 2010). Larkins has made a list of ten infamous islands which have been used for exile, these include Patmos (Greece), Sado Island (Japan), Île Sainte-Marguerite (France), Robinson Crusoe Island (Chile), Devil's Island (French Guiana), St. Helena (Brazil), Coiba Island (Panama), Galápagos Islands (Ecuador), Robben Island (South Africa) and Alcatraz, San Francisco (California, USA) (Larkins 2010). In 2013, when the Australian government determined not to allow any asylum seekers and refugees coming by boat to get in, around 2,000 people were kept in detention centres on the pacific island of Papua New Guinea and Nauru. They were kept in the island for four and a half years from 2013 to 2018 when Amnesty International raised a strong voice against this act. While Australia claims that they did for protection, Amnesty International in 2018 declared that 'this is a punishment' (The Amnesty International 2018). In the case of Rohingya in Bangladesh, many could think the GoB's planning to relocate Rohingya to Bhasan Char is a punishment. But this is completely opposite since the Rohingya relocation to Bhasan Char, as my research finds, is motivated by three objectives: (a) to reduce crowding in the already overcrowded camps in Ukhia and Teknaf, (b) to decrease the massive presence of Rohingya refugees in the locality and (c) to provide a decent life to the Rohingya far better than the life in Ukhia and Teknaf.

Bhasan Char has come into focus very recently soon after authorities announced that it is ready to receive Rohingya refugees from Ukhia and Teknaf though it was under preparation and a matter of on-and-off discussion for the last three years (Bhattacharyya 2020). Since the people outside the 'authority' have no access to Bhasan Char, the information circulated by the authority became the only source of knowledge about the island. Therefore, it has created a lot of curiosity, suspicions and confusion among the general public, media, rights bodies and the international communities. Rohingya refugees also have very little idea about Bhasan Char since they have come to know about the island from some speculative news by curious media, social media networks and negative campaigns by some rights groups. Due to some kinds of hide-and-seek strategies and non-transparency in the dissemination of information, some human rights organizations started raising concerns about relocating Rohingya to Bhasan Char.[8] Also, some UN bodies showed great concerns due to their non-engagement in the entire preparation of the project and the relocation process (The UN, Bangladesh 2021). The EU also showed their concerns over the relocation project since 'they have limited knowledge' about Bhasan Char.[9] Though from September and October 2020, the media started regular reporting and telecasting on the preparation of Bhasan Char to accommodate interested Rohingya (Molla 2020), it created a huge positive impression among the general public in Bangladesh, but could not change the tone of negative camp as the media reports were considered among the Rohingya refugees as mostly state-sponsored publicity. Besides, the media personalities and journalists who were taken to Bhasan Char were controlled and guided by the authorities and there was no scope left for any independent visit to Bhasan Char (Ibrahim 2020).

No independent investigator, researcher, human rights organization and UN bodies were allowed to Bhasan Char, which rather contributed to the growing suspicion about the 'floating island'. Instead, allowing them to visit the island and letting them express their first-hand experience could really create a trustworthy impression among the Rohingya refugees and also could alter the tone of negative camps. Five internationally acclaimed human rights organizations[10] applied to the authority to allow them to visit Bhasan Char, but their appeals

---

[8] See for details, *The Dhaka Tribune*, 3 December 2020.

[9] See for details, *The Financial Express*, 3 December 2020.

[10] The five human rights organizations are Fortify Rights, Amnesty International, Refugees International, Robert Canady Human Rights and ASEAN Parliamentarians for Human rights.

were declined. The UN also offered to do a technical assessment (The UN, Bangladesh 2020) to reconfirm whether the island is safe, secured and liveable for the people, but the offer was not accepted. All these reasons created confusion, suspicion and a lack of clarity. The reality has also come to the light of experience soon after the entire arrangement has been disclosed amid a wider campaign and publicity by the electronics and print media at home and abroad yet sponsored by the state and heavily controlled by the authority

Forty Rohingya leaders called *majhee* (unit head of the camp) were taken to Bhasan Char to inspect the entire arrangements (*The Daily Star* 2020) so that they could share their experience with others living in Ukhia and Teknaf. The *majhee* were seemingly very pleased to see the arrangements, but they could motivate and convince literally none of the Rohingya living in Ukhia and Teknaf to move to Bhasan Char. Though GoB's action of taking *majhee* to Bhasan Char to give a first-hand experience was appreciated by all stakeholders, but it did not work out properly. Besides, there was no follow-up action during the post-visit activities of the *majhee*. Later on, a team of NGO workers was also taken to Bhasan Char to provide a clear idea about what kind of preparations have been taken so far to host the Rohingya on the island, but it also made little positive impact since most members of the team were from pro-government NGOs. A team of local journalists was taken to visit Bhasan Char to have a feel about the island. The team members highly appreciated the preparation the authority has taken so far. But the confusion and suspicion remain at a larger stake since no credible, trustworthy and independent voice supports the project and encourages the Rohingya to move to the island. So, the contestation of myths and realities is still going on among both the Rohingya and the general public of Bangladesh.

It must be admitted that structurally Bhasan Char has been designed in a far better way than the Rohingya have in Ukhia and Teknaf. An area of 40 square kilometres has been used to establish the settlements in Bhasan Char, an island of landmass 13,000 acres. 440 clustered sheds have been built four feet above the plain-land to protect against any potential floods and tidal surges. Every shed has 12 houses and each house has 16 rooms. Each room has two storied two beds, which are designed for a four-member family. According to the UN standard, each refugee is entitled to 37 square feet (UNHCR 2007), but the rooms at Bhasan Char are far more spacious than the UN standard. Bhasan Char has 120 cyclone centres which could accommodate the entire refugee population in case of any unexpected floods and cyclone. Besides houses and living rooms, Bhasan Char has schools, mosques, hospitals, playgrounds, wider roads, solar system, storage for food preservation, sanitation system, adequate water supply, mobile telephone operator towers, super shop, saloon, lighthouse, day-care centres, marketplace, community centres and a police camp to ensure law and order situation (*The Business Standard* 2019). A small port station has also been built for the smooth transportation of goods and people. Besides, Bhasan Char project has scope for livestock rearing, sewing and making handicrafts to run cottage industry, poultry firms, fishing facilities, small-scale milk production industry, agriculture and horticulture. Though the Bhasan Char project is very well planned, well designed and has an adequate safety net to protect the people from floods, tornados, cyclones, tidal surges and any other natural calamities, it fails to convince human rights organizations (Human Rights Watch 2020). This is the reality, but due to the information gap it becomes a myth for the Rohingya living in Ukhia and Teknaf. Also, whether all sorts of arrangements are good enough for people to live in a very remote, isolated and solitary island leaving many friends, fellows, co-villagers and relatives far away in Ukhia and Teknaf is a big question that has been left unaddressed in every corner.

15.4. What's Wrong with Relocation?

This section provides empirical data as it presents the views, perceptions and perspectives of different stakeholders that I have gathered by applying ethnographic research techniques.[11] I have interviewed many Rohingya in Ukhia and Teknaj camps and tried to understand

---

[11] Since the information is collected through ethnographic research techniques, the data is descriptive, qualitative, empirical and narrative in nature. For details, see Gobo (2008).

the reasons for their refusal to move to Bhasan Char. I found largely four reasons behind their reluctance: (a) fear of being washed away by floods and monsoon tide, (b) the lack of proper information about the newly built Bhasan Char, (c) the UN bodies and some international human rights organizations' objections and (d) some NGOs' activities to discourage the move.

15.4.1. Fear of being Washed away by Floods and Tidal Surges

Many Rohingya living in Ukhia and Teknaf refugee camps believe that Bhasan Char is a very low-lying island and still not ready for habitation. They believe that a standard and modest flood or cyclone could easily wash them away and wash away their life and property. Even the water of regular tides or tidal surge could become dangerous to their lives in Bhasan Char. That is the reason why it is called a 'floating island' (Paul, Baldwin and Marshal 2018). Hasan Mia,[12] a Rohingya informant explained to me in December 2020,

> We escaped a definite death in Rakhine and came to Bangladesh to save our lives. If we go to Bhasan Char, our lives will fall in danger again since there is *jiboner nirapotta* (no security of life) in Bhasan char. Flood water could easily cross over the island and hence it can easily wash us away anytime. For example, we are sleeping at night, but in the morning we will find ourselves in the middle of the Bay of Bengal. It could happen any time. So, we don't want to put our lives at further risk. We will not go anywhere. If we should go, we will go back to Rakhine, our homeland, but not Bhasan char.

What Hasan Mia said clearly indicates that many Rohingya are refusing to move to Bhasan Char due to the fear of being washed away by floodwaters or the frequent tidal surges. This seems to be the collective notion prevalent among many of the Rohingya in Ukhia and Teknaf.

---

[12] Hasan Mia is a Rohingya informant of 56 years old. He crossed the border on 4 September 2017. Now, he lives in Balukhali refugee camp in Ukhia. The interview was taken in December 2020 in Ukhia.

15.4.2. Lack of Proper Information about Bhasan Char

Till now, the kind of preparations taken so far in Bhasan Char has not been disseminated adequately to the Rohingya, but it was done more among the general public of Bangladesh amidst a series of media reports (*The Daily Star* 2020) published and telecasted in Bangladesh. I interviewed many Rohingya and very few of them knew about the schools, hospitals, playgrounds, mosques, super shops for shopping, mobile operators and day-care centres being built to facilitate the Rohingya in Bhasan Char. Forty Rohingya *majhee* were taken to visit Bhasan Char in September who were seemingly very pleased to see the overall arrangements and management of the island. It was expected that they would motivate other Rohingya living in Ukhia and Teknaf and inform them of all sorts of preparation taken and share a positive experience of visiting Bhasan Char. But they did nothing meaningful to motivate even a single Rohingya. Besides, there was no monitoring from concerned authorities to follow up the activities of the Rohingya leaders during the post-visit period as mentioned in the earlier section. It means the policy of taking some Rohingya leaders to Bhasan Char to convince and motivate others did not work at all. Besides, a team of journalists was taken to Bhasan Char to observe the overall preparation of the island in October 2020, who wrote very positive reports encouraging the Rohingya to move to Bhasan Char, but it did not also work well mainly because the majority of Rohingya living in Ukhia and Teknaf neither frequently visit media portal online nor read newspapers in print. A very small number of Rohingya refugees watch TV regularly and have come to know about the management and arrangements of Bhasan Char, but they have little trust in media reports as they believe that these are prepared and prescribed by the GoB. Nurul Amin,[13] a Rohingya informant told me in December 2020,

All these reports are made of prescriptions given by the Government agencies to motivate us. But the reality is different. Out of 300 Rohingyas[14] currently living in Bhasan Char, three are

---

[13] Nurul Amin is a Rohingya informant of 56 years old. He came to Bangladesh in October 2017. Now he lives in Balukhali. I interviewed him in December 2020 at a tea stall in Ukhia Paan Bazar, the entry point of Balukhali refugee camp.

[14] See for detail, *Dhaka Tribune*, 20 May 2020.

my relatives. They have informed us that this is a confined island like an open prison and they are constantly under surveillance by the security forces. They have no freedom of choice as they have to depend on the security personnel for everything. Even they want to come back to Ukhia and are not allowed to do so. Therefore, why should we go there?

Like Nurul Amin, many Rohingya have little knowledge about Bhasan Char. In fact, the lack of information and widespread misinformation is another reason why many Rohingya are reluctant to move to Bhasan Char.

15.4.3. Objections of UN Bodies and International Human Rights Organizations

Many Rohingya know that the UN suggested (The UN, Bangladesh 2020) the GoB to engage the refugees in the construction, preparation and the entire relocation process, but the GoB declined. Many Rohingya also know that the UN wanted to visit Bhasan Char for doing a technical assessment to justify whether the island is liveable or not before the relocation process kicks off. But the GoB declined their proposal which also created suspicion among the Rohingya. Many Rohingya asked me the reason for the refusal of the UN proposal, but I did not have any informed answer to respond to them. Fazal Karim,[15] a Rohingya informant at a marketplace in Lambashia of Kutupalong, asked me while I was doing a focus group discussion (FGD),

if the Government has taken all necessary preparations for the relocation of 100000 Rohingyas, then what's their problem for them to allow the NU delegates to make an assessment? It indicates that there is something wrong and the GoB is playing a sick-and-hide

[15] Fazal Karim is a 59-year-old Rohingya informant. He crossed the border in Bangladesh in October 2017. He now lives in Lambashia camp in Khutupalan camp-2. I was holding an FGD with seven Rohingya including males and females across ages and education at a marketplace in Lambashia of Kutupalong in December 2020. While I was discussing about their knowledge on Bhasan Char, Fazal Karim asked me many questions about Bhasan Char.

game with us. Given the context how could we trust the GoB promises of providing a better life in Bhasan Char?

Fazal Karim's question was very strong and I noticed similar suspicions among others attending my FGD. When a similar question was raised by many credible national and international media just after the first and second phase of relocation, the Foreign Minister of Bangladesh categorically rejected the suspicion saying that 'The UN did never give any formal proposal to visit Bhasan Char'. Rohingya people are also informed well that five international human rights organizations applied to the GoB seeking permission to visit Bhasan Char before the relocation process begins, but they were also refused. The Rohingya in Ukhia and Teknaf very rapidly know this information through NGO workers and the workers attached with various UN agencies in the camp because Rohingya people have everyday interaction with them. Besides, diaspora Rohingya activists and Rohingya human rights organizations widely circulated this information. Also it was spread up through social media as many Rohingyas I met knew about it. I interviewed many Rohingya and found them very suspicious about the relocation process mainly because of the non-engagement of the UN bodies and declination of international human rights organizations' proposals. It works as another major reason behind the Rohingya's reluctance to move to Bhasan Char.

15.4.4. NGOs' Activities to Discourage the Move

Hundreds of NGOs are working in Ukhia and Teknaf Rohingya refugee camps and a majority of them are doing a really good job and truly supportive as far as my experience goes. It would be difficult for the GoB to manage more than one million Rohingya refugees without the active help and support of many national and international NGOs. Particularly, following the massive influx in August 2017, many NGOs and INGOs came forward to stand by the Rohingya with various forms of supports, programmes and activities which help the GoB tackle the situation very nicely. Gradually it turned into a system through well-coordination by the GoB and other stakeholders working in the camp. But the GoB is blaming some NGOs for working against the government's move to relocate Rohingya to Bhasan Char (see *The Daily Prothom-Alo* November 15, 2020). In my research, I also found that some NGOs, not many, and some workers in the camp continuously discouraged Rohingya refugees to move to Bhasan Char. Many Rohingya told me in their interviews that some NGO workers told them not to move because if they move from Ukhia and Teknaf, they will not be supported adequately and will not get what they need. And many NGOs will not be able to work in Bhasan Char since it is heavily controlled by the naval forces. Also, Bhasan Char is an isolated island that will keep them away from the whole world and the human settlement. If the Rohingya move to Bhasan Char, they will be locally locked in the dangerous island and cut off from the world. And they will not be able to come out of this trap in their lifetime. Many Rohingya were also informed that if they would stay in Ukhia and Teknaf, they might have the scope to escape the camp to socially integrate into Bengali society what they cannot do from Bhasan Char. Also, if they get any opportunity, they might leave the country to take asylum in a developed country which they cannot do from Bhasan Char. This kind of discussion regularly takes place between many Rohingya and many NGO workers is what I found from many interviews. I found another reason for NGO workers to discourage Rohingya to move because many NGO workers enjoy a very metropolitan life in Cox's Bazar with abundant facilities of the modern living standard including hotels, motels, sea-beach, wonderful restaurants and all modern and urban amenities what they cannot get in Bhasan Char. So, some NGO workers want to remain in Cox's Bazar and it is only possible if the Rohingya remain in Ukhia and Teknaf. This is an untold and hidden transcript behind the Rohingya reluctance to move to Bhasan Char, what I found in my field visits and interviews in Ukhia and Teknaf refugee camps during September–December 2020.

15.4.5. Perspectives of the Rohingya

I visited Rohingya camps a couple of times during September–December, 2020, in an effort to understand the Rohingya perspectives about their relocation to Bhasan Char. I found in fact mixed perspectives though 'non-interested' was the dominant portion in the findings. I could categorize the findings in three ways: non-interested, less-interested and growingly interested. The majority of Rohingya are 'not interested' to move to Bhasan Char due to the lack of information about the island, some misconceptions about insecurity owing to floods, tornado, tidal surge and cyclone, fear of being detached from family and relatives, losing their hopes of social integration or third country resettlements and scared of being isolated and locally locked in a 'floating' island. Some Rohingya are 'less interested' because they want to see first what happens to those who move to Bhasan Char. They want to observe the consequences of the relocation and know more from their people other than the media and the GoB agencies. They also want to see the position of the UN and international human rights organizations and their clearance because if anything happens or any sort of unavoidable circumstances come up, they want to keep a space for breathing. Khalilur Rahman,[16] a Rohingya informant told me in Mochara, Kutupalon Ukhia in December 2020, that,

> I will go but I want to make sure that it is safe, better and secure for my life and future. I am looking forward to having a clearance from the UN and international human rights organizations because they always care about us. Bangladesh Government is also doing a lot for us but still, we trust the UN more than the Government. If we fall into any trap, who will come forward to rescue us? Whom will we appeal to? We want to keep a space for any sort of potential problem in the future.

Khalil works with an NGO in a refugee camp in Ukhia and is quite aware of the rights and entitlements of the Rohingya. Therefore, he is over-conscious about the relocation of Rohingya to Bhasan Char. I found similar sentiments among many Rohingya whom I interviewed and talked with. Some Rohingya are 'growingly interested' knowing different facilities, scopes and opportunities of Bhasan Char which are far better than they have in Ukhia and Teknaf. Unfortunately, I found hardly any Rohingya who are interested to move to Bhasan Char and I could make a category 'interested one' until November, 2020. But I found a lot of Rohingya among my interviewees in December who are

---

[16] Khalilur Rahman is a Rohingya informant of 41 years old. He migrated Bangladesh in September 2017. Now he lives in Kutupalong Camp-4. I interviewed him in Mochara, Kutupalan, Ukhia in December 2020.

growingly interested to move to Bhasan Char because the Rohingya who have already migrated there are telling a lot of good stories about the island. Many of their relatives and co-villagers are encouraging the Rohingya living in Ukhia and Teknaf to move to Bhasan Char for a better life compared to the lives in the camps. Now, many Rohingya are getting gradually interested to move to Bhasan Char. I found some Rohingya being interested mainly because to take the leading role in Bhasan Char as the earliest migrants to the island. Mohammad Azad,[17] a Rohingya informant told me in Shaplapur camp in November 2020,

> Even if we want, we can't but go to Bhasan Char. The GoB policy seems we all will be relocated to Bhasan Char gradually over the years and it is immaterial whether we want or not. That's why I think it's better to go earlier and hold a position to lead others in the island. Besides, I think if I go earlier, I could get additional care and privilege. That's the reason why I have decided to go to Bhasan Char.

It is mentionable here that Mohammad Azad with his family of five members has already moved to Bhasan Char in the first batch of relocation on December 4, 2020.

15.4.6. Response from the International Community and Media

Relocation of the Rohingya to Bhasan Char drew huge international attention and got massive media coverage (*The Guardian* 2020). In the age of globalization, no state can do anything alone particularly if it is related to migration and refugee issue since it entangles with rights and entitlements of human beings under international jurisprudence and the framework of global justice (Uddin 2020b). Just before the relocation process started the UN declared that it has no involvement in the relocation process (The United Nations, Bangladesh 2020). The EU said in a press release that they have 'very little information about the Rohingya relocation to Bhasan Char'. International players including Human Rights Watch, Amnesty International, Fortify

---

[17] Mohammad Azad is a Rohingya informant of 53 years old. He migrated to Bangladesh in October 2016. He now lives in Shaplapur camp in Teknaf. I interviewed him in Shaplapur Bazar in November 2020.

Rights, Refugee International and others expressed deep concerns (*Al-Jazeera* December 03, 2020) about the relocation process raising questions about whether it is coerced or voluntary relocation. Many internationally acclaimed global media outlets published reports on the Rohingya relocation to Bhasan Char, but the tone of the majority of media was negative[18] as they claimed the relocation was done against the will of the Rohingya refugees. Many Rohingya organizations heavily criticized the role of the GoB for executing this relocation programme by forcibly sending the Rohingya to Bhasan Char. Why the international community, global media and international human rights organizations are opposing this relocation process is not quite clear because they are raising questions whether the relocation of Rohingya was done forcibly or voluntarily. The GoB has time and again insisted that it was completely a voluntary relocation (*The Daily Star* March 27, 2019) and nobody was forced to leave Ukhia and Teknaf to move to Bhasan Char. I also talked to some of the Rohingya and found that many of them are excited to move and ready to accept a 'new life' though some were uncertain about their future. Another question what the international community and media brought to light is about the suitability of the island for human living in terms of safety and security. From my keen observation and intensive follow-up of the relocation process, I feel that the authority could not convincingly disseminate the facts and figures of the safety and security measures taken into consideration while preparing the Bhasan Char. It is known to all that Bangladesh is one of the role models of disaster management (*The Daily Sun* October 14, 2019) because of its perennial experience of coping strategies and indigenous knowledge of disaster management. So, definitely, Bangladesh should have taken enough and adequate preventive measures to protect the relocated Rohingya from potential tidal surges, monsoon floods and seasonal cyclones. But it was not adequately and convincingly disseminated among all concerned and shared with the international community, the UN bodies, human rights organizations and international media which could reduce the debate about the relocation process.

[18] See for details, *The Economist*, 12 December 2020; *The New York Times*, 8 December 2020; *CNN*, 8 December 2020; *the Indian Express*, 29 December 2020; Al-Jazeera, 3 December 2020; *The Guardian*, 28 December 2020.

15.4.7. From the Perspective of the General Public in Bangladesh

Following the declaration of Bhasan Char being ready for the Rohingya relocation, it created enormous attention and curiosity among Bangladeshis because of its beautiful architectural design, very colourful bird's eye look, attractive facilities with all modern forms of amenities and huge investment from the taxpayers' money since it is built completely with self-funding policy without any financial involvement from donors (*Reuters* March 27, 2018). Some Bangladeshi people also expressed dissent to it saying why Bangladesh should spend so much of taxpayers' money to prepare a better living place for the Rohingya refugees. Some others said that the relocation of Rohingya to Bhasan Char may delay the repatriation process. Some others remarked that the Rohingya refugees should be kept on the borderland and bringing them to the mainland could create many other problems for the country. But, the majority of Bangladeshi people praised the overall preparation, arrangements and management plan of the Bhasan Char. However, many people are confused thinking about the point of return through this relocation programme by investing a huge amount of public money. I talked to many people to know their reaction to the Bhasan Char issue and found that the majority of people believe that the GoB has taken a good decision to reduce the load of massive Rohingya presence in Ukhia and Teknaf which will help the host community to have a better atmosphere in their locality. But, many Bangladeshi people whom I talked with showed serious anger knowing that the majority of Rohingya are reluctant to move to Bhasan Char and they found no reason for refusal. Instead, the Rohingya, they think, should be happy that Bhasan Char has better facilities than that of Ukhia and Teknaf. One of my colleagues[19] at the University of Chittagong put across an interesting observation that,

> The Rohingya people don't want to go to Bashan Char because they have made Ukhia and Teknaf as if their homeland. They can do everything whatever they want in Ukhia and Teknaf. They are

[19] I am not mentioning her name here as per research ethic, but I took her permission to use her remark in my writing on anonymity.

the kings in their kingdom. But, if they go to Bhasan Char they will become general refugees losing their kingdom in Cox's Bazar. Many of them are involved in illegal border trade, smuggling, drug business and extortion in the camp. They just don't want to lose it.

One can find similar remarks in the leading dailies in Bangladesh which reflect the populist paradigm of 'blaming the victims'. In fact, the growing anti-Rohingya public discourse has been fuelled further by their refusal to move to Bhasan Char.

15.5. What Could Be Done More?

There is little doubt that the GoB has done as much as it can to support and help the Rohingya refugees in Bangladesh since they crossed the border in 2017 so that they can lead a better life. The GoB's efforts to shelter and take care of more than one million Rohingya in its land have been highly appreciated and hailed in various international arenas time and again. Even though international aid is gradually decreasing, Bangladesh has done its level best to provide all necessary goods and services during the last four years. Preparing Bhasan Char and the idea of subsequent relocation of the Rohingya is also an extension of the GoB's support to provide them with a better life as long as they are not returned to Myanmar through voluntary repatriation. However, Bhasan Char project particularly relocating Rohingya triggers some debates due to some unclear reasons. Because why the UN has not been involved in the relocation process and what is the point for Bangladesh to do it alone and what is the point of return of such solitary movement is not quite clear to many. It is also evident that the extent of preparation and the quality of settlement pattern of Bhasan Char is way better than that of Ukhia and Teknaf. Therefore, it would be nice if the debate could be avoided through the involvement of the UN in the relocation process. But, still, there is ample scope for Bangladesh to engage the UN agencies in the Bhasan Char project because those who have already been shifted there seem very happy with the preparation, arrangements, facilities and management of Bhasan Char. The planning of relocating 100,000 to Bhasan Char should not be used as a space of discomfort between Bangladesh and the UN while more than one million still should be dealt with, with the help of the UN agencies. Bangladesh now must convince international partners that the relocation planning is for the betterment of both the Rohingya and the host community because it will reduce the overcrowded atmosphere in the camps and demographically unload the host community. The gap is only in the gap of information, but there is no gap in objective, motives and movement and that should be clear to all. It is very encouraging to learn that the GoB has arranged a four-day tour for the 18-member UN delegation to Bhasan Char on March 17–20, 2021. The delegation observed the facilities and amenities of the island and talked to the Rohingya refugees living there. The UN delegation has meanwhile submitted a report which seems positive about the Bhasan Char project based on what the foreign ministry source informed us (*The Daily Star* April 16, 2021). It brings a real light of hopes and wind of spring for all stakeholders including the general people of Bangladesh.

15.6. Conclusion

Bhasan Char has appeared as a new issue in the discussion and scholarship on the Rohingya people. It has triggered both appreciation and criticism though the point of return is still quite unclear from Bangladesh's part through the relocation of 100,000 out of more than one million Rohingya to Bhasan Char. In order to redress the Rohingya crisis, Bangladesh from day one tried to repatriate them to Myanmar amid a bilateral agreement. During the last four years from 2017, two repatriation attempts were made—the first one on 15 November 2018, and the second one on 22 August 2019—but they failed due mainly to the non-cooperation, non-interest and non-preparation from Myanmar's part. After that, no repatriation attempt was made due to the COVID-19 situation which has affected the world. Myanmar has been showing reluctance from day one to make successful repatriation though Bangladesh has extended all sorts of cooperation. The international community is also playing a dubious role and not supporting the repatriation process wholeheartedly under the pretext of an unsuitable human rights situation in Myanmar. But they did little to improve the human rights situations in Myanmar. Therefore, the repatriation process is not finding the light of the day.

Given the context, Bhasan Char has appeared as a new issue and the GoB paid more than required efforts to the relocation process though it received some unexpected and unnecessary criticisms. Paying much attention to and investing more than required for the relocation process may hamper the potential of the repatriation process. Since repatriation to Myanmar is the lasting, sustainable and potential solution left for both Bangladesh and the Rohingya, the GoB should pay more attention to repatriation rather than relocation.

References

Abrar, C. R. 2020. 'Rohingya Refugees: Contentious Case of Relocation to Bhashan Char'. *The Daily Star*, 7 December. Available at: https://www.the-dailystar.net/opinion/news/rohingya-refugees-contentious-case-relocation-bhashan-char-2007033 (accessed on 20 April 2021).

Ahmed, Imtiaz. 2020. *The Plight of the Stateless Rohingyas: Responses of the State, Society & the International Community*. Dhaka: The University Press Limited.

Al-Jazeera. 2020. 'Bangladesh begins Rohingya Relocation Despite Rights Concerns'. *Al-Jazeera*, 3 December. Available at: https://www.aljazeera.com/news/2020/12/3/rights-groups-urge-bangladesh-to-halt-rohingya-relocation (accessed on 2 January 2021).

Amnesty International. 2020. 'Bangladesh: Halt Relocation of Rohingya Refugees to Remote Island'. Amnesty International, 3 December. Available at: https://www.amnesty.org/en/latest/news/2020/12/bangladesh-halt-relocation-of-rohingya-refugees-to-remote-island/ (accessed on 9 January 2021).

Bhattacharyya, Rajeev. 2020. 'Bhasan Char: A New Home for Rohingya Refugees'. *The Diplomat*, 22 December. Available at: https://thediplomat.com/2020/12/bhasan-char-a-new-home-for-rohingya-refugees/ (accessed on 9 January 2021).

Crisp, Jaff. 2004. 'The Local Integration and Local Settlement of Refugees: A Conceptual and Historical Analysis'. *New Issues in Refugee Research*, Working Paper No.102, UNHCR, Geneva, p. 1. Available at: https://www.unhcr.org/research/working/407d3b762/local-integration-local-settlement-refugees-conceptual-historical-analysis.html (accessed on March 15, 2021).

Fielden, Alexandra. 2008. 'Local Integration: An Under-Reported Solution to Protracted Refugee Situations'. *New Issues in Refugee Research*, Working Paper No.158, UNHCR, Geneva, p. 3. Available at: https://www.unhcr.org/486cc99f2.pdf (accessed on 20 March 2021).

Gobo, Giampietro. 2008. *Doing Ethnography*, translated by Adrian Belton. London: SAGE Publications.

Human Rights Watch. 2020. 'Bangladesh: Cyclone Endangers Rohingya on Silt Island'. Human Rights Watch, 20 May. Available at: https://www.hrw.

org/news/2020/05/20/bangladesh-cyclone-endangers-rohingya-silt-island (accessed on 20 December 2020).

Ibrahim, Azeem. 2020. 'If Rohingya must be Moved, Bangladesh has to Allay Fears'. *Arab News*, 8 December. Available at: https://www.arabnews.com/node/1774381 (Accessed on January 03, 2021).

Kozinets, Robert. 2010. *Netnography: Doing Ethnographic Research Online*. London, California, Delhi and Singapore: SAGE Publications.

Larkins, Karen. 2010. 'Ten Infamous Islands of Exile'. Smithsonianmag.com, 22 July. Available at: https://www.smithsonianmag.com/history/ten-infamous-islands-of-exile-1947938/ (accessed on 12 December 2020).

Moinuddin, A. K. M. 2021. 'Bangladesh to Demand 10pc of Funds for Rohingyas in Bhasan Char'. *Dhaka Courier*, 23 April 2021. Available at: http://dhaka-courier.com.bd/news/Reportage/Bangladesh-to-demand-10pc-of-funds-for-Rohingyas-in-Bhasan-Char/3395 (accessed on 16 May 2021).

Molla, M. Al-Masum Molla. 2020. 'Bhasan Char: All Set to Take in Rohingyas.' *The Daily Star*, 19 October. Available at: https://www.thedailystar.net/frontpage/news/bhasan-char-all-set-take-rohingyas-1980345 (accessed on 3 January 2021).

Paul, Ruma, Baldwin Clare and Marshal Andrew. 2018. 'Floating Island: New Home for Rohingya Refugees Emerges in Bay of Bengal'. *Reuters*, 22 February. Available at: https://www.reuters.com/article/us-myanmar-rohingya-island/floating-island-new-home-for-rohingya-refugees-emerges-in-bay-of-bengal-idUSKCN1G603T (accessed on 2 January 2021).

Reuters. 2018. 'Bangladesh Sees Little Foreign Funds for Rohingya Refugee Island: Minister'. *Reuters*, 27 March. Available at: https://www.reuters.com/article/us-myanmar-rohingya-bangladesh/bangladesh-sees-little-foreign-funds-for-rohingya-refugee-island-minister-idUSKBN1H306P (accessed on 2 January 2021).

The Amnesty International. 2018. 'Punishment, not Protection: Australia's Treatment of Refugees and Asylum Seekers in Papua New Guinea'. The Amnesty International. Available at: https://www.amnesty.org.au/wp-content/uploads/2018/02/Manus-briefing-FINAL4.pdf (accessed on 12 December 2020).

The Business Standard. 2019. 'An Inside Look at Bhashan Char—the New Home for Rohingyas'. *The Business Standard*, 30 December. Available at: https://tbsnews.net/rohingya-crisis/inside-look-bhashan-char-new-home-rohingyas (accessed on 20 December 2020).

The Cable News Network. 2020. 'Fears of Forced Removals as Bangladesh Moves Hundreds of Rohingya Refugees to Remote Island'. *The Cable News Network*, 8 December. Available at: https://edition.cnn.com/2020/12/03/asia/rohingya-relocations-bhasan-char-intl-hnk/index.html (accessed on 2 January 2021).

The Daily Star. 2019, 27 March. 'Rohingya's Bhasan Char Relocation to be Voluntary: FM'. *The Daily Star*. Available at: https://www.thedailystar.net/rohingya-crisis/rohingya-relocation-to-dhaka-bhasan-char-may-not-happen-1721098 (accessed on 20 December 2020).

The Daily Star. 2019, 28 February. The Philippines offers Rohingyas Citizenship'. *The Daily Star.* Available at: https://www.thedailystar.net/asia/news/philippines-offer-citizenship-rohingya-refugee-1708015 (accessed on 5 January 2021).

The Daily Star. 2020, 5 September. '40 Rohingyas Reach Bhashan Char to Visit Accommodation Project'. *The Daily Star.* Available at: https://www.thedailystar.net/40-rohingya-refugees-their-way-visit-bhashan-char-project-1956293 (accessed on 5 January 2021).

The Daily Star. 2020, 19 October. 'Bhasan Char: All set to take in Rohingyas'. *The Daily Star* 2020. Available at: https://www.thedailystar.net/frontpage/news/bhasan-char-all-set-take-rohingyas-1980345 (accessed on 2 January 2021).

The Daily Star 2021. 'Rohingya Relocation: UN Positive about Bhasan Char'. *The Daily Star*, 16 April. Available at: https://www.thedailystar.net/rohingya-crisis/news/rohingya-relocation-un-positive-about-bhasan-char-2078465 (accessed on 15 May 15 2021).

The Daily Prothom-Alo. 2020. 'Int'l Agencies, NGOs Hinder Rohingyas Relocation to Bhasan Char: Momen'. *The Daily Prothom-Alo*, 15 November. Available at: https://en.prothomalo.com/bangladesh/intl-agencies-ngos-hinder-rohingyas-relocation-to-bhasan-char-momen (accessed on 2 January 2021).

The Daily Sun. 2019. 'Bangladesh becomes Role Model In Disaster Management: PM'. *The Daily Sun*, 14 October. Available at: https://www.daily-sun.com/arcprint/details/431042/Bangladesh-becomes-role-model-in-disaster-management:-PM/2019-10-14 (accessed on 2 January 2021).

The Dhaka Tribune. 2020. Rights groups: Halt relocation of Rohingya to remote island. December 03. Available at: https://www.dhakatribune.com/bangladesh/rohingya-crisis/2020/12/03/bangladesh-halt-relocation-of-rohingya-to-remote-island (accessed on 2 January 2021).

The Dhaka Tribune. 2020. '300 Rohingyas in One Cyclone Shelter at Bhashan Char'. *The Dhaka Tribune*, 20 May. Available at: https://www.dhakatribune.com/bangladesh/rohingya-crisis/2020/05/20/300-rohingyas-in-one-cyclone-shelter-at-bhashan-char (accessed on 2 January 2021).

The Economist. 2020. 'Bangladesh is moving Rohingyas to a Remote Island'. *The Economist*, 12 December. Available at: https://www.economist.com/asia/2020/12/12/bangladesh-is-moving-rohingyas-to-a-remote-island (accessed on 2 January 2020).

The Guardian. 2020. 'Bangladesh Moves More Rohingyas to Remote Island Despite Rights Concerns'. *The Guardian*, 28 December. Available at: https://www.theguardian.com/global-development/2020/dec/28/bangladesh-moves-more-rohingyas-to-remote-island-despite-rights-concerns (accessed on January 02, 2021).

The Indian Express. 2020. 'Bangladesh Rohingya Relocation to Isolated Island Criticized by Rights Groups. *The Indian Express*, 29 December. Available at: https://indianexpress.com/article/world/bangladesh-rohingya-relocation-to-isolated-island-criticized-by-rights-groups-7092867/ (accessed on 2 January 2021).

The New York Times. 2020. 'From Crowded Camps to a Remote Island: Rohingya Refugees Move Again'. 8 December. Available at: https://www.nytimes.

com/2020/12/04/world/asia/rohingya-bangladesh-island-camps.html (accessed on 2 January 2020).

The UN Human Rights Council. 2020. 'UN Expert Urges Independent Assessment of Bhasan Char and Verification of Voluntary Relocation'. The United Nation Human Rights Notice, 10 December. Available at: https://www.ohchr.org/SP/NewsEvents/Pages/DisplayNews.aspx?NewsID=26590&LangID=E (accessed on 2 January 2021).

The United Nations High Commissioner for Refugee or UNHCR. 'Solutions for Refugee.' Chapter 7. In *10-Point Plan*. UNHCR. Available at: https://www.unhcr.org/en-us/50a4c17f9.pdf (accessed on 5 January 2021).

The UNHRC. 'What is Refugee Resettlement?' *Frequently Asked Questions about Resettlement*, Available at: https://www.unhcr.org/524c31666.pdf (accessed on 15 May 2021).

The UNHCR. 2007. *Handbook of Emergencies*. 3rd ed. UNHCR: Geneva.

The United Nations, Bangladesh. 2020. 'United Nations Statement on the Relocation of Rohingya Refugees to Bhasan Char'. The United Nations, 2 December. Available at: https://bangladesh.un.org/en/103285-press-statement (accessed on 15 March 2021).

Uddin, Nasir. 2012. 'Of Hosting and Hurting: Crises in Co-existence with Rohingya Refugees in Bangladesh'. In: *To Host or to Hurt: Counter Narratives on Rohingya Refugee Issue in Bangladesh*, edited by Nasir Uddin, 83–98. Dhaka: Institute for Culture and Development Research.

Uddin, Nasir. 2017a. *Not Rohingya, but Rooinga: Stateless People in the Struggle for Existence* (in Bengali). Dhaka: Murdhanna.

Uddin, Nasir. 2017b. 'State of the Stateless People: The Plight of the Rohingya Refugees in Bangladesh'. In: *Human Rights to Citizens: A Slippery Concept*, edited by Rhoda Howard-Hassmann and Margaret Walton-Roberts, 62–77. Philadelphia, PA: The University of Pennsylvania Press.

Uddin, Nasir. 2018. 'Ongoing Rohingya Repatriation Efforts are Doomed to Failure'. *Opinion, Al-Jazeera*, 22 November. Available at: https://www.aljazeera.com/opinions/2018/11/22/ongoing-rohingya-repatriation-efforts-are-doomed-to-failure (accessed on January 09, 2021).

Uddin, Nasir. 2020a. *Rohingya: An Ethnography of 'Subhuman' Life*. Delhi: Oxford University Press.

Uddin, Nasir. 2020b. 'The World Must Stand by the Rohingya'. *Culturico*, 7 December. Available at: https://culturico.com/2020/12/07/the-world-must-stand-by-the-rohingya/ (accessed on December 20, 2020).

About the Editor and the Contributors

Editor

Nasir Uddin is Professor of Anthropology at the University of Chittagong, Bangladesh. He studied and carried out research at the University of Oxford (UK), School of Oriental and African Studies (SOAS) at London University (UK), the London School of Economics (LSE) at London University (UK), Heidelberg University (Germany), VU Amsterdam (the Netherlands), Ruhr-University Bochum (Germany), Delhi School of Economics at Delhi University (India), the University of Hull (UK), Kyoto University (Japan), and the University of Dhaka (Bangladesh). He has received prestigious awards and fellowships including the MEXT Scholarship, the British Academy Visiting Scholarship, the Alexander von Humboldt Foundation Fellowship, a Visiting Scholarship at LSE, a Visiting Fellowship at Oxford University and Asian Studies Fellowship at East-West Center, Washington, DC, USA. His latest edited book is *Deterritorialised Identity and Transborder Movement in South Asia* (2019, co-edited with Nasreen Chowdhory). His latest monograph is *The Rohingya: An Ethnography of 'Subhuman' Life* (2020).

Contributors

Bayes Ahmed (PhD) is Lecturer in Risk and Disaster Science at the Institute for Risk and Disaster Reduction at University College London (UCL), UK. His background includes research into the field of disaster risk reduction (DRR), conflict and migration, climate change adaptation, community vulnerability and resilience and climate justice. He works in the intersection between conflict and disaster with a vision to help to improve the living standards of forced migrants and stateless population. He teaches quantitative and qualitative research methods, application of geographic information system (GIS) and remote sensing in disaster science, risk-sensitive land use planning and landslides. He is passionate about working with grassroots people to understand their disaster vulnerabilities and producing effective policy recommendations to address their problems.

Meherun Ahmed, Professor of Economics, joined Independent University, Bangladesh (IUB) on June, 2021. She is serving as dean of School of Business and Entrepreneurship. Before IUB she worked as associate dean of faculty at Asian University for Women (AUW), Bangladesh. She has received both her Ph.D. and M.A. in Economics from the University of Washington in Seattle, Washington, USA. She completed her Bachelors and Masters in Economics from University of Dhaka. Her research focuses on the microeconomic analysis of household behavior, with an emphasis on investment in education and health, forced displacement, crisis coping mechanisms, wellbeing, poverty, as well as labour force supply. Before Joining AUW, she was an assistant professor at Carleton College in Minnesota, USA. She has worked for many national and international development agencies and think tanks like the World Bank, The International Monetary Fund, International Organization of Migration and Institute of Microfinance. She has published in reputed journals and presented her research in numerous conferences.

Mohammad Shaheenur Alam is Assistant Professor in the Department of Peace and Conflict Studies, University of Dhaka, Bangladesh. He completed his master's in Social Science from the Department of Peace and Conflict Studies, University of Dhaka. He completed MPhil in 2012 from the Department of International Relations, Jadavpur University, India. His areas of research interest include migration and conflict, ethnicity, conflict and conflict management, approaches to peace and peace theories, regional approaches to peace and development.

S. M. R. Arfanul Alam studied International Relations at the University of Dhaka. Currently, he works as a research fellow at the Centre for Genocide Studies, University of Dhaka in a project collaborated between the UCL and the University of Dhaka. He worked for various national and international research organizations before he joined teaching as a fellow of Teach for Bangladesh. Besides specializing in qualitative research, he has field-level experience of the primary education sector in Bangladesh. His research interests include refugees and internally displaced persons, environment, security studies, governance and globalization.

Syeda Kaosar Jahan Barkha has recently completed her master's degree in Economic Policy in Global Markets from Central European University (CEU), Budapest, Hungary. She completed her undergraduate degree from AUW with a major in economics and a minor in Mathematics in 2017. During her studies, she also worked as a part-time math teacher in a school for a year. She was also an intern research officer at Bangladesh Institute of Development Studies, which is a renowned multidisciplinary government research institution. Barkha has worked on research projects on topics including maternal health in Bangladesh, socio-economic status and educational status of mothers in Bangladesh. Her research interests include health economics, development economics and economic policy issues.

Anurug Chakma is PhD Scholar in the School of Politics and International Relations at the Australian National University, Australia. Prior to commencing his doctoral studies, he was Assistant Professor in the Department of Peace and Conflict Studies at the University of Dhaka. He has published several peer-reviewed research articles on the peacebuilding of the Chittagong Hill Tracts, identity conflicts, human rights of indigenous peoples, the Kashmir conflict, the South Asia refugee crisis and terrorism in the *Asian Journal of Peacebuilding*, *Journal of Human Rights and Peace Studies*, *Society and Change*, *Social Science Review* and *Journal of Sociology*.

Yuriko Cowper-Smith has just completed his PhD in Political Science (with a major in Comparative Politics and a minor in Public Policy) in the Department of Political Science at the University of Guelph. Her main research interests lie in migration, statelessness and social movements, and her dissertation research investigates migrant-led social movements. For two years, she has worked with the Rohingya community in Canada by volunteering, organizing and attending events and raising public awareness about the crisis through her writing and research. She currently volunteers with The Sentinel Project, an NGO that tracks early signs of genocide, and the Canadian Centre on Statelessness. Yuriko visited the Rohingya refugee camps in Cox's Bazar, Bangladesh, in the fall of 2018. Additionally, she has extensive experience working in academic and community-based research. For three years, she worked on research projects with various community partners as a part of her role at the Community Engaged Scholarship Institute at the University of Guelph. Yuriko's research has been supported by an Ontario Graduate Fellowship and an Ontario Graduate Scholarship.

Paul Chaney (PhD) is Senior Faculty of Politics and Policy at Cardiff University. He is Co-Director of Wales Institute of Social, Economic Research and Data (WISERD). He has been a member of a number of public advisory bodies including the UK government Steering Group on the Equality and Human Rights Commission. He was a panel member/special adviser to the RAE (2008) and REF (2010–2011). He was on the Management Board of *Policy and Politics* (Policy Press) and co-editor of the peer-reviewed journal *Contemporary Wales: An Annual Review of Economic, Political and Social Research* (2003–2014). He has authored and edited 14 books and written over 60 papers in international peer-reviewed journals. His research and teaching interests include territorial politics, public policymaking, civil society and equality and human rights.

Bebek Kanti Das is a development and research activist working in Center for Environment and Disaster Studies (CEDS) as Associate Director-Research and Programme in Cox's Bazar since 2012. He received master degree on Geography and Environmental Studies from the University of Chittagong in 2012 and then 2nd master degree on Environmental Economics from the University of Dhaka in 2018. He has nine years long professional experience in several projects with recognized research organization, national & international NGO and govt. level institution. He has accomplished his experience on DRR, humanitarian response, early response and protection in emergency. He has experience in the research arena, for example, evaluation, impact study, development plan etc. Protection concern of children, adolescent girls and women in the camp is an increasing factor. Bebek has an interest to work with these vulnerable groups to assist to get their dignity.

Fahima Durrat is Assistant Professor of Peace and Conflict Studies at the University of Dhaka, Bangladesh. She received an MSS degree in Peace and Conflict Studies in 2009 from the University of Dhaka and an MSc degree in Development Studies from the School of Oriental and African Studies in 2012. Her areas of interest are political economy, social movements, conflict resolution and peacebuilding.

Manas Dutta is Assistant Professor in the Department of History in the Aliah University, Kolkata, West Bengal, India, and his current area of research covers issues related to War and Conflict in South Asia, with a special focus on civil–military relations in the Global South. Along with this, he is also investigating, as part of his recent research on War and Genocide Studies, the involvement of native Indian soldiers in the First World War, with a special emphasis on their performance in the Western Front. He has received the Charles Wallace India Trust Fellowship for collecting research materials in the British Library, United Kingdom in 2016. In 2018, he was awarded the summer fellowship by the Institute for Critical Social Inquiry in the New School for Social Research, New York, USA. He has completed the project 'New Social Movement, Media an Paradigm Shift in Political Aspirations in Contemporary India' under the aegis of the Indian Council of Social Science Research, New Delhi in 2019 and received research project grant from the Nazrul Centre for Social and Cultural Studies, Kazi Nazrul University, West Bengal, for conducting research on 'Nazrul and War-front' in 2020.

Matteo Fumagalli is a Senior Lecturer at the School of International Relations, University of St Andrews, UK. His research interests lie at the intersection of the study of identities, ethnic conflict and violence and the politics of natural resources. He has conducted research in the post-Soviet space (especially Central Asia and the Caucasus) and East Asia (especially South Korea, Taiwan, Laos, Myanmar and Bangladesh). He has authored several books, more than 20 peer-reviewed articles and many book chapters. His monograph *New Silk Roads, Growing Inter-Asian Connections: South Korea's Quest for Energy and New Markets in Central Asia* is forthcoming in 2021.

Azeem Ibrahim (PhD) is Research Professor at the Strategic Studies Institute, US Army War College and Director of the Center for Global Policy in Washington, DC. He received his PhD from the University of Cambridge after which he completed fellowships at the universities of Oxford, Harvard and Yale. He is also an official columnist for the magazine *Foreign Policy* and has published hundreds of articles in the likes of the *New York Times*, *Washington Post*, *Daily Telegraph*, *The Times* (UK), *Chicago Tribune*, *LA Times*, *Newsweek*, *National Interest*, *Yale Global* and many other publications around the globe. He has been researching the Rohingya issue for more than a decade and is the author of the well-regarded book *The Rohingyas: Inside Myanmar's Hidden Genocide* (2016). He is also a well-known expert on international affairs and the failure of traditional multilateral bodies such as the UN to respond to China's new assertiveness.

Md. Touhidul Islam is Associate Professor in the Department of Peace and Conflict Studies, University of Dhaka, Bangladesh, and has a keen knack on conducting analysis of conflict and situations alike. He holds an MA in Peace Studies from the University of Bradford, UK and has published a number of research articles on peace accord, conflict resolution, peacebuilding and conflict transformation, both at home and abroad. His current research interests include migration, host–refugee relations, community engagement and resilience, conflict and peace processes, peacebuilding, climate change, fragility and resilience.

Jenny Lamb has over 17 years of professional experience in the humanitarian, development and private sector in the fields of water, sanitation, hygiene, public health, and environmental engineering. In the international aid sector, she has operated in a broad range of countries and contexts. Geographically she has experience in the Middle East, Africa and Asia, including Myanmar and Bangladesh where she has been a keen advocate from the outset for equality and human rights for the Rohingya. Jenny has a holistic comprehension of WASH; research ethics; ethnographic research methods; social anthropology; human rights and the social, cultural, economic and environmental conditions that exist for global communities. She has recently completed an MSc in Social Anthropology of Development from SOAS, University of London. During her anthropological studies, she carried out ethnographic research in Cox's Bazar where she examined how the Rohingya cope with their encampment and liminality, through their own agency.

Mursheduzzaman is a postgraduate researcher and development and climate change research activist working with Disaster and Development Organization in Chittagong since 2016 and Climate Change Adaptation, Mitigation Experiment & Training Park in Dhaka and different parts of coastal Bangladesh since 2018. He received his master's degree in Geography and Environmental Studies from the University of Chittagong in 2019. He has a four-years long professional experience in several projects with recognized research organizations, national and international NGOs and government institutions. He has accomplished his experience on climate change and human adaptation, risk management, emergency response and child protection in emergency, humanitarian response. He has experience in the research arena of climate change, nature-based solutions, DRR, evaluation, impact study, etc., in coastal Bangladesh and children protection concern, adolescent girls and women's health in the camps. Mursheduzzaman has an interest to work with these vulnerable groups to assist to mitigate the problem with dignity.

Sagarika Naik has completed her M.Phil at the University of Delhi and is now working as a researcher at Princeton University, USA. She has previously worked as a research assistant at Confluence Media Pvt Ltd, with the project titled *Integration of Indian Princely States*. Currently, she is working as a research associate for National Archive of Trinidad and Tobago, where she is constantly working with the archival records including Census Report, Immigration and Emigration Files, Famine Reports, Gazetteers and Annual Administrative Reports. She has presented and participated in different national and international conferences, seminars, workshops, including The Rise of Asia in Global History and Perspective, La Montee De L'Asie En Historie et Perspective Globales, France, North American Labor History Conference (NALHC), Wayne State

University, Detroit, Michigan, USA, University of East London, V. V. Giri National Labor Institute, etc. Her research interest focuses on Labour History, Migration Studies, Gender and Sexuality, Human Trafficking, South Asian Studies. Her recent research explores the Rohingya refugee crisis, where she examines the diverse issues regarding the practice of belongingness, place-attachment and mobility, refugee crisis and sex trafficking. Her upcoming publications include 'Indian Ocean: Free and Coerced Migration in the Age of Global Empire' (at Marquette University), 2021 and *Voiceless Rohingya: From Refugees to Modern Slaves*, which are under review.

Syeda Naushin Parnini is Research Fellow at the Centre for Democracy and Election (UMCEDEL), University of Malaya, Kuala Lumpur, Malaysia. Dr Parnini did her master's and PhD in International Political Economy at the Graduate School of Humanities and Social Sciences, University of Tsukuba, Japan. She completed her bachelor's degree and master's in International Relations in the Department of International Relations, University of Dhaka. She had been Senior Lecturer, University of Malaya, Kuala Lumpur from 2009 to 2014. She was a Guest Lecturer at University of Nottingham and Guest Fellow at the University of Freiburg (FRIAS), Germany. She was a Visiting Fellow at the Department of Government and International Affairs, University of South Florida, USA. Dr Parnini has published several books, monographs and research articles in internationally reputed journals.

Obayedul Hoque Patwary is Assistant Professor at the Department of Peace and Conflict Studies, University of Dhaka, Bangladesh. He has completed his bachelor's and master's degrees in Peace and Conflict Studies at the University of Dhaka, Bangladesh. He has obtained his second master's degree in Peace and Conflict Transformation from the University of Tromsø, Norway. His research interest includes climate change and conflict, conflict transformation, environmental refugees and terrorism and counterterrorism.

Alak Paul (PhD) is Professor of Geography and Environmental Studies at the University of Chittagong, Bangladesh. He received his MSc from Dhaka University, Bangladesh in 1999 and PhD from the

University of Durham, UK, in 2009. Being an empirical geographer for last twenty years, his research and teaching interests span over public health; society and environment; disaster management, among others. Dr Paul emphasises on marginalised and stigmatised people in his studies using qualitative approach and looks at the everyday geographies of various vulnerable people where he establishes how place plays a role in (re)shaping the life of people or environment. He has over 50 peer reviewed research publications in reputed journals along with seven book chapters to his credit. His latest edited book is *Geography in Bangladesh: Concepts Methods and Applications* (Routledge, 2019, co-edited with Sk Tawhidul Islam). His latest authored book is *HIV/AIDS in Bangladesh: Stigmatized People, Policy and Place* (Springer, 2020).

Md. Atiqur Rahman is Associate Professor of Geography and Environmental Studies, University of Chittagong, Bangladesh. His research activities are focused on climate change assessment and climate modelling, agricultural water management and environmental management issues related to climate change and water problems of Bangladesh. He obtained his master's degree in Geography and Environmental Studies (Chittagong University). Later, he received training on technology for integrated water management from the University of Ghent and the University of Antwerp, Belgium. He obtained his doctoral degree from Nanjing University of Information Science and Technology, PRC. His PhD research work was on the assessment of climate change and associated impacts on irrigation demands of dry season rice in Bangladesh. Currently, he is working on climate change impacts assessment on different components of the hydrological cycle. He uses both the observed and model data and applies different tools like R-programming, ArcGIS, GrADS in his work.

Peter Sammonds (PhD) works at the interface of natural and social sciences. His research and knowledge exchange are on natural hazard risks, disasters and recovery. He has worked on earthquake mechanics, volcanoes and ice physics in the Arctic. He works on research council, British Academy and Royal Society-funded projects on Increasing

Resilience to Environmental Hazards in Border Conflict Zones and Resilience Futures for the Rohingya Refugees. He has advised the UK research councils on the increasing resilience to natural hazards programme; been a member of Earthquake Engineering Field Investigation Team, contributing to inter-disciplinary reports on disaster, taken up widely by government for policy advice; and been a Commissioner on the UCL–Lancet Commission on Migration and Health, 2017–2018, whose report has been influential. He is currently the Gender and Intersectionality Ambassador for the UKRI network+ GRRIPP project led by the IRDR Centre for Gender and Disaster.

Shaila Sharmin is a teacher of Bangladesh Studies at Presidency International School. She holds BSc and MS both in Geography and Environmental Studies from the University of Chittagong, Bangladesh. She has completed her MS thesis on health issues of Rohingya refugee women. Her research interests include women health vulnerability, sexual harassment, social and mental health of vulnerable people.

Bulbul Siddiqi is currently serving as Associate Professor in Anthropology and Sociology at the Department of Political Science and Sociology. He is also serving as Director of Confucius Institute at North South University. Dr Siddiqi completed his doctoral research from Cardiff University on the Tablighi Jamaat (a revivalist piety movement) in the UK and Bangladesh following an ethnographic research method. He also earned MA in Global Citizenship, Identities and Human Rights from the University of Nottingham, UK. He has published books and journals (Scopus indexed) from international reputed publishers. Currently, he is jointly editing a book titled, *The Displaced Rohingya: A Tale of a Vulnerable Community'* to be published by Routledge. He is also contributing to two chapters in this book. His present research on the Rohingya crisis focuses on 'Exploring the Roles of "National Development Experts" in International Development: A Critical Analysis of the Rohingya Refugee Crisis in Bangladesh'.

Parvin Sultana is currently working as Assistant Professor in Pramathesh Barua College. She is pursuing her PhD at Gauhati

University. Her research interests include gender, migration, minority politics. She has written research papers and book reviews for journals such as *Social Change, The Book Review,* etc. Her research papers have been published in journals like *Meridian Critic, Journal of Identity and Migration Studies, Policing,* etc. She also writes regularly for newspapers, webzines and magazines both in English and in vernacular. Apart from teaching, she works also with the community in spreading awareness about girls' education and women's rights in far-flung areas of Assam.

Index